The Outdoor Handy Book

For Playground, Field, and Forest

DANIEL CARTER BEARD

rse Publishing

Originally published in 1896 by Charles Scribner's Sons.

Library of Congress Cataloging-in-Publication Data is available on file.

ISBN-10: 1-60239-268-4
ISBN-13: 978-1-60239-268-7

10 9 8 7 6 5 4 3 2 1

Printed in China

CONTENTS

SPRING.

CHAPTER I.

CHAPTER II.

CHAPTER III.

CHAPTER IV.

SUMMER.

CHAPTER XII.

CHAPTER XIII.

CHAPTER XIV.

CHAPTER XV.

CHAPTER XVI.

CHAPTER XXIII.

CHAPTER XXIV.

CHAPTER XXV.

CHAPTER XXVI.

CHAPTER XXVII.

CHAPTER XXVIII.

CHAPTER XXIX.

CHAPTER XXX.

CHAPTER XXXI.

AUTUMN.

CHAPTER XXXII.

CHAPTER XXXIII.

CHAPTER XXXIV.

CHAPTER XXXV.

CHAPTER XXXVI.

CHAPTER XXXVII.

WINTER.

CHAPTER XXXVIII.

Spring

The Outdoor Handy Book

CHAPTER I

MARBLES

Marble Time—History of the Game—Sakya-Muni and Humphrey Potter—How Marbles are Made—Marble Names, Marble Terms, and Expressions—Games from Bull Ring to Long Ring.

Marble Time.

In the early spring time, while the white frost still jewelled the grass in the mornings and the ground was alternately frozen at night and thawed by the morning sun, marble time used to begin, and on Long Island the custom of playing marbles as soon as old winter has taken off his coat of snow is still in vogue.

How my knuckles used to smart where the cold wind had chapped them and "knuckling down" had ground the mud into the raw places. But, pshaw! What did I care for raw knuckles, as with a pocketful of assorted varieties of marbles I watched eagerly for a playmate, and as soon as one appeared, shouted, "First for keeps!"

In those days I thought that gambling consisted only in playing games for money.

Four hundred years before the first incidents occurred that are written of in the New Testament, old Sakya-Muni was dead and buried, but, like John Brown, his spirit keeps marching on.

Sakya-Muni was a great man, but I doubt if any of my young readers would like him. Mr. Muni founded a great religion, but he was narrow-minded. Boys in those days were just like the boys of this day—they were fond of fun, fond of games, and they made little windmills, and they enjoyed seeing the wheels buzz in the breeze.

Old Sakya-Muni thought this sinful and silly. He forgot that he was ever a boy himself, so he forbade windmills as "detrimental to progress in virtue." Sakya-Muni, or Gautama Buddha, was an ancient Puritan; he was down on chess or checkers, hop-scotch he abhorred, jack-straws to him were the invention of the evil one, ball was a game of perdition, drawing pictures, blowing horns, racing, archery, and marbles, were equally bad and forbidden sins.

There are many estimable, narrow-minded, half-developed people of to-day who think just as Buddha did so long ago, but fortunately for the young people no one now takes them seriously.

Sakya-Muni had no intention or desire to be of assistance to the author of this book. No doubt if the old pagan were alive he would forbid its publication, but nevertheless he is introduced to the reader because his denunciations of these games prove that the youngsters of his day found entertainment in the same games that occupy the leisure of the school-boys at the close of the nineteenth century.

Not many years ago there was a boy named Humphrey Potter, who, sad to relate, in spite of Mr. Muni's harangue against games, would rather play marbles than work; but he was a poor boy, and he would rather work than see his parents deprived of the comforts that his little earnings could procure. Humphrey was only a boy; he did not know anything. Not one of the great men who had invented the awkward, puffing old steam-engines that were used in those days would have condescended to consult Hump in regard to his invention.

The poor little chap had to sit all day on a stick of wood for a stool, and, with one hand on the steam-cock and the other on the water-cock, alternately turn on steam and water. When he turned on the steam this vapor rushed into the cylinder and forced a heavy piston up; when he turned on the water, that fluid rushed in, cooled off or condensed the steam and down came the piston. So that without a boy at the steam and water cocks this great invention of full-grown men would not work.

But Hump had a better head than these men, and the lad wanted to play marbles. So down went his hand into that junk-shop which every boy has, but which he calls his pocket, and out came a piece of string—most likely it was a top-string—and Hump harnessed up the piston to the valves.

It was as simple as falling off a log. The piston opened and shut the valves itself, and Humphrey played marbles and drew his pay at the same time.

Simple as falling off a log, but like many things it was too simple for a man to think of, and yet simple as it was Humphrey Potter's invention lifted the steam-engine from the plane of a clumsy machine chiefly used for pumping purposes to the higher field where its uses are so manifold as scarcely to be numbered, and Humphrey was only a boy and an inveterate marble-player at that.

Boys, when you hear the thunder of the railroad train, the hum of the factory wheels, or the whistle of the big steam-boats, rattle the marbles in your pockets, and say,

"Well, if it were not for one of us, where would all your wonderful inventions be, you great, big, bald-headed, bearded boys that build your cities without leaving us room for a Bull Ring?"

Terms Used in the Game.

Before going any farther, I might as well give the meanings of the principal terms used in marbles—the phrases which mean so much to boys and so little to those who are unfamiliar with them.

The Taw or **Shooter,** is the marble used for shooting.

The **Taw Line** or **Tie Line,** or **Scratch,** as it is often called, is the line drawn for a starting-point in games like the Long Ring.

Ducks are the marbles to be shot at.

Dubs* means that you take all the marbles knocked out of the ring by one shot.

Fen Dubs† means that you must put back all but one marble.

Lofting means shooting through the air. When you loft you knuckle down and your taw goes through the air and does not strike the ground until it hits the duck aimed at, or a spot near it.

Knuckling down means what the name implies, resting the knuckles on the ground during the act of shooting.

Hunching means shoving your hand over the mark as you shoot. Hunching is unfair, and if a good shot is made and the player making it is caught in the act of hunching he should be made to shoot over again and shoot fair.

Histing is holding the hand some distance above the ground. Histing is not allowable in the Bull Ring or in Meg-on-a-String.

---

* An abbreviation of doubles. † An abbreviation of defend doubles.

Roundsters means taking a new position on one side or the other of some obstruction. This is not fair in Bull Ring.

Sidings means to move your taw from one side to the other in a straight line when about to shoot, and is not allowable in Bull Ring.

Burying is the term applied to the act of placing your taw in a good spot and then forcing it into the ground with the heel of your shoe. Burying is sometimes allowed in all games of marbles, but only by unskilled players; with the others "Fen buryings" is the unwritten rule of the game.

Laying in is similar to burying, with the exception that your taw is left on top of the ground. This is also a "baby" game and not often resorted to. "Laying in" also means placing the marbles in the ring.

Clearances means removing stones, sticks, or other objects between your taw and the ducks.

Sneaking is the act of shooting for a position.

Babying is shooting with little force, so as not to knock the ducks far or to cause your taw to fly far. Babying is not of much use in large rings, but is often resorted to in small rings and in such games as Follerings. There is no rule that can make you stop babying, so the other players always try ridicule. This never succeeds to any extent, though it eases the minds of the unsuccessful players when another boy is "skinning" the ring by babying.

Playing **for Keeps** is a game in which all the ducks won are kept. Playing **for Fair** is an Eastern term with the same meaning, and **for Fun** means of course that all the marbles are returned to their original owners when the game is over.

The Right Spirit.

It is not necessary to gamble with marbles, as many suppose, and in fact there is little doubt that the game was first played "for keeps" centuries ago when pebbles were used for marbles and the pebbles won were only valued as trophies or counters. In reality a marble won is a point won in the game, and it is not necessary to keep the marbles after the game is over, any more than it is necessary to keep the balls and bats of the defeated base-ball players or the balls and rackets of the defeated lawn-tennis players or the foot-ball of the defeated foot-ball players. What the American boy plays for is to *win the game*, not the implements of the sport. It is only the occasional "tough" who manages to get into the game who has the real instincts of the gambler, and he is the boy who always cries "grinder," and "snatches up" or "swipes" the marbles of smaller or more timid lads. Such a boy should be avoided just as respectable men avoid the gambler and black-leg.

Knuckle Dabsters.

Every boy who plays marbles should possess a knuckle dabster; these can be made from bits of soft woollen cloth,

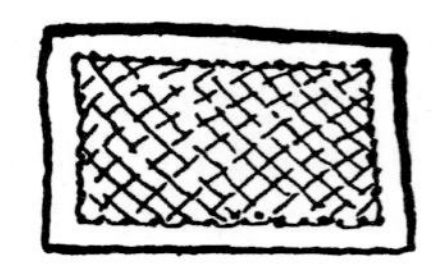

FIG. 1.—A Quilted "Knuckle Dabster."

FIG. 2.—Mole Skin "Knuckle Dabster."

felt, or the skin of small animals. Mole skins make the softest and prettiest of knuckle dabsters, but any piece of fur will answer. Some boys wear them fastened to the hand, but the most expert players seem to prefer to throw them down at the spot from which they are about to shoot and then knuckle down on the soft fur or woollen cloth.

A knuckle dabster prevents one's knuckles from becoming sore and raw, and adds greatly to the comfort of the player.

Your sister, mother, aunt, or grandmother can in a few moments stitch two pieces of thick, soft cloth together for you when marble time arrives, and if they will add to this favor by making you

A Marble Bag

with strings to draw the mouth together, you are ready for the season. The marble bag should be small enough to slip into your pocket, where it will prevent the loss of many marbles that might work their way through that hole that is always to be found in a boy's pocket after he has worn his clothes for a short time.

FIG. 3.—Marble Bag.

FIG. 4.—Same with Strings Drawn.

I remember how I used to plan leather and buckskin pockets that would not wear out, and I made up my mind that when I was old enough to make money and buy my own clothes the tailor should be instructed to put in leather pockets.

Alas! when I reached that age it took so much cash to buy the clothes that there was never enough in the pockets to wear them out.

Whom to Play Marbles With.

If Little Lord Fauntleroy had been born in a Western town his life would not have been worth living. He was a gentle little "sissy" aristocrat, who would never have been tolerated by the "Huck" Finns and Tom Sawyers inhabiting the valleys of the Mississippi and its tributaries.

Imagine, if you can, such a little chap wearing the clothes with which Mr. Birch, in his beautiful illustrations, so appropriately dressed him; imagine him down on one knee, with his girlish hand chapped with the wind and the cracks filled with grime, knuckling down and lofting on the ducks in the middle of a bull ring, or with doubled fists standing over his marbles, defending his property against some young highwayman from the rolling mill on the river bank!

As the New York boys would say, "He wouldn't be in it." No, the house is the place for him. This is a rough world, and it requires experiences outside of a gentle, loving mother's care or the sweet lady-like tuition of a governess to fit a lad for the battle of life.

What we want for a playmate is a fair and square fellow, who will stand by a friend through thick and thin, and, without being quarrelsome, defend his rights and never "weaken." It is unnecessary to say that such a lad's love of justice will always prevent him from imposing upon smaller boys and his manliness will cause him to treat his companion and the girls with courtesy. You need not watch him in any game, for he will not cheat. Among my old schoolmates I have known many such fellows, and, to a man, they are all good fellows now; good citizens, good fathers, and they still enjoy watching the boys play the games in which they used to excel themselves.

How Marbles Were First Made.

With the aid of frost and sun nature splits the rocks, dropping the fragments into the water, and the ever moving water rolls the fragments over each other and against other stones until they become smooth pebbles, many of which are almost as round as the marbles sold in stores. Away back before history was written the children used these natural marbles to play with, but there is nothing to tell us whether they used a "long ring" or a "bull ring," or what rules governed the game.

When the Tammany Halls of Rome and the citizens in general became wicked and corrupt it made nature very ill, and she broke out in volcanoes. While the terrible fires from the bowels of the earth were spouting and scattering their ashes and lava over towns and cities, Pompeii was buried with all its streets and houses and with some of its people and dogs. Among the many curious things found in the ruins by the antiquarians who have unearthed the old cities were—what? Marbles left by the boys in their flight from the doomed city, and, I think, if the truth were known, some of the little rascals delayed their departure long enough to secure and carry away with them their "megs," as the New York boys would call the ancient marbles.

Marbles in America.

One hundred and twenty-eight years after Columbus discovered America, and when many of the ancestors of this generation of boys could call themselves Americans, the Dutchmen imported marbles to England, and it is very probable the old Knickerbockers introduced them here, but it matters little who had the honor of introducing them to

America. They came to stay, and now, from California to Maine, and from the Calumet and Hecla mines at Red Jacket, Mich., to New Orleans, the boys all play marbles.

Made Abroad Nowadays.

Where do they all come from? Some of you win them, some of you trade postage-stamps for them, but some person bought them, probably, at the little store around the corner.

When I attended the Eighth Street District School in Cincinnati we used to replenish our stock from "Malaney's." I do not recollect the real name of the proprietor of the little store, but that is the name it went by among the boys. There we bought our butterscotch and bull's-eye candy; our match-sticks for kites, our elastic bands for slings, our tops and top-strings.

Local Names of Marbles.

But Malaney must have secured his supply from somewhere, because I know he did not make them himself, and he always had a quantity on hand of "potteries," "plasters," "chinas," "crystals," "agates," "alleys," and "commies."

Atlantic coast boys do not use these names, but they use the same marbles. We had a tradition that the potteries were made at a pottery near the Brighton Hotel in the suburbs of Cincinnati. What truth, if any, there is in this tradition I am unable to state. In New York I seldom see this rich brown mottled marble, whose glossy surface is marked by three rough dots.

The "crockery" never had the splashes of white that distinguished the "burned agate" of New York, nor the green of the "moss agate" of the same place. Both of the latter were unknown to the Western boys twenty-five years ago.

At the beginning of this century marbles were sometimes called "bowls," and all came from Nuremberg, down the Rhine to Rotterdam, and thence to all other parts of Europe.

How Marbles are Made.

They are now manufactured in immense quantities in Saxony for exportation to the United States, India, and China. The common marble is manufactured of hard stone quarried near Coburg, Saxony, and the process is practically the same as that used by nature in grinding out the little round pebbles originally used by the children of long ago.

Nature, though constantly busy, is slow. We do not want to wait a thousand or maybe a million years for her to get our marbles ready. Our fingers might be too old to shoot with them, so we adopt nature's principles, but make more haste. In place of frost man uses a hammer to break the stone into fragments.

The hammer breaks the hard stone into small squares, or, more properly, cubical shaped blocks. These are placed on a large millstone one hundred or two hundred at a time. The millstone has several grooves cut in it in the form of rings, one ring inside another, or, as your Geometry would put it, in the form of concentric circles. Over this a block of oak of the same size as the lower stone rests on the small square fragments and is kept turning while water flows upon the bottom stone.

Power is supplied by a water-wheel, and when the machinery is set in motion the little cubes are compelled, by the pressure and motion of the upper piece, to roll over and over in their circular tracks, and round and round and round they travel like circus horses in a ring. In fifteen minutes' time the mill does what nature takes years to accomplish, and the little blocks of stone are turned into small stone balls. These are the unfinished marbles and need smoothing.

One such mill can turn out two thousand marbles a week, and if there are four or five sets of millstones running, eight thousand or ten thousand a week can be manufactured.

In another part of the establishment the water-wheel turns a number of wooden barrel-shaped receptacles, something like the copper ones used for making candy in this country. Inside the wooden casks are hard stone cylinders. These revolving cylinders smooth the marbles, which are compelled by the motion of the machinery to keep up a constant rubbing against each other and against the stone cylinder. When they are smooth enough the dust made by the last process is emptied from the casks and fine emery powder substituted. This gives finish and polish to the marble.

Common Marbles.

The small, gray marbles are what the Western boys call "commies" or "combos." They are often painted bright colors, but the paint soon wears off and they look like little dried clay balls. They are not much valued, and five "commies" usually represent the value of one "plaster."

The Century Dictionary gives an "alley" as one of the definitions of a marble. On what ground it bases this information I am unable to state. "Agate," "meg," "duck" or "real" would be just as good a definition. "Meg" or "duck" would be better, inasmuch as, in different sections of the country, both of these terms are used to define marbles of any description; while "alley" in almost all parts of the country means a particular kind of marble.

The Alley.

In some parts of Ohio and Kentucky the marble designated by the latter name is a small, hard sphere with a yellowish-white ground, streaked with wavy lines of bluish green. These are not the same as the "Croton alley" or "Jasper" of New York. The latter, I believe, are made of glazed and unglazed china marbled with blue, and are generally larger marbles than the so-called alleys of the West.

The China and Plaster.

In Cincinnati and the adjoining cities of Covington and Newport, Ky., a china is what its name implies—china. This term, when I was a boy, was used only to designate a glazed china; the unglazed ones we called plasters, from their resemblance to that substance.

Both of the latter marbles are decorated with lines of various colors, sometimes crossing each other, forming plaids, and again arranged in circles and called bull's eyes. They are made in wooden molds and are dried, baked, and painted like any other chinaware.

The Bumbo and Peawee.

"Bumbo," "bumboozer" or "bowler" are names applied to very large marbles of any description. A "peawee" is the name used for any very small marble.

Crystals

is a general name applied in many parts of the country to all glass marbles, including "opals," "glimmers," "bloods," "rubies," etc. They are all very beautiful, but their beauty is only skin deep, and when used much they become dull and full of nicks. Some of these glass marbles are called "agates" in the East, and hence the genuine agate is called a "real," to distinguish it from the counterfeit glass one. Glass marbles are made by melting the glass and pressing the hot substance in polished metal molds, the halves of which fit so neatly that no trace of a seam or line is visible on the glass to mark where the parts of the mold join.

The "Lucky Taw."

Our lucky taw, or the marble we used when a skilful shot was required, was carefully selected for its weight and symmetry, and was generally an agate or real. Agates are beautiful gems of agate or carnelian, varying in color from a smoky gray to a blood red, or variegated with mottlings or stripes of different colors. Agates are made into marbles at Oberstein. The workmen are very skilful. The stone is first broken into fragments of the proper size, and then, by means of a hammer, clipped into rude balls; these balls are then worn down on the face of a large grindstone, and are managed with great dexterity by the workmen, who in a few minutes bring them into perfect spheres, after which they are polished by hand on lapidary wheels.

FIG. 5.—"Cunny Thumb."

Cunny Thumb or Scrumpy Knuckled.

If Little Lord Fauntleroy played marbles, any boy could tell you how he would shoot. He would hold his hand vertically, place his taw or shooter against his thumb-nail and his first finger. He would shoot "cunny thumb style," or "scrumpy knuckled." The thumb would flip out weakly (Fig. 5), and the marble would roll on its way.

Tom Sawyer would lay the back of his fist on the ground or on his mole-skin "knuckle dabster," hold his taw between the first and second joints of the second finger and the first joint of the thumb, the three smaller fingers closed and the first finger partially open (Fig. 6). From this animated ballista the marble would shoot through the air for four or five feet, alighting on one of the ducks in the middle of the ring, sending it flying outside, while the taw would spin in the spot vacated by the duck. Tom or Huck Finn would display as much skill with his taw as an expert billiard player would with the ivory balls.

FIG. 6.—As Tom Would Shoot.

FIG. 7.—Western Reserve and New York.

FIG. 8.—Another and Better Style.

A Southern Way.

Down in Dixie I have frequently seen grown men, white and black, playing marbles, and one or two of the expert players held their taw on their second finger, holding the second finger back with their thumb; then suddenly removing the thumb and straightening out the finger, they sent the marble, like a bullet, straight to the mark. This manner of shooting must require much practice, and I doubt if it is more accurate than the one just described as Tom's method. Some boys, skilful in the game, squeeze the marble they shoot with between the thumb and the forefinger, wetting it with their mouth to make it slip quickly.

The Arabian Way of Shooting.

The dark-faced little Arabs have a curious manner of shooting. They place their taw in the hollow between the middle and the forefinger of the left hand, the hand being flat on the ground with the fingers closed. The forefinger of the right hand is then pressed firmly on the end joint of the middle finger, which pushes the middle finger suddenly aside, and the forefinger slips out with sufficient force to propel the shooter very accurately.

There are innumerable games of marbles in vogue in different sections of the country. I have watched the boys play in every State east of the Mississippi River, and between the Gulf of Mexico and the Great Northern Lakes, and will describe the most popular games.

CHAPTER II

"FAT" AND OTHER FAMOUS GAMES OF MARBLES.

The Uncertainties of "Fat," Sometimes Called "Yank" or "Yankey" —Stand-up Marbles—Follerings—Knucks, the Long Ring, and Patterson—The Scientific Bull Ring—Duck in a Hole.

Fat.

MAKE a ring that will measure a foot and a half or two feet across the centre. Then draw a straight line through the centre from top to bottom, and another straight line from right to left at right angles to the first through the centre of the ring, thus dividing it into quarters (Fig. 9).

Each player lays in a duck, that is, puts a marble in the ring. Where only two play, place one duck on the right and the other on the left hand side of the ring. If four boys play, place a marble at the end of each cross line, and if more boys are in the game put the marbles around the ring, one for each player.

Beginning the Game.

About ten feet away from the ring scratch a taw or tie line to shoot from. Here the first player places his knuckle dabster, knuckles down and shoots at the marbles. If he is a good marksman and knocks a marble out of the ring he shoots again from the spot where his taw or shooter rests and so continues to shoot until he makes a miss, pocketing all the ducks he knocks out. When he has failed to hit and knock out a marble, his turn is over and he must allow his shooter to lie where it rolled.

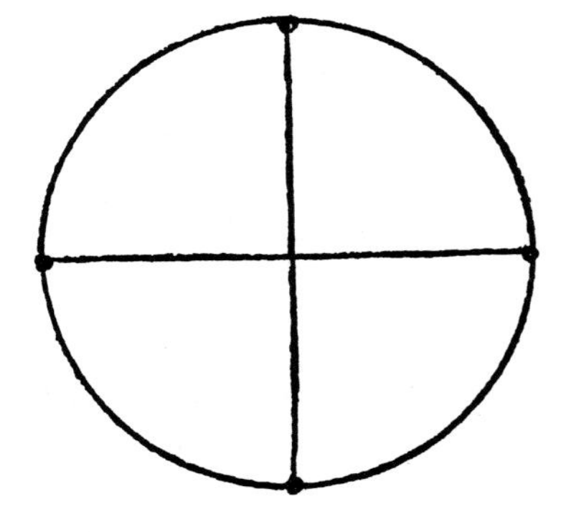

FIG. 9.—Fat Ring.

Number Two's Play.

Number two now takes his turn. Knuckling down at the taw line, he shoots as number one did, or if number one's taw is within range, he shoots at that, and if he is fortunate or skilful enough to hit number one's taw, then number one must hand over to number two all the ducks he (number one) has knocked out of the ring. If number two's luck still continues and he is able to hit number one's taw again, then number one is considered "killed," that is, he must put his taw in his pocket and quit playing until another game is started.

When number two misses, number three knuckles down at the taw line and shoots at the ducks in the ring, or at his opponent's taw, if that marble is within range.

"Killing."

When only two boys are playing if one "kills" the other, of course the killer wins the game, and more ducks are laid in and a new game started. The first man killed is the last to shoot in the next game, and the second man killed is next to the last to shoot, etc. In some sections of the country when three boys are playing the third boy is required always to shoot his taw across the ring, whether he shoots at the other taws or at the ducks.

The Uncertainties of "Yank."

It will not take a beginner in this game long to learn that his safety lies in keeping his own taw as far as possible away from his neighbors', and when he shoots in their direction he will shoot hard. One player may secure all the ducks but one and then miss, and the next player by striking the first's taw compel him to turn over to him all the ducks he has knocked out.

It does not require much wit to see that there is more to be gained by shooting at your neighbor's taw if the neighbor has been lucky than there is shooting at the one lone duck in the ring.

It sometimes takes good players a half, three quarters, or a full hour to finish one game. Often two or three unlucky players will combine against a lucky one and peg away at the lucky one's taw until he is compelled to give up the ducks he has knocked out. Another way to play this game is to make the player whose taw is hit replace in the ring all the marbles he has previously succeeded in knocking out.

Stand-up Marbles.

There is no skill required in this game, and the only excuse for its existence is that the rapid growth of our big cities has had the effect of so covering the boys' play-grounds with buildings and other obstructions that the boys are compelled to adopt such games as they can play under the existing conditions. So "Stand-up Megs" has become popular in many places.

Make a two-foot ring about six inches from a convenient house or fence. Use a "bumboozer" for a taw and stand at the taw line about six feet from the ring. Hold up your taw and take aim with your right eye, and shoot by hunching at the marbles in the ring. If you miss, pick up your big taw and let the next boy shoot. If any one knocks one or more ducks out, he continues to shoot until he fails. Each boy takes his turn until all the ducks are knocked out of the ring. Another way to play the game is to make a hole in the ground and place a duck for each player in the hole, then standing at the taw mark the players with their "bowlers" or "bumboozers" shoot as already described. If a player's taw or shooter fails to knock out any megs and remains in the hole, then he must put in as many ducks as "are up" before he is allowed to remove his taw.

"Follerings," or Followings,

is a travelling game, generally played by the boys on their way to school, or often, I am afraid, when they are sent on errands by their mothers. Although this game is a travelling game it is unnecessary to say that it does not lend haste to the traveller. In fact, it must be acknowledged that more speed can be made by a boy on an errand if he omits to play the game on his way.

The rules of "Follering" are simple. "First" shoots his marble in the direction he wants to travel, and "Second" shoots his marble at the "First's" taw. Thus they shoot each in turn until one boy is lucky enough to hit his opponent's taw. That means a duck for the fortunate one, or else a point in the game and another shot at his opponent's marble. He continues to shoot until he misses, and so the game goes on.

"Everything," and "Fen everything!" are the cries in this game. If one player before he shoots cries "Everything" before his opponent can cry "Fen everything," then the shooter may "hist," that is, as already explained, hold his marble up and shoot, or he may remove a brick, can, old shoe, or whatever object accident may place between him and his opponent's marble, or he may take "roundsters," going one side or the other of any object that may be in the way. But he cannot go any nearer the other boy's marble than his first position. If, however, the other player cries "Fen everything!" first, then the shooter must knuckle down and make the best of it.

The Art of Babying.

If one player hits his opponent's taw and knocks it into a gully, a hole, or the gutter and his own taw does not fly far away, he shouts "Everything!" if possible before the other player can say "Fen," and then he commences a series of soft, easy shots, each of which counts just the same as a long, difficult one. With care a good shot can baby away until his opponent shouts himself hoarse with cries of "Fen babying! Fen everything! Fen histing! Fen roundsters! Knuckle down." To all these cries the player pays no attention, but continues to shoot until he carelessly makes a miss. Then the other player has his revenge and babies away, to the great discomfort of his opponent.

Follerings starts where the two lads meet and lasts until the school-house or some other objective point is reached. It can be played almost anywhere, and is quite exciting enough to meet the approval of most boys.

Knucks.

This is a game of give and take. One boy, called "knucks," places a small marble between his knuckles and rests his hand on the ground. The other player knuckles down at the taw line four or five feet away and shoots at the marble between the fingers of his playmate. It is customary to knuckle down and loft, or shoot through the air, and not bowl along the ground. The taw marble or shooter used is of medium size. Every time the marble in "knucks'" hand is hit it counts one; every time "knucks'"

FIG. 10.—A Game of Knucks.

knuckles are hit it gives "knucks" a shot at the first shooter.

Suppose that it is agreed that each player should have three shots, and there are two in the game. Number one shoots three times, hits the marble once, and the knuckles twice. Then number one wins one count, and number two, who has been "knucks," takes his three shots, and two shots to pay for the two raps he had on his knuckles. That makes five shots he has at number one.

Unless number two is an expert he is going to hit number one's knuckles a number of times in his five shots, but number one grins and bears it, as he knows that the rules of the game will give him satisfaction. There is no end to this game, and it only stops when both boys agree that their knuckles demand a rest.

If one boy is a good player and the other a poor one the good player wins the most points, but the bad player makes the other's knuckles suffer for their skill.

The Long Ring.

About eight feet beyond the taw line, make a ring composed of two parts of a circle crossing each other at the ends (Fig. 11), a fish-shaped ring with its head toward taw line. Draw a straight line through the centre of the long ring to lay the marbles on. If only two boys are playing and each lays in a duck, one marble should be at each end of the ring. If more than two play, or if more than one duck apiece is laid in, then they should be placed along the line in the centre of the ring.

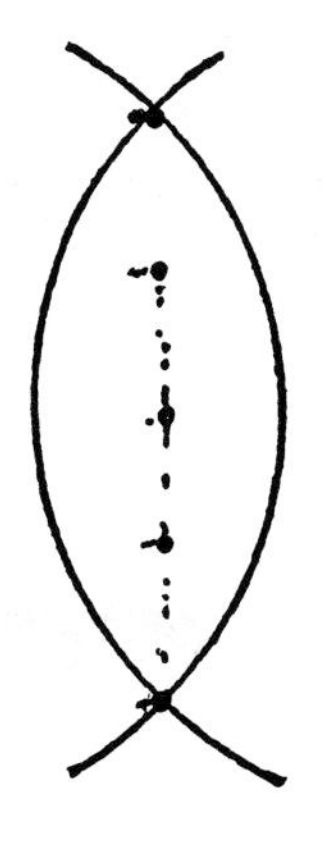

FIG. 11.—The Long Ring.

When number one shoots, if there are only two marbles he generally "sneaks," that is, he bowls, as some call it, or shoots his marble with just sufficient force to cause his taw to roll slowly along and come to a rest as near as possible one of the marbles in the ring.

In doing this number one runs the risk of being killed by number two, whose turn it now is to shoot, and if there are only two in the game, and number two kills number one, this gives the game to number two, but if there are more in the game it puts number one out. and number two has another shot at the ducks in the ring, and continues to shoot until he misses. Then number three shoots, or if number one is not dead, and only two are playing, number one shoots from the spot where his taw lies.

Any player can sneak whenever he thinks he dare risk it. Of course a sneak is a shot and he must run the chance of being killed; but if he is killed he can, when his turn comes around, lay in as many ducks as he did at first, and then placing another duck near the taw line, knuckle down and shoot, hitting the near duck on one side so as to cause his taw or shooter to fly down toward the ring. It often happens that in this way he can make up for what points he lost by being killed. If he makes a miss he leaves his taw where it rests, and the next player takes his turn.

Patterson.

This game is played like "Fat," previously described, and often goes by that name, but in place of the round ring used in real Fat the Patterson boys use the taw line and the oblong or fish-shaped ring of the Long Ring game. The principal difference between Long Ring and Patterson is that you must hit your opponent's taw twice to kill him, and he cannot come to life again by laying in when his turn comes and shooting at a duck near the taw line. The first time you hit his taw you win all the points he may have made, the second time you strike his taw you put him out of the game and there is one less to fight against; hence there is not much sneaking in Patterson.

Gambling Games.

"Sports" among boys may frequently be seen trying to entice other boys to pay a stated number of marbles a shot at a notched and numbered shingle. The "sport" holds the shingle with his hand and rests the edge with the notches in it on the ground, while the player shoots from taw at the notch with the biggest number. He seldom goes through, but if he succeeds, the "sport" pays him back as many marbles as are designated by the number over the notch his marble went through. This is a great game for cheating; a slight movement of the shingle from one side to the other will make the best shot miss, and, like all gambling games, create ill feeling, and frequently the game is only decided by the fists of the players.

The Bull Ring.

One of the really scientific games is the old-fashioned Bull Ring, which is from four to ten feet in diameter. The ducks are placed a few inches apart on a cross scratched in the middle of the ring. The number of ducks varies according to how many "a whack," or how many "up" or to "lay in" may be agreed upon. If four or five boys are in the game, "one up" makes a nice pot of ducks to shoot at.

If but two boys are playing they sometimes lay in three, four, or even more ducks apiece, according to their wealth. The boy who cries "First" soonest is accorded the first shot, and the others in their order. In case of dispute they "lag" for turn. Each player knuckles down and shoots for the opposite side of the ring, and their turns come in the order of their success; the nearest first and the most distant last.

Of course the object of the game is to knock out all the ducks if possible. Sometimes the first player, by a combination of luck and skill, will "skin the ring" before the others have had a shot. The first player knuckles down and lofts at the ducks in the middle of the ring. If he strikes one properly, his taw should stand or spin in place of the fleeing duck. The duck must reach or pass the line that makes the ring to be out and pocketed by the player, who now shoots from the place where his taw stands.

Sometimes his shooter will fly out of the ring, but if the duck is knocked out he continues to shoot, again knuckling down on the ring. In case he misses one shot, number two takes his turn. Whenever a slip is made or a hit fails to knock the duck from the ring and the shooter comes to

FIG. 12.—A Game in a Bull Ring.

rest inside the bull ring, it must remain where it is until the player's turn comes again or until the shooter is knocked out by one of the other players. If the shooter or taw in the ring is knocked out by another player's taw, the owner of the latter is out of the game, or killed, and there is one less to fight against. The player who knocks the taw out not only has another shot, but is entitled to pick one of the ducks from the ring as a reward for his luck. He continues to shoot until he misses.

In case two or more ducks are knocked out at one shot, if the player succeeds in crying "Dubs!" before the others cry "Fen dubs!" he is entitled to all he knocks out, otherwise he must replace all but one marble, but continue to shoot until he fails to knock out a duck. If a player is caught "hunching," that is, shoving his fist beyond the ring while shooting, and makes a lucky hit, he must replace the marble and shoot over again. "Histings" and the use of "bowlers" are debarred in the bull ring.

Sneaking or Dribbling.

Sneaking is allowed; that is, shooting the taw slowly, so that it will stop in or near the centre. This counts as a turn, and the marble is allowed to rest there until the sneaker's turn comes round again, in which case, if he has not been killed by some other player, he shoots from the spot occupied by his taw.

If a dead man's turn comes around and there are enough ducks in the ring to warrant the risk, the dead man may re-enter by laying in the middle twice as many ducks as the game required at first and placing still another duck near the edge of the ring to carom on. He shoots at the carom duck with the hopes of knocking it out and flying in the centre, where, if he is "any good" he will "skin the ring." Often the dead man is unsuccessful and the game goes on.

Duck-in-a-Hole.

This game is played with three shallow holes in a line at right angles with a taw line which should be about ten feet distant from the first hole. The holes are three feet apart. The object of each player is to shoot his marble so that it will go in and remain in the first hole. If successful in this he is allowed to place his thumb on the edge of the first hole, and using his hand as a pair of dividers, by a twist of the wrist he describes, that is, traces with the ends of his fingers, a curved line on the ground.

This is called taking a span, and the player then knuckles down on the span line and shoots for the second hole. Taking another span he shoots for the third, and if successful he now takes a span back toward the middle hole and shoots for that. If he again succeeds he takes a span and shoots for the first hole, and if he fails not in this he is a "duck" and can take two spans from the spot where his marble lies every time he shoots. When he has gone forward and backward twice he is allowed three spans, and when he has gone backward and forward three times he is a "King Duck" and can take four spans.

If the first player misses the first hole, player number two shoots. If number two's marble rolls in the first hole and stays there he looks around for the first player's taw, and when he discovers it, if he feels certain he can hit it, he takes a span, knuckles down and cracks away at number one's taw. If he hits it he places his own marble in the second hole and proceeds to try for the next until he misses. Then the next player tries his luck.

When number one's turn comes around again he shoots for the first hole, knuckling down on the spot to which number two knocked his (number one's) taw.

King Duck.

Each player strives to be King Duck first. Each time one player hits another player's taw the lucky player counts one point, and the one hit loses a point.

When one player is King Duck it is hard on the others, because as soon as they miss a hole he is on them. For his four spans from the nearest hole will almost always bring him within short shooting distance of any marble that has missed a hole, and when he hits that marble he generally manages to hit it hard enough to send it flying.

By the time three boys have won the title of King Duck the game is over. At the advent of the second King Duck the first monarch divides with him and gives him one of the end holes to command, and he keeps the other two. When the third man is King the first King assigns him the remaining end hole and retains command of the middle hole, but by this time the boys are ready to stop for a rest. Each time a player hits a marble it counts one point, and the game may be for ten points or ten thousand points.

Meg-in-a-Hole

differs from the preceding game of Duck-in-a-Hole, first, in the fact that there is no taw line. The first player shoots from one end hole at the middle hole. After he succeeds in shooting into the middle hole he is entitled to a span, but he has no more than a span until he is King, having gone backward and forward three times.

The King can take one foot (his own foot for a measure) and a span from the first hole, two feet and a span from the second hole, and three feet and a span from the third hole before shooting at any other player's marble that has made a miss.

This gives the King great power, and it is hard to escape him. It often happens that the King knocks the other marbles fifteen or more feet away from their holes, and it is no easy matter for the unfortunate player to approach the holes again.

If a second player wins the title of King, the first King assigns him the first hole to guard, because there is less shooting for it, for the players only go in it three times, while they go six times in the middle hole. The third hole is next best to the middle, or, as I heard one boy put it, "next worse to the first hole." If a player misses it and a King is loafing around, the player does not stand much chance of getting near it again. When all have become Kings the game is over.

Meg-on-a-String.

This is a game of skill, and at this day finds little favor. The boys seem to prefer the less skilful and ruder games, such as Stand-up marbles, a game I notice the lads playing under the lamp-posts after dark; and so primitive has the sport become in the great cities, that in place of the beautiful agate for a taw these boys use stones, which they hold up to one eye, then pitch at a group of shamefaced marbles huddled together in a hole in the ground.

But Meg-on-a-String requires a higher sort of skill to play, and the successful player must be a good shot at fair knuckling-down shooting.

In a crack in a friendly fence a small stick is so thrust that its free end is about three feet outside the fence line. From near the end of the stick threads are hung about three inches apart, and on the ends of the threads are small lumps of shoemaker's wax. By pressing the wax against a small alley, commie, crystal, china, plaster, or agate, the marbles will adhere and swing from the ends of the threads. The latter should be so adjusted that the marbles clear the ground by an inch or two.

There is no ring in this game, but a taw line is scratched about four feet from the meg stick, and a marble for each player hangs from the stick. It is all knuckling down and lofting in this game, and the swinging marbles are kept in motion, it being against the rules for any boy to shoot at a stationary duck. He is only allowed to wait until the marbles cease to strike against each other, then he must shoot.

When the first player misses, the second player shoots. If the first player's taw is within reach he may shoot at that, and if he hits it then the owner of the unlucky taw is dead and out of the game, and the boy who killed him has another shot at the swinging marbles, or if there are only two players, he wins the game.

What Counts.

To make a successful hit it is deemed necessary to knock the swinging duck off the string, otherwise the shot does not count. When a player's taw is too near the fence he can cry "Sidings," and move to one side far enough to enable him to shoot with comfort. But if the other boys cry "Fen Sidings" before he cries "Sidings," then the player must make the best of his ill luck and shoot. It is allowable to sneak, that is, to shoot with so little force that your taw will only roll to the spot near the swinging marbles and rest there, but a sneaker always runs the risk of being killed and put out of the game by the next in turn.

"Dubs" and "Fen dubs," "Sidings" and "Fen sidings" are all the cries in this game, because the rules of the game are "Fen histings," "Fen clearances," "Fen, fen everything," except sidings and dubs, and it is even fen to these if a player shouts the word in time.

The reader can readily see that no bad shot at marbles need try this game with any hope of success, but to the real sportsmen among the boys the game will be popular. Old players try to get a position flanking the swinging ducks, as this position has a double advantage. First, if the player misses the first marble, he is liable to hit one of the others, and second, as it is necessary to loft and shoot hard in order to knock a marble off the string, if he misses his taw he strikes against the fence and bounds back to practically the same position he shot from, in place of hurtling off ten or twelve feet, or away or back over the taw line.

For over two thousand years boys have been playing marbles, and have developed some really scientific games, which much older people might play without loss of dignity. But since the game is confined practically to the youngsters, it behooves them to see to it that the noble and ancient games of marbles are not degraded into shingle gambling boards and pitch rock.

Block or Square Ring.

After reading over the preceding description of marble games to a young Brooklyn friend of mine, he exclaimed, "Well! You have left out Block. We play Block in Brooklyn."

Now it is not the intention of the author to slight Brooklyn in this book, and a game that they can play there must be adapted to any large city. Block is played with a square ring, if we may be allowed to call a square a ring, and the ring is quartered as it is in Fat, a game to which Block is akin. As in Fat, the marbles are laid in on the intersections of the cross lines, but the taw line is about thirty feet away.

This game is sometimes called Injun, a corruption of Indian, probably because the game is a game of extermination. For, in order to win, you must kill all the other players. Hence, you can see that "First" plays at a disadvantage, there being no one for him to kill; if he knocks out a duck he must replace it. If a taw stops inside the ring, that is a fatal shot, for he has killed himself and is out of the game. So when the first player shoots he does not knuckle down, but toes the taw line and tosses his taw for a good position near the ring.

For good and sufficient reasons the second player has no desire to get near the first, so he throws his marble with sufficient force to send it through the ring out of reach of First, hoping that his taw may be fortunate enough to knock out a duck on its way. Because if number two knocks out a duck, he can, before replacing the duck, go back to taw and holding the duck in his left hand shoot his taw with his right so that it will strike on the top or side of the duck and fly off near First's taw, which he may then hit and kill.

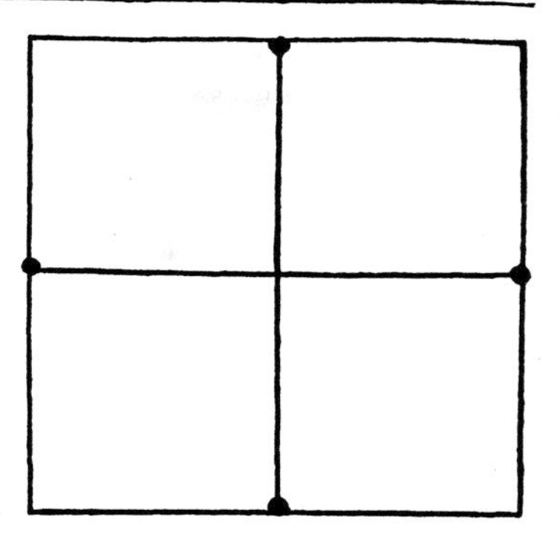

TAW LINE.

FIG. 13.—The Block or Square Ring.

If number two misses the duck, number three pitches his marble off to one side, and thus the game goes on, each boy doing his best to guard his own taw and to hit and kill his neighbor's taw, knocking out ducks when the opportunity comes for the sake of the privilege of going back to taw and making a flying shot from the duck to the neighborhood of his playmate's marble.

At the end of the game the same number of ducks of course remain in the ring that were placed there. If any player misses the duck that he is trying to make a fly shot on he loses his turn, and has the mortification of seeing his taw roll dangerously near an opponent, where he must allow it to remain and run the chance of being killed. When all but one are killed the survivor is "Big Injun" and has won the game. A similar game is played in other places with the moon ring (Fig. 14).

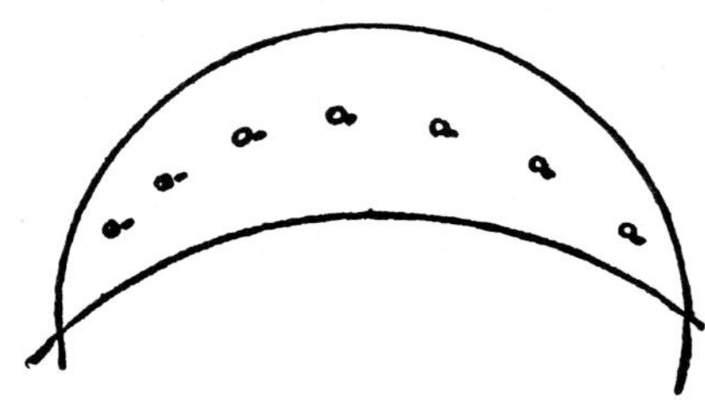

FIG. 14.—The Moon Ring.

There are numerous other games played in the cities which are the outgrowth of the cramped spaces the boys have for play-grounds, but as they differ in different cities and also in different parts of the same city and are only modifications of the games given here, they will be omitted.

FIG. 15.—Top Time in the City. A Game of Plug in the Ring on the Housetop.

CHAPTER III

TOP TIME

Whip Tops — Home-made Tops — Peg Tops—Plug in the Ring—Chip Stone — Racing Tops.

THERE is no doubt about it—boys are the most conservative people in the world. Nations have been born, grown great, and died, leaving only mouldering ruins to tell of their former grandeur, but when those nations were young, boys were whipping tops, and to-day boys are belaboring their tops with a lash of soiled rags with as much vigor and enthusiasm as if the latter were newly discovered toys.

In fact the boys are more enthusiastic than they would be over a new toy. No game or toy is considered respectable unless its ancestry is lost in the murky atmosphere that covers the pre-historic past. Ever since I can remember each season has brought forth some novelty in tops, but the whip-top and the peg-top still hold their own and the novelties are lost and forgotten.

In the house, an American boy will occasionally condescend to spin a musical top or a whistling or humming top to amuse his little sister, but he never thinks of taking such toys on the play-ground or in the street to spin before his comrades and school-fellows.

With all these facts before me I dare not propose a new style of top or suggest a new game, because both would go to the land of useless toys, a land grown-up men spend time and labor to supply with toys which boys will not use and games which boys will not play. I say a land for lack of a better name. No one knows what becomes of all the wonderful inventions for boys that boys do not want unless they go to a place where very bad boys go who are compelled to play these new-fangled games and spin these wonderful tops as a punishment for sins committed in this glorious world, where good boys have the old reliable peg-top and its even more ancient brother, the whip-top.

Home-made Tops.

As for home-made tops, those made of a spool are the favorites, and are usually made to spin by a twist of the finger and thumb. To make one it is only necessary to whittle a stick to a diameter a trifle greater than the hole in the spool, and hammer it in so that a part of the stick will protrude at both ends. Then whittle off one of the flanges of the spool, and bring the stick at that end to a point for a peg. Cut off all but about an inch of the stick from the other end, and your spool top is finished.

A boy that I had in my studio made a top with an old tin blacking-box and some lead pipe, which he melted and poured into the mould. When it was cool he had a flat leaden disk. But first he took a wooden spool, and cut off one flange and whittled the end to a blunt point. Next he cut a hole in the blacking-box, so that the spool could be forced in, and made to stick there.

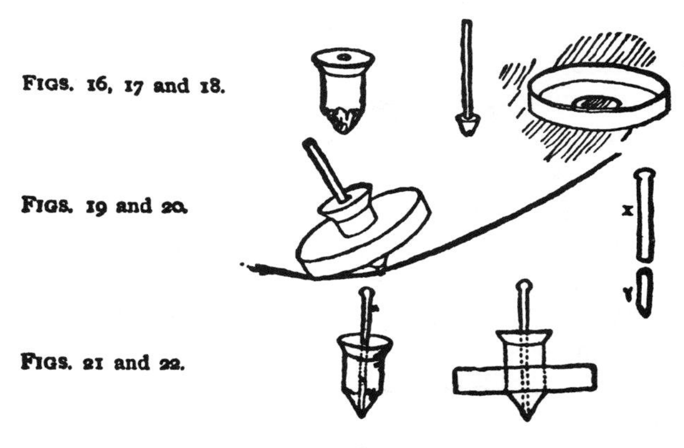

CONSTRUCTION OF HOME-MADE TOPS.

FIGS. 16, 17, 18, 19, and 22 show construction of slack-rope dancing top; x and y, Figs. 20 and 21, show parts of top with double peg. FIG. 22 is a top with a solid peg for spinning on the table.

I asked him what sort of top he was making, and he replied, "A slack-rope dancer."

This proved to be the case, for he made a peg for the top with a notch in one end, and he spun the top for me on a string for a slack rope. Figs. 16, 17, 18, and 19 show the construction of this ingenious toy.

Afterward he made another somewhat similar top with a movable stick and fixed peg, spun it, removed the stick, and inserted pieces of bent wire, which, when the latter were whirled around, looked like glass goblets, vases, and various other objects.

The materials are cheap, and the labor light, in making this top. Try it!

Plug in the Ring.

The "plugger" is the top you spin, the "bait" is the top or tops you try to strike with your "plugger."

A top is "asleep" when it stands perfectly erect and apparently motionless while spinning. A "gigler" is a top that goes dancing and hopping about. "A dead top" is one that has ceased to spin; all bait tops are necessarily dead tops.

Boys use as much care in selecting their pegger or plugger as they do in choosing their taw or shooter in marbles. Some prefer a rather long spindle top, others a short, heavy boxwood plugger. All tops should have screw pegs, for these are rarely driven up through the top so as to split them. Besides, the screw top is not so apt to drop out as the common ringed peg.

Get a Good String.

As a rule, I think, the string sold for top string in New York is too light. A cord half as thick again gives better results.

Select for a string a rather heavy cotton cord, about a yard long. At one end fasten a wooden button mould, or, better still, an old bone button. About an inch and a half from the other end tie a hard knot in the string and allow the end to fray out below the knot (see Figure 23). Wet the end of the string and plaster it diagonally up the side of the top. Then wind tightly until the string covers the bottom nearly to the top of the top, leaving enough string to wrap around the hand. Slip the string between the first and second fingers, so that the button fits on the outside of the hand; then wind the slack around the hand until the top fits tightly, with the big end grasped by the first finger bending over it. The peg should rest on the outside of the thumb between the first and second joints.

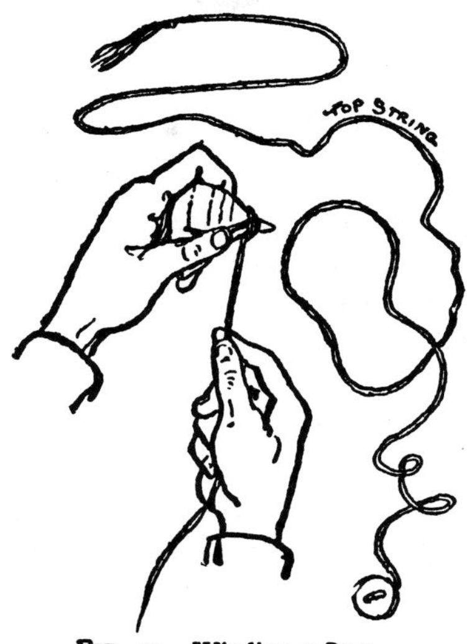

FIG. 23.—Winding a Top.

To spin the top, raise your hand above and back of your head (see second boy, Fig. 15); bring it down forcibly and throw the top six or eight feet in front of you (see third boy, Fig. 15). Don't jerk back. If you have made a proper throw the top will spin "for all it is worth."

Now for the game: Mark out a bull ring about six feet in diameter and in the centre mark a smaller ring about a foot in diameter. Put as many tops in the centre as there are players, and toss up for first shot or decide your turns in any manner you may agree upon. Many boys play without turns, each spinning his top as soon as he can wind it.

The first player winds up his plugger with care and grasps it firmly in his hand, then with his left toe on the outside ring he tries to hit the tops in the centre. If he misses and fails to spin, or if he strikes outside of the centre circle, he must put another top in the middle and await his next turn. If he strikes the tops with the big end of his plugger it counts a miss, and all he knocks out must be replaced; but if the peg of his plugger strikes a top and sends it out of the little centre ring he pockets the bait top and spins or plugs again.

If his plugger strikes in the small ring and spins there, and by knocking against the tops knocks them out, it is called a hit—he wins the tops knocked out and has another turn. A good player will sometimes spin his plugger in the small ring and fail to knock out any tops. In this case the player must allow his top to stop spinning before he touches it, and if, when it tires out, or "dies," as the boys call it, it fails to roll out of the ring, he must place another top in the centre.

A Great Honor.

Good players will often split one of the tops in the middle ring by the force and accuracy with which their plugger's peg strikes the "bait." This is considered a great honor, but, of course, it ruins the bait top.

You cannot play Plug in the Ring until you learn to hold and throw a top as described above. The baby manner of spinning by jerking back the string is never accurate and has not enough force to split a pea. Neither must you hold your top like a girl, with the greater part under the forefinger and the peg sticking into the ball of the thumb.

I have frequently seen this game played "for keeps," but the bait was composed of toothless, battered wrecks of tops that had no other value than as trophies of victory. The proper game is to use the bait you win as marks or scores, and after the game is finished return them to their proper owners. The object of the game is not to win tops, but to derive pleasure from a test of skill.

Chip Stone.

In the gravel-pit or somewhere along the river, creek, lake, or sea-shore may be found disk-shaped stones called "skippers" or "sailors," because the boys can make them sail through the air or skip over the surface of the water. These stones are used for counters in the game of Chip Stone. The pure white or semi-transparent skippers, about the size of an old-fashioned copper cent, are the kind selected.

A bull ring about five feet in diameter is made on the ground, or two taw lines about five feet apart are drawn on the sidewalk, and each boy, as in marbles, "lays in" a counter. If the game is on the sidewalk the skippers are placed in a row between the two taw lines. If in a bull ring the stones are placed in a small circle in the centre of the ring.

In turn each player spins his top and plugs at the skippers in the ring or between the taw lines; if his top fails to spin he "lays in" another skipper.

If his top "dies," that is, stops spinning inside the ring, he "lays in" another stone. But if his top spins as it should he takes it up on a little wooden shovel and drops it so that the peg hits the edge of a counter; he continues to scoop up and drop the top so long as it will spin, or until it has knocked a counter over the taw line or outside the ring, in which case, as in marbles, he has another turn.

Chip Stone is really a game of marbles in which sailors or skippers are used for ducks and tops are used for taws. Of course each boy takes great pride in his collection of trophies, each of which he considers as a medal won by his superior skill as a top spinner. No clumsy, awkward top spinner can hope to have many sailors in his pocket unless he hunts them in the gravel-pit in place of competing for them at the bull ring or between the taw lines.

Fig. 24 shows the wooden shovel or spoon which each player should make for himself with his own pocket-knife. Sweet smelling red cedar is the choice wood, but almost any other kind will answer.

Whip-Tops—Eel-skin Whips the Best.

As a rule boys use old rags for their whips. These soon become very much soiled and look untidy, but the real

Fig. 24.—The Wooden Chip Stone Shovel.

sportsman, be he man or boy, takes great pride in his guns, fish-rods, skates, golf-sticks, or top-whips; and such boys prefer for a top-whip an eel-skin fastened to a short wooden handle.

Country boys catch their own eels, city boys get the skins at the fish market.

A whip-top can be made of any sort of wood, and in place of a peg a brass hollow-headed furniture-tack is driven into the point where the peg of an ordinary top is located.

To Spin the Top.

Put your whip under your left arm and take the top in your right hand, and grasping it with your thumb and second finger give it a smart twirl. If this is skilfully done the top will spin long enough for you to grasp the handle of your eel-skin whip and give it a lash, striking outward and drawing the whip toward you at the end of the stroke.

Fighting Tops.

At the word "Go!" two boys spin their tops and then thrash the poor things until they bump together. The top that knocks its opponent out of the bull ring in which they are spun is the King Top. It is considered a foul for one boy to strike his opponent's top with his whip or in any way interfere with it except by guiding his own top in the path of the other. A top that stops spinning is beaten, not with the whip, but by the other top that keeps alive.

Racing Tops.

Two taw lines are drawn on the hard ground or sidewalk, and at the word "Go!" all the boys in the game spin their tops and belabor them with might and main, endeavoring at the same time to compel them to travel over the space between the taw lines before their opponents can cover the distance. It requires no little skill to drive a successful race.

Whipping tops, like most of the favorite games of boys, is a very old sport. The little boys in Old Testament times played the game just as you are playing it now. West of the Allegheny Mountains the whip-top is not as often seen as in the neighborhood of New York City.

FIG. 25.—Kite Time.

Though marble time can't always last,
Though time for spinning tops is past,
The winds of March blow kite time here,
And April fools' day, too, draws near.

CHAPTER IV

LATEST THINGS IN KITES

For Practical Uses — Steering Kites — Life Savers — Men Lifters and Other Novel Forms—Kites as Motive Power—The Malay Variety.

KITE time begins with March, or used to when the writer was a boy, in Cincinnati. Even the blustering March wind must be weaker in the Ohio River Valley than here on the coast. If some one had imported an ordinary New York kite into Ohio and shown it to the boys there they would have told him to go and get a shingle and it would fly better, but now the author must modify his judgment and admit that the heavy sticks and apparently careless pasting on the Atlantic-coast kites are necessary to give them strength to brave the gales from off the ocean. In place of the twine used in New York we flew our kites with cotton thread, and it was only an extra large kite that required white cotton string. The dainty tissue-paper covered kite, with its framework of delicate match sticks that is used in the interior of our country, would be wrecked by the first blast of the boisterous March wind on the coast.

Grave professors and men of dry scientific minds often take to boys' sports in a heavy, ponderous fashion, and try to demonstrate some pet theory of their own by means of the boys' playthings. Old Ben Franklin did not think it beneath his dignity to fly a kite. Had Benjamin consulted the modern American boy he would have been told not to use the European bow kite, but to take the coffin-shaped or American hexagonal kite for his experiment, or one of the tailless kites that have lately become so popular with grown-up scientific kite flyers.

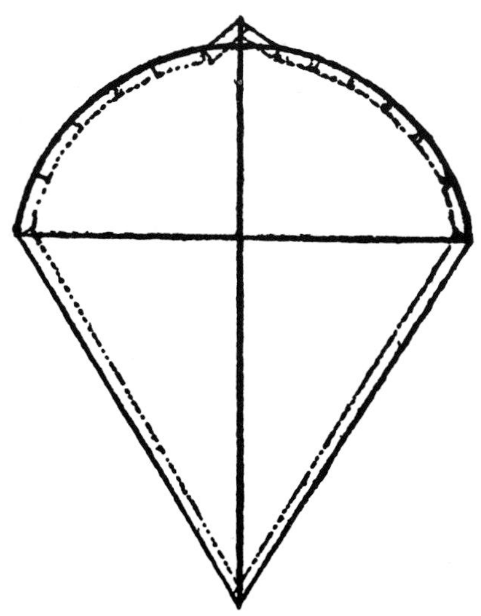

FIG. 26.—The Inevitable Bow Kite. Sticks are Represented by Thick Lines. Strings are Represented by Thin Lines. Where the Paper is Folded and Pasted the Edges are Represented by Dotted Lines.

Kites for Practical Uses.

The engineers who constructed the first bridge across

Niagara River did not refuse to accept as a means of communication between the shores a line placed there by a kite. Sixty years ago an Englishman by the name of Ward suggested the use of a kite as a means of establishing communication between vessels wrecked upon the off-lying rocks of a lee shore and the mainland. Being an Englishman, he selected, of course, the inevitable bow kite (Fig. 26), with its tail festooned with bunches of paper in the manner made respectable by ages of use.

I give his method because it may be of use to boys in accomplishing some other object, such as stretching a home-made telephone line across the intervening space between two big apartment houses, or across a river or lake in the country, or for a thousand other purposes dear to a boy.

FIG. 27.—The Pulley and Weight Kite.

The Pulley and Weight Kite.

Mr. Ward's method of using a kite as a means of suspending and conveying a line ashore is as follows:

At a short distance below the kite's bellyband, attach to the kite-string a loop and suspend from the loop a pulley light enough in weight not to impede the flight of the Weight and Pulley Kite. Over this pulley pass a second string and fasten the weight to the end, the other end of the string being aboard the ship. When the kite has sailed through the storm until it floats over the land, no more line is given out, and the kite becomes a stationary point, from which the weight attached to the end of the line is allowed to drop, and thus form a communication between the ship and the shore. In an experiment made by the inventor, the kite was found to fly best with the weight hung at least ten yards below the kite. (See Fig. 27.)

In 1893 the New York underwriters took to flying immense star kites covered with oil-cloth. These kites had two bellybands and two strings to guide or steer the kites by, and tails of jute, with a life buoys attached.

The two-stringed star kite is an invention of Professor J. Woodbridge Davis of New York. (See Fig. 29.)

Steering Kites.

Seven years ago the professor began to experiment in flying kites, and being displeased with the stationary position ordinarily assumed by them, and not satisfied with the wig-waggle of the short-tailed or the darting of the light-tailed variety, which imparts so much excitement to the young novice, he added two bellybands and two strings, by means of which after a little practice he was able to steer his kite around the sky and make it perform all manner of queer and absurd antics, to the great delight of the small boys.

It is said that the professor became so proficient with his kite that he could make it cut out letters in the sky, dance and dive, and do other marvellous things. He also found that he could make it go off the wind many degrees. In speaking of what he could now make the kite do, he said it would not sail upon the wind as the Vigilant and Valkyrie did, but it could make some very remarkable tacks.

Driving a Kite Attached to a Wagon.

A couple of his pupils last summer took a carriage ride on the shore of Long Island, in the vicinity of Arverne, and the nag they drove was a star-shaped kite, seven feet in diameter.

These two young men conceived the idea of propelling a wagon by means of one of these kites. They arranged a four-wheeled vehicle with a platform, placing a seat in the

FIG. 28.—Wagon Attached to Kite. FIG. 29.—The Double Belly-Banded Kite.

rear, in front of which is a long box wherein to place one's feet, so that the weight can be as low as possible. The arrangement allows one plenty of room to manipulate the cord of each windlass by means of a crank and a brake. The other passenger sits on a little more elevated seat near the front, where he can work a sort of brake, the shaft of which is connected with a simple device for steering the front wheels. The wheels are all the same size, three feet four inches, and are strongly made. The tray is four feet eight inches.

A favorable breeze sent up the kite, and soon the wagon was following the new motor along the beach. By being able to steer the kite to right or left they were enabled to follow the line of the shore.

If any of the readers of this book are ambitious to make an experiment, they had better try a small hand wagon with a much smaller kite for motive power (Fig. 28). Kites will pull a wagon, as has been demonstrated many times, and if the kite can be steered then the greatest difficulty is overcome.

Why not Use a Sled?

Attached to a sled in winter time such a kite would afford royal sport, and something entirely new. There are many places where a sled could be used on the smooth snow or ice that would be impracticable for any kind of a wagon.

Keeled Buoys Towed by Kites near New York City.

Boys! Keep your eyes on Bayonne, New Jersey. There appears to be a nest of inveterate kite-fliers there. First we hear of one thing and then of another in the kite line, and each time some man from Bayonne is mixed up in it, or at least he is at one end of the line.

Lately Mr. Eddy has been experimenting with Professor J. Woodbridge Davis's keeled kite buoy. The buoy here referred to is a float, not a boy, as the old song has it:

> " Meaning a buoy for the ship what sails,
> And not a *boy* of the juvenile males."

The kites used in the experiment were from the " stables" of Mr. Eddy. The five-foot tailless kite that Commodore Vermilye and Mr. Eddy first sent up on this occasion had a perforated centre, which allowed some of the wind to escape through the hole or holes in the kite, and made it less liable to pull hard suddenly, when struck by a squall or wind puff. In other words, the perforation answered for, and was the kite's safety-valve.

The First Experiment.

The buoy was sent out from the Port Richmond side, while the kites went up from the Bergen Point side, for the reason that the wind was southerly, southwesterly, and westerly, often carrying the kites inland, beyond the Bergen Point shore.

The keel buoy was put in a rowboat and rowed to Port Richmond. A six-foot kite was flying, attached to about four hundred feet of cord which was fastened to the buoy in the boat rowed by John A. Weaver, with Mr. Eddy holding the kite cord.

The buoy was dropped overboard and cut loose at 4.20 P.M., the wind having shifted to westerly, and although the kite pulled eastward, the buoy moved northward, the adjustment being such that the buoy tacked under the side pull like a yacht. Its speed was very unequal, owing to the irregular pull of the kite, but the buoy reached the marsh above the Port Johnson coal docks at 4.29, making the distance of a mile in nine minutes. Mr. Weaver rowed for the Port Richmond side at 4.35, Mr. Eddy holding the string, the kite maintaining its position as long as the boat moved westward against the wind. But when Port Richmond was reached the westerly wind died out and dropped the kite into the water at 4.45 P.M.

The kite was recovered, but the experiment was abandoned because a fog settled over the water, the wind completely reversing and suddenly setting in from the east. Much was learned of the management of kites on the water in calms. There are indications that the buoy can tack against the wind when the kite pull is adjusted at different angles.

Of what interest is all this to the boys? Of great interest; on account of the weather the most satisfactory results were not obtained, but enough was learned to suggest the possibilities of a new sport to the boys, that of using

Kites for Sails for Small Boats.

Probably ever since kites were invented boys have attempted to use them for motive power, to make their boats go with no other sail than the one soaring in the sky, and no mast but the slender line leading from the boat to the kite.

In almost every attempt the boys have been partially successful, but as the boats could only go before the wind and follow the kites, the direction of their course had to depend entirely upon the whims of the weather clerk, and kite-sailing never became a sport. But the late experiments with towing-floats and the invention of the double belly-band has opened new possibilities for the future of kite-fliers.

The advantage of the star kite for sailing purposes is first in its strength which the three sticks give it. Since all these sticks cross in the centre it makes a kite of practically six sticks, and the sticks on each side supply a good strong support for the two belly-bands.

For sailing purposes build your kite about three and one-half feet in diameter, cover it with good Manilla paper, and treat your paper with a coating of hot paraffine to make it water-proof. Use a paint brush and put the paraffine on as if you were painting the paper. Mr. Woglom's storm kites are of paper covered with paraffine, and he has flown them when it rained so hard that he was wet to the skin, but the kites did not suffer. When kite-sailing there is always the chance of your sail-kite falling into the water, and if your sail is not water-proof your fun is over for at least that day.

Kites for Swimming.

As the writer grows older he becomes more and more modest in his claims for originality. For it has often happened that his brightest and most treasured original ideas are found upon investigation to be claimed also by some one who lived long ago.

A kite for swimming is one of those ideas, and the writer really thought it a brand new one. But, alas! he has discovered that that rare old American, Ben Franklin, has a prior claim which, since Ben lived first, the author cannot dispute. But Ben only floated on his back and allowed the kite to tow him, and you can at least improve upon Mr. Franklin's idea by using a plank for a float, which will allow you to see where you are going, and a double belly-banded kite that you can guide in the direction you wish to go. All who have tried this sport pronounce it delightful, and it will be preferred by many to kite-sailing. Of course the kite-swimmer must be careful not to hitch his kite to his float, or if he does to guard both float and kite, for his steed will run away upon the first opportunity and never stop running until the wind fails or some obstruction is met.

There are only a few days in which all these kite sports can be enjoyed in some of the inland parts of the country, but in other sections there is seldom a day the year 'round that there is not wind enough and to spare.

The Belly-bands.

The way to make a star kite is fully described in the "American Boy's Handy Book," and it is not our intention to duplicate anything there described. But the two belly-band steering apparatus is something new and properly belongs here. The star kite has three sticks of equal length, which cross each other in the centre; they are strung so that when the ends of the sticks are equal distances apart they form a six-pointed star, thus, and the belly-bands may be fastened at equal distances from the centre, one each side, to the sticks in this manner shown by Fig. 30. The tail-band, of course, is simply a loop fastened to the sticks at the bottom so that it will hang below the kite. It is taken for granted that the reader knows that the belly-band of all kites is on the paper side of the kite and not on the same side as the sticks. In the latter case the wind would tear the covering off the kite at once.

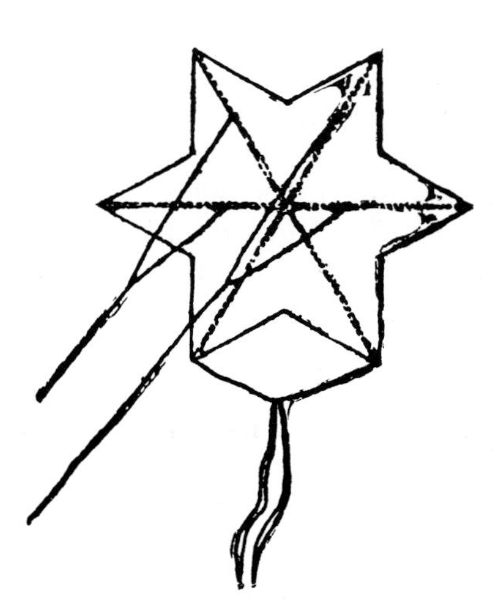

Fig. 30.—The Star Kite.

"Kite Broken Loose!"

That was the cry that used to send a thrill through every youngster and start them all on a hot race after the fugitive kite. Twenty or thirty years ago the runaway kite always became the property of the one who first captured it. Such was the unquestioned though unwritten law among the boys, and it appears from the items that occasionally appear in the papers that to this day there is a strong tendency on the part of the boys, and even men, to adhere strictly to this old law.

One of Mr. Eddy's tandem teams of kites broke away and the kite-string slid over the neck of a man working on a coal-barge. The coal-heaver, upon putting up his hands to investigate the cause of the tickling of his neck, to his great astonishment found himself holding a team of funny tailless kites, which were bobbing around in the sky. When Mr. Eddy demanded his runaways he had considerable difficulty in persuading the man to give up the prize.

A Team of Eight Kites Loose.

In July, 1894, the same gentleman lost a team of eight kites which he was flying at Bayonne. One kite caught in a tree and the rest broke away and sailed over the Kill von Kull. Then the bottom kite struck the ground, and again the upper ones broke away, leaving their unfortunate comrade. The six remaining kites went scudding over Staten Island until the dangling string caught on a telegraph wire and brought the six runaways up standing. Mr. Eddy had to journey by train and boat before he could cover the distance travelled by the fugitives and effect their capture.

A Runaway's Experience.

The writer once saw a kite pull the stick the twine was fastened to from the hands of a boy who was perched upon the roof of a tenement-house. The building was near the East River on the New York side, a good wind was blowing and the kite lifted the stick over the intervening house-tops until it dangled over the water. Here the lack of resistance caused the kite to settle, and down came the stick into the water. The water offered sufficient resistance to the stick to send the runaway kite up again, and the stick was towed diagonally across the river until it reached the Brooklyn side, where the string became entangled in the rigging of a ship that was being loaded with sugar. When last seen the runaway tenement-house kite was bravely flying from the ship.

Kite at Boothbay Tows a Plank.

While spending summer at Ocean Point, near Boothbay, Me., the author sent up an ordinary Japanese hawk kite and attached the string to a nail in a piece of plank which was placed in the ocean. The plank presented resistance enough to keep the kite aloft, and it sailed away past Squirrel Island, Pumpkin Rock, and out to sea.

Two days afterward when the mackerel fleet came into port, the writer learned that the crew of one of the smacks had been surprised to find a kite floating from a line entangled in the rigging of the main-mast. Where it came from was a mystery, until the skipper and the writer chanced to meet while the latter was making a drawing of the mackerel fishers.

Some one in New Jersey once sent a kite out to sea attached to a float, and it was picked up on the coast of Virginia.

Notes to Neptune.

Boys who live near the lake-side or sea-shore, or those who visit these places for their vacation, can send messages out to sea whenever the wind is " off shore," that is, blowing from the shore toward the sea.

Address the note to Mr. Neptune, Atlantic Ocean or Pacific Ocean or Lake Erie, according to the location of the sender. The contents can be worded to suit the taste of the writer, but it should end up with a request that the finder communicate with the sender and tell him when, where, and under what conditions the note was found; and do not forget to give your address as carefully as you do when writing to some one for an autograph.

Seal the note and enclose it in some water-proof material or a tightly corked bottle. Lash the package or bottle securely to a short plank and drive a nail securely in one end of the plank.

After sending up your kite attach the string to the nail and let the plank go out to sea. If no accident happens to your kite it is almost certain to attract some one's attention, and as a rule any one receiving such a message at sea will enter into the spirit of the thing and send a reply on the first opportunity. In this manner you can learn how far the kite travelled with its tow.

Messengers up the Kite String.

It used to be a favorite amusement with the boys to send messengers up their kite strings after they had succeeded in raising their good kite to a respectable height. These messengers are simply round pieces of colored paper with slits cut in them to holes in their centres. The slits are for the purpose of sliding the string through to the hole. The latter is just large enough to allow the paper to slip over the string with as little friction as possible. (See Figs. 31 and 32.)

The wind takes these papers up the string and hence they are called messengers to the kite.

High Fliers.

In 1884 Mr. E. Douglass Archibald, of the Royal Meteorological Society, sent up two diamond-shaped kites, one seven feet and the other four feet in diameter, both attached to one string. These kites, like Ben Franklin's,

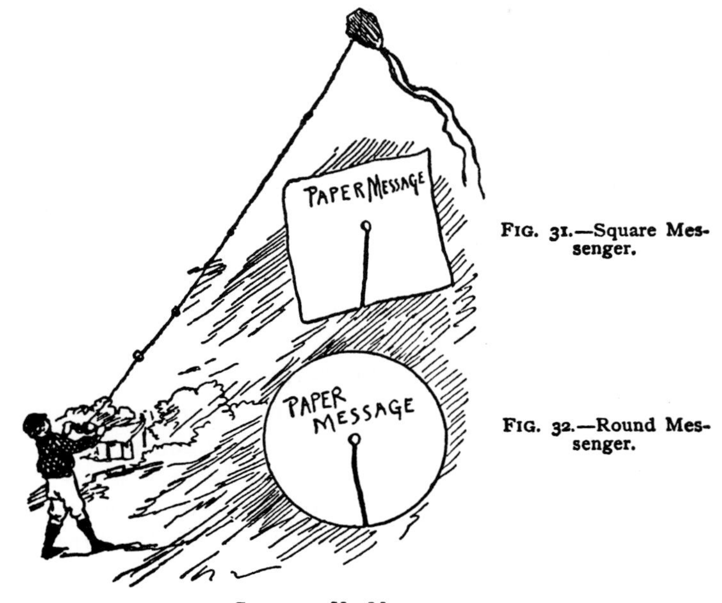

FIG. 31.—Square Messenger.

FIG. 32.—Round Messenger.

SENDING UP MESSENGERS.

were covered with silk; they carried scientific instruments 2,200 feet into the air. "Pshaw," said some Americans, "how is this for high?" and they sent a tandem team of kites 6,000 feet up in the air; over a mile high!

That is kite flying! Why, if any one of the boys had been able to do such a thing when the author was a lad flying kites on the banks of the Ohio River, that boy would have achieved fame enough to satisfy even the vaulting ambition of a young Ben Franklin. The writer's experiments had no scientific ends in view; his mission was to introduce new shapes of kites and prove by experiment that they would fly. He felt more pride in holding by main strength the heavy hempen twine to which a six-foot, straddle-legged-man kite was attached, than ever was experienced by any of those learned professors with their tandems of tailless kites loaded with scientific instruments.

But all boys will be interested in Lawrence Hargrave's kites. This great Australian inventor of flying machines wanted some sort of an apparatus from which to send off his flying machine, and so he invented

The Queerest Kite Ever Made.

In appearance there is nothing to suggest a kite; but then this is not surprising in a country where moles have the bills and feet of ducks and are credited with laying eggs, where poll-parrots kill sheep, and where savages have war clubs which when thrown at an enemy not only knock the enemy over but immediately return to their owners' hands. If the inhabitants of such a country fly kites we expect something unheard of in the kite line, and Lawrence Hargrave's kites do not disappoint us.

Imagine two boxes with their sides removed and connected by rods and you have the form of the Hargrave kite. Mr. Hargrave calls these boxes "cells," but you must not mind that any more than you do when Mr. Eddy, Mr. Woglom and Professor Clayton call their kites "aëroplanes." They mean all right by it. After you grow up to man's estate and dignity, you too will be hunting up out-of-the-way terms for common things. But now, while you are boys, be charitable to the poor men and let them keep their dignity with big words, while you use simpler ones which answer the purpose better.

Mr. J. B. Millet Tests its Qualities.

Mr. Millet spent three summers experimenting with the Malay or Eddy kite and then constructed a Hargrave kite, and seems to be well satisfied with the action of this double dry-goods box, for that is what it most resembles.

Mr. Millet, in comparing the Hargrave with the Holland, Malay, or Eddy in the *Aëronautical Annual*, No. 2, 1896, says that "the Hargrave was the steadier, the less likely to break or lose its shape in the air, and lifted much more per square foot of lifting surface." He further says that it is a kite that can be anchored in the wind and left there without fear of disaster. It will fly steadily and not require constant mending or balancing.

It is evident at a glance that the Hargrave kite must possess "rigidity" of frame. It is also evident that this is a most difficult quality to be secured without adding weight to the structure. Hence this kite is generally considered as unfit for light winds.

How to Make a Hargrave Kite.

Take eight slender, stiff pieces of bamboo,—what the inland boys know as fishin' pole or cane. These sticks must be as evenly balanced as possible and exactly the same length, eighteen inches and three-quarters long. Next cut six sticks each eleven inches long and as nearly alike as possible. These are for the middle uprights and end stretchers. Find the middle of each of your first eight sticks and lash them together in pairs at their middle (Fig. 33 A). Use waxed shoe-thread to bind the middle points together, and make the spread between *a* and *c* just eleven inches. Notch the ends of the sticks.

You now have four pairs of cross sticks neatly fastened together, and you must take one of your eleven-inch uprights and bind it to the ends of two pairs of cross sticks. (Fig. 34 B.) Take the other eleven-inch upright and fasten the other two pairs of cross sticks in the same manner.

Next cut two "booms," "spines," or connecting-rods, also of stiff bamboo, and let them each be thirty inches long, and like the two uprights, as nearly alike as it is possible for you to select them. Now, with your waxed thread, or shoe thread, bind the two booms over the ends of the eleven-inch stretchers or uprights (Fig. 35 C). The boom must fit like the top of a letter T over the stretchers, and be perfectly square, that is, at right angles with the stretcher, *b*, *d*, Fig. 34 B. Each end of the booms must protrude beyond the uprights five and one-half inches, that is, the end *b*, *k*, the end *d*, *l*, the end *m*, *b*, and the end *a*, *n*, must each be five and one-half inches long, which leaves nineteen inches between *b*, *b* and *d*, *d* (Fig. 35 C). Bind the other four stretchers to the ends of the sticks *a*, *c*, etc., as shown in Fig. 36 D. Now string the frame, so that all the sticks (with the exception of the diagonal or cross sticks, Fig. 33 A) shall be, as the boys say, perfectly square with each other, or, more correctly speaking, at right angles. Take an old paint-brush and a pot of hot glue, and paint all the joints with glue.

The frame is now finished, and it only needs a cover. The frame should now measure thirty inches in the longest dimension of the box or cell, eleven inches in the height of the cell, and eleven inches in the breadth of the cell, that is, 11 by 11 by 30 inches for each box or cell, and thirty inches for the length of the two booms, and eight inches between

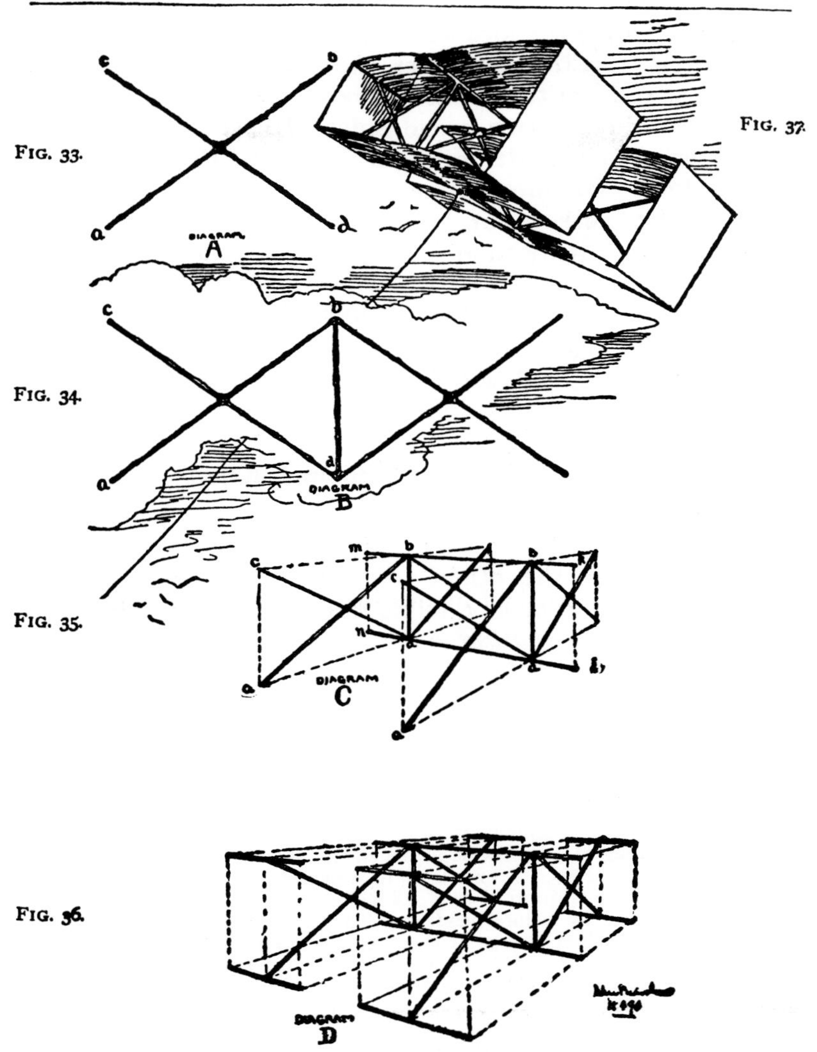

FIGS. 33-37.—The Funny Hargrave Kite.

the cells. Cover the kite with light, strong cloth that will not stretch. Fit the cloth over the frame neatly, and sew it on so as to form two boxes covered at the top, bottom, and ends. But the two broad sides of each are left open for the wind to whistle through. Hem all the raw edges of the cloth. On the bottom boom, at or near the inside edge of the cloth cover, lash with waxed thread a small brass ring for a belly-band (Fig. 37).

Double and Triple Kite.

All of the diamond-shaped, tailless kites may be made double or triple, and will fly as well as, if not better than, the single kites.

How to Make Compound Kites.

Use a backbone or spine stick twice the size you intend your kites to be. Then on the same spine stick make two kites, one above the other, or make the backbone three times as long, and make a triple kite. The courtesy of the editor of the *Aëronautical Annual* places before the reader this

Explanation of Triple Malay Kite.

"Spruce frame. Backbone FL is curved as shown in the upper figure. MN, OP, etc., are spruce uprights ½ inch × ¾ inch and 12 to 20 inches in length, according to position. MO, etc., NP, etc., and also the diagonal lines, are taut steel wires. Backbone is 18 feet long, ½ inch thick, 1½ inch wide in the centre, tapering to ⅞ inch wide at the ends. From L to A measured on the stick 1 feet 6 inches. From A to K, 9 inches. From K to B, 3 feet 9 inches. From B to C, from D to E, 18 inches each. GH, QR, and ST are bows each 5 feet long before bending. They are ½ inch × ¾ inch. When bows are bent the bow-strings in their centres are about 5 inches from the wood. The surfaces BGAH, DQCR, and FSET are equal.

"The curves of the backbone and the three cross-bows have their convex sides toward the wind. This kite is covered with very strong Manila paper. Weight of the whole kite, 6 pounds. Textile fabric made impervious to air and moisture would make a better covering. SR, TQ, QH, RG, SQGL,

TRHL, are taut steel-wire stays. The kite is bridled as follows: Find a point on the backbone between D and E 4 inches from D, here attach two cords, each 2 or 3 feet long, drop them so that one will be on one side and the other on the opposite side of the wire NP, unite the ends of the two cords, and rig a chafing-gear on the wire NP, so that the cords may not be cut.

"Attach a long single cord to the cords just united. Pull taut and measure off 16 feet 3 inches from the point of attachment between D and E. Call this point on the cord W. Let the cord fall in a bight and secure

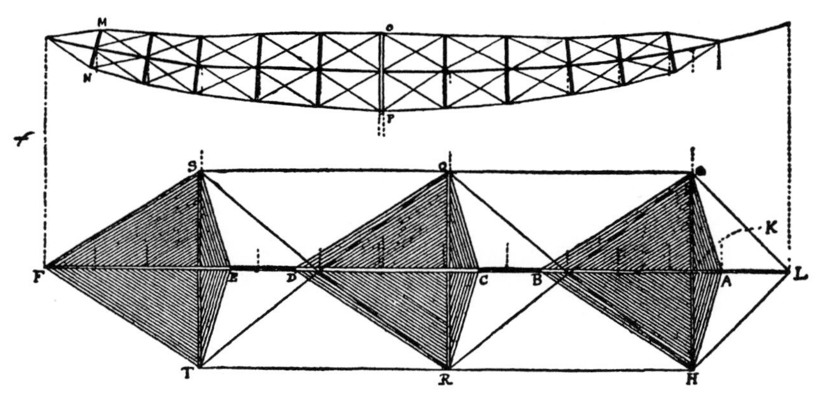

FIG. 38.—The Professional's Compound Kite.

W to the backbone at A. Now take four or five galvanized iron-rings and fasten them by marline to the cord, the first one about 7 feet 4 inches from A, the next about 7 feet 7 inches, and so on at intervals of 3 inches. At the end of the line from the reel place a small snap-hook. When this is snapped into the ring 7 feet 10 inches from A, the remainder of the bridle measuring 8 feet 5 inches, the kite will be bridled as when last flown. Still, no two kites are alike, and it may be that better results will be obtained from a new kite if the snap-hook is fastened to one of the other rings. Be particular to preserve the symmetry in framing and covering, or your labor will be wasted."

Kite String.

Inland, where the wind is light, good, strong, linen thread answers all purposes for small kites, but when the kites are larger or the wind is stronger the best string is a close-twisted linen line. At the famous Blue Hill "kite stables" a string called blocking-cord is the favorite line with the kite-fliers. Blocking-cord is used in blocking hats. Cable-laid twines are also good for kite string. Knots are safer than splices in a kite string. Don't tie a granny knot or you will lose your kite. Look in your "American Boy's Handy Book," and in the chapter on knots, bends, and hitches you will see how to tie knots that will not slip.

CHAPTER V

MALAY AND OTHER TAILLESS KITES

Some Famous Experiments—How the Malays and Other Oriental Kites Are Made—Kites in Tandem—Cannibal and Chinese Butterfly Kites.

Malay Kites.

In a New York newspaper in October, 1894, there appeared an article describing Professor Clayton's experiment, and showing how he sent up a series of kites, all attached by short lines to one kite string. The kites were tailless, bowed, diamond-shaped; kites which the writer called "Malay kites." The only Malay kites that the author of this book ever saw were at the World's Fair at Chicago, and in the collection of Mr. Chase, the artist. These kites differed from the Holland kites and the Eddy kites in the fact that they possessed two cross sticks, one straight one and one a bow over the straight stick. The Malay kite is said to fly without a tail, like most of its Oriental brothers.

In the last edition of the "American Boy's Handy Book" the diamond-bowed tailless kite is described, and there called a Holland kite by the gentleman who sent in the description to the author in 1883, long before it burst into popularity under the name of the Malay kite.

Part of the Celebration.

During the Columbian parade in New York City these kites were used to help celebrate. As on all occasions of the kind where large bodies parade, there "came a long wait, the tedium being only occasionally relieved by the frantic efforts of the policemen to drive the crowd back by leaning against the foremost and pushing desperately, but generally unavailingly. Then there came another break in the monotony. Gilbert T. Woglom, the well-known experimenter with aëroplanes—actually tailless kites—sent up six gaudily colored fliers from the Judson Memorial Tower, south of the arch. When they were so high that they were almost invisible a large American flag was attached to the kite line and raised far into the air, until it was over a thousand feet above the earth. There it fluttered grandly, outlined sharply against the unclouded beauty of the Venetian sky that glorified the city's holiday, until the celebration was ended."

This was an interesting sight, but not new, as Captain Jack Walker, of the Nereus Club, used to do the same thing during the Fourth of July Regattas of the club on Flushing Bay. The captain's kite-line was attached to the top of the flag-pole on the club-house. An illustrated account of this experiment appeared in the *St. Nicholas Magazine* several years ago.

How to Make the Tailless Kite.*

The vital difference between this and the old-fashioned diamond kite consists in using instead of the cross stick, a bow, as may be seen in the accompanying diagram. The sketch also shows how the belly-band is attached and its proportions, the latter being taken from a kite made in

* "Mr. Eddy had one convex kite in his collection at Blue Hill last summer, which he called the Beard Kite. Mr. Beard has given to kite-fliers (in "The American Boy's Handy Book") the earliest working drawings of a tailless kite which the Editor has yet found."—*Aëronautical Annual*, 1896.

Rochester, which flew very satisfactorily. The centre stick or spine is four feet long, the cross stick, of ash, or hickory, is three feet long.

Mr. Woglom began his experiments with this sort of a kite in 1894, and he now keeps a regular "stable" of

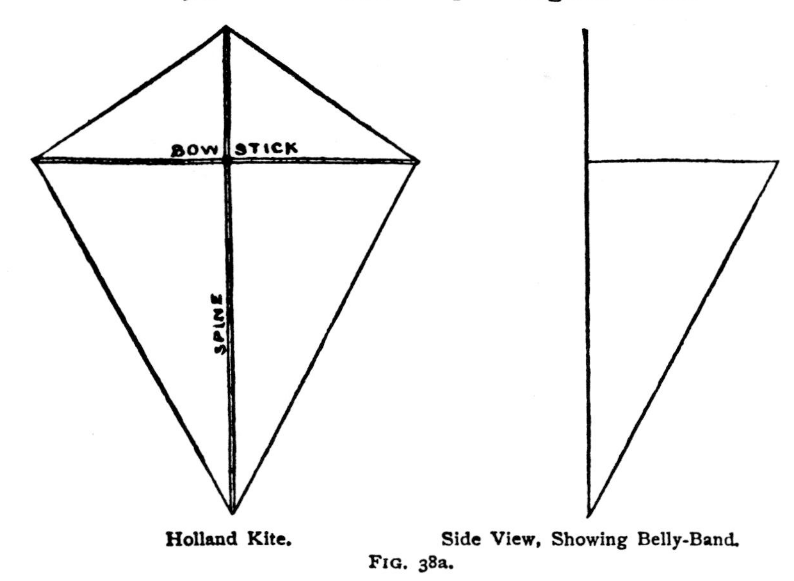

Holland Kite. Side View, Showing Belly-Band.

Fig. 38a.

kites of all sizes. But he does not call them kites, he calls them aëroplanes, and he has sent his aëroplanes 5,590 feet into the sky—that is, the top kite was three hundred and ten feet more than a mile above the earth.

The Woglom Kite—How it is Made.

Take two sticks of equal length. At a point on the upright or spine stick, one-fifth of the length from the top of the spine, place the centre of the cross or bow stick and fasten it there. Bend the bow so that the curve is as perfect as possible, and fasten it with a string. Then string the kite as you would an ordinary diamond kite. Mr. Woglom uses piano wire for the bow, and silver-plated copper wire for guys running around the kite from end to end of the sticks. Few boys, however, have access to such material, and string will answer their purpose.

Mr. Eddy's Kite.

Mr. William A. Eddy, of Bayonne, is also a celebrated kite enthusiast. He uses his kites for ascertaining how hot, cold, or damp it is up among the clouds. There is a

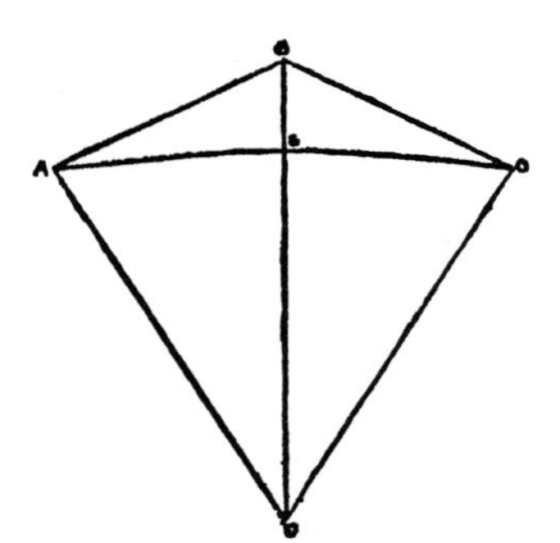

FIG. 39.—The Eddy Kite.

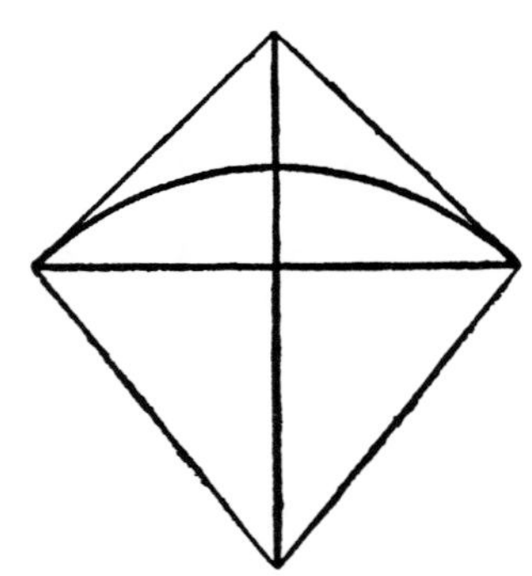

FIG. 40.—The Malay Kite.

vacant lot near his house where he flies his kites, or, to use a new term in vogue among these grown-up kite-fliers, he "dismisses a gang of kites" from the vacant lot.

Mr. Eddy is the proud owner of a "stable" of five hundred kites. He began his kite-flying with the good old American hexagonal or coffin-shaped kite, but in using more than one kite on a string there was always a chance of the tail becoming entangled in the line. At the Columbia Exposition he saw the Malay kite and that settled the tails. He now uses no kites with tails.

How It is Made.

The following are his directions for building a kite as given in one of the New York papers:

"The longitudinal stick shown in the cut (Fig. 39), at the line B D should be of spruce about three-eighths by one-half inch. For ordinary purposes sixty inches is a convenient length, but it can be varied to any extent so long as the other dimensions are kept in proportion. The cross piece A C should be a similar stick of equal length. When in position it is bent about four per cent. of its length. It should cross B D at E, so that B E shall be 18 per cent. of B D. The frame A B C D should be of light spruce, the same size as the cross-pieces, and great care should be used to have A B just equal to B C, and A D equal to C D. When the frame is finished cover loosely with manila paper, allowing some concavity on the face of the kite on each side below the cross stick, so that it will act as a sail. Bind the edges with thin wire, which stretches less than string. Then go out and fly your kite. It will not be necessary to wait for the wind, for this kite will fly in a very slow breeze. If the kite is a large one, an important part is the string. It should have a breaking strength of from thirty to seventy-five pounds, in accordance with the strength of the winds it is used in. In any case not more than one-third of the breaking strain should be used, two-thirds being left as a reserve for emergencies. For very high flying silk cord is the best, as it possesses the greatest strength for its weight."

Seven Kites in Tandem.

Mr. Eddy sent up seven kites tandem that reached a height of 3,700 feet. This sort of kite-flying is not a boy's sport, at least not *a small* boy's sport, as the pull is often so great that no small boy could hold the kite, and sometimes it is dangerous, as another kite-flier, Mr. A. A. Merrill, discovered when the line of a large kite caught him around the waist. Fortunately, there was help near by, or the accident might have proved serious.

Among the things that will interest boys is the fact that Mr. Eddy has sent a camera up attached to his kite string, and by means of a line to pull, in place of touching the button, he has taken photographs of the landscape from a kite's point of view. These were reproduced in a New York newspaper. To use the scientists' term let us now "dismiss" these aëroplanes and turn our attention for awhile to some novelties in the kite line, which will be less scientific but just as interesting to the boys, and in the description of which we shall not have to use quotation marks, as the kites are our own invention.

How to Make Wing and Wing.

This is an entirely new form, designed especially for the boy readers of this book as a novelty for kite-time. The framework is indicated by heavy lines and the strings by light lines, and in Wing and Wing the sketches show the gradual evolution from a bow and a straight pine stick to a schooner under full sail going wing and wing, topsail set, wind astern.

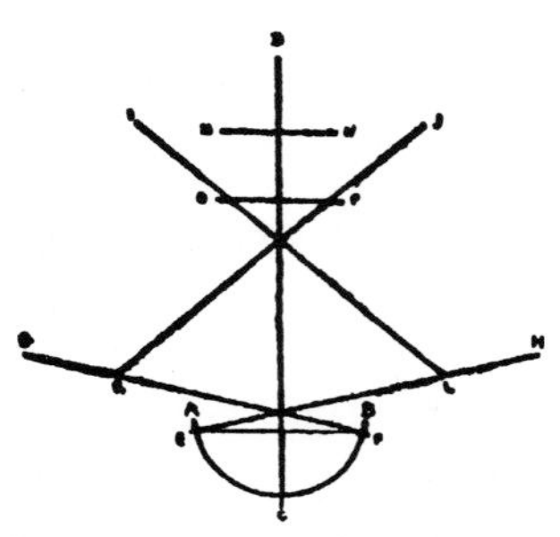

FIG. 41.—Sticks of the Ship-Kite.

Take an elastic stick three and one-half feet long and bend it in the form of a bow, so that the bow string will measure two and one-half feet from A to B in the diagram. For a mast take a straight pine stick (C D) seven feet long, allow three inches to extend beyond the bow to form a keel at C. Fasten the mast to the exact middle of the bow and again to the exact middle of the bow string, as shown in the diagram. Next cut two boom sticks, each five feet long, and be careful that they are exactly the same length; fasten the ends of the boom stick at E and F, a trifle below A and B, the ends of the bow. Allow them to cross the mast and each other at a point on the mast one and one-half feet above the keel end of the mast stick, as G F and E H cross in the diagram. The sprit sticks, L I and J K, in the diagram should be also exactly the same length; *i.e.*, six feet each, and should cross the mainmast at a point about four feet three inches above the keel end of the mast. At a point on the mast four feet nine inches above C, the keel end of the mast stick, put the yard O P for the square topsail. Five feet ten inches from C place the second cross stick, M N; square your yards, as the sailor would say—that is, see that they are neither tipping up nor down, but at right angles with your mast, D C.

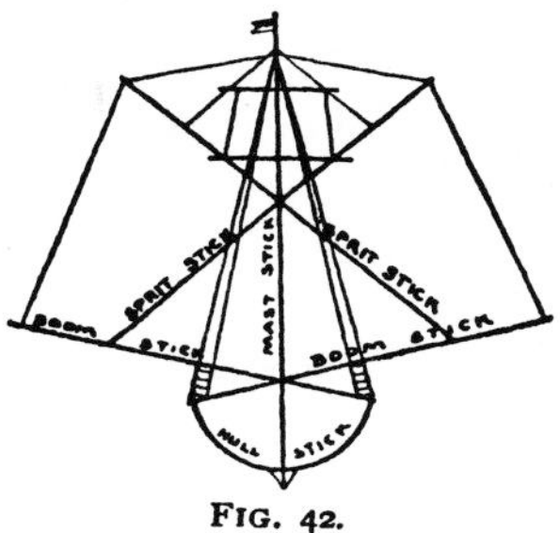

FIG. 42.

The framework is now done and you must fix the "ropes," made of string, as shown in the diagram (Fig. 42). Your kite is then ready to cover. Feet and inches have been used in this description only for convenience; of course it is not necessary nor desirable, as a rule, to make a kite seven feet high, and very few boys, or even men, would be able to hold such a monster; but remember that when feet are used it is only to give the proportions: inches or half feet would answer just as well. For instance, the main mast pine stick, C D, would then be seven *half feet* long, that is, three and a half feet. This will make a kite of very good size that a boy can manage. In other words, use the proportions given in the description, and not, necessarily, the same unit of measure.

To Cover and Paint it.

Select white paper for the sails and dark paper for the hull. Spread your paper on the floor and lay the frame upon it, holding it firmly with paper-weights or books to keep it in place. Then, with a good, sharp pair of shears, cut carefully around the frame, leaving a margin of paper to fold over. At each angle cut a slit in the margin to the angle in the frame, and upon curves cut similar slits every few inches. This will prevent wrinkles and make a neat job.

With good flour-paste cover the margin, section by section, turning each section over the frame and pressing it down with a towel or rag to make it adhere. Continue this until the whole frame is covered as in the diagram marked "Wing and Wing" (Fig. 43). When it is dry, with a small paint-brush paint the reef points on the sails with ink or black paint. Paint a white cutwater up the middle of the hull, and tie cross strings on the stays, rope-ladder fashion, where they show above and below the mast.

Fig. 43.—Wing and Wing, the Ship-Kite.

All that is necessary now is to put a little flag or pennant on the topmast and your ship is ready to sail its course through the fleecy billows of cloud ocean.

Tail and Belly Bands.

Attach a loop of string to the hull from either side of the keel and it will form the tail-band. Attach the belly-band to the two sprit sticks and allow it, like the sticks, to cross in the middle of the kite. Tie your kite-string to the belly-band and adjust it to the proper point by sliding up or down as the trial flights of the kite may dictate.

Only the other day the author met a lady with a boy walking down the street. The boy carried affectionately in his arms a man kite larger than himself. The man kite was made upon the plan published in the "American Boy's Handy Book." This is mentioned only to show that boys can still build their own kites, for several points about this particular kite indicated that the lad who carried it had made it himself. If his father made it for him the workmanship was not above criticism, but for a boy's work it was first rate and it undoubtedly will fly.

To Make a "Dancing Bear."

The "Dancing Bear" is another original kite design especially for this book. It is made like a man kite, but with shorter arms and legs, and the addition of two extra sticks in the head for ears. The heavy black lines in Fig. 44 show the pine sticks that make the skeleton; the strings are the lighter lines. The construction is not difficult, and I think the reader can, if he lays the diagram in front of him, trust to his eye for the proportions. If not, he may call the spine or middle stick six feet or else six inches long, then the two leg sticks will also be six feet or six inches each, the arm stick four and one-half, and with these figures he may guess at the size of the head, feet, and hands.

The only real difficulty will be in painting the kite. Cover it with brown paper, and with this book open before you, with black paint or a bottle of ink and a brush paint on the claws, the black triangles of shadow under the arms and above the legs, a black collar around the neck, leaving a notch for the lower jaw, and a black mouth having two teeth showing, the outline of the nose, two nostrils, two wrinkles, two round dots for eyes and two black triangles for the inside of the ears, and if it doesn't look like a bear it will look like some sort of a beast.

As far as the likeness to a bear is concerned, after you have done your best in the artistic line, let it go; it will

FIGS. 44, 45.—The Dancing Bear.

be a better-looking bear than some of the drawings that pass for this beast in current magazines and natural histories.

Try a "Tandem,"

that is, send up one kite first until it has reached a point as high as you may desire. Then send up another kite far enough so that its tail will not interfere with the first kite string. Make the second kite-string fast to the line of the first kite and let out more string. Mr. Clayton, late of Blue Hill Observatory, gives the following as

The Best Tandem Arrangement.

"In the summer of 1890, while experimenting with hexagon tail kites at Bergen Point, I found that the best tandem system was not to fasten one kite to the back of another, but to give each kite its individual string and allow it to branch upward from a main line. This method was so successful that on May 9, 1891, at Bergen Point, with a ten or twelve mile wind from the west and with five hexagon tail kites to lift the main line, the top kite became a very distant speck, estimated at 4,000 feet high by those looking on, although no triangulation of the altitude was made. I have since become convinced that the probable altitude was 6,000 feet, but as it was not measured, I have not so far included it in my records of altitude.

Tailless Kites the Best.

"The hexagon tail kites carry up a wonderfully steep string, but they call for long individual lines to each kite to prevent the kite-tail from becoming entangled with the line below. But the Malay tailless kites excel them. I have Malay tailless kites that fly with a steeper string than a hexagon, and require no hauling down if the wind increases from eight to thirty-five miles an hour—conditions which will bring to the ground a tail kite.

"Since the Malay kite has only two light sticks, and can be built of very light paper as well as cloth, it is at home in mild winds of from four to eight miles an hour. The cloth-covered kites are much heavier and are for use in stronger winds."

Now if the reader has proved himself a good kite-flier

he should have a fine "stable" of kites of his own manufacture, and since from the authorities quoted it is evident that kites with tails can be made to fly tandem he can produce a great sensation by taking an example of all the different forms of kites and by sending up the largest one first. At-

FIG. 46.—All the Novelties in the Air.

tach the string of another to the first kite string and let it go. Let him pay out more line and hitch on another kite, and so on until he has a whole navy or zoölogical garden floating over the heads of the astonished spectators, and though he may discover no new law in science, he will have a "heap" of fun. (Fig. 46.)

A Strange Country and the Home of a Strange Kite.

In a land where street-car drivers on duty wear wreaths of flowers on their hats or around their necks; where centipedes have lost their venom, where savages no longer murder, but divide their time between decorating each other with flowers and working to heap up wealth for the white strangers who have seized their land; in a land where the eruption of a volcano is hailed with joy because, like the centipede, it has lost its sting and does its little eruption act apparently with the sole object of furnishing entertainment for the people;—in such a curious land we have a right to expect novelties in the kite line, and are not surprised when we find

Cannibal Kites

that not only do not eat each other but are perfectly harmless and gentle in their deportment. If you happen to be at Honolulu and are taking a day off to see old Kilaue during an eruption, you will probably take the *Kinau*, the regular *Hilo boat*, and with a jolly party all bedecked with flowers sail over that wonderful sea under that wonderful sky southward. You will pass the extreme southwest point of Molokai, and skirt the emerald shores of Lanai and the rocky Kahoolawe, and then, turning in a northeasterly direction, enter the channel that separates Hawaii from Maui.

This is far enough for our purpose at present, for it is at Maui that the cannibal kites flourish. A number of Gilbert Islanders emigrated from their own island home to Maui and brought their kites, or the art of making them, with them. The whites call the Gilbert Islanders cannibals because of the supposed habits of these people's ancestors, and hence their beautiful bird-like toys have the terrible name of cannibal kites.

In form this kite is what might be termed a wide bow-kite. It is about five times as wide as it is high, and not at all like the stiff old-fashioned English bow-kite. The bow has the curve of the spread wings of a bird, and like them ends at both ends in points, very much on the same plan as the wings of Lilicnthal's wonderful flying machine (Fig. 47).

FIG. 47.—The Live-Man Kite.

But while thc Gilbert Islanders, now in the Sandwich Islands, have evolved the wings of a flying machine, it has apparently never occurred to them to use their invention for any other purpose than a beautiful toy. On a thirteen-foot kite the bow stick is half an inch thick, and the lateral cross stick is of the same thickness, but the bottom sticks are only a quarter of an inch in thickness. The longer sticks of this kite are made, like a split bamboo fishing rod, of a number of pieces or strips of wood neatlv spliced together. In place of paste the Gilbert Islanders use thread, and tie the sticks to the paper covering so neatly that it has the appearance of being glued on. The kite is a delicate affair, and is only used in fair weather, but much stronger wings can be made to suit the winds of the Atlantic coast, while the boys of the Ohio and Mississippi valleys can build their kites as delicately as the original cannibals did theirs.

How to Make a Cannibal Kite.

A piece of spruce wood well seasoned and absolutely free from knots is what you want for your kite frame.

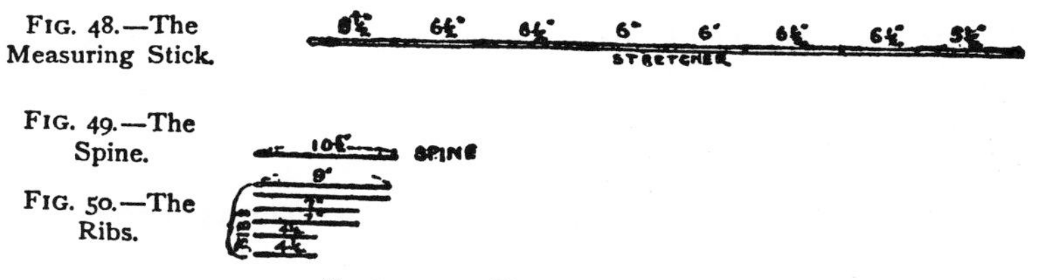

FIG. 48.—The Measuring Stick.

FIG. 49.—The Spine.

FIG. 50.—The Ribs.

STICKS FOR CANNIBAL KITE.

You can make the kite as large as you choose, but in this description we will suppose that the frame is to be only about four feet from tip to tip of the wings.

First select a good strong piece of wood of any kind, a little over four feet long, for a stretcher or measuring stick, and mark off on it, from the centre both ways, forty-nine inches divided thus: Five and one-half inches, six and one-half inches, six and one-half inches again, then six inches. (See Fig. 48.) Now make seven kite sticks, one for the spine or middle stick, ten and one-half inches long (Fig. 49); two more, each nine inches long; two, each seven inches long, and two short ones four and one-half inches in length (Fig. 50). Make all these sticks a trifle longer than the length given, to allow for slight errors in bending the bows and for protruding ends. Next select the best piece of wood you have for the bow, and trim it so that it will bend easily and evenly into the required form. Make the bow five feet long. At the exact middle of the bow, lash the longest upright stick or spine (Fig. 51). Use strong waxed thread

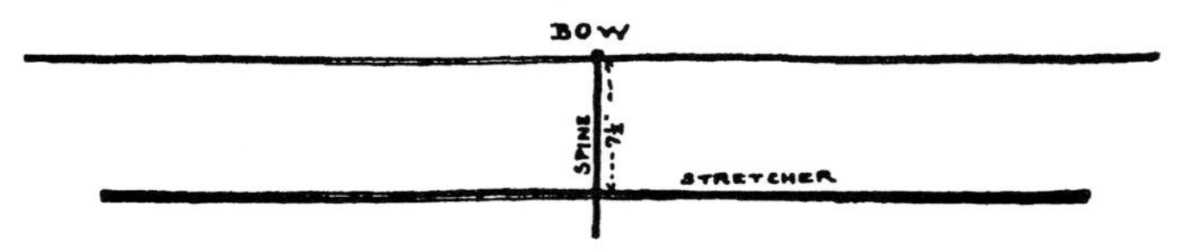

FIG. 51.—Cannibal Kite Sticks in Position.

and tie in square knots. (See Fig. 122, Chapter XIII.) Seven and one-half inches from the top of the spine make a mark, and at the mark bind the spine to the stretcher (Fig. 51).

Now bend the bow until the two ends cross the stretcher at the two extreme points marked on it, fasten the bow in this position and bind the ends of the other sticks to the bow in their proper order, as marked out

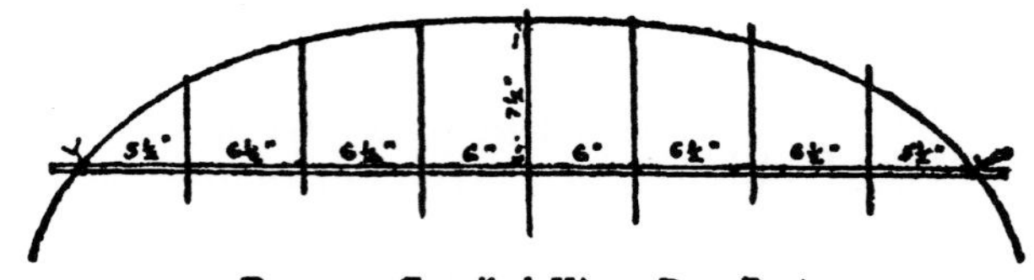

FIG. 52.—Cannibal Kite. Bow Bent.

on the measure stick, five and one-half inches from the end marks for the two short sticks. The next ribs are each six and one-half inches from the short ones, and the longest ribs six and one-half inches from the last, and six inches from the middle stick or spine (Fig. 52). Make another bow of good spruce wood a trifle shorter than the first, and lash the middle of this last bow to the middle stick or spine at a point six and one-half inches below the first bow. At a point six and one-quarter inches below the first bow make the lower bow fast to the two longest ribs. At a point five and one-half inches below the top bow make the lower one fast to the next pair of ribs. (See Fig. 53.)

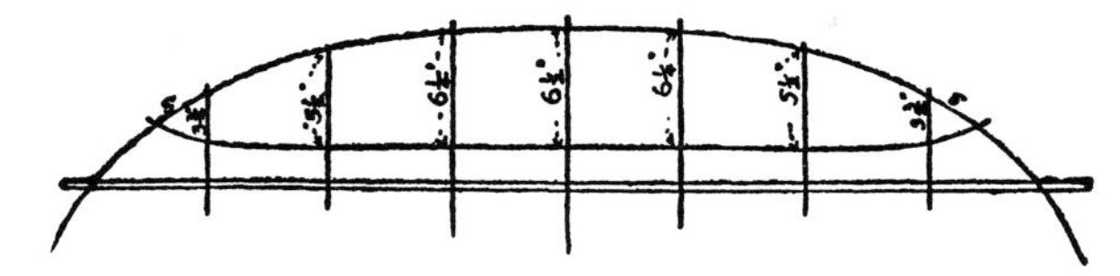

Fig. 53.—Cannibal Kite. Reverse bow bent and fastened in place.

Use the greatest of care during this process, and see that you keep the ribs and spine at exact right angles with the temporary stretcher or measure-stick. At a distance of three and a quarter inches below the top bow, bind the bottom bow to the two shorter ribs. Then bring the ends up slightly to a point on the top bow about three inches beyond the juncture of the short rib and the bow, lash it

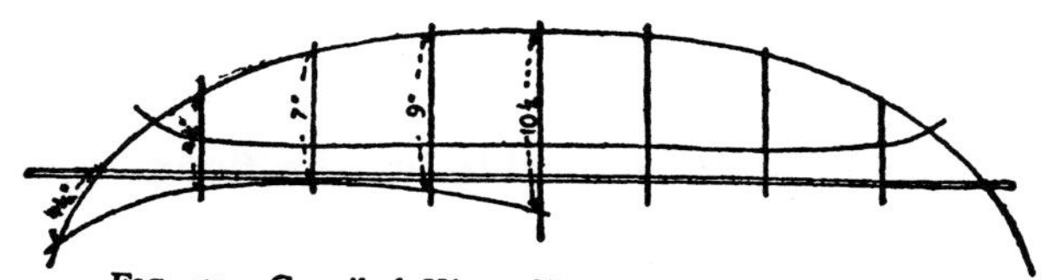

Fig. 54.—Cannibal Kite. First bottom bow in place.

securely in place and then cut off the protruding ends. Make two more bow sticks, each about half the thickness and half the length of the first one described, and with your strong waxed thread bind the two ends crossed on the bottom end of the spine stick. Then firmly bind the ends of the first pair of ribs in place, and bind the bottom bows to the remaining ribs at points nine, seven, and four and one-half inches respectively below the top bow, and to the top bow at the point four and one-half inches below where the

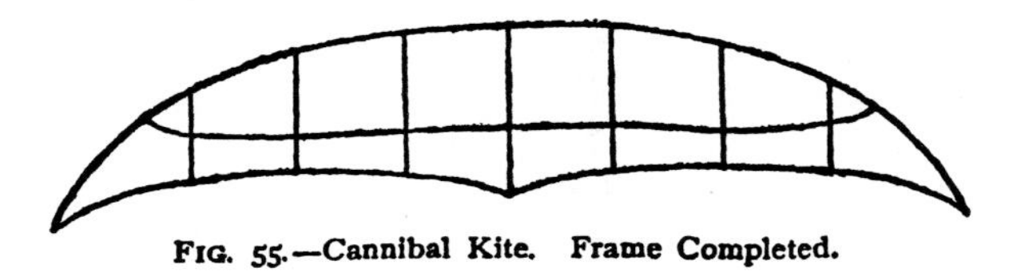

FIG. 55.—Cannibal Kite. Frame Completed.

latter crossed the temporary stretcher. Cut off the protruding ends, and the temporary stretcher may now be removed, and your frame will have the form of Fig. 55.

Kite Covering.

Of course it is admitted that silk is the ideal covering for a kite, but silk costs money, and that is an article usually absent from the museum concealed in a boy's pocket. But for big kites common silesia, such as is used in dress linings, is an excellent substitute. We will suppose, however, this to be a paper kite.

How to Cover the Cannibal.

Spread your paper smoothly on the floor. Lay your frame on the paper and hold it in place by some paper-weights, books, or other handy weights. With a sharp pair of shears cut the paper into the form of the frame, leaving just sufficient margin to turn over and paste.

About every six inches make a cut from the outer edge to the frame. When this is done, you can begin pasting, using good flour paste and pasting one section at a time, pressing each down with a towel until it adheres firmly.

The Belly Band.

Attach each end of a piece of string, about six inches long, to the bow each side of the spine. Fasten another string to this, and connect it with the spine where the middle bow crosses. This string should be between eight and nine inches long. Attach the kite string to the bellyband at a point about three inches from the top loop (Fig. 56).

FIG. 56.—The Great Cannibal Kite.

These are approximate figures for a kite of the dimensions described, but each kite varies so that the flier must by experiment find the proper manner of adjusting the string of the belly-band.

Mr. W. C. Bixby after some difficulty procured one of these kites from some natives and gave a short description of it in *Harper's Young People* of April 15, 1884. His kite had a spread of thirteen feet and a height of thirty-four and one-half inches.

For a fair-weather kite for tandem teams the "cannibal" should excel the short, dumpy Eddy or the Holland kite. Possibly it will never be a favorite in the East, where strong winds blow, but it should fly beautifully in the central parts of this country.

A Chinese Butterfly Kite.

The *Aëronautical Annual*, published in Boston by W. B. Clarke, is really a kite-flier's magazine and it is edited by an enthusiastic kite-flier, Mr. James Means. When this gentleman was attending the Centennial Exhibition at Philadelphia, he saw in the Chinese exhibit a tailless butterfly kite which he has since flown with great success. The form of this butterfly kite so nearly approaches that of the Wing and Wing that there is scarcely room for doubt that with longer booms the latter kite will also fly without a tail, which will add immeasurably to its popularity.

Mr. Means has had great success with double kites, that is, two or three kites one above the other with one spine, boom, or middle stick to answer for all. Mr. C. H. Lanson, of Portland, Me., uses two Malay kites with only one backbone.

It would be well for all boys who enter into this sport to make experiments in this line. There can be scarcely a doubt that a double Cannibal kite would be a grand flier.

Messrs. William H. Pickering, Albert A. Merrill, and James Means, the Executive Committee of the Boston Aëronautical Society, offer five prizes for kite-fliers to compete for. Here is a chance for some bright American boy, some youthful Ben Franklin, to distinguish himself. The writer is unable to state what the prizes are, but the real value of such a prize lies in the glory of winning it, and there is no good reason, why a boy should not win any or all of them.

The McAdie-Hammon California Barrel Kite.

From the latest reports from the Pacific it would appear that our Far West does not intend to be left behind in kite building and they are now flying a paper barrel with a bowsprit in place of a belly-band, the description of which I must quote from the San Francisco *Chronicle*.

"For some months past W. H. Hammon and A. G. McAdie, of the United States Weather Bureau, have been experimenting with a great variety of sizes and shapes in kites, in the hope of finding one that will safely carry an aluminum thermograph to a height of 1,000 feet, so that the instrument may record, and, when returned to earth, inform them of the condition of the atmosphere far above the house tops. From some such observations they would be able to foretell many of the pranks of the weather, but their service in this line would be of most value to shipping, as the fact that a fog was coming in could be ascertained so long before its arrival as to give ample time for warning every ship in the bay of the danger which threatened moving vessels.

"On Tuesday Hammon and McAdie tried a queerly shaped apparatus, which rose into the air with such a remarkable willingness as to highly elate its inventors. In appearance the new kite bears a close resemblance to a paper barrel, with bowsprit projecting from one end.

Its form is cylindrical. It is about four feet long and two feet in diameter. It is made up of four very light hoops, and braced together with thin strips of wood. The twelve-inch space between the pair of hoops at either end is covered with a collar of paper, and the string by which the kite is held is attached to a stick which passes diagonally through the inside of the cylinder from end to end, projecting from that end nearest the operator. The arrangement is something of a modification of the Australian kite, invented by Professor Hargrave, but a wonderful improvement over his apparatus, as shown by Tuesday's test. Hammon and McAdie worked on their new kite for some weeks before giving it a trial, and as they have met with many disappointments expected little else when they hoisted their paper barrel. The trial took place in the ten-acre lot just north of the German Hospital, and there were fifty or sixty boys of the neighborhood on hand to guy the inventors had their latest device proved a fizzle. McAdie held the odd-looking object, and Hammon walked off with the string tied to the bowsprit in his hand. He looked ahead of him to see that there were no boys over which to stumble and cried out:

"'All right, McAdie!'

"McAdie let go the kite, Hammon ran and the new-fangled kite soared up into the air, not so gracefully, but with less apparent effort than a sea-gull shows as it flits across the waters of the bay. For a few minutes Hammon had all he could do to let out string, but McAdie, who was at leisure after the hoisting, gazed at the object of their labor with a delighted smile and yelled, 'Eureka!' while the small boys cheered the artificial bird on its upward flight.

"In the air the body of the kite maintains a horizontal position, and the bowsprit attachment, of course, points downward. Although at Tuesday's trial the new kite did not rise to as high an altitude as have some of the Malay or flat kites which the weather men have experimented with, it carried the string which held it to an angle much nearer a perpendicular than any of the others have. This tendency of the new kite to stand more nearly over its anchor, when in the air, leads to the belief that ultimately it will be an easy matter to send the kite up 1,000 feet.

"McAdie recently informed the Chief of the Weather Bureau at Washington, Willis Moore, that he would surprise him some day by sending him in a report of the atmospherical conditions existing 1,000 feet above San Francisco. He and Hammon propose that the San Francisco Bureau shall be the first to officially record such observations."

CHAPTER VI

AËRIAL FISH AND DRAGONS

WHEN a gang of kites is sent up tandem, each kite helps to lift the string and prevent it from sagging. Consequently not only flags but all manner of queer things can be attached to the main kite-string. Paper streamers of bright colors and large paper Japanese fish and dragons weigh very little, and will make a display most wonderful to behold. The author attached a Japanese fish about five feet long to the string of an old-fashioned hexagonal kite, the latter was about three feet high. With the aid of a good wind the kite kept that great fish flapping up aloft all day.

FIGS. 57, 58.—Paper Dragon and Paper Fish.

Paper Dragon or Fish for Kite Strings.

With a pencil mark out a pattern on a piece of wrapping paper, and after you have secured the shape you desire, cut it out with the scissors. Take some red or yellow tissue paper and cut it according to the brown-paper pattern. You will see by the diagrams (Figs. 57 and 58) that the mouth should be very large. This is because a hoop is pasted in the mouth to admit the breeze which is to inflate the dragon or fish. After cutting out two tissue-paper dragons, according to your pattern (Figs. 59 and 60), paste the edges together, except at the mouth (Fig. 61), which must be left open. When the paste is perfectly dry take the scissors and cut slits of about half an inch long all around the mouth opening (Fig. 64). For the hoop use any light elastic wood that you can bend into a circular form. Make a hoop of this material the exact size of the mouth opening of the

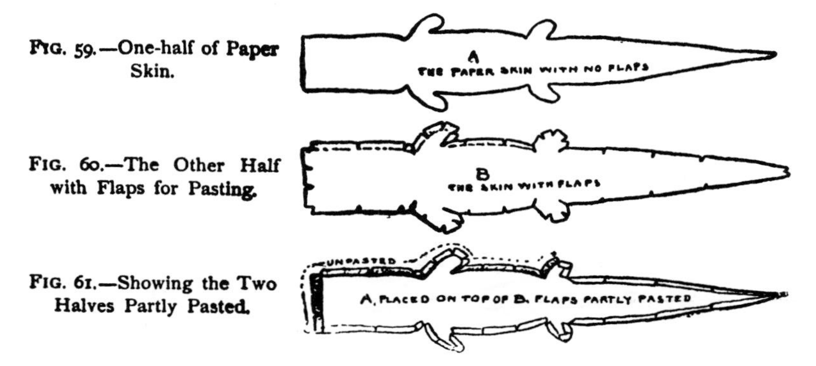

FIG. 59.—One-half of Paper Skin.

FIG. 60.—The Other Half with Flaps for Pasting.

FIG. 61.—Showing the Two Halves Partly Pasted.

dragon or fish (Fig. 63), and then paste it in by folding the parts divided by the slits over the hoop as in Fig. 65, and allow it to dry. When it is dry attach strings to the hoop from opposite sides and let the loops form a sort of belly-band (Figs. 57, 58 and 65).

The fish will then be ready to be attached to the kite-string, and when it is aloft it will swell out like a balloon and look very comical in the air. (Fig. 46, Chap. IV.) If a heavy black line is painted on each side of the head to represent the mouth, and two big black circles to represent the eyes, it will add greatly to the effect. (Figs. 57 and 58 show how to paint the dragon and fish.)

Pennants

Can be made by simply cutting a triangle from colored tissue paper and pasting the edges together, as described with the fish. A hoop must also be fastened in at the larger

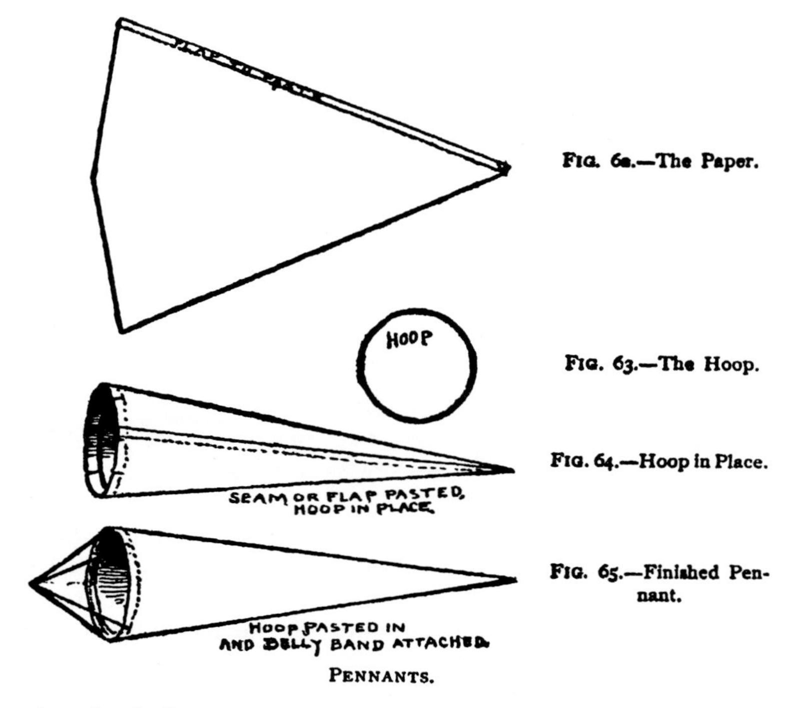

FIG. 62.—The Paper.

FIG. 63.—The Hoop.

FIG. 64.—Hoop in Place.

FIG. 65.—Finished Pennant.

PENNANTS.

end and a belly-band arranged as described in the case of the fish. (See Figs. 62, 63, 64 and 65.)

Comical Figures.

Not only reptiles and beasts, but men and women can be made in the same manner and with little difficulty. Use pink paper for the hands and face of the men and women and put the hoop in the top of their heads, as shown in the accompanying diagrams of dragon and fish.

A good tandem team of five or six kites will support quite a number of these queer devices and will reward your trouble with no end of fun. You need not fear that your work will be unappreciated, for when the passers-by see fish, alligators, and men and women bobbing around in the sky they not only will stop and look, but will linger and look again and again ; and as the pay of all who appear before the public is public applause you will be well paid.

A Live-Man Kite.

In the " American Boy's Handy Book," there is described a man kite, but since then a real live-man kite has appeared in the person of Mr. Otto Lilienthal of Berlin. His kite consists of two wooden frames covered with cotton twill, or in other words, two cloth-covered kites one above the other. These kites are capable of being folded up when not in use. Mr. Lilienthal jumps off of high places and then by means of his kite sails a long distance. From a hill a hundred feet high he can sail like a flying squirrel about seven hundred feet. See illustration from a photograph of a live-man kite in Chapter IV.

If Mr. Lilienthal would build himself a number of big Cannibal kites and send up a tandem of them, he might take his wings with him and go up with the kites five or six hundred feet. From such a perch he could easily soar nearly a mile! Or since his wings are really kites, he might, if he is brave enough, and no one doubts his cour age; fasten a string to himself and go up like any other kite as far as he could, and then cast loose the string and sail down. But seriously, the wonderful advancement in kites and flying machines is so rapid that there is reason to believe that some such feat as suggested will actually be performed before what has been written here can go through the printer's hands and come out in the form of a book. Do not try to forestall these experiments. Give the gentlemen already in the field a chance first, and then the author of this book will not feel that he is responsible to parents for the broken heads or limbs of his boy readers.

CHAPTER VII

HOOPS AND WHEELS

The Old and the New Fangled Hoops—How to Trundle a Wheel—Sport with Tin-Can Covers.

SEVERAL years ago an effort was made to make wire or iron hoops popular. They were neatly made, and propelled by an iron hook, which kept the hoop upright and pushed it along in place of being propelled by a succession of blows, as in the old-fashioned primitive barrel hoop. But the very points that the manufacturers thought would recommend these toys to the small boys, eventually caused their downfall and the substitution for them of a wooden hoop, much neater than the clumsy barrel hoop, and better adapted to the boy's ideas than the metal one.

Like the former, it is propelled by means of a short stick, with which the boy belabors his toy. This has retained its popularity for the last twenty-five years. Various attempts have been made to improve on it by adding bells and metal jinglers of odd shapes, producing what was expected to be pleasant and popular noises; but no boy out of kilts will sacrifice the dignity of his knickerbockers by causing them to chase after such a baby rattle. So these elaborate affairs are relegated to the little girls and kilted boys, while the sturdy legs of the real small boy run tirelessly after the old wooden hoop.

A Reminiscence.

The greatest triumph of my hoop-time days was when my parents bought some sugar hogsheads, which were cut up for kindling-wood. I secured the largest of the hoops, which stood some distance above my head, and from one of the staves of the hogshead made myself a beautiful club to hammer my giant with. Then I sallied forth, and

FIG. 66.—Hoop-time.

when I bore down on a street full of my play-mates rolling this giant hoop in front of me, all the metal store-hoops and wooden barrel hoops ceased rolling, while the boys stood respectfully aside to let me pass. It was a great triumph, and was talked about long afterward as the lads gathered on the sidewalk to play Jack and the Çandles in the dusk of a summer evening. There was one freckled-face boy who tried to mar my triumph by securing a big cart wheel, but he only caused a laugh, because he could not manage his heavy-spoked and hubbed hoop, which insisted upon going its own gait and taking its own direction, in spite of the severest clubbing, to the great alarm of passing pedestrians. But small

Wheels

are very popular during hoop-time, and make an interesting toy, requiring more skill to guide than the ordinary hoop. To trundle a wheel the boy uses a long stick, one end of which he places under the hub, and with which he both pushes and guides the wheel in a very interesting and skilful manner, as he runs after it.

FIG. 67.—Trundling a Wheel.

Tin-Can Cover.

Generally it is the top of a big, old-fashioned blacking-box that is used for this purpose. First, the boy finds the centre of the box-lid, after a manner known to himself, but not recorded in any work on geometry. Next, he places the lid on a board, and, with an old rusty nail for a puncher, and half of a brick or a cobble-stone for a hammer, he drives the nail through the centre of the tin. From the mysterious depths of his pocket he produces about a yard of top-cord, and, putting one end of the string in his mouth, he brings the ravelled end to a point, which he threads through the hole in the box-cover. At the other end he makes a big, round hard-knot, and pulls the string through until the knot rests against the cover.

This accomplished, he starts to run, and, by the exercise

of his art, he causes the tin to trundle on the side-walk along side of him.

There are no very new things in hoops, and if any man should attempt to bring his scientific experience and knowledge to bear upon the subject, and invent a new toy in that line, he would find it a difficult operation when he attempted to persuade the conservative small boy to adopt his invention. What a boy uses, it seems, must be what has been tried for centuries by his predecessors and proved faithful, and any change in form must be the gradual and almost imperceptible growth of natural evolution, caused by the change of surroundings or, as their parents would say, environments.

FIG. 68.—Racing with the Tin Wheel.

CHAPTER VIII

HOW TO MAKE THE SUCKER

Leather Suckers and Live Suckers — Turtle-Fishing with Suckers.

A PIECE of sole-leather, three or four inches square, is the first thing necessary in order to make a sucker. A sharp knife is the next thing, and a bright boy who can use the knife without cutting his fingers is the third. Let the boy trim the corners of the leather until the edges are circular in form, or, as he would say, round. Lay the leather on a flat surface, and pare or bevel off the edge until it is thin enough to be called a paper edge.

Now the boy may bore a small hole through the centre of the sucker, just large enough to force the end of a good strong top-string through. Near the end of the top-string, which has just been pushed through the leather, tie a good hard-knot, and make it big enough to prevent the possibility of its slipping back through the leather. It is now only necessary to pull the string through the leather until the knot fits against the under part of the sucker, and to cut off the superfluous string beyond the knot.

How to Use the Sucker.

Soak the leather in water until it is very soft and "flabby." Find a loose brick, place the sucker on top of the brick, and, with one foot, press it as flat as possible. Then slowly and carefully try to lift the sucker by the

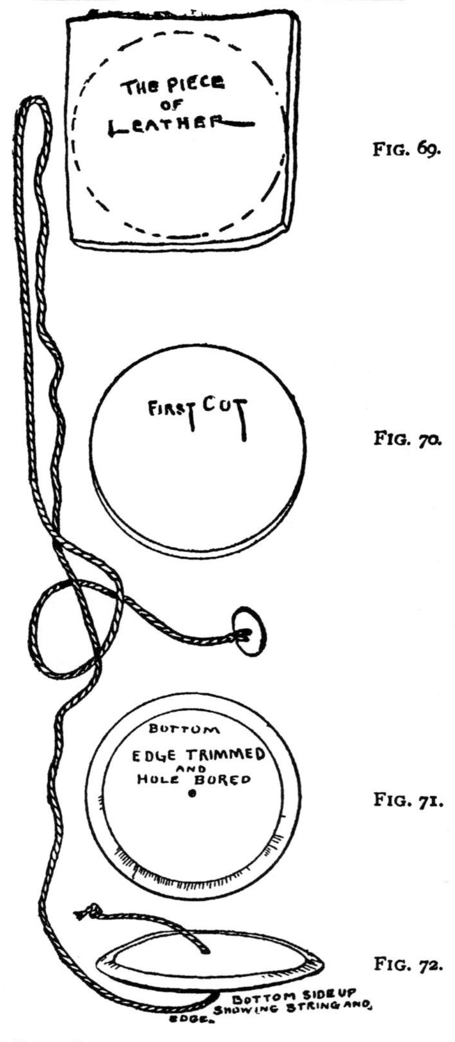

FIG. 69.

FIG. 70.

FIG. 71.

FIG. 72.

FIGS. 69, 70, 71, 72.—How to Make a Sucker.

string. Air is heavy, as your school-books will tell you, and it will press so hard all around the leather, that, if your sucker is a good one, you may lift the brick before the sucker will loosen its hold.

There is a fish in the Atlantic Ocean that the author has seen and sketched from life, which has an arrangement on top of its head made on the same principle. Fishermen call it the "shark-sucker," although its proper name is the remora. When the remora wants to travel fast, and is too lazy to do so by his own exertions, he steals up to some terrible old shark and noiselessly and gently flattens his sucker on the shark's belly or side, and there he sticks fast. The shark may be a terrible man-eater or, worse than that for the marine world, a voracious fish-eater, but it matters little to the remora, he is safer sticking to the shark's body than anywhere else, and does not need to even wag his tail, but goes tearing through the water as fast as the shark can swim.

A Live Sucker for Turtles.

This remora has been used, according to some French writers, to catch turtles. A line having been fastened to a rubber ring around the remora's tail, the fish is allowed to swim off, and when he sees a turtle he sticks fast to him, and the fisherman pulls both in. So it may be that to the remora belongs the honor of suggesting the boy's sucker.

CHAPTER IX

UP IN THE AIR ON STILTS

How to Make all Kinds—Stilt-Walking Shepherds—Hand or Arm-Stilts are Best for Beginners—Queer Stilts Used in Various Countries.

THE other day a magician appeared to me. Instead of a peaked cap he wore a derby hat, and, in place of the long black gown, his garb was the ordinary suit of a New York man. There was nothing mysterious in his manner, but, with a smiling face, he looked into my studio and said: "The boys want a new book, and put in something on stilts."

Tom's Wooden Legs.

I believe in magic. Let me try it on myself and see if I can bring back a scene of my youth in Kentucky.

Ab-ra-ca-dab-ra Stilts!

Who is that pale-faced, curly haired boy straddling over the blue-grass lawn on long, wooden legs? Why, it's my old playfellow, Tom! Hello, Tom! Where did you get those stilts? But what a foolish question! I might know what the answer would be: "Made 'em."

Jt took me all one Saturday to finish a pair of wooden legs like Tom's. I begged a pair of Aunt Annie's clothes-poles for the sticks, and sawed them off the proper length, then, with my jack-knife, I shaped the handles and smoothed them with a piece of sand-paper. Next I took a sound piece of two-inch pine board, and marked with a piece of soft brick the outline of one block. With a hand-saw I soon cut this out, and, placing it on the remains of the two inch plank, outlined a duplicate block. After this the blocks were smoothed off with my knife.

Hand Stilts.

I then heated a small piece of iron and bored holes for the nails and screws, and fastened the blocks on to the sticks. We called these "hand-stilts," because the sticks are just long enough above the block to reach the hands of the walker. (See Fig. 73.)

In those days there were only a few of us who had money in our pockets, but that is about the only thing that was not there—bits of string, marbles, tops, leather slings, with old nails as "hummers" to throw from them, jack-knives, occasionally one with a whole blade, "rubber" buttons for finger-rings, in all stages of manufacture, with sand-paper, buckskin and pumice-stone for polishing them, "lucky

FIG. 73.—Tom's Wooden Legs.

stones " from the head of a fish, to make us certain winners at marbles; two or three buck-eyes for ballast, fish-lines, hooks and sinkers, and an apple or two for lunch between meals. These were some of the things that were always in our pockets.

FIG. 74. FIG. 75.

In the twilight, after tea, Tom and I sauntered out on our hand-stilts to visit some boys on the next street. I am afraid our visit was not altogether prompted by friendship; we knew that those boys did not dare use straps over their feet for fear of a fall, and that the sticks of their stilts were awkward and long, poking up from behind their shoulders, and for reasons of timidity the blocks were set low. So we wandered over to show off and let those " girl boys " (Fig. 75) just see what reckless, wild fellows we were.

A Short-Lived Triumph.

As we approached, the boys on the next street lined up against a brick wall, and stood watching us swagger by, but our triumph was short-lived, for, as we neared the corner, we met Dick, another playmate, and he was not walking on the side-walk, but striding over the uneven limestone-paved street, with his hands carelessly thrust into his pockets, and his mouth puckered up, whistling, "Way Down South in Dixie."

Was he on stilts? Of course he was; but he not only had straps over his feet, but straps on his legs, and the sticks only came to the knee, leaving the hands free. He could not even see us until we hailed him with "Hello, Dick!"

Then he only stopped whistling long enough to say, "Hello, fellows," and continued on his way.

We watched him disappear down the street and nothing was said until he strode out of sight. Then Tom remarked: "Ain't Dick stuck up? Poo! we can make stilts like his; that's nothing!"

"I'll bet we can," I replied, to which Tom nodded his head by way of assent, and, as a smile spread over his face, said: "Well, I don't care; we can lick salt off of those fellows' heads, anyhow," referring to the "girl boys," and to the fact that our stilt-blocks were enough higher than theirs to render this feat possible.

The Japs Use Stilts.

No one knows when stilts were first introduced by mankind, nor for what purpose they were invented. I never heard of an American Indian walking on them, but away off in Japan the little shaven-headed boys walk on bamboo stilts of quaint design (Fig. 77). The blocks are mortised on to the sticks and bound in place by withes. The blocks project backward, instead of sideways, and the children hold on by their big toes (Fig. 76), allowing the stick to pass, like a sandal-band, between their great and their smaller toes.

FIGS. 76 and 77.— Japanese Stilts.

I would not recommend this style for American boys, as I hardly think the wearing of heavy shoes is a proper preparation of the foot for such uses.

Tattooed Stilt-Walkers.

The first travellers who visited the Marquesas Islands found them peopled with a magnificent race, of which every member was an athlete; an artistic race whose beautiful clothes lasted until death put an end to the wearer, for their costume was the skin with which the Creator covered their bodies—but which the islanders had beautifully decorated with tattooing, from the crowns of their heads to the tips of their toes. One of the chiefs, when measured, was found to stand six feet eight inches in his bare feet.

They were great stilt-walkers, and went through performances which would excite the envy of any modern acrobat. They ran races, jumped and danced on their

FIG. 78.—Stilt Walkers, Marquesas Islanders.

beautifully made and superbly decorated stilts, and thought it great fun to trip each other up.

In place of straps the block of the Marquesas stilt curves over so as to hold the foot. They used hand-stilts like those of the Western boys (Fig. 78).

Anti-Gadabouts.

At the close of the sixteenth century it was the style in Southern Europe for the women to wear, under their dresses, stilts which, they claimed, gave them height and

Fig. 79.—Sixteenth Century Anti-Gadabouts.

dignity of bearing; but it is hinted that their fathers and husbands introduced the style so as to make it difficult for them to walk, and cause them to stay at home, just as the Chinese of to-day keep up the style of cramping and deforming their women's feet to prevent them gadding about.

These anti-gadabouts of the sixteenth century are all too heavy and clumsy for American boys, but a modification of the French shepherd's stilts are the very reverse, and might be properly called "gadabouts."

Shepherds on Stilts.

The French shepherds, perched on

FIG. 80.—Shepherds on Stilts.

their long wooden sticks, look like ungainly storks, but they can spy a sheep when a man on the ground would be unable to detect him, and they can wade a stream dry shod, or, rather, with dry feet, for I believe they wear no shoes.

In fact, Dick's stilts, strapped on his sturdy legs (Figs. 74 and 81), are only a modification of these shepherd's wooden legs, and, if we give Dick the shepherd's long cane or pole, and shorten the distance to the ground, we have a pair of gadabouts, which, though requiring some skill to use, will not be dangerous. and will admit

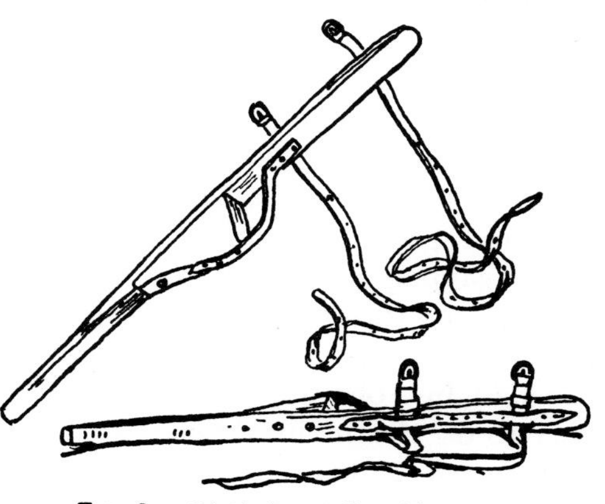

FIG. 81.—Dick's Leg Stilts with Straps.

of the free use of the hands. Gadabouts are sometimes used in Brooklyn, but I have never seen them in New York.

Best for the Boys.

The long-armed, strapless stilts of the "girl boys" are first-rate for beginners. The hand-stilts are good all-round walkers, and the gadabouts are the best for the sturdy American boys, because they require skill in their manufacture and use.

They develop just those qualities of ingenuity and pluck that have made us the nation we are. Remember that you boys of to-day are the men of to-morrow, and it is to you that we must leave this great country to success or to ruin, according to the faculties you develop now while you are yet boys.

Trick Stilt-Walking.

While I was a member of the gymnasium at Cincinnati, the youngsters were intensely interested in a group of professionals, who practised there during the winter months. They were mostly circus men, quite gentlemanly sort of men, not at all what people generally suppose circus men to be.

One bald-headed man, of particularly dignified and austere looks and manners, was in the summer time a painted clown of the saw-dust ring. At a certain hour each day, as regular as a clock, this bald-headed man appeared, and strapped a pair of long stilts to his legs, while we looked on with awe at the dreadful proceeding. Then he began his practice. He did not walk, skip, hop or jump. He had but one object in view, but one ambition, and that was to do the inebriate act, although he was a man who never used ardent spirits. So, for an hour or more each day, he hung on to a rope suspended from the ceiling, and swayed his body around, as we have all seen the clown do at the circus, when he comes in and pretends to become intoxicated while walking on stilts, All winter the bald-headed man practised this one act, and the Spring birds had begun to appear before he dared, without keeping a firm hold of the rope, to do " the drop," as he called the peculiar limp stagger that he had practised all winter.

Since then, when I attend a circus, and the ridiculous clown appears in the ring, and does his part in the clown's peculiar off-hand manner, I forget to laugh, for I am lost in wonder, thinking of the constant study, application, and hard work that he must have gone through, in order that we may think him a funny old fool. This incident is related to show what practice it takes to acquire skill in difficult feats. Few boys are willing to devote so much time and thought to learn anything, and certainly not to learn one trick on stilts.

Skating on Stilts.

Alfred Moe skates on stilts, doing the inside and outside edges with ease and grace. He cuts a figure 8, and all the various other figures well known to skaters. Moe began his public career as a roller-skater, and claims to have opened the first roller-skating rinks in this country and in England. He evolved the idea of stilt-skating in 1868, and gave his first performance in St. Louis.

From my observation of the clown, I am satisfied that the stilt-skater must have done some hard work practicing before he dared appear in public. Such things are novelties, but not suitable to the ordinary boy, who, if he becomes expert enough to run, jump, hop, and skip on his wooden legs, has acquired all the skill that is necessary to enjoy the fun of stilt-walking.

Ocuya, or Giant Dance.

If you will look on your map of Africa, just below the equator and between longitude 11° and 12° east, you will see where the Aponos dwell, a merry tribe of celebrants and revelers.

FIG. 82.—Ocuya, the Aponos' Dance, Africa.

For several months each year this tribe does nothing but dance, sing, and drink palm wine. When the wine season is over they settle down to ordinary pursuits, and would find no place in this book if it were not for the fact that one of their weird dances is performed on stilts.

This entertainment is called the Ocuya, or Giant Dance. Ocuya is made of wickerwork, with a big wooden head and wooden arms. Monkey skins furnish the head - dress, and a long skirt of grass-cloth hides the stilt-walker. It is unnecessary to add that the native must be a skilful stilt-walker to take the part of Ocuya.

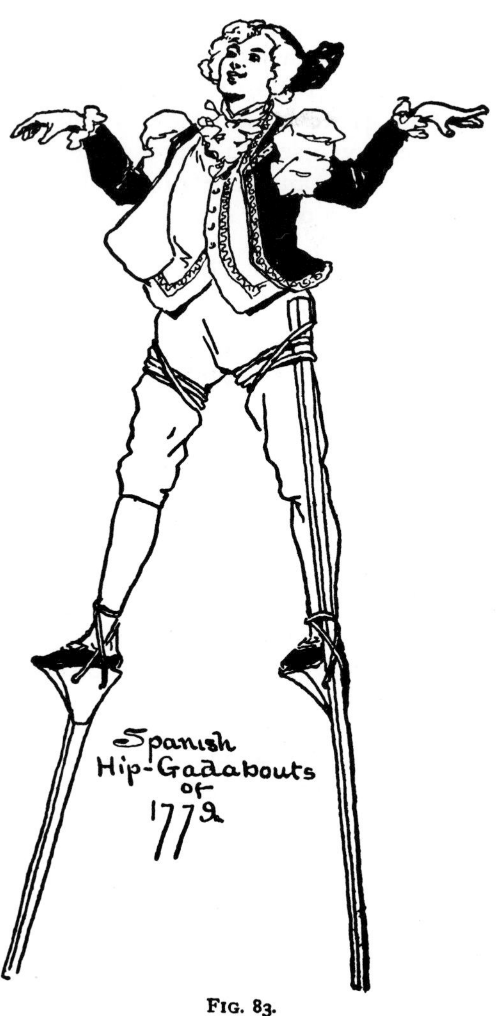

FIG. 83.
(From an old engraving made in 1779.)

New Woman on Stilts.

According to the newspapers, walking on stilts is the very latest fashionable amusement of the "new woman" in London. If there is any truth in this statement, it is safe to say that it will not be long before you boys will be called upon to make stilts for your sisters. There can be little doubt that the time is coming when a book written for boys will be the only one girls will read, or, rather, every book will be written for young people, and will be addressed to both boys and girls. Just why girls should not walk on stilts or engage in any similar sport no one yet has given a satisfactory answer. Twenty-five years ago the boys used to make stilts with very low blocks for their sisters, and the girls seldom would use them, but insisted upon using their brothers' high-blocked stilts.

Tomato-Can Stilts.

In the cities, where wood is scarce, it is quite pathetic to see the boys tramping around on old tomato-cans for stilts. The tomato-cans have strings tied to them in place of poles, and these strings are held by the hands.

Lath-Stilts.

One bright boy, on Fourth Avenue, New York City, has a pair of stilts made of old laths, from the ruins of some dismantled house. Three laths nailed together form each stilt pole, and the blocks are made of a graduated lot of pieces of lath nailed together.

Now, if a small boy in the tenement-house district can make himself a good, serviceable pair of stilts out of some old laths, there can be no doubt that the boys who read this book will be able to find material and tools to build themselves beautiful gadabouts.

CHAPTER X

BAIT, LIVE AND DEAD

Salt-Water Worms that Live on Land—Angle-Worms, Hellgramites, Minnows, Crawfish, Grasshoppers, Crickets, Frogs, and "Lampers"—How to Catch and How to Keep Them.

ALL modern naturalists will tell you how long, long ago an adventurous marine worm, little by little, accustomed himself to living out of water, until at length he was able to sustain life on land, so long as there was moisture enough to keep his body moist. His descendants throve in their new home, and multiplied and spread all over the face of the earth, and to-day they may be called land animals, although they still breathe as a leech does, and are still dependent upon water in the form of moisture to support life. In a dry atmosphere and dry earth they die.

All day long these busy worms eat their way through the earth, and grow fat on the food on which they live. With no eyes, they know light from darkness; without noses, they can smell out food buried in the earth; without ears, they hear the approach of an enemy, and every ring and invisible bristle on their slimy bodies is keenly sensitive to the slightest touch.

After a rain in June how the robins laugh to see the angle-worms enjoying the wet grass of the lawns! But, if Mr. Robin expects to catch many, he must be prepared for work, for at the sound of the bird's light foot-fall the angle-worm quickly disappears in his hole. Often the robin secures a piece of the retreating tail, but that is a matter of little importance to the worm, for there are plenty of tails where that came from, and he grows himself another.

If you take an earth-worm in your hand and smooth him with your fingers from his tail to his head, you will distinctly feel the invisible bristles, four pair of which grow at each ring of his body. Now, if you stroke the worm from his head to his tail, no resistance will be felt; he is as slippery as an eel. The reason for this is that the bristles point backward, and thus enable him to crawl. For they keep his tail fixed while he is stretching his head forward, and then he holds on with hooked bristles on the forward end of his body while pulling his tail up. By repeating this operation the worm manages to crawl on the surface or below ground.

The Work which Angle-Worms Do.

Painstaking scientific men have made careful calculations, and claim that an acre of ordinary land suitable for worms contains fifty-three thousand angle worms! If bait is ever scarce, it is because the worms in a long-continued drought or during very cold weather burrow deeply into the ground, sometimes to the distance of eight feet, which is too long a distance to dig for bait.

It takes very little imagination on the part of the reader to consider that fifty-three thousand worms, all busy taking earth from below and piling it above ground, can do a great deal in a few thousand years.

To our common, despised earth-worm, Mr. Darwin says we are indebted for the preservation of many noble statues and works of art. For, when the priceless art treasures of an older civilization were left to decay amid the ruins of the ancient cities, the earth-worms went silently to work to bury them, which, in course of time, they accomplished, thus protecting the statues and carvings from the ruinous action of the elements, and from vandal human hands. Without the assistance which angle-worms render, by preparing the soil to receive the seeds, many plants would become extinct. We reward the creature by impaling his wriggling body on hooks, and by using him as bait for fish. Digging for worms is always laborious work, and all fishermen should know

How to Collect Angle-Worms

at night, when they are above ground, and you need no spade and laborious digging to catch them. If there has been a warm shower, the conditions for a big harvest of worms is perfect. Take a lantern and a pail or a box and sally forth. If you step softly, and hold your lantern close to the ground, you will see hundreds of worms in the wet grass, in the open foot-path and by the road-side—great fat fellows called night-crawlers, that will make any hungry fish's mouth water.

Last summer I saw a mysterious light moving over my front lawn, and when I investigated its origin, I discovered a boy with a pail and a lantern, catching worms. When he saw a worm, he would snatch it as quickly as any robin.

But that is not the best manner to capture them. When you see a worm lying on the ground, you will discover, if you look carefully, that it has one end of its slippery body hidden in its burrow, but what you cannot see is that the stiff bristles are firmly hooked in the soil in the hole. At a moment's notice the worm can draw itself out of sight, by simply contracting its muscles. If you will gently place your finger on the end of the earth-worm's body at the burrow, you will frighten this end of his body, so to speak, and cause it to let go its hold. But as soon as the worm, in its endeavor to escape from the enemy at home, does this, it is helpless, and you may pick it up and put it in your pail, which will soon be filled with good bait.

Different Varieties.

There are many varieties of angle-worms known to the fisherman. Whether they are varieties recognized by the scientist or not, is of no importance here, but we all know that some worms are strong, lusty, dark in color, and will live some time on the hook; while others are weak, flabby, light in color, and soon die on the hook. Mr. J. Harrington Keene, in *Harper's Young People* for July 23, 1889, describes worms, which he calls the garden-worm, the brandling, a manure-heap-worm, the cockspur, with golden spots on its tail, the marsh-worm, to be found in boggy places, and the flag-worm, found at the roots of the sweet flag.* Fish will bite at all of these worms, but for large fish I have found the night-crawlers and the marsh or mud-worm, the most tempting. Since writing the last sentence I tried a big night-crawler with success upon a sly old trout which has resisted the tempting bait of anglers for years. After you have collected your bait the next thing to know is

How to Keep Angle-Worms Healthy and Well.

Put them in any sort of clean tin box. Place the cover of the box on a piece of soft plank, and with a hammer

* In Isaac Walton's "Complete Angler," he speaks of the garden-worm as the "lob-worm," and then enumerates the other varieties as the red-worm of the manure-heaps, and the brandling or yellow-worm, ringed with red, of manure-heaps and tan-heaps. His description of these worms seems to correspond to the varieties enumerated by Mr. J. Harrington Keene.

and nail, make a number of holes in the cover to admit air. Gather some fresh moss, and cover your angle-worms with it. Put in plenty of moss, and no earth, except that which naturally adheres to the moss. The moss should be moist but not *wet*. Leave enough space between the top of the moss and the cover to form an air-chamber.

In this box your bait not only will not die, but will grow stronger and better day by day. When you wish a fresh bait, pull out the wad of moss, and you will find the worms hanging from the bottom like so many bits of string. Keep the box in some damp, cool place, where it will be sheltered from the rain and sun.

I have often heard that if you tap on the ground the worms will come out of their holes. This is probably an ancient legend without truth. Some old Long Islanders, however, assert that the worms will think the noise to be rain, and hasten above ground to prevent being washed out and drowned.

How to Bring the Worms Out of their Holes.

A writer in *La Nature* makes the statement that the earth-worms can be quickly forced to come above ground, by pouring a solution of blue vitriol (cupric sulphate) on the ground. Ten grammes of blue vitriol to a quart of water is given as the proper mixture. Ordinary soap-suds is good for the same purpose, and, if the water is pretty warm, it acts all the quicker. There is little danger of scalding the bait, for the water cools very rapidly when dashed on the ground. I have frequently noticed the earth-worms crawling around where the laundresses have emptied their tubs. Cold, fresh water will doubtless have the same effect, though possibly the worms will take more time in making their appearance upon the surface.

In a publication of the Lakeside Library, called "Fish and Fishing," the following directions are given for preserving worms for bait:

"Procure some fresh mutton suet, cut it fine, and boil it in a quart of water till dissolved; then dip into this two or three large pieces of coarse, new wrapper, large enough to supply each variety of worms, which should not be mixed together. When these are cold, put them into separate

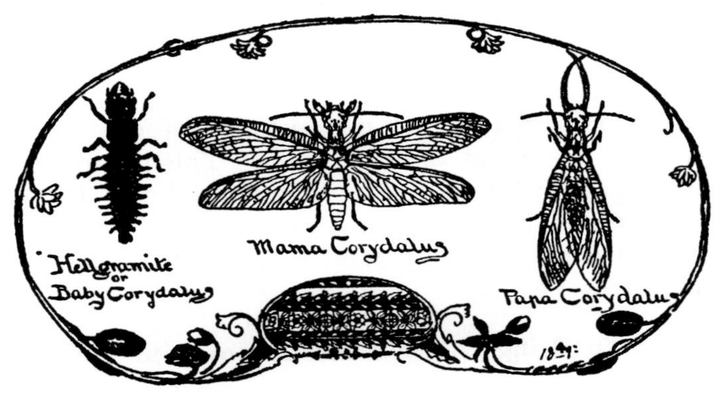

FIGS. 84, 85, and 86.—The Young and Adult Corydalus.

earthern jars, with some damp earth and the worms which are to be kept, and tie over all a piece of open, coarse muslin."

Hellgramites, Bogerts, Hojack, Dobsons, or Clippers.

The first one of these frightful, black, squirming creatures that I ever remember of seeing, inspired me with a terror it has taken years to overcome. I was bathing in a pool in the little muddy stream of Bank-lick, near Covington, Ky. I had advanced far enough in the art of swimming only to be able, with safety, to swim across the pool.

While I was about half way across on one of these trips, a sudden pinch on my back announced the fact that I had been attacked by some native of the stream.

I looked over my shoulder in alarm, and there I saw what was to me then an unknown animal. It was about as long as my finger, black as could be, and apparently with as many legs as a centipede. It had fastened its pincers in my back, and hung on until I reached the opposite shore, where one of my companions picked it off, to my great relief.

Since then I learned that this was only a good black bass bait which had so terrified me, and that, although it can pinch quite sharply, it is a harmless insect.

Another Adventure.

The next adventure I had with a hellgramite was at Niagara Falls. It was when the old tower still stood upon a rock on the brink of the cataract, but a large sign marked

DANGER !

warned all visitors off the bridge leading to the tower.

Boy-like, I traversed the bridge to the point where the sign barred farther progress, and here I leaned upon the barrier and watched the green water tumble over the falls. And as I watched I saw a living thing on a rock upon the very brink of Niagara. It was in the act of crawling out of its old skin. There was no doubt in my mind that what I saw was an insect, but it was such an insect as I had never before encountered. Gradually it shook out its beautiful lace-like wings, and then I climbed over the danger sign, threw myself flat on the rock, reached over the edge, picked the insect from its giddy perch, transferred it to my hat, put my hat on, and hastened to the hotel to examine my prize.

It looked like a sort of comical dragon-fly, with very long pincers, which opened and closed in a most threatening manner, but I knew the thing could do no harm, because it was still soft, like a soft-shell crab. This was a large male corydalus in its perfect form. It was a full-grown hellgramite, and the first adult insect of its kind I had ever seen.

Fishing for Hojacks with a Net.

From the foregoing it may be seen that this bait passes part of its life in the water and part in the air and on land. With the perfect insect we have little to do, but the ugly black babies we need for perch and bass, and we must catch them with a small dip-net made of mosquito-netting.

Wading up stream, and coming to a flat stone, place the net on the down-stream side of the stone, and then lift up the stone. The bait that are underneath will float into the net. Some, however, may be glued to the stone by their sticky tails, and these must be picked off and placed in your pail or box. Along the edge of the stream in the wet sand or gravel, under the stones, is also a lurking-place for bogerts.

The Time when Bogerts are Best.

About the 1st of June, when the young corydalus feels that it is about to change into a lace-winged insect, it scrambles out of the water and crawls rapidly about in search of a suitable dressing-room, where it may change its clothes. The under surface of an old board, stone, or log, or even the undersides of the shingles of a house, not too far from the water, are the places chosen. At this time the insects are best suited to the purposes of the fishermen, being exceedingly tough and hard to kill. One bait frequently serves to catch several fish. At this stage the hellgramites are called crawlers.

Within a rude earthen cell the crawler remains in a sort of mummy-like condition until about the 1st of July, when it bursts forth from its shell (pupa) a perfect-winged insect. The female has short pincers and the male ferocious-looking long ones. Both sexes, however, are perfectly harmless.

How to Keep Dobsons or Clippers Alive.

Select a good wooden box, about two feet by a foot at the base and six inches or a foot high. Bore holes in the lid of the box to admit air. Cover the bottom of the box with *dry* gravel, and dump in your dobsons, clippers, bogerts, or hellgramites, as the larva or young corydalus is variously called, according to the part of the country you happen to be in. Keep the box in a dark, cool place.

I have kept hellgramites in a box of this description for thirty days without losing a single insect, all of them being apparently tougher and livelier at the end of a month than they were when first placed in the box.

Mr. J. Harrington Keene, in *Harper's Young People*, says that hellgramites can be kept alive in a can in which some water has been placed and damp moss added, but I doubt if the bait will live as long and be as strong and healthy kept in this way as they are when kept dry.

White Grub-Worms.

These are the young or larvæ of beetles, and may be found by digging in rich soil or in old rotten logs and stumps. They make good bait for trout, bass, perch, cat-fish, and sunfish. Keep them in the manner described for keeping the earth, angle, or garden worm.

Gentles, or Young Blue-Bottle Flies

are not pleasant creatures to look upon, or pleasant to capture, or pleasant to handle. But there is no accounting for tastes. It is evident that fish do not look upon the white carrion-eating baby-fly in the same light that we do,

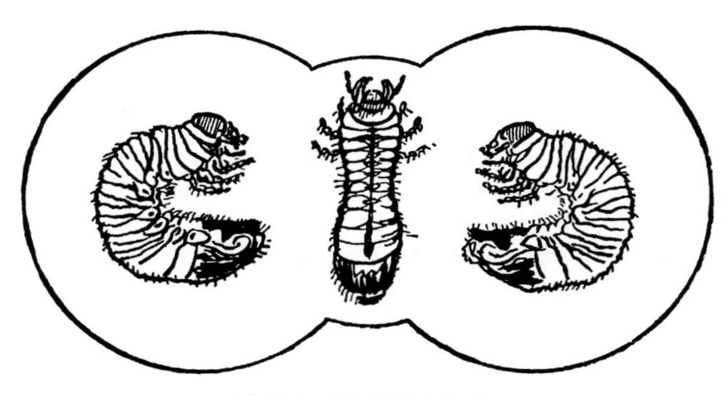

FIG. 87.—The White Grub.

for they are very fond of gentles; and from quaint old Walton down to the present time this little grub has been, and still is, used for bait. The beautiful, dainty, red spotted trout, in his cool spring-water stream, is passionately fond of the larvæ of the blue-bottle fly. If you are camping out or living near your fishing-grounds, take any old offal and put it in an old can, bucket, or other deep vessel in a shady out-of-the-way place, where mink or other small animals will not disturb it.

Wandering blue-bottle flies will soon discover the tempting display and deposit their eggs in it, and in a few days there will be plenty of bait. When they are full grown carefully remove them by gently knocking the larvæ with a stick on a piece of birch bark or paper.

How to Keep the Trout Bait.

Place them in a box of sand or bran. Here they will soon cleanse themselves and become of a milk-white hue, losing all their disgusting features. Keep them in a damp, cool place to stop them from maturing, or going into the chrysalis state, preparatory to becoming blue-bottle flies.

Katydids

are very difficult to obtain in quantity sufficient for use as bait, on account of their habits of living in trees. Once, when I was fishing among the Thousand Islands, in the St. Lawrence River, I became weary of trolling for big muskallonge that would not bite, and made the guide put me ashore upon a little rocky island, covered with small shrubbery and stunted trees. These I found to be full of great, green, handsome katydids. I soon filled my handkerchief with them, and in less than one hour's time caught a good string of fish of assorted kinds, but principally fine bass.

Among other things, I caught the largest fresh-water eel I have ever seen; but as I was dressed in summer-resort fishing clothes, and feared the effects of eel slime on my trousers, I cut the eel loose, allowing him to depart in peace with my hook in his mouth.

Black Crickets.

These are good bait for almost all kinds of game fish, and are killing bait for bass and trout. Frequently, when bass will not notice a live minnow, crawfish, hellgramite, or frog, he will eagerly snap at a black cricket.

There is but one way to catch this bait, so far as I know, and that is to seek it under the loose stones and chips, where crickets delight to hide. I have had the best luck in open, sunny spots, hilltops, and pathways. Mr. Keene, in his interesting notes on bait in *Harper's Young People*, advises his readers to look for crickets in a cool, damp place; but he evidently found them, as I have, under chips

FIG. 88.—Crickets.

and stones. Mr. Keene caught one hundred and twenty-four trout in one stream with black crickets.

Handle your crickets with care, not for fear that they might hurt you, but because they are easily injured, and their usefulness is thus impaired. After you have collected a sufficient quantity for your purpose, hasten to place them in some roomy receptacle, the bottom of which is plentifully supplied with damp gravel and small chips for hiding-places. Otherwise they will eat each other.

Grasshoppers

are another good bait. Often a fish will take hold of a grasshopper when nothing else will tempt him to bite.

Every boy knows where and how to catch these long-legged insects, but to keep them alive for any great length of time is more difficult.

FIG. 89.—The Grasshopper.

How to Make a Grasshopper Box.

Take an old cigar box, make a square hole about two by three inches in the lid; cover the hole with a piece of wire netting. Make another hole just large enough to admit a finger. Make a sliding door of a small paddle-shaped piece of wood, fastened with a screw at one end in such a manner as to allow the other end to slide over the hole (Fig. 90). Half fill the box with green grass.

FIG. 90.—*A*, the sliding door; *B*, the grasshopper hole; *C*, the air window protected by wire netting.

"Lampers."

This is the fisherman's name for what is generally known as the lamprey eel, and what is generally known as lamprey eel is no eel at all. In spite of all this, the "lampers" are great bait for bass. Near Binghamton, last summer, with a good lamprey for bait, I caught a bass weighing four pounds, two ounces, and my friend, Mr. James Johnson, caught several weighing over three pounds, while Mr. Johnson's wife landed a six-pounder! These fish were all weighed, measured, and recorded with their outlines in Mr. Johnson's book, kept for that purpose. I say this because any one who has fished for black bass knows that a three-pound fish can send a thrill down the spine of even old fishermen, and that the "four-pounders" are generally the fish caught around the camp-fire, and not the real live fish of the streams.

FIG. 91.—The "Lamper."

Habits of the Lamprey.

Last summer's experience compels me to speak of the lamprey with the greatest respect. If the fish are passionately fond of the lamprey, the lamprey is also passionately fond of fish, especially of shad, as may be seen from the following interesting account, which appeared in the New York *Sun* about the time I was making my first trial with them for bait.

"The lamprey leaves the ocean in great numbers in March, proceeds to the head of tide-water in the rivers, and there actually lies in wait among the rocks for the shad that will soon be pushing their way up stream to spawn. The lamprey follows the shad on this interesting journey, fastening itself to the delicate fish by its mouth, which is simply an armed sucking disc with extraordinary adhesive power. The lamprey is always found fastened at the orifice from which the shad drops her eggs, and from which it sucks the roe, at the same time rasping the tender flesh of the fish with its sharp-toothed tongue, drawing blood from the shad to wash down the raped roe into its maw. The shad having by June become of little profit to the lamprey, the latter sets about attending to its own family affairs.

"The female lamprey builds her nest in a swift current, making an excavation sometimes two feet deep. She frequently removes as much as a wheelbarrow load of stones in preparing her nest. She has such strength that she can haul up from the bottom stones weighing five pounds or more. Gluing her mouth to a stone, she works backward, drawing the stone after her. John G. Sawyer, of Sawmill Rift, once speared a lamprey in the Delaware as she was in the act of hauling up a stone in this way, and so firmly attached was she to the stone that it was lifted into the boat with her, she being pulled out of the water by the tail.

"The male lamprey hovers about the spot while his mate is building the nest, watching her tugging away at the stones, but never offering any aid. As soon as the big nest is ready the female lamprey deposits her eggs in it, and swims away and dies. I can remember when the shores of the upper Delaware were lined, during the month of June, with dead lampreys and dead shad. As soon as hatched the young lampreys go ashore and bury themselves in the sand, where they are found by eager fishermen, who seek them for bait for other fish.

"Properly cooked, the lamprey is good. There isn't a bone nor a suspicion of a bone in it. Place a lamprey in the sun and keep it there, and it will melt like so much butter, the only evidence that it ever existed being a grease-spot. A peculiarity of the lamprey's flesh is that, although it will melt away in the sun, it becomes tough when put in the frying-pan over a fire, and becomes tougher and tougher the longer it is fried. The only way it can be cooked so as to be fit for the table is by stewing it."

How to Catch Lampreys.

This is downright hard work, and anyone who digs his own lampreys earns all the fun he derives from their use as bait. With a spade in hand he wades in the water above his knees, and digs the soft sand and mud from the bottom, quickly throwing the contents of the shovel on the bank, where a companion looks it over for young lampreys. It takes a strong man to lift one of the shovels full of water and mud clear of the water. To buy lampreys is expensive, for no man we could find would dig them for less than four cents apiece, and some charged ten cents apiece for them.

How to Keep Lampreys.

Put them in the ice-chest in a pail of aquatic grass and ice, or, where it is possible, make a long, wooden box, and cover the bottom with clean sand. Set the box where the water from a spring can run through holes bored in the sides near the top for that purpose. Other holes in the opposite sides near the top allow the overflow water to run off. Have a good cover for your box, and wire netting over the air- and water-holes, or you will discover that some land animals are almost as fond of your expensive bait as the bass are.

This box is also an excellent contrivance for keeping bull-heads and other minnows alive. The wire netting over the holes keeps out the garter and other snakes that need only a hint to avail themselves of the opportunity of feeding on your bull-heads.

Lampreys are expensive to buy, to keep, and to handle. When taken out of the box to use, put them in a pail with grass and some big pieces of ice, and cover the whole up well with something to protect it from the sun. When you take a bait out you will find him so numb that it is not difficult to bait him. After he is once overboard, the warm water thaws him out so that he becomes exceedingly lively and tempting to the fish.

Frogs

are highly esteemed as bait by many fishermen, and there is no doubt that some fish are fond of them, and that most fish will bite at them at times. Wall-eyed pike, or Jack salmon, as these fish are called in Ohio, pickerel, bass, and large perch are caught with half-grown and not infrequently with full-grown frogs.

How to Bait a Live Frog.

Some fishermen put the hook through the frog's lips, some through the web of one foot, some through the skin of the leg at the thigh, and others through the skin of the back. For my part, a live frog is a very unpleasant bait. Its human-like form and its desperate struggles to free itself by grasping the hook with its queer little hands, are too suggestive of suffering.

To those who wish to use this bait, however, it will be a comfort to know that it is claimed that the frog is really

FIG 92.—Frogs.

less sensitive to pain than many other baits. As a rule, you should put a heavy sinker on your line when using a live frog, and frequently lift him out of the water, so that he may have a chance to breathe.

At times, under certain conditions, it is an excellent plan to remove all sinkers and allow the frog to swim at will until he is gobbled up by some big fish which has been quietly resting under an old log or the lily-pads, watching for some foolish creature to swim by his ambush.

How to Catch Frogs.

One way is to walk alongside of the stream or pond and drive the frogs into the water. They will not go far, but make great pretensions of doing so, and kick up the mud so as to deceive and blind you as to their real hiding-place. A few moments' waiting, however, will allow the mud to settle, and then, near the shore, you will see a suspicious lump of mud, and you need not doubt that the frog has doubled on his track to mislead you. It may be that from this lump of mud two bulging eyes appear. At any rate quietly slip your hand in the water, and with a quick motion grasp the lump, and you will have the frog.

Some boys acquire great skill in catching live animals. When I was a small chap I watched with interest the movements of a cat while in pursuit of birds, and discovered that its plan of action was simply this: slow, deliberate movement, with frequent and long pauses whenever the prey showed signs of alarm, no violent motion until the game was within reach; then a sudden stroke with a curved paw and extended nails seldom failed to grapple or hook the victim.

Long I pondered over this, and then began a series of experiments, and could soon proudly boast of the capture with bare hands of a gray squirrel, several pigeons, a cage full of gold-finches, turtles and frogs by the gross—not little, half-grown frogs, but great yellow-throated, green-backed, full-grown bull-frogs.

Once I crept up upon a big Virginia horned owl, and could undoubtedly have caught him, but I was a little chap, and when I looked at his great hooked talons my heart failed me, and I simply pushed him off his perch and fled as the astonished owl silently flew away. Since then I have seen a Virginia horned owl sink his talons through a heavy cowhide shoe.

In such parts of the country where the streams have muddy margins and over-hanging banks, the boys walk along the bank, and when they see a frog squatting in the mud below, throw a piece of wood at it and bury the frog in the mud, where it is easily captured.

Red Flannel Frog-bait.

A full-grown frog will bite at almost any object that moves near it, except a snake. In some experiments I made with two frogs they both showed great alarm when a little baby garter-snake was put in the same aquarium with them. Yet one of these frogs afterward swallowed his mate, and attempted the same feat with my young alligator. Taking advantage of this desire of the frog to put himself outside of everything that moves, the boys bait their hooks with bits of red flannel, and dance the gaudy cloth in front of the frog's nose until he grabs it, and the hook grabs him.

Three Hooks

knitted together like a grapple, and fastened to a short line on a long pole, will enable the boy to catch frogs a long way from shore, among the lily-pads. The hook will not alarm the frog in the least, and a sudden jerk of the line when the hooks are under the frog will never fail to bring him kicking through the air safely ashore. Any sort of small live creature can be caught with these grapple hooks.

How to Keep Frogs.

Put them in a covered vessel of any kind that will hold water, but do not make the common mistake of filling or half filling the vessel with water, or you will drown all your frogs. Put a lot of gravel, mud, moss, or sand in the bottom of your frog-bucket, and add only enough water to saturate thoroughly the material at the bottom of your bucket. Use a perforated tin or wooden cover that will admit plenty of air, or a cover made of wire netting, or an old piece of mosquito netting, or any other cloth with open meshes that will admit plenty of air.

In such a home the frogs will retain their health and vigor for any length of time. I have kept them for over a year alive and apparently happy. It is not necessary to feed them more than once in three weeks, so you need have no fear of starving them: as it is, you will seldom want to keep them longer than a week.

Live Minnows.

This bait, on the whole, is more satisfactory than any other live bait. It is more easily obtained than lampreys,

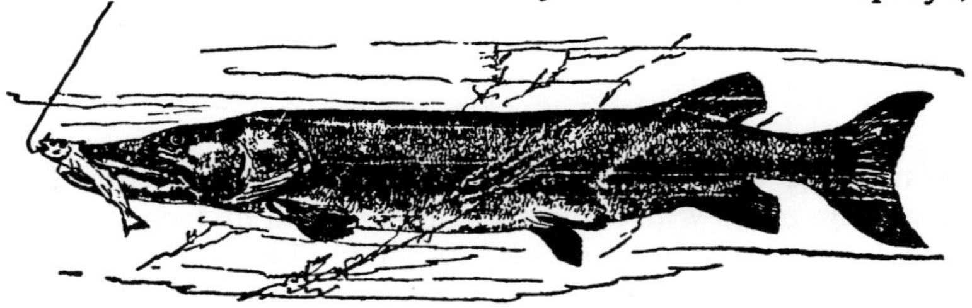

FIG. 93.—Live Bait.

is not as disagreeable to handle as insects and worms, and either suffers less, or at least appears to suffer less, than the frogs. Possibly a hook may hurt a minnow as badly as it does a frog, but the little fish has not the power of showing his discomfort or suffering so graphically. Besides all this, if you bait a minnow through the lips it can cause no more pain than cutting your own finger-nail.

To me the minnow is the king of live bait. When, as a child, I used to visit my grandmother in Northern Ohio, I was delighted to find the little brooks full of small fish, with bright red stripes on their sides. These are the famous "painted" minnow, and form excellent bait for the big black bass of Lake Erie.

How to Catch Minnows.

Where the bait is in small streams, the best thing to use is a rectangular net, with corks on the top edge and sinkers on the bottom, the net attached to two poles, one at each end. A home-made minnow net is described in the "American Boy's Handy Book." Take off your shoes and stockings and wade in the brook, one boy at each pole; slant the tops of the hand-pole down stream, being careful to keep the lower edge of the net on the bottom. Now move up stream, carefully plodding your way along so as not to foul your net on snags and stones in the bottom.

When you think you have gone far enough, bring one end of the net quickly but carefully around to the shore where the other end is. Slide the bottom of the net up to the dry land and lift it all out of water. One haul should be enough to fill your minnow-bucket.

How to make a minnow-bucket is also described in the "American Boy's Handy Book;" but, since the introduction of cheap wire netting in the market, any boy who calls himself an American should be able

To Construct a Serviceable Minnow-bucket

by taking an ordinary tin pail and making a wire-netting cylinder that will fit loosely inside the tin pail, then cut a circular piece of netting for the bottom, and fasten it there with copper wire. A lid can be made of the same material as the cylinder and hinged on with wire, so that it may be opened and closed at will, or secured with a staple and pin. The object of the open work inside the pail is to make it easy to change the water without losing the bait; or the wire pail may be hung to the boat side in such a manner that the water will flow through it and keep the bait alive.

How to Catch Minnows in Ponds, Lakes, or Deep Streams.

Where the water is deep, minnows have the habit of congregating in great schools, and may be best captured with dip-nets, either by sinking them and waiting until the bait gathers over them, or by sinking the nets and then coaxing the bait over the traps by means of a handful of bread or cracker crumbs. A favorite, but slow, method in Pike County, Penn., is to fish for the minnows among the lily-pads with a small hook and piece of thread attached to a switch, and baited with a wee bit of an angle-worm, fish, or fresh-water mussel.

How to Keep Minnows Alive.

Keep them in a box similar to the one described for lamprey eels, or in a wooden box perforated with small holes and sunk in shallow water, or in a box made of wire netting and sunk in shallow water. Always be careful to fasten the box securely, because mink and coons have a disagreeable way of robbing minnow-boxes that are carelessly fastened and what they leave the water-snakes devour. I have more than once lost more than a pailful of minnows in one night in what appeared to be a most mysterious manner, until the imprint of little hand-like feet in the muddy banks near my box gave me a clew to the robber. In transporting minnows by rail or wagon they will live in a crowded bucket, because the agitation of the water keeps it fresh, but as soon as a long stop is made they will all die, unless the water is frequently changed.

Crawfish

may be caught by a net in streams with muddy, grass-grown bottom, or by digging in the banks, or by lifting up the stones in shallow water. In lakes or ponds look for crawfish in the bottom, sand, or mud at the mouths of in-flowing brooks or springs. It is a fact not generally known that there are no crawfish on Long Island.

How to Keep Crawfish Alive.

Keep them in boxes or pails with damp moss, gravel, or aquatic plants. Put in only enough water to saturate the plants. Do not flood them. Keep in a cool, damp place.

Miscellaneous Bait.

Butterflies, moths, caterpillars, bumble-bees, May-flies, caddis-flies (Fig. 94, E), blue-bottle flies, and meal-worms, all

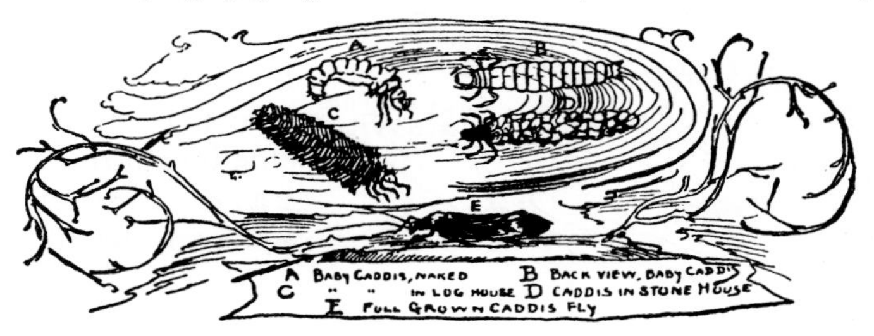

FIG. 94.—The Caddis.

make good bait at times. The last-named are to be found around old flour-mills, and with little trouble may be reared at home in musty meal.

Looking-glass Bait.

A fish is not a vain animal, but he is a very jealous creature, and looks with suspicion upon all his kind. A pet fish will not tolerate the introduction of a stranger in the aquarium, and, like a dog or a chicken, if a fish sees a companion secure a piece of food, that is the piece of food the first fish wants.

FIG. 95.—The Envious Fish.

So, I am inclined to place some credence in the story of the *Petit Journal*, to the effect that a Mr. William R. Lamb, of East Greenwich, R. I., has taken advantage of the jealous disposition of the fish. By fastening a mirror to his line below the hook, he deceives the fish that may come smelling around his bait. Immediately upon approaching the bait, the fish discovers his reflection in the glass, and hastily snaps at the hook, so as to get it before his rival can do so.

According to one authority Mr. Lamb is an Englishman, but according to another he is an old fisherman of Greenwich, R. I. It matters little where the inventor hails from; here is his contrivance:

Take a small rod with a ring in the middle and one at each end, and fasten a line to each ring. About six or eight inches above the rod bring the lines together, and tie them in such a manner that the two side lines are exactly equal, and form what your geometry would call an isosceles triangle, with the middle line running through the centre.

If possible, procure a circular or oval mirror, about a foot and a half in diameter, and fasten it by a ring in the frame to the cross-rod. Attach your fish-line to the points where the three lines meet, and fasten a short line with hook attached to the ring at one end of the cross-rod in such a manner that the bait will hang in front of the glass. (Fig. 95.)

Mr. Lamb claims that this scheme has proved successful, and there appears to be no reason why it should not. Still, when the novelty is worn off, it seems probable that a fish on the end of a clean line would feel better to the fisherman than one attached to a line hampered with a great, flat looking-glass.

Bottom Bait—Bran and Bread.

The buffalo-fish of the Western rivers, the German carp, lately introduced in many of our lakes and ponds, goldfish, and many other small fish, are fond of bread or dough, but these articles are difficult to manage, for the water washes them off the hook.

I have seen fishermen on the Ohio River mix corn-meal with cotton, or roll it into balls, and tie them up in bits of mosquito netting, and bait their hook with these balls. Another method is to soak some bread until it is thoroughly saturated, then squeeze the water out and knead it with bran and meal until it becomes tough, like putty.

Dead Bait.—Meat.

Salt pork, cut in small chunks, bits of fresh meat, and the refuse of fish already caught, form tempting bait for eels, cat-fish, and other bottom fish.

How to Pick Up a Live Eel.

To pick up a live eel, grasp its throat between your hooked first and second finger, the rest of your fist being doubled up. (See Fig. 96.) If there is a dry, sandy, or dusty spot near at hand, toss the eel into it, and again pick him up. This time, on account of the dust or sand, you will find it much less difficult to hold him.

How to Skin Him.

After picking him up, throw him down on the ground with all your force. This will stun the animal, and you may now take a sharp knife and make a circular cut below the first or pectoral fins (Fig. 97). Then, with the finger-nails, peel the skin back until you can get a good hold of it with your hands, which you have previously covered with dust.

Now take hold of the head with one hand, and strip the skin back with the other hand as shown in the third position (Fig. 98).

Eel-tail Bait.

When you have skinned the eel to a point about three or four inches above the tail, cut the tail off with a sharp knife, but leave it adhering to the skin. Turn back the skin still further, and cut off the turned-over portion of the skin about half way down. A sharp pair of scissors will be best for this purpose.

Now take your fish-hook and run it through the flesh

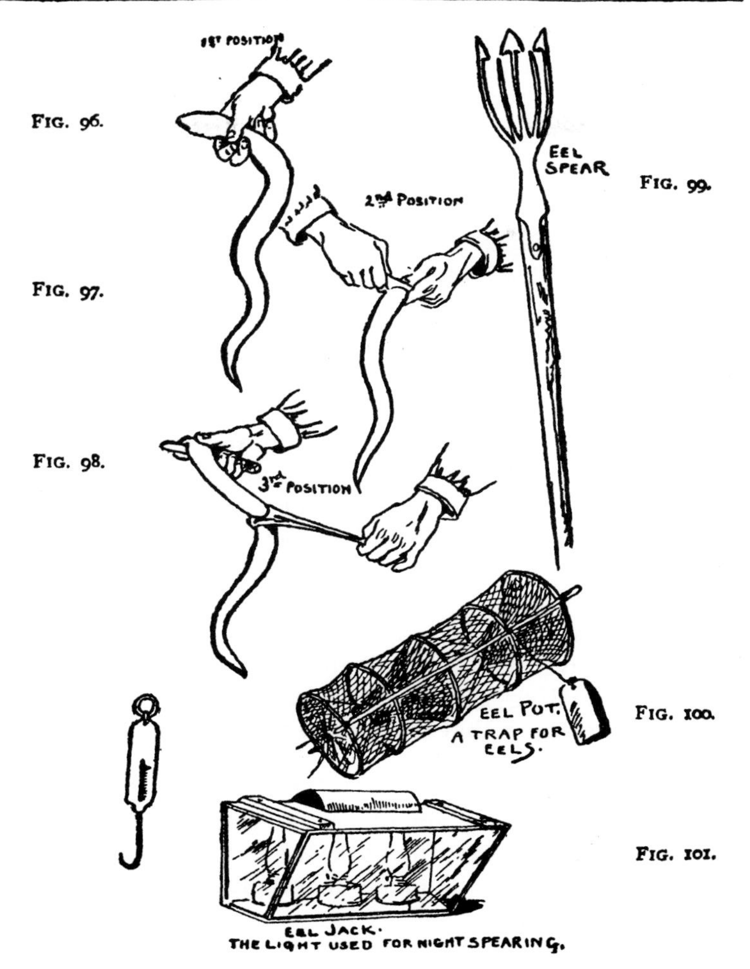

FIGS. 96, 97, and 98.—How to Hold and Skin an Eel. FIG. 99.—Eel Spear. FIG. 100.—Eel Pot. FIG. 101.—Eel Jack for Spearing at Night.

Sketched on Long Island for the American Boy's Book of Sports.

of the eel until the point of the hook protrudes at a point between one and two inches from the tip of the tail. The sinker, a split buck-shot, should be fastened to the snell just above the hook, and the skin must now be turned back above and cover the sinker. Here it must be tightly tied with waxed silk thread or fine twine. Now turn the skin down again so that it comes about half-way between the gathered end of the skin at the top and the point of the hook at the bottom. With a needle and some strong, well-waxed thread sew the edge of the skin to the body bait. You understand, of course, that the point where you cut the body of the eel off depends altogether upon the size of the eel used.

FIG. 102.—The Eel-Tail Bait.

The eel-tail bait is tough, and will last a long time. It has a beautiful bluish color that pleases the fish, and in trolling or casting the free end of the tail wiggles in so tempting a manner that it makes a very killing bait.

How to Keep Eels for Bait.

Put them away in jars of coarse salt. In using salted eels for bait it is best to soak them for an hour or so in fresh water. This will make them plumper and improve the color.

Skittering.

For skittering, a dead frog or dead minnow is just as good as a live one, inasmuch as the constant twitching of the pole or rod causes the bait to skitter over the surface of the water. The action is so violent that live bait never survive more than one or two casts. Some large fish are caught by skittering, and at certain times of the year no other method seems to meet with much success. My first awkward effort at skittering in Pike County, Pa., was rewarded with a three and one half pound bass. When you are fishing at such times it will be useful to know

How to Preserve Dead Frogs or Minnows,

so that you may keep a supply on hand. One way is to put your dead minnows in salt, or in sugar, or in alcohol and water, or in whiskey, gin, or rum. But sweet-oil will keep them firm and fresh for perhaps the greatest length of time. Put the frogs or minnows in a pail of oil and this into a pot of boiling water, and keep it there until the oil reaches the boiling point. Then immediately remove it. Do not boil your bait, or you will make it soft, tender, and unfit for use.

Other Bait.

Boys, as a rule, are all fond of fishing, and, furthermore, are almost without exception bait fishermen, leaving the use of artificial flies, spoon-hooks, and other like devices to their fathers and older brothers.

The almost universal bait of the small boy is the earthworm, garden-worm, angle-worm, or fish-worm, as it is variously called; but there are other equally as good, if not better, baits named in this chapter, so that the boys may not be at a loss for lack of knowledge of what to use as bait.

As a rule, almost any small live creature will serve in an emergency. Even live mice make good bait for large trout, and I have known fish to swallow small birds that fell in the water while fighting. Cheese is a good bait for chubs, and boiled shrimp for perch and even salmon. Paste made of bread or dough and mixed with mashed shrimp, or sweetened with sugar or honey and colored red to attract attention, Isaac Walton and some modern writers claim is good for dace, carp, etc.

Fish-spawn is called a poacher's bait. Caddis-worms, to be found in the bottom of ponds and brooks, are a killing bait. Caddis-worms build themselves little log-cabins or houses of stone, which they carry around, as a snail does its shell. They may be picked off the underside of stones and plants, and kept in a can with wet moss or aquatic plants (Fig. 94, A, C, B and D).

Fish bite when they are so inclined, and no bait that I have ever used is certain to tempt them. I have used live hellgramites and minnows with no luck, while a boy beside me caught a four-pound bass on an angle-worm. Experience, observation, and an assortment of bait are what fill your fish-basket.

FIG. 103.—Bottom Fishing (?).

CHAPTER XI

COMMON-SENSE PRECAUTIONS IN FISHING

Why and How Fish are Easily Frightened—The Lessons of Nature and of Experience.

If you will sit perfectly quiet on the bank of a clear stream or lake, it will not be long before the inhabitants of the water will venture out of their hiding-places and swim around in plain view of the observer. What does this mean? If you shoot a pistol over your head, and make no quick motion with your arms or hands, even then the creatures under the water will not flee. What does this mean?

Of course, my reader can answer for himself that all this means that sound has not much, if any, effect upon the fish, but that their eyes are quick to detect the slightest suspicious movement overhead or on shore. If you are in a boat and make a noise with your feet or anchor, the case is different, because you jar the water and that frightens the fish, but if you sit still, you may talk with no danger of alarming the game.

Some may doubt this; nevertheless, I have fired a pistol over the water and killed a frog with the bullet without alarming the other frogs or the fish in plain sight. But as soon as I made a movement to gain possession of the dead frog, not only all the other frogs plumped into the water and all the turtles slipped off the logs where they had been peacefully baking their backs in the sun, but every fish in sight darted away to be out of reach of the dangerous two-legged animal they saw approaching.

Nature as a Teacher.

The inference is that we must keep as motionless as possible when fishing, and when compelled to move, do so with great deliberation. If any one of my readers has ever watched a black-crested night-heron or any kindred bird as it fished in the shallow water, the motionless poise or the slow, deliberate movement of the bird could not have escaped notice. When you want to learn nature's secrets go to nature to find them out. Watch how the hunters with four legs and fishers with feathers act, and the nearer you conform your methods to theirs the greater will be your success.

It is understood, of course, that in fly-fishing, casting, and skittering, motion is constant and unremitting, but even then the better you are concealed, the better will be your luck.

In the woods of Pike County, Pa., there is a bright, noisy little brook that comes gabbling and gurgling down the mountain-side, now diving under moss-covered roots, and hiding a while, only to jump out and surprise you in an unlooked-for spot. After rambling along in a happy-go-lucky manner under the deep shade of tall pine-trees, it suddenly leaves the woods and sweeps out in a broad, deep pool into a pasture-field.

Out of Sight of the Pool.

Fishing down this stream a few summers ago, I came suddenly upon the pasture, but in place of climbing the fence, I cautiously poked my rod through the bushes until my fly hung directly over the spot where I supposed the pool to be. Then I gently allowed the fly to settle down, and I only knew when it struck the water by the sudden pull on the line.

Without once seeing the pool, I landed fourteen fine trout; there were no very large ones. But I had enough fish for breakfast and returned home.

Effect of Being Seen.

The next time I visited the brook I fished up the stream, and when I struck the pasture I climbed the fence and cast my fly from the bank; but I had been seen, and not one trout came near my hook.

In approaching this hole on my first trip I was shouting and breaking my way through the underbrush with great noise, purposely, in order to make my whereabouts known to a companion, who was somewhere in the glen. The last time I made no noise, but approached on tiptoe. The first time I was unseen, and I think that I could, had I wished, have taken every trout out of that pool. But when they saw me on the second occasion, I had better gone on my way and not wasted time by fishing for panic-stricken trout. There is but one big trout in this brook and I hope some day to land him; he is in a round, deep hole in an open, exposed place, devoid of shelter, besides which the hole is a network of strong sunken sticks, a veritable snare for a fisherman's line; and the only apparent way to catch him is with a strong line and a sudden jerk. Yet this trout has not lived for years in his hole for nothing, and it is probable if any one ever captures him, it will be by meeting cunning with cunning, and not by brute force.

Trolling with a Spoon.

In trolling, the longer the line the better, for the very palpable reason that the boat frightens the fish, but with a long line the fish has time to recover from his fright before the spoon comes glinting by him. Of course, a spoon does not look like any sort of a live creature when it is stationary, but a darting silver sheen is all that can be seen in the water, and that does look like a very brilliant and very lively young fish disporting himself with youthful impudence under the very noses of his cannibalistic grandsires; and it is no wonder they snap at it, if only to teach the young rascal a lesson. But, alas! they find that they are the pupils in the severe school of experience, and seldom do they live to relate their adventure to their companions.

A Word about Fly-fishing.

Now, in regard to fly-fishing, fly-rods, reels, lines, hooks, fly-hooks, and all the numerous accessories of the modern fisherman, there are books and books written upon such subjects, and there is not room here for a hundredth part of what might be and has been well said upon these topics; but bait-fishing and bottom- or still-fishing are the choice methods for boys, and could not be well left out of the spring sports.

Summer

CHAPTER XII

AQUATIC SPORTS

Rowing Clothes—How to Make a Bathing-suit—How to Avoid Sunburn—Points about Canoeing.

FROM the parent's point of view, nowhere that a boy's restless nature impels him to go is fraught with so much peril as the water, and nowhere is a boy happier than when he is on the water, unless it is when he is in it. Nowhere can be found a better school for his young mind and body than that furnished by boating. Hence it appears to be the imperative duty for parents personally to see that their children are taught to swim as soon as their little limbs have strength enough to make the proper motions.

Boating Clothes.

In aquatic sports of all kinds, if you expect to have fun, you must dress appropriately. You should have a suit of old clothes that you can change for dry ones when the sport is over. When boating, it is nonsense to pretend you can keep dry under all the varying conditions of wind and weather. If your purse is small, and you want a good rowing-suit, it can be made of last winter's woollen underclothes, and will answer for the double purpose of rowing and bathing.

How to Make a Bathing-suit.

First take an old woollen undershirt and cut the sleeves off above the elbows. Then coax your mother, aunt, or sister to sew it up in front like a sweater, and hem the edges of the sleeves where they have just been cut off.

Next take a pair of woollen drawers and have them sewed up in front, leaving an opening at the top about four inches in length; turn the top edge down all around to cover a piece of tape, that should be long enough to tie in front. Have this hem or flap sewed down to cover the tape, and allow the two ends of the tape to protrude at the opening in front. The tape should not be sewed to the cloth, but should move freely, so that you can tighten or loosen it at will. Cut the drawers off at the knees and have the edges hemmed, and you will have a first-class bathing- or rowing-suit.

If woollen clothes are not to be had, cotton will do, but wool is coolest and warmest as the occasion may require.

When rowing wear old socks, woollen ones if you have them, and old shoes cut down like slippers. The latter can be kicked off at a moment's notice, and, if lost, they are of no value, and may be easily replaced.

When on shore a long pair of woollen stockings to cover your bare legs and a sweater to pull over your sleeveless shirt are handy and comfortable, but while sailing, paddling, or rowing in hot weather the rowing-suit is generally all that comfort requires. Of course, if your skin is tender, you are liable to be terribly sunburned on your arms, neck, and legs, but

Sunburn

may be avoided by gradually accustoming your limbs to the exposure. Dearly will you pay for your negligence if you go out for a day with bare arms or legs in the hot sun before you have toughened yourself, and little will you sleep that night.

I have seen young men going to business the day following a regatta with no collars on their red necks, and no shirt over their soft undershirts, the skin being too tender to bear the touch of the stiff, starched linen, and I have known others who could not sleep a wink on account of the feverish state of their bodies, caused by the hot sun and a tender skin. Most boys have had some experience from sunburn, acquired while bathing. If care is taken to cover your arms and legs after about an hour's exposure, you will find that in place of being blistered, your skin will be first pink and then a faint brownish tint, which each succeeding exposure will deepen until your limbs will assume that dark, rich mahogany color of which athletes are so proud. This makes your skin proof against future attacks of the hottest rays of the sun.

Besides the pain and discomfort of a sudden and bad sunburn on your arms, the effect is not desirable, as it is very liable to cover your arms with freckles. I have often seen men with beautifully bronzed arms and freckled shoulders, caused by going out in their shells first with short sleeves and then with shirts from which the sleeves were entirely cut away, exposing the white, tender shoulders to the fierce heat, to which it was unaccustomed.

It is a good plan to cover the exposed parts of your body with sweet-oil, vaseline, mutton-tallow, beef-tallow, or lard. This is good as a preventive while in the sun, and excellent as an application after exposure. Any sort of oil or grease that does not contain salt is good for your skin.

Clothes for Canoeing.

In canoeing I have found it convenient to dress as I would in a shell-boat, but I generally have had a sweater and a pair of long trousers stowed away, ready to be pulled on over my rowing clothes when I landed. Once, when I neglected to put these extra clothes aboard, I was storm-bound up Long Island Sound, and leaving my boat, I took the train home, but I did not enjoy my trip, for the bare legs and arms and knit cap attracted more attention than is pleasant for a modest man.

Do not wear laced shoes in a canoe, for experience has taught boating-men that about the most inconvenient articles of clothing to wear in the water are laced shoes. While swimming your feet are of absolutely no use if encased in this style of foot-gear, and all the work must be done with the arms. But if you have old slippers, they may be kicked off, and then you are dressed practically in a bathing-suit, and can swim with comfort and ease.

Possibly these precautions may suggest the idea that a ducking is not at all an improbable accident, and it must be confessed that the boy who thinks he can learn to handle small boats without an occasional unlooked-for swim is liable to discover his mistake before he has become master of his craft.

Stick to Your Boat.

Always remember that a boy's wet head is a very small object in the water, and liable to be passed by unnoticed, but that a capsized boat can scarcely fail to attract attention and ensure a speedy rescue from an awkward position. As for the real danger of boating, it cannot be great where care is used. Not one fatality has occurred on the water among all of my large circle of boating friends, and personally I have never witnessed a fatal accident in all the years I have spent rowing and sailing.

Life-preservers.

All canoes should have a good cork life-preserver in them when the owner ventures far away from land. I never but once ventured any distance without one, and that is the only time I was ever in need of a life-preserver. The ordinary cork jacket is best. It can be used for a seat, and when spread on the bottom of your canoe, with an old coat or some similar article thrown over it for a cushion, it is not at all an uncomfortable seat. Most canoes have air-tight compartments fore and aft—that is, at both ends—and the boat itself is then a good life-preserver. Even without the air-tight compartments, unless your boat is loaded with ballast or freight, there is no danger of its sinking. A canvas canoe, as a rule, has enough woodwork about it to support your weight when the boat is full of water.

An upset canvas canoe supported me for an hour and a half during a blow on Long Island Sound, and had not a passing steamer rescued me, the canoe would evidently have buoyed me up as long as I could have held onto the hull.

CHAPTER XIII

THE LAND-LUBBER'S CHAPTER

Common Nautical Terms and Expressions Defined—How to Sail a Boat—Boat Rigs.

THERE are a few common terms with which all who venture on the water should be familiar, not only for convenience, but for prudential reasons.

Accidents are liable to happen to boats of all descrip-

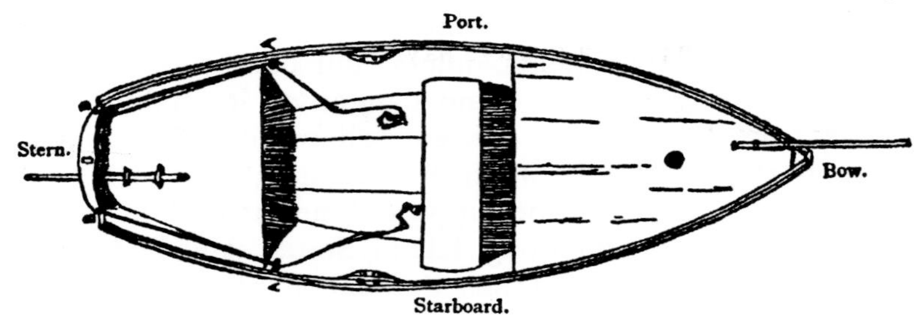

FIG. 104.—Top View of Small Boat.

tions, and often the safety of property and life depend upon the passengers' ability to understand what is said to them by the officers or sailors in charge of the craft.

To those who are familiar with the water and shipping it may seem absurd to define the bow and stern of a boat, but there are boys who will read this book who cannot tell the bow from the stern, so we will begin this chapter with the statement that

The bow is the front end of the boat, and

The stern is the rear end of the boat.

Fore'ard is toward the bow of the boat.

Aft is toward the stern of the boat. Both terms are used by sailors as forward and backward are used by landsmen.

The hull is the boat itself without masts, spars, or rigging. A skiff and a birch bark canoe are hulls.

The keel is the piece of timber running along the centre of the bottom of the hull, like the runner of a skate, and used to give the boat a hold on the water, so that she will not slide sideways.

When you are sitting in the stern of a boat, facing the bow, the side next to your right hand is the right-hand side of the boat, and the side next to your left hand is the left-hand side of the boat; but these terms are not used by seamen; they always say

Starboard for the right-hand side of the boat, and

Port for the left-hand side of the boat. Formerly the left-hand side was called the larboard, but this occasioned many serious mistakes on account of the similarity of the sound of larboard and starboard when used in giving orders.

Red and Green Lights.

After dark a red light is carried on the port side and a green light on the starboard side of all vessels in motion. If you can remember that port wine is red, and that the port light is of the same color, you will always be able to tell in which direction an approaching craft is pointing by the relative location of the lights.

> "When both lights you see ahead,
> Port your helm and show your red!
> Green to green and red to red,
> Your're all right, and go ahead!"

If you are a real land-lubber, the verse quoted will be of little service, because you will not know how to port your helm. In fact, you probably will not know where

FIG. 105.—Helm—Lever, or Stick for Tiller.

to look for the helm or what it looks like; but only a few of our readers are out-and-out land-lubbers, and most of them know that the helm is in some way connected with the steering apparatus.

The rudder is the movable piece of board at the stern of the boat by means of which the craft is guided. The rudder is moved by a lever, ropes, or a wheel.

The tiller is the lever for moving the rudder, or the ropes used for the same purpose (Fig. 105).

The wheel is the wheel whose spokes end in handles on the outer edge of the rim or felly, and it is used for moving the rudder (Fig. 106).

The helm is that particular part of the steering apparatus that you put your hands on when steering.

The deck is the roof of the hull.

The centre-board is an adjustable keel that can be raised or lowered at pleasure. It is an American invention. The centre-board, as a rule, is only used on comparatively small vessels. Mr. Joseph H. Tooker, in a note to the New York *Sun*, November 24, 1895, says that the inventor of the centre-board is Mr. Salem Wines, who kept a shop on Water Street, near Market Slip, and, when alive was a well-known New York boat-builder. His body now lies in Greenwood Cemetery, and upon the headstone of his grave is the inscription, "The Inventor of the Centre-Board."

For sailing, the boat or hull is rigged with masts and spars for spreading the sails to catch the wind.

FIG. 106.—Helm—The Wheel.

The masts are the upright poles or sticks that hold the sails.

The yards are the poles or sticks at right angles with the masts that spread the sails.

The boom is the movable spar at the bottom of the sail.

The gaff is the pole or spar for spreading the top or head of the sail (Fig. 107).

The sail is a big canvas kite, of which the boom, gaff, and masts are the kite-sticks. You must not understand by this that the sail goes soaring up in the air, for the weight of the hull prevents that; but if you make fast a large kite to the mast of a boat it would be a sail, and if you had a line long and strong enough, and should fasten any spread sail to it, there can be no doubt that the sail would fly.

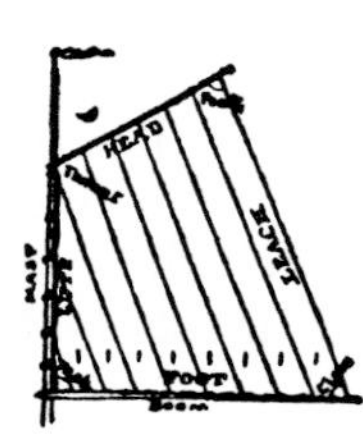

FIG. 107.—A Sail.

The spars are the masts, bowsprit, yards, and gaffs.

The bowsprit is the stick or sprit projecting from the bow of the boat (Fig. 137, Sloop).

The foremast is the mast next to the bow—the forward mast (Fig. 135, Ship).

The mainmast is the second mast—the mast next to the foremast.

Mizzen-mast is the mast next to and back of the mainmast (Fig. 135, Ship).

The rigging of a boat consists of the ropes or lines attached to its masts and sails, but a boat's rig refers to the number of masts as well as to the shape of its sails.

Stays are strong ropes supporting the masts, fore and aft.

Shrouds are strong ropes reaching from the mast-heads to the sides of the vessel; supports for the masts, starboard and port.

Ratlines are the little ropes that form the steps or foot ropes that run cross-wise between the shrouds.

The painter is the rope at the bow of a small boat, used for the same purpose as is a hitching-strap on a horse.

The standing rigging consists of the stays and shrouds.

The running rigging, of all the ropes used in handling yards and sails.

The sheets are the ropes or lines attached to the corners of sails, by which they are governed (Fig. 108).

The main sheet is the rope that governs the mainsail.

The jib sheet is the rope that governs the jib sail.

The gaskets are the ropes used in lashing the sails when furled.

The braces are the ropes used in swinging the yards around.

The jib stay is the stay that runs from the foremast to the bowsprit.

The bob stay is practically an extension of the jib stay and the chief support of the spars. It connects the bow of the boat with the bowsprit and prevents the latter from bobbing up and down.

Besides the port and starboard sides of a boat there are the windward and leeward sides. Do not understand by this that the boat has four sides like a square. Windward may be the port or the starboard side, according to the direction the wind blows; because

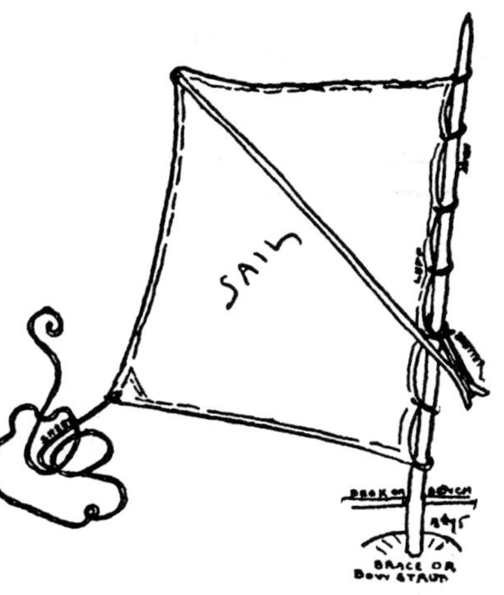

FIG. 108.—Sail and Sheet.

Windward means the side of the boat against which the wind blows; the side where the wind climbs aboard; or it may mean the direction from which the wind comes. The opposite side is called

Leeward—that is, the side of the boat opposite to that against which the wind blows, where the wind tumbles overboard, or the side opposite to windward. When you are sailing you may be near a

Lee Shore.—That is, the shore on your lee side against which the wind blows, or a

Windward Shore.—That is, the land on your windward side from which the wind blows.

All seamen dread a lee shore, as it is a most dangerous shore to approach, from the fact that the wind is doing its best to blow you on the rocks or beach. But the windward shore can be approached with safety, because the wind will keep you off the rocks, and if it is blowing hard, the land will break the force of the wind.

In a canoe or shell the boatman sits either directly on the bottom, or, as in the shell, very close to it, and the weight of his body serves to keep the boat steady, but larger crafts seldom rely upon live weights to steady them. They use

Ballast.—That is, weights of stone, lead, iron, or sand-bags used to balance the boat and make her steady.

As has been said before in this chapter, the sail is a big canvas kite made fast to the boat, and called a sail, but the ordinary kite has its covering stretched permanently on rigid sticks.

The sail, however, can be stretched to its full extent or only partially, or it may be rolled up, exposing nothing but the masts to the force of the wind. To accomplish all this there are various ropes and attachments, all of which are named.

It is quite important that the young sailor should know the names of all the

Parts of a Sail.

Luff.—That part of the sail adjoining the mast—the front of the sail (Fig. 109).

Leach.—That part of the sail stretched between the outer or after end of the boom and the outer end of the gaff—the back part of the sail (Fig. 109).

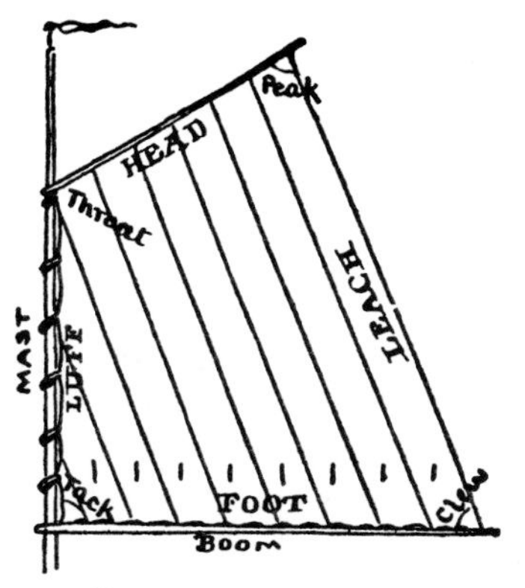

FIG. 109.—Parts of Sail.

Head.—That part of the sail adjoining the gaff—the top of the sail.

Foot.—That part of the sail adjoining the boom—the bottom of the sail (Fig. 109).

Clews.—A general name for the four corners of the sail.

Clew. — The particular corner at the foot of the sail where the leach and boom meet (Fig. 109).

Tack.—The corner of the sail where boom and mast meet (Fig. 109).

Throat or Nock.—The corner of the sail where gaff and mast meet (Fig. 109).

Peak.—Corner of the sail where the leach and gaff meet (Fig. 109).

How to Steer a Boat.

When you wish your boat to turn to the right push your helm to the left. This will push the rudder to the right, and turn the boat in that direction. When you wish your boat to turn to the left push your helm to the right. In other words, starboard your helm and you will turn to the port (Fig. 110). Port your helm and you will turn to the starboard (Fig. 111).

From a reference to the diagram you may see that when you **port your helm** you move the tiller to the port side of the boat, and when you **starboard your helm**

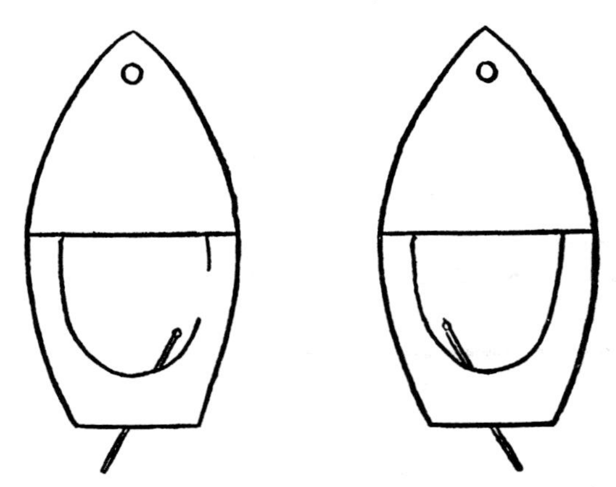

FIG. 110.—Starboard Helm. FIG. 111.—Port Helm.

you move your tiller to the starboard side of the boat (Fig. 110), but to **ease your helm** you move your helm toward the centre of the boat—that is, amidships.

How to Sail a Boat.

If you fasten the bottom of a kite to the ground, you will find that the wind will do its best to blow the kite over, and if the kite is fastened to the mast of a toy boat, the wind will try to blow the boat over.

In sailing a boat the effort of the wind apparently has

but one object, and that is the upsetting of the boat. The latter being well balanced, is constantly endeavoring to sit upright on its keel, and you, as a sailor, are aiding the boat in the struggle, at the same time subverting the purpose of the wind to suit your own ideas. It is an exciting game, in which man usually comes out ahead, but the wind gains enough victories to keep its courage up.

Every boat has peculiarities of its own, and good traits as well as bad ones, which give the craft a personal character, that lends much to your interest, and even affects your sensibilities to the extent of causing you to have the same affection for a good, trustworthy craft that you have for an intelligent and kind dog or horse.

A properly balanced sailboat, with main sheet trimmed flat and free helm, should be as sensitive as a weathercock and act like one—that is, she ought to swing around until her bow pointed right into the "eye of the wind," the direction from which the wind blows. Such a craft it is not difficult to sail, but it frequently happens that the boat that is given to you to sail is not properly balanced, and shows a constant tendency to "come up in the wind"—face the wind—when you are doing your best to keep her sails full and keep her on her course. This may be caused by too much sail aft. The boat is then said to carry a weather helm.

Weather Helm.—When a boat shows a constant tendency to come up in the wind.

Lee Helm.—When a boat shows a constant tendency to fall off the wind—that is, when the wind blows her bow to the leeward. This is a much worse trait than the former, and a boat with a lee helm is a dangerous boat. It may be possible to remedy it by adding sail aft or reducing sail forward, which should immediately be done.

In spite of the fact, already stated, that the wind's constant effort is to capsize a boat, there is little or no danger of a properly rigged boat upsetting unless the sheets are fast or hampered in some way. When a sailboat upsets it is, of course, because the wind blows it over. Now, the wind cannot blow a boat over unless the boat presents some surface larger than its hull for the wind to blow against, and the sail is the only object that offers enough surface to the breeze to cause an upset.

If the sheet is slackened, the sail will swing around until it flaps like a flag and only the thin edge is presented to the wind; and a boat that a flag will upset is no boat for beginners to trust themselves in. True the boom may be very long and heavy enough to make it dangerous to let so much of it overboard, but this is seldom the case. A good sailor keeps his eyes constantly on the sails and trims them to take advantage of the slightest favorable breeze. In place of losing control of his sail by letting go the sheets he will ease the tiller so as to "spill" part of the wind—that is, let the forward part or luff of the sail shake a bit. Or, in case of a sudden puff of wind, he may deem it necessary to "luff"—that is, let her shake—and slacken the sheets, too.

Trimmed Flat.—Sheets hauled in until the boom is only a little to the leeward of the helm (Fig. 112).

Close-Hauled.—Sheets trimmed flat and the boat pointing as near as possible to the eye of the wind. Then the sail cannot belly, and is called flat (Fig. 112).

To Sail Close-Hauled.

The skipper must watch that his sail does not flap or ripple at the throat, for that means that he is pointing too close to the wind and that some of the breeze is blowing on both sides of his sail, which even a novice can see will retard the boat.

Upon discovering a rippling motion at the luff of the sail put the helm up—that is, move the tiller a little to windward until the sail stops its flopping.

Before the Wind.—When the wind is astern; sailing with the wind; sailing directly from windward to leeward (Fig. 113).

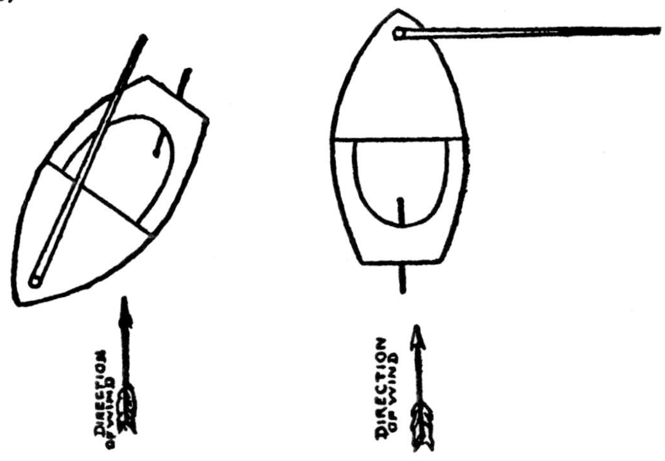

FIG. 112.—Close Hauled. FIG. 113.—Before the Wind.

In order to reach the desired point it is often expedient to sail before the wind, but unless the wind is light, beginners had better not try this. To sail before the wind you let your sheets out until the boom stands at almost right angles with the boat. Keep your eye on the sail and see that it does not flap, for if the man at the helm is careless and allows the boat to point enough away from the direction of the wind to allow the wind to get on the other side of the sail, the latter will swing around or jibe with such force as to endanger the mast, if it does not knock some one overboard.

The price of liberty is constant vigilance, and the price of a good sail is the same. I have seen a mast snapped off clean at the deck by a jibe, and once when out after ducks every one was so intent upon the game that proper attention was not paid to the sail. The wind got round and brought the boom with a swing aft, knocking the captain of our boat club overboard. Had the boom hit him in the head and stunned him, the result might have been fatal.

Wing and Wing.—When a schooner goes before the wind with one sail out at nearly right angles on the port side and the other in the same position on the starboard side she is said to be wing and wing, and presents a beautiful sight.

Tacking.—Working to the windward by a series of diagonal moves.

Legs.—The moves or diagonal courses made in tacking. It is apparent to the most unthinking observer that no vessel propelled by sail can move against the direct course of the wind, that is, nothing but electricity, naphtha, steam, or some such power can drive a boat into the eye of the wind. But what cannot be accomplished in a direct manner can be done by a series of compromises, each of which will bring us nearer to the desired point.

First we point the boat to the right or left, as the case may be, as near or as close to the wind as the boat will sail. Then we come about and sail in the other direction as close as practicable to the eye of the wind, and each time we gain something in a direct line.

When your boat changes its direction on a tack it is done by "jibing" or "coming about."

Jibing.—With the wind on the quarter, haul the main boom aft or amidships with all possible speed, by means of the main sheets (Fig. 115), and as the wind strikes the

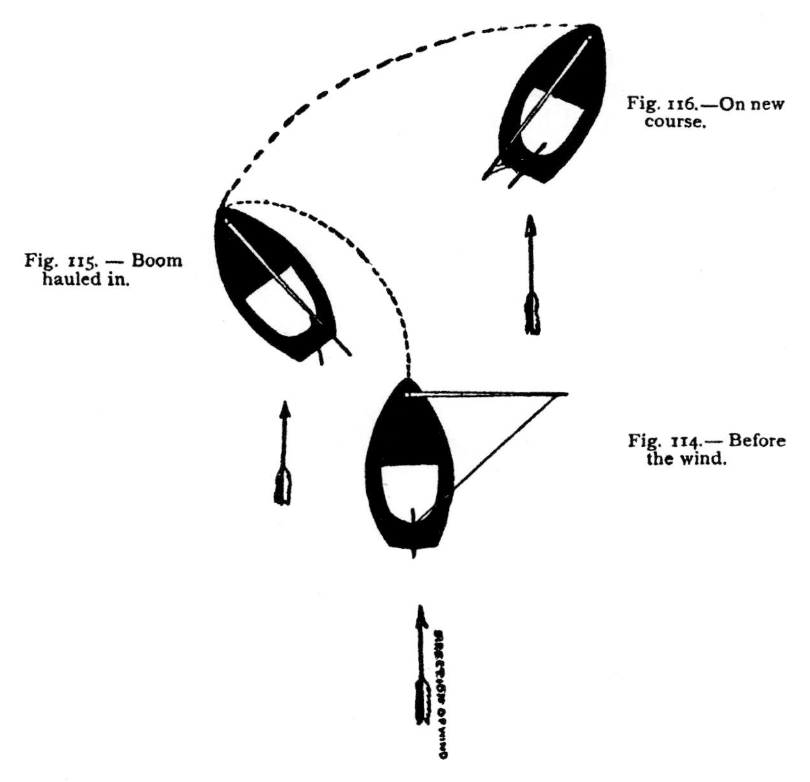

Fig. 116.—On new course.

Fig. 115. — Boom hauled in.

Fig. 114.— Before the wind.

FIGS. 114, 115 and 116.—Jibing.

sail on the other side let it out as deliberately as possible until it reaches the position desired (Fig. 116).

Beginners should never attempt to jibe, for if there is

more than a capful of wind, the sail will probably get away from them, and, as described in going before the wind, some disaster is liable to occur. Experts only jibe in light winds, and frequently lower the peak, so as to reduce sail, before attempting a jibe.

When you wish to come about see that all the tackle, ropes, etc., are clear and in working order, and that you are making good headway, then call out: "Helm's a-lee!"

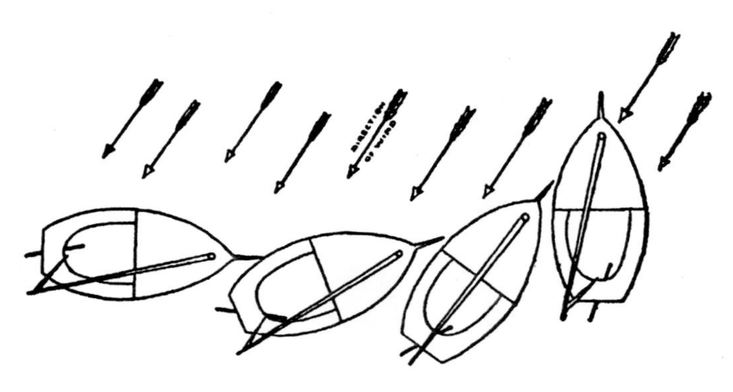

FIGS. 117, 118, 119 and 120.—Coming About.

or "Ready about!" and push the tiller in the direction opposite to that from which the wind blows—that is, to the lee side of the boat. This will bring the bow around until the wind strikes the sail upon the side opposite to that which it struck before the helm was a-lee (Figs. 117, 118, 119, 120).

If you are aboard a sloop or schooner, ease off the jib sheet, but keep control of it, so that as the boat comes up to the wind you can make the jib help the bow around by holding the sheets so as to catch the wind aback. When the bow of the craft has passed the eye of the wind and the sail begins to fill give the order to make fast or trim the jib, and off you go upon the opposite tack, or on a new leg.

If the wind is light, or if, for any cause, the boat works slowly, you can sometimes help her by trimming in the main sheet when you let the jib sheet fly. In the diagram of coming about no jib is shown.

Wearing is a term sometimes used in place of jibing.

In a Thunder-Storm.

A thunder-storm is always an uncertain thing. There may be a veritable tornado hidden in the black clouds that we see rising on the horizon, or it may simply "iron out the wind"—that is, go grumbling overhead—and leave us becalmed, to get home the best way we can; generally by what the boys called a "white-ash breeze"—that is, by using the sweeps or oars.

On Long Island Sound a thunder-storm seems to have certain fixed rules of conduct. In the first place, it comes up from the leeward, or *against the wind.* Just before the storm strikes you for an instant the wind ceases and the sails flap idly. Then look out! for in nine cases out of ten you are struck the next moment by a sudden squall from exactly the opposite direction from which the wind blew a moment before.

What to Do.

Make for the nearest port with all speed, and keep a man at the down haul ready at a moment's notice to lower sail. The moment the wind stops drop the sail and make everything snug, leaving only bare poles. When the thunder-squall strikes you, be it ever so hard, you are now in little danger; and if the wind from the new quarter is not too fresh, you can hoist sail again and make the best of your way to the nearest port, where you can "get in out of the wet."

If the wind is quite fresh keep your peak down, and with a reefed sail speed on your way. If it is a regular howler, let your boat drive before the wind under bare poles until you can find shelter or until it blows over, and the worst mishap you are likely to incur is a good soaking from the rain.

Shortening Sail.—Just as soon as the boat heels over too far for safety, or as soon as you are convinced that there is more wind than you need for comfortable sailing, it is time to take a reef—that is, to roll up the bottom of the sail to the row of little ropes or reefing points on the sail and make fast there. This, of course, makes a smaller sail, and that is what you wish.

While under way it will be found impossible to reef a sail except when sailing close-hauled. So the boat is brought up into the wind by pushing the helm down, as if you intended to come about. When possible it is better to lower the sail entirely before attempting to put in a reef.

To Reef Without Lowering Sail.

It sometimes happens that on account of the proximity of a lee shore, and the consequent danger of drifting in that direction, or for some other equally good reason, it is unadvisable to lower sail and lose headway. Under such circumstances the main sheet must be trimmed flat, keeping the boat as close as possible to the wind, the helm must be put up hard a-lee, and jib sheet trimmed to windward (Fig. 121).

When this is done the wind will hit the jib, "paying her head off," or pushing her bow to leeward, and this tendency is counteracted by the helm and mainsail, bringing the bow up into the wind. This keeps the boat squirming. Lower the mainsail until the row of reef points is just on a line with the boom, keeping to the windward of the sail. Tie the first point—that is, the one on the luff rope—then the one on the leach, being careful to stretch out the foot of the sail. Then tie the remaining points, always making a square or reefing knot. Tie them to the jack stay on the boom or around the boom.

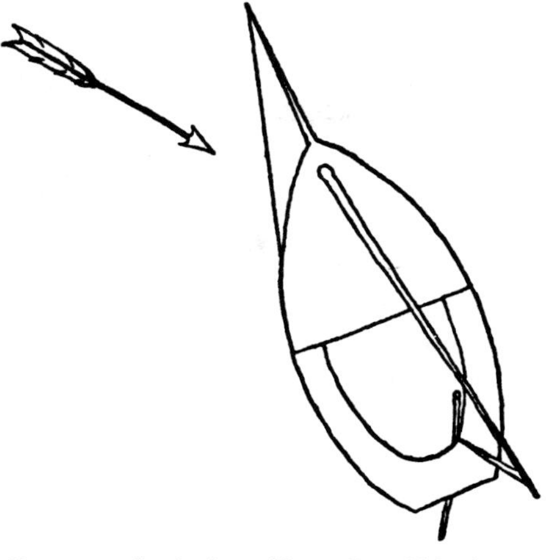

FIG. 121.—Squirming; Jib on Port Side, Boom Close-hauled on Starboard Side.

The Reef or Square Knot

is most frequently used, as its name implies, in reefing sails. First make a plain overhand knot, as in Fig. 122. Then repeat the operation by taking the end and passing it over and under the loop, drawing the parts tight, as shown in Fig. 123. Care should be observed in crossing the ends so that they will always lay fairly alongside the main parts. Otherwise the knot will prove a *granny*, and be comparatively worthless.

FIG. 122 and 123.—Square or Reef Knot.

To Shake Out a Reef,

untie the knots, keeping to the windward of the sail. Untie the knot at the leach first, next the one at the luff.

and then the remaining points. In lowering a sail you use a rope called the down haul.

Starboard Tack.—When the main boom is over the port side.

Port Tack.—When the main boom is over the starboard side.

Right of Way.—All boats sailing on the starboard tack have the right of way over all those on the port tack. In other words, if you are on the starboard tack, those on the port tack must keep out of your way. Any boat sailing close-hauled has the right of way over a boat sailing free.

Lights for Canoe.

A canoe under sail at night should have an uncolored lantern hung to her mizzen-mast to notify other craft that she is out and objects to being run down. The light is put on the mizzen so that it may be behind the skipper and not dazzle him.

What you have read in the foregoing pages will not be found very difficult to remember, but there is only one way to learn to sail and that is by *sailing*. If possible, sail with some one who is a good seaman. If this sort of companion cannot be had, try it alone on smooth water and with short sail until you accustom yourself to the boat and its peculiarities. No boy ever learned to skate or swim from books, but books often have been helpful in giving useful hints to those who were really learning by practical experience.

Some Do Nots.

Do not overload the boat.

Do not carry too much sail.

Do not sail in strange waters without chart or compass.

Do not forget your anchor.

Do not forget your paddles or oars.

Do not attempt to learn to sail before you know how to swim.

Do not sit on the gunwale.

Do not put the helm down too suddenly or too far.

Do not let go the helm.

Do not mistake caution for cowardice.

Do not be afraid to reef.

Do not fear the ridicule of other land-lubbers.

Do not fail to keep the halyards and sheets clear.

Do not jibe in a stiff wind.

Do not fail to keep your head in times of emergency.

Do not make a display of bravery until the occasion demands it.

Do not allow mistakes or mishaps to discourage you.

You will soon become an expert and be able to engage in one of our most exhilarating, healthy, and manly sports and earn the proud distinction of being a good small-boat sailor.

CHAPTER XIV

RIGS OF ALL KINDS FOR SMALL BOATS

How to Distinguish between a Ship, Bark, Brig, and Schooner—Merits and Defects of Cat-Boats—Advantages of the Sloop—Rigs for Canoes—Buckeyes and Sharpies.

THE two principal rigs for vessels are the fore-and-aft and the square rig.

Square rigged consists in having the principal sails extended by yards suspended at the middle. (Fig. 135.)

Fore-and-aft rigged is having the principal sails extended by booms and gaffs suspended by their ends (Figs. 124, 125, 126, 132, 138 and 137).

Barks, brigs, and ships are all more or less square rigged, but schooners, sloops, and catboats are all fore-and-aft rigged. In these notes the larger forms of boats are mentioned only because of the well-known interest boys take in all nautical matters, but no detailed description of the larger craft will be given. All that is aimed at here is to give the salient points, so that the youngsters will know the name of the rig when they see it.

The Cat.

There is a little snub-nosed American who, in spite of her short body and broad waist, is deservedly popular among all our amateur sailors.

The appreciation of her charms is felt and acknowledged by all her companions without envy, not because of her saucy looks, but on account of her accommodating manners.

Possessing a rare ability for quick movement, and a wonderful power to bore her way almost into the very eye of the wind, or with double-reefed sail to dash through the storm or gently slide up alongside of a wharf or dock as easily as a rowboat, the American catboat, with her single mast "chock up in the eyes of her," has made a permanent place for herself among our pleasure craft, and is omnipresent in our crowded bays and harbors.

FIG. 124.—The Snub-nosed American Cat.

Knowing that there is little danger of the catboat losing its well-earned popularity, and being somewhat familiar with many of her peculiarities, I am free to say that this rig, notwithstanding its numerous good points, has many serious defects as a school-ship, and the beginner had better select some other rig with which to begin his practice sailing.

First, the great sail is very heavy and difficult to hoist and reef. Second, in going before the wind there is constant danger of jibing, with serious results. Third, the catboat has a very bad habit of rolling when sailing before the wind, and each time the boat rolls from side to side she is liable to dip the end of her heavy boom in the water and "trip herself up." When a boat trips *up* she does not necessarily go *down*, but she is likely to upset, placing the young sailors in an unenviable, if not a dangerous, position. Fourth, when the craft begins to swagger before the wind she is liable to "goose neck," that is throw her boom up against the mast, which is another accident fraught with the possibilities of serious mischief.

The catboat has no bowsprit, no jib, and no topsail, but that most graceful of all single-stickers,

The Sloop,

possesses several jibs, a bowsprit, and topsail. Besides these, when she is in racing trim, a number of additional sails are used. All our great racers are sloops, and this rig is the most convenient for small yachts and cutters.

Racing Sloops.

A racing sloop (Fig. 137) carries a mainsail, A, a fore staysail B, a jib, C, a gaff topsail, D, a club topsail, E, a baby jib topsail, F, a No. 2 jib topsail, G, a No. 1 jib topsail, H, a balloon jib topsail, J (Fig. 133), and a spinnaker, K (Fig. 133).

Jib and Mainsail.

A small sloop's sails are a mainsail, jib, and topsail. A sloop rig without topsail is called a jib and mainsail (Fig. 125).

While every small-boat sailor should know a catboat and a sloop when he sees them, and even be able to give the proper name to their sails, neither of these rigs is very well suited for canoes, sharpies, or other boats of the mosquito fleet; but the

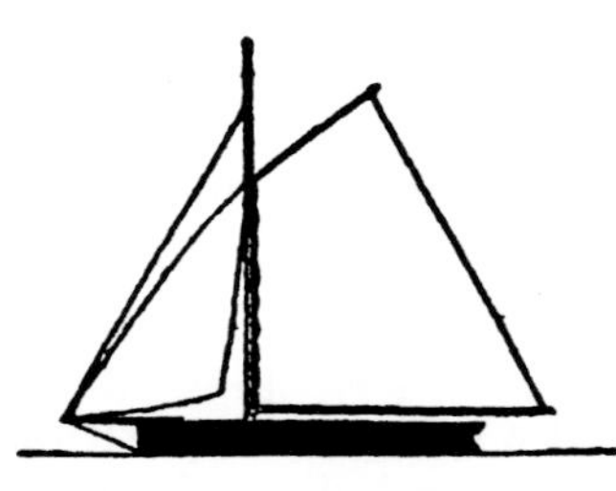

FIG. 125.—Jib and Mainsail.

Schooner Rig,

which is the form of boat generally used for the larger yachts, is also very much used for open boats. As you can see, by referring to Fig. 126, the schooner rig consists of a bowsprit, fore and main mast, with their appropriate sails. Lately freight schooners have appeared with three or more masts. For small boats two adjustable masts and an adjustable bowsprit, as described in the Rough and Ready, Chapter XIV., are best. The sails may be sprit sails, Fig. 143, balance lug, Fig. 127; standing lug, Fig. 128; leg of mutton, Fig. 129, or the sliding gunter, Fig. 139.

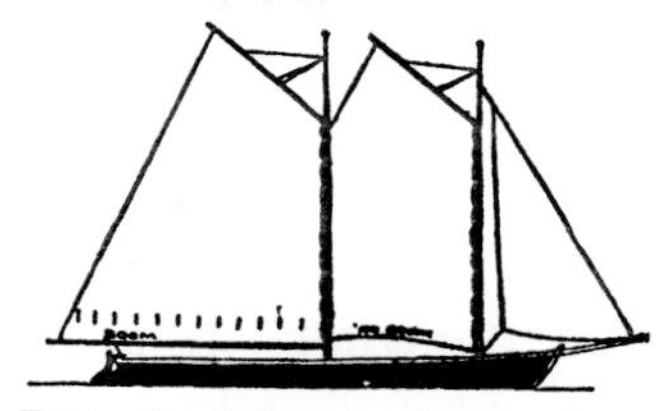

Fig. 126.—Schooner Rig for Open Boat. Boom on Mainsail, none on Foresail.

In the chapter on how to build the Rough and Ready, the sprit sail is depicted and fully described.

The Balance Lug

comes as near the square sail of a ship as any canvas used on small boats, but you can see, by referring to the diagram, Fig. 127, that the leach and the luff are not parallel and that the gaff hangs at an angle. To boom out the can-

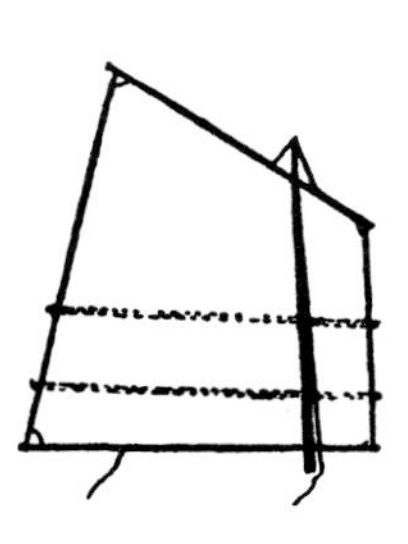

Fig. 127.—The Balance Lug.

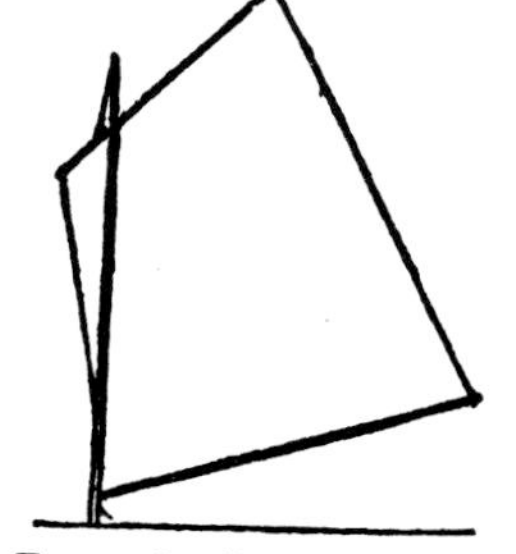

Fig. 128.—Standing Lug.

vas and make it sit flat there are three sticks extended across the sail from the front to the back, luff to leach, called battens. This has caused some people to call this a batten lug. Like the lateen sail, part of the balance lug hangs before the mast and serves the purpose of a jib. This rig is said to be easily managed and to possess good sailing qualities.

The Standing Lug

is another sail approaching the square in pattern, and, as any novice can see, is a good canvas with which to scud before the wind. It is very convenient for open boats built to be propelled by paddles. While the standing lug cannot point up to the eye of the wind like a schooner or cat, it is very fast on the wind or when running with the wind astern. Probably the safest form of sail used is the old reliable

Leg-of-Mutton Sail.

This is used by the fishermen on their stanch little dories away up on the coast of Maine, and by the "tide-water" people in their "buckeyes" on Chesapeake Bay. The latter boat is very little known outside of the locality where it makes its home, but like the New Haven sharpies, it is very popular in its own waters.

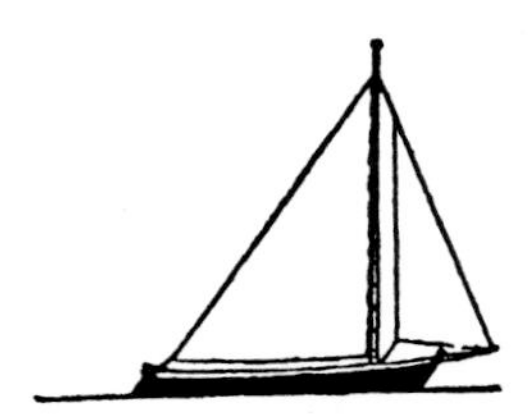

FIG. 129.—Leg of Mutton Sail. Jib and Mainsail Rig.

The Buckeye,

or "bugeye," as it is sometimes vulgarly called, has a great reputation for speed and sea-going qualities. When it cannot climb a wave it goes through it. This makes a wet boat in heavy weather, but when you travel at a high rate of speed you can endure a wet jacket with no complaint, especially when you feel that, in spite of the fast-sailing qualities of this boat, it is considered a particularly safe craft.

The construction of a **buckeye** has been evolved from

FIG. 130. FIG. 131. FIG. 132.

FIG. 135. FIG.

FIGS. 130–137.—RIGS

Fig. 134.

Fig. 133.

Fig. 137.

...at we Meet at Sea.

the old dugout canoe of the Indians and the first white settlers. America was originally covered with vast forests of immense trees. Remnants of these forests still exist in a few localities. It was once possible to make a canoe of almost any dimensions desired, but now in the thickly settled regions big trees are scarce.

FIG. 138.—The Buckeye.

So the Chesapeake Bay boat-builders, while still adhering to the old dugout, have overcome the disadvantage of small logs by using more than one and bolting the pieces together. Masts and sails have been added, and since the increased proportions made it impracticable to drag such a craft on the beach when in port, anchors and cables are supplied. Two holes bored, one on each side of the stem, for the cables to run through, have given the boat the appearance of having eyes, and as the eyes are large and round, the negroes called them buckeyes, and this is now the name by which all such craft are known.

At first only two masts with leg-of-mutton sails were used, but now they have a jib and two sails. With the greatest width or beam about one-third the distance from bow to stern, sharp at both ends, its long, narrow, and heavy hull is easily driven through the water, and makes both a fast and stiff boat.

The buckeye travels in shallow as well as deep waters, and hence is a centre-board boat, but there is nothing unnecessary on the real buckeye—no overhanging bow or stern, for that means additional labor; no stays to the masts, for the same reason. The lack of stays to stiffen the masts leaves them with "springiness," which in case of a sudden squall helps to spill the wind and prevents what might otherwise be a "knock-down."

The foremast is longer than the mainmast and does not rake aft so much, but the mainmast has a decided rake, which the colored sailors say makes the boat faster on the wind. Sometimes in the smaller boats the mainmast can be set upright when going before the wind.

Wealthy gentlemen on the Chesapeake are now building regularly equipped yachts on the buckeye plan, and some of them are quite large boats. A correspondent of the *Forest and Stream*, in speaking of the buckeye, says:

> "Last summer I cruised in company with a buckeye, forty-two feet long, manned by two gentlemen of Baltimore city. She drew twenty inches without the board. In sudden and heavy flaws she was rarely luffed. She would lie over and appear to spill the wind out of her tall, sharp sails, and then right again. Her crew took pleasure in tackling every sailing craft for a race; nothing under seventy feet in length ever beat her. She steered under any two of her three sails. On one occasion this craft, on her way from Cape May to Cape Charles, was driven out to sea before a heavy northwest blow. Her crew, the aforesaid gentlemen, worn out by fatigue, hove her to and went to sleep. She broke her tiller lashing during the night, and when they awoke she was pegging away on a southeast course under her jib. They put her about, and in twenty hours were inside Cape Henry, pretty well tired out. Buckeyes frequently run from Norfolk to New York with fruit. For shallow waters, I am satisfied there is no better craft afloat. Built deep, with a loaded keel, they would rival the English cutter in seaworthiness and speed."

When the hardy, bold fishermen of our Eastern States and the brave fishermen down South both use the leg-of-mutton sail, beginners cannot object to using it while practising; knowing that even if it is a safe sail, it cannot be called a "baby rig." Another safe rig, differing little from the leg-of-mutton, is the

Sliding Gunter.

In this rig the sail is laced to a yard which slides up or down the mast by means of two iron hooks or travellers (Fig. 139). No sail with a narrow-pointed top is very serviceable before the wind, and the sliding gunter is no exception to the rule. But it is useful on the wind, and can be reefed easily and quickly, qualities which make it many friends.

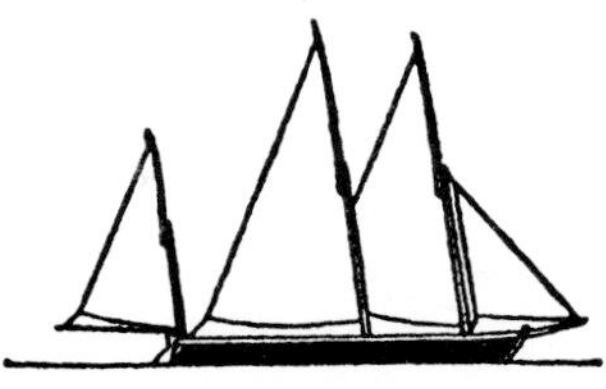

FIG. 139.—The Sliding Gunter.

In the smooth, shallow waters along the coast of North Carolina may be seen the long, flat-bottomed

Sharpies.

Without question they are to be ranked among the fastest boats we have. These boats are rigged with a modification of the leg-of-mutton sail. The ends of the sprit in the foresail

FIG. 140.—Sharpie with Sprit and Club Leg-of-Mutton Sails.

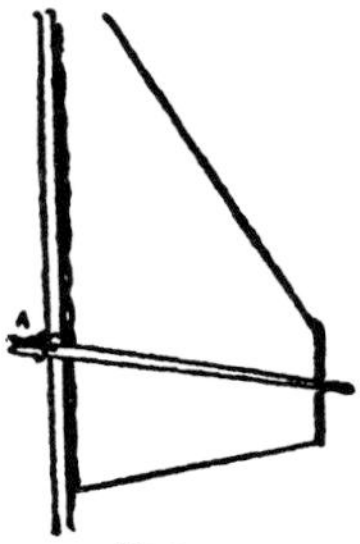

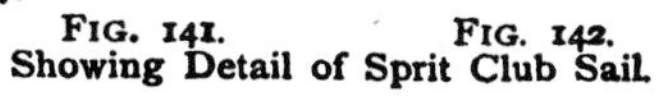

FIG. 141. FIG. 142.
Showing Detail of Sprit Club Sail.

project at the luff and leach. At the luff it is fastened to the mast by a line like a snotter at the leach. It is fastened to a stick sewed into the sail, called a club. The sheet is attached to the end of the sprit (Figs. 140, 141, 142, 144, and 145).

The Sprit Leg-of-Mutton Sail

has this advantage, that the clew of the sail is much higher

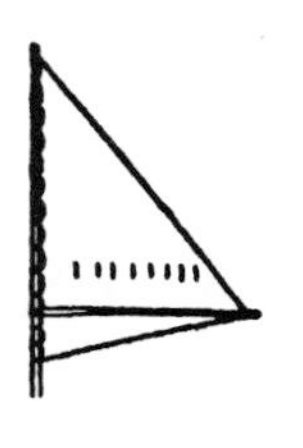

Fig. 143.—Plain Sprit Leg-of-Mutton.

Fig. 144.

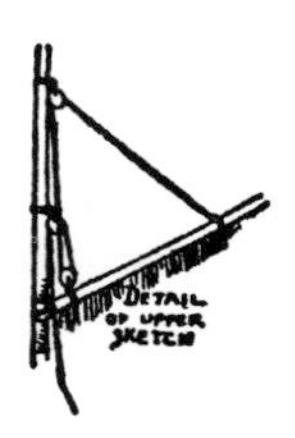

Fig. 145.

Another Form of the Sprit Sail.

than the tack, thus avoiding the danger of dipping the clew in the water and tripping the boat.

The Dandy Jigger, or Mizzen Rig,

is named after the small sail aft, near the rudder-head. This jigger, mizzen, or dandy may have a boom, a sprit, or be rigged as a lug. (See Figs. 146, 147, 149, 150, 151, 152, 154, 156, and 160, which show the principal mizzen rigs in use.)

In puffy wind and lumpy water the main and mizzen rig will be found to work well.

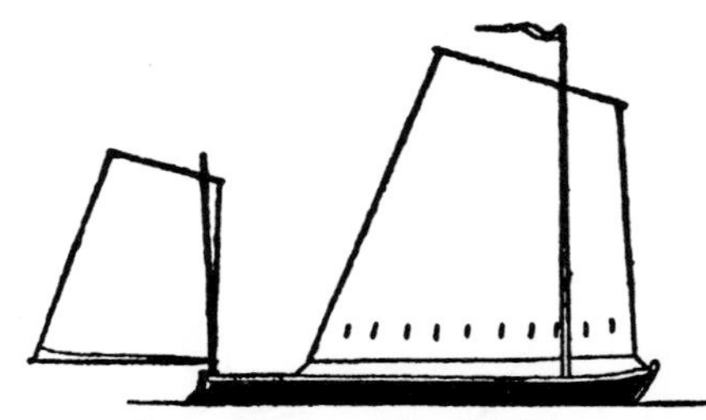

Fig. 146.—Lug Rig with Jigger.

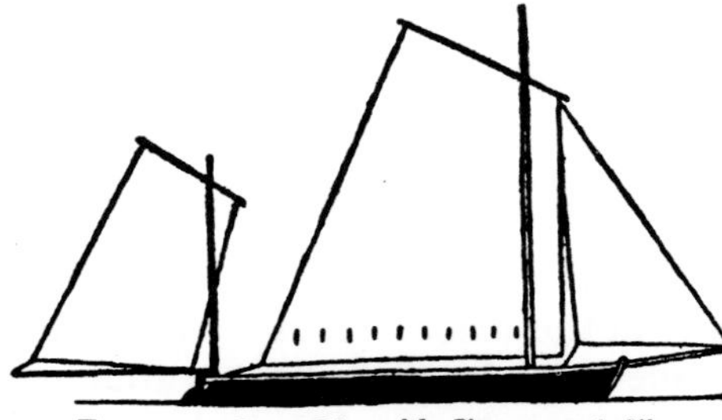

Fig. 147.—Lug Rig with Jigger and Jib.

The little sail aft should be trimmed as flat as possible. It will be found of great help in beating to the windward, and

FIG. 148.—Jib. FIG. 149.—Sprit Sail, Schooner Rig, with Dandy. FIG. 150.—Sprit Sail Jib and Dandy.

will keep the nose of the boat facing the wind when the mainsail is down. Different rigs are popular in different localities. For instance:

The Lateen Rig

is very popular in some parts of the Old World, yet it has only few friends here. It may be because of my art training that I feel so kindly toward this style of sail, or it may be from the association in my mind of some of the happiest days of my life with a little black canoe rigged with lateen sails. At any rate, in spite of the undeniable fact that the lateen is unpopular, I never see a small boat rigged in this style without a feeling of pleasure. The handy little stumps of masts, end in a spike at the top, and are adorned by the beautiful sails lashed to slender spars, which, by means of metal rings, are lightly, but securely, fastened to the mast by simply hooking the ring over the spike. I freely acknowledge that when the sails are lowered and you want to use your paddle the lateen sails are in your way. It

FIG. 151.—The Lateen Rig with Dandy.

is claimed that they are awkward to reef, and this may be true. I never tried it. When the wind was too strong for my sails I made port or took in either the large or the small sail, as the occasion seemed to demand.

The Ship.

When you are out sailing and see a vessel with three masts, all square rigged, you are looking at a ship proper, though ship is a word often used loosely for any sort of a boat (Fig. 135).

The bark is a vessel with square-rigged foremast and mainmast and a fore-and-aft rigged mizzen-mast (Fig. 136).

The brig is a vessel with only two masts, both of which are square rigged (Fig. 134).

The brigantine has two masts—foremast square rigged and mainmast fore-and-aft rigged (Fig. 131).

The barkentine has three masts—mainmast and mizzen-mast fore-and-aft rigged and foremast square rigged. (See Fig. 130.)

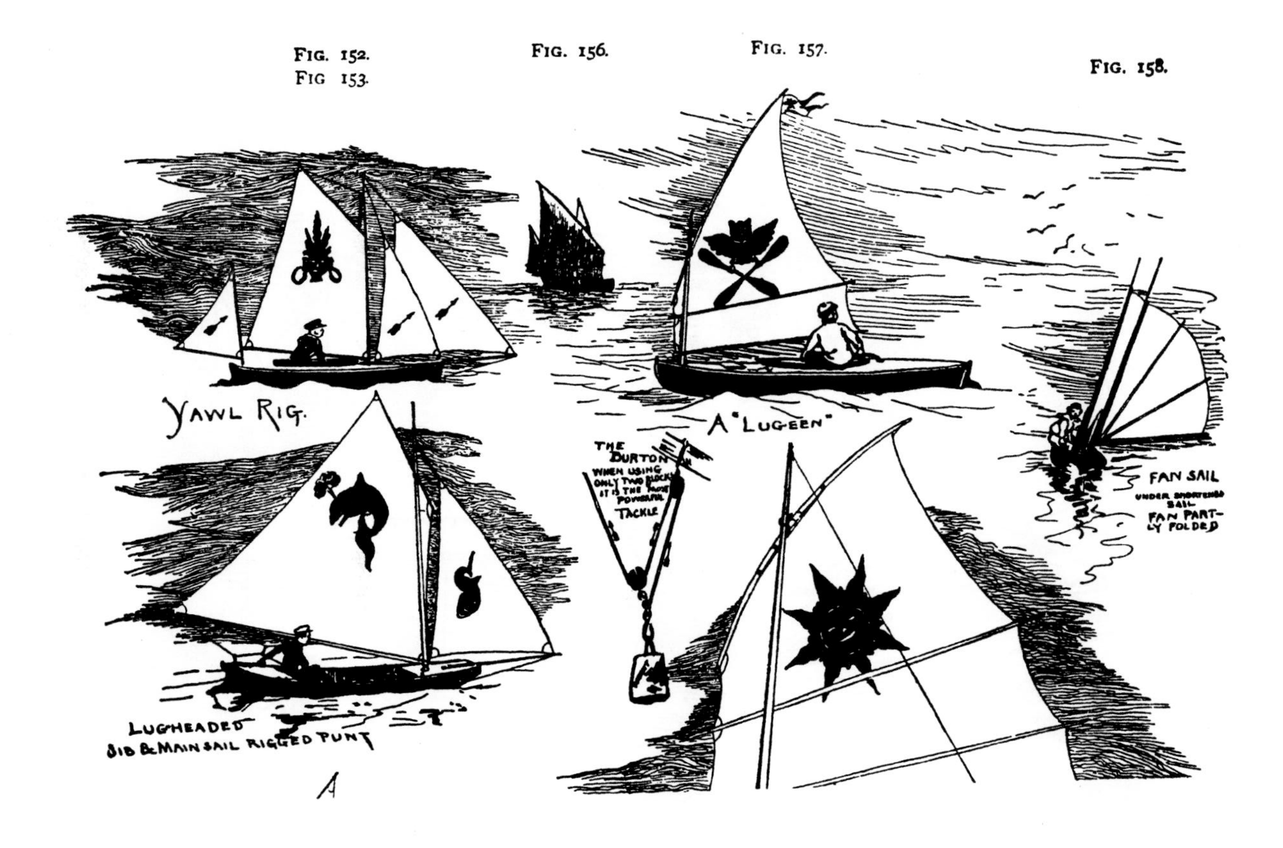
FIG. 152.
FIG 153.
FIG. 156.
FIG. 157.
FIG. 158.
YAWL RIG.
A "LUGEEN"
THE BURTON
WHEN USING ONLY TWO BLOCKS IT IS THE MOST POWERFUL TACKLE
FAN SAIL
UNDER SHORTENED SAIL
FAN PARTLY FOLDED
LUGHEADED
JIB & MAIN SAIL RIGGED PUNT
A

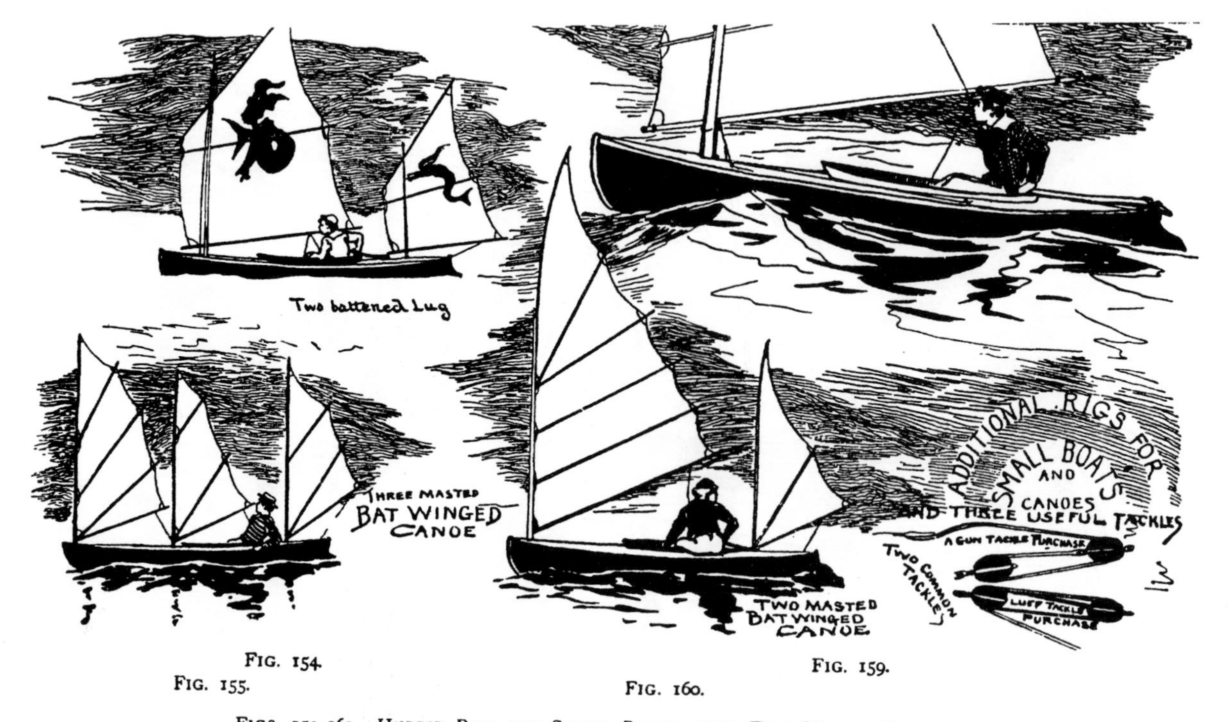

FIG. 154
FIG. 155.
FIG. 160.
FIG. 159.

FIGS. 152-160.—HYBRID RIGS FOR SMALL BOATS, ALSO TWO USEFUL TACKLES

CHAPTER XV

A "ROUGH AND READY" BOAT

Just What an Ingenious Boy Must Do to Build It—Detailed Instructions as to How to Make the Boat and How to Rig It.

GOOD straight-grained pine wood is, without doubt, the best "all-around" wood for a boy's use. It is easily whittled with a pocket-knife; it works smoothly under a plane; can be sawed without fatiguing the young carpenter; it is elastic, pliable, and cheap; therefore use pine lumber to build your boat.

Examine the lumber pile carefully and select four boards nearly alike. Do not allow the dealer or his men to talk you into taking lumber with blemishes. The side-pieces should be of straight-grained wood, with no large knots and no "checks" (cracks) in them, and must not be "wind shaken."

Measure the wood and see that it is over twenty-two feet long by one foot four or five inches wide and one inch thick. Trim two of the side-pieces until they are exact duplicates (Fig. 160a). The stem-piece (or bow-piece) should be made from a triangular piece of oak (Fig. 166), and it is wise to make it a few inches longer than will be necessary, so that there may be no danger of finding, after all your labor, that the stick is too short; much better too long, for it is a simple matter to saw it off. Make a second stem-piece (Fig. 167) of oak about one inch thick and the same length as the first, and two or three inches wide, or twice as wide as the thickness of the side boards.

The Stern-Piece.

The stern-piece can be fashioned out of two-inch pine boards, and may be made as wide or narrow as you choose.

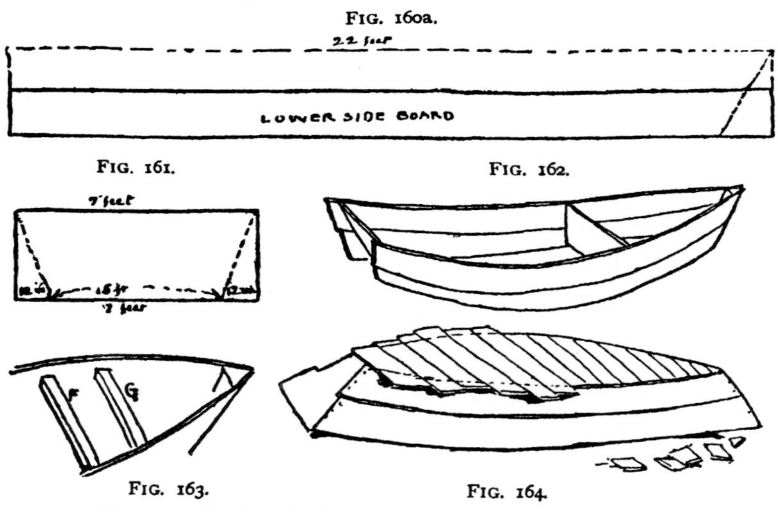

Diagrams Showing the Construction of the Rough and Ready.

A narrow stern makes a trim-looking craft. With your saw cut off the corner of the tail-piece, so that it will be in the form of a blunted triangle (Fig. 168), measuring three feet ten and one-half inches across the base, three feet four inches on each side, and nine and one-half inches at the apex. The base of the triangle will be the top and the apex will be the bottom of the stern-board of your boat.

Now make a brace on which to model your boat. Let it be of two-inch pine wood, two and one-half feet wide and seven and one-half feet long (Fig. 161). Measure twelve inches on one edge of this board from each end toward the centre and mark the points; then rule lines from these points diagonally across the width of the board (A, B and C, D—Fig. 161), and saw off the corners, as shown by the dotted line in Fig. 161.

Lay the boards selected for the lower side boards on a level floor and measure off one and one-half foot on the bottom edge, then in a line with the end of the board mark a point on the floor that would be the top edge of the board if

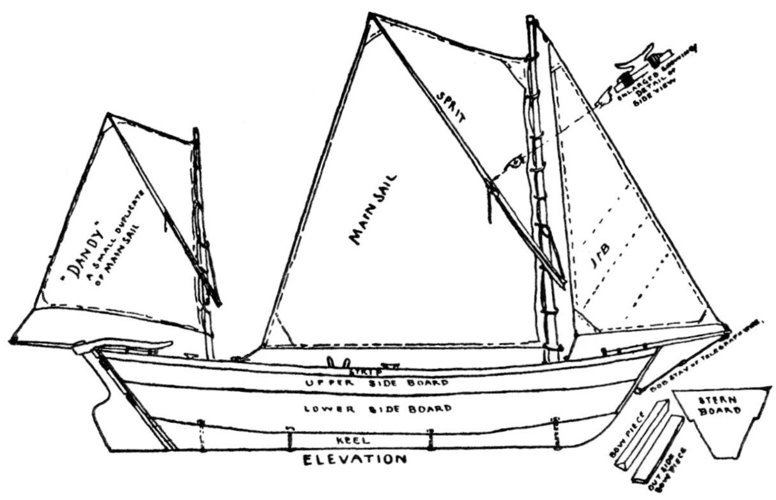

FIG. 165. FIGS. 166, 167, and 168.

The Rough and Ready.

the board were two and one-half feet wide; rule a line from the point on the floor to the point marked on the board and saw off the corner as marked; make the other side-piece correspond exactly with the first (Fig. 160a).

Use Rope for Binding.

Set the side-pieces upon their bottom or shorter edges and place the brace between the sides. Now bind the stern ends with a rope and bring the bow-pieces together until they touch; rope them in this position, and when all is fast push the brace up until it rests at a point nine feet from the bow; fasten it here with a couple of nails driven in, but leaving their heads far enough from the wood to render it easy to draw them out. Now adjust the bow-piece, and use the greatest of care in making the sides exactly alike, otherwise you will wonder how your boat happened to have such an unaccountable twist in it. When the stem is properly adjusted fasten on the side boards with screws. Do not try to hammer the screws in place, but bore holes first and use a screw-driver.

Take your stern-piece and measure the exact width of the stern end of the bottom boards and mark it at the bottom of the stern-piece; or, better still, since the stern-board will set at an angle, put it temporarily in place, bind it fast with the ropes, and mark with a pencil just where the side boards cross the ends of the stern-board. Remove the stern-board and saw out a piece one inch wide, the thickness of the bottom board, from the place marked to the bottom of the stern-board. Because the top side board overlaps the bottom one at the stern, there must be either a large crack left there or the stern-board notched to fit the side boards (Fig. 168). Replace the stern-board and nail side boards fast to it; now loosen the ropes which have held your boat in shape, and fit on the upper side boards so that at the stern they will overlap the lower side boards an inch. Hold in place with your rope, then bring the bow end up against the stern-piece over the top of the lower side board and fasten it in place with a rope. With your carpenter's pencil mark the overlap, and with a plane made for that purpose, called a rabbet, trim down your board so that it will have a shoulder and an overlap to rest on the bottom board, running out to nothing at the bow. When the boards fit all right over the lower ones bind them in place and then nail them there (Fig. 162). If you can obtain two good boards of the requisite size, you need have but one board for each side of your boat; this will obviate the necessity of using the rabbet, and be very much easier; but with single boards of the required dimensions there is great danger of splitting or cracking while bending the boards.

Planing the Bottom.

Turn the boat upside down and you will see that there is a decided arch extending from stem to stern. This would cause the boat to sink too deep amidships, and must be remedied to some extent by cutting away the middle of the arch, so that the sides in the exact centre will measure at least four inches less in width than at the bow and stern, and reducing the convex or curved form to a straight line in the middle, which will give a sheer to the bow and stern. A good plane is the best tool to use for this purpose, as with it there is no danger of cutting too deep or of splitting the side boards. Saw off the projecting ends of the side boards at the stern.

Make the bottom of three-quarter-inch boards. Lay the boards crosswise, nail them in place, leaving the irregular ends projecting on each side. The reason for this is obvious. When you look at the bottom of the boat you will at once see that on account of the form no two boards can be the same shape, and the easiest way is to treat the boat bottom as if it were a square-sided scow. Fit the planks closely together, nail them on securely, and then neatly saw off the projecting ends (Fig. 164).

The Deck.

The brace may now be removed by carefully drawing the nails, so that a bottom plank trimmed to fit the bow and the stern can be securely nailed in place (Fig. 169). Cut a notch in your brace to fit tightly over the bottom plank just laid. Plane off the top of the brace so that when in the boat the top of the brace will be four inches below the top of the side boards. Replace the brace and securely nail it. Next cut two small cross-pieces (F, G, Fig. 163) and place them near the bow, four inches below the top of the sides of the boat. Drive the nails from the outside through the side boards into the end of F and G, the cross-brace. Cut out a bow-piece to fit from the middle of G to the bow and nail it in place, driving the nails from the outside into the edge of the bow-piece. Fasten a small cleat along the boat from the solid board brace to F on each side and deck the space over with light lumber.

Of the same material make a trap-door to fit in between the braces F and G. This door should be big enough for a boy to creep through, for this compartment is intended as a safe place to store cooking utensils, foods, etc., as well as a water-tight compartment. At a point five feet from the stern put another cross-brace, similar to the ones in the bow, four inches below the top of the sides. At the same level nail a cleat on the stern-piece and make a stern seat by boarding over between the cross-piece and the cleat. When your boat is resting securely on the floor or level ground rig a temporary seat, then take an oar and by experiment find just where the rowlock will be most convenient and mark the spot. Also mark the spot best suited for the seat. On each side of the spot marked for the rowlock cut two notches in the side-boards two inches deep, one and a half inches wide, and three inches apart. Saw two more notches exactly like these upon the opposite side of your boat. These will make the rowlocks when the side strips are nailed on (Fig. 169).

The side strips should each be made of one-inch plank three inches wide and a few inches longer than the side boards. Nail the strips on the outside of the boat flush with the top of the side boards. Make your thole pins of some hard wood, and make two sets of them while you are

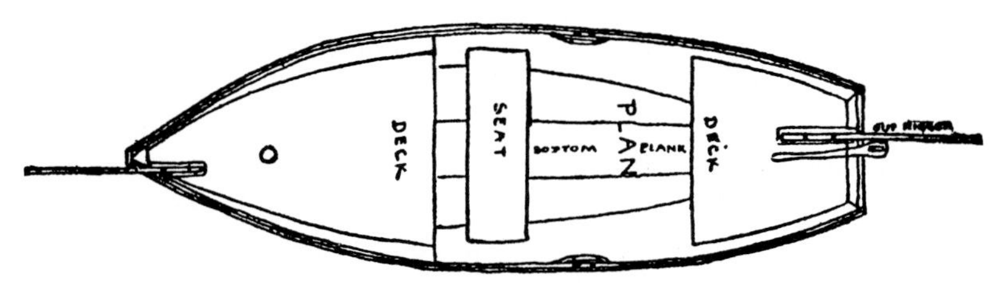

FIG. 169.—Top View of Rough and Ready with Tiller Stick.

about it, "one set to use and one set to lose." Screw a hardwood cleat on the inside of your boat over each pair of rowlocks, as shown in Fig. 169.

Ready for the Water.

Fasten the remaining bow-piece securely over the ends of your side boards, and the nose of your craft is finished.

Put a good, heavy keel on your boat by screwing it tightly in the stern to the hardwood rudder-post that is fastened to the centre of the stern ; bolt your keel with four iron bolts to the bottom of the boat, and the ship is ready to launch, after which she can be equipped with sails and oars.

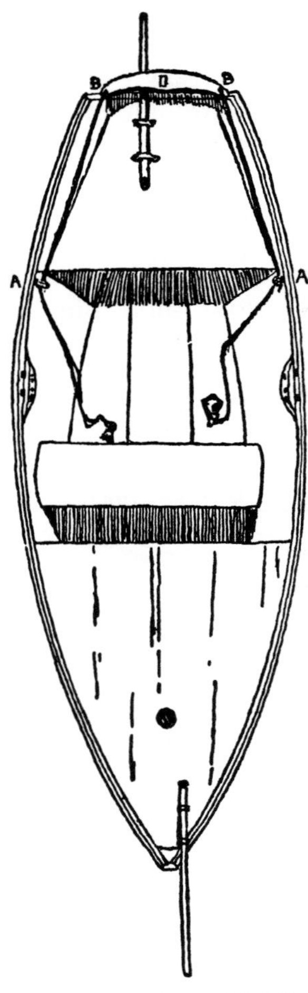

FIG. 170.—Rudder, with Tiller Lines.

Of course, you understand that all nail-holes and crevices should be puttied up, and if paint is used, it must be applied before wetting the boat. But if you have done your work well, there will be little need of paint or putty to make it tight after the wood has swelled in the water. Fasten your rudder on with hooks and screw-eyes, and make it as shown in the diagram (Fig. 165). Step your mainmast in the bow through a round hole in the deck and a square hole in the step, which must, of course, be screwed tightly to the bottom before the bow is decked over.

Step your jigger or dandy-mast in the stern after the same manner. These masts should neither of them be very large, and are intended to be removed at pleasure by unstepping them, that is, simply pulling them out of their sockets. An outrigger will be found necessary for your dandy-sail, and since the deck aft is below the sides of the boat, a block of wood will have to be nailed to the deck to the starboard or right-hand side of the rudder-post. If the builder chooses, he can make the decks flush with the sides of the boat, and thus avoid blocks. A couple of staples for the out-rigger to slip through are next in order. They must be fastened firmly in the block or stick of wood just nailed to the deck. A similar arrangement can be made for the bowsprit, but as it is a movable bowsprit, and the stem of the boat is in the way, put it to the port or left-hand side of the stem of the craft (Fig. 169).

How to Make the Sail.

Secure for a sail material as strong as you can find, but it need not be heavy. Unbleached muslin is cheap and will make good sails. Turn over the edges and sew or hem them, as in the diagram. Make eyelets like buttonholes in the luff of the sail—that is, the edge of the sail nearest the mast. Sew a small loop of rope in each corner of the sail. Through the eyelets lace the luff of the sail to the mast.

From spruce or pine make a sprit two inches in diameter. For a "sheet"—that is, the rope or line that you manage the sail with—tie a good, stout line about a dozen feet long to the loop in the loose corner of the sail. Trim the upper end of the sprit to fit the loop in the top of the sail and make a simple notch in the other end to hold the line called the "snotter."

Now, as you can readily see by referring to Fig. 165, when the sprit is pushed into the loop at the top of the sail the sail is spread. To hold it in place make a cleat like the one in the diagram, and bind it firmly with a cord to the sprit; pass the snotter or line fastened to the mast through the notch in the sprit up to the cleat and make fast, and the sail is set. The jigger or dandy is exactly like the mainsail except in size, and the sheet rope is run through a block or pulley at the end of the out-rigger and then made fast to a cleat near the man at the rudder or helm. The jib is a simple affair hooked on a screw-eye in the end of the bowsprit. The jib halyard, or line for hoisting the jib, runs from the top of the jib through a screw-eye in the top of the mast, down the port side of the mast to a cleat, where it is made fast. When the jib is set the jib-sheets are fastened to a loop sewed in the jib at the lower or loose end. There are two jib-sheets, one for each side of the boat, so that one may be made fast and the other loosened, according to the wind. The remaining details you must study out from the diagrams or learn by experiment.

How to Reef Her.

When the wind is high reef your sails by letting go the snotter and pulling out the sprit. This will drop your peak and leave you with a simple leg-of-mutton sail. Only use the jib in light weather.

In this boat, with a little knowledge of sailing, you may cruise for weeks, lowering your sails at night and making a tent over the cock-pit for a sleeping-room.

When the author described the Rough and Ready for the New York *Press*, Mr. Curtis Brown, the genial editor of the Sunday edition of that paper, was delighted with it. He had had letters from boy readers asking the rules for building just such a boat. After the article was published Mr. Brown received more letters asking for descriptions and rules for building a rowboat. The writer had already told how to build a rowboat, under the head of a "Yankee Pine" in the "American Boy's Handy Book." If the young boat-builders do not have a "Handy Book" they can reduce the dimensions of the Rough and Ready, leave off the decks, and they will have a serviceable rowboat.

CHAPTER XVI

A RAFT THAT WILL SAIL

And a Home-Made Catamaran—The Raft is Just the Thing for Camp Life—Pleasurable Occupation for a Camping Party Where Wood is Plentiful—You Will Need Axes and Hatchets and a Few Other Civilized Implements.

FIRST we will select two pine logs of equal length, and, while the water is heating for our coffee we will sharpen the butt or larger end of the logs on one side with the axe, making a "chisel edge," as shown in Fig. 171. This gives us an appetite for breakfast and makes the big fish in the lake, as they jump above the water, cast anxious looks toward our camp.

Breakfast finished, we will cut some cross-pieces to join our two logs together, and at equal distances apart we will bore holes through the cross-pieces for peg-holes (Figs. 172, 173, and 174). While one of the party is fashioning a number of pegs, each with a groove in one side, like those shown in Fig. 175, the others will roll the logs into the water and secure them in a shallow spot.

Shoes and stockings must be removed, for most of the work is now to be done in the water. Of course, it would be much easier done on land, but the raft will be very heavy and could never be launched unless under the most favorable circumstances. It is better to build the craft in the element which is to be its home.

Cut two long saplings for braces, and after separating

the logs the proper distance for your cross-pieces to fit, nail your braces in position, as represented by Fig. 171.

This holds the logs steady, and we may now lay the two cross-pieces in position and mark the points on the logs carefully where the holes are to be bored to correspond with the ones in the cross-pieces. Bore the holes in one log first; make the holes deep enough and then fill them with water, after which drive the pegs through the ends of the cross-pieces and into the log. The grooves in the pegs (Fig. 175) will allow the water to escape from the holes and the water will cause the peg to swell and tighten its hold on the log and cross-pieces.

Now bore holes in the other log under those in the cross-pieces and fill them with water before driving the pegs home, as you did in the first instance. Fig. 176 is a Man-Friday raft.

The Deck.

Before placing the bow in position we must go ashore and make a dry deck. Selecting for the springs two long elastic ash or hickory poles, trim the ends off flat on one side, as shown by Fig. 177. This flat side is the bottom, so roll them over, with the flat side toward the ground, and if you can find no planks or barrel staves for a deck, split in half a number of small logs and peg or nail them on the top side of the springs, as in Fig. 178.

Now all hands must turn out and carry the deck down to the raft and place it in position, with the flattened sides of the springs resting on top of the logs at the bow. Prop it up in this position, and then bore holes through the springs into the logs and peg the springs down. Over the flat ends place the heavy bow cross-piece, bore the peg holes, and fasten it in position (Fig. 179).

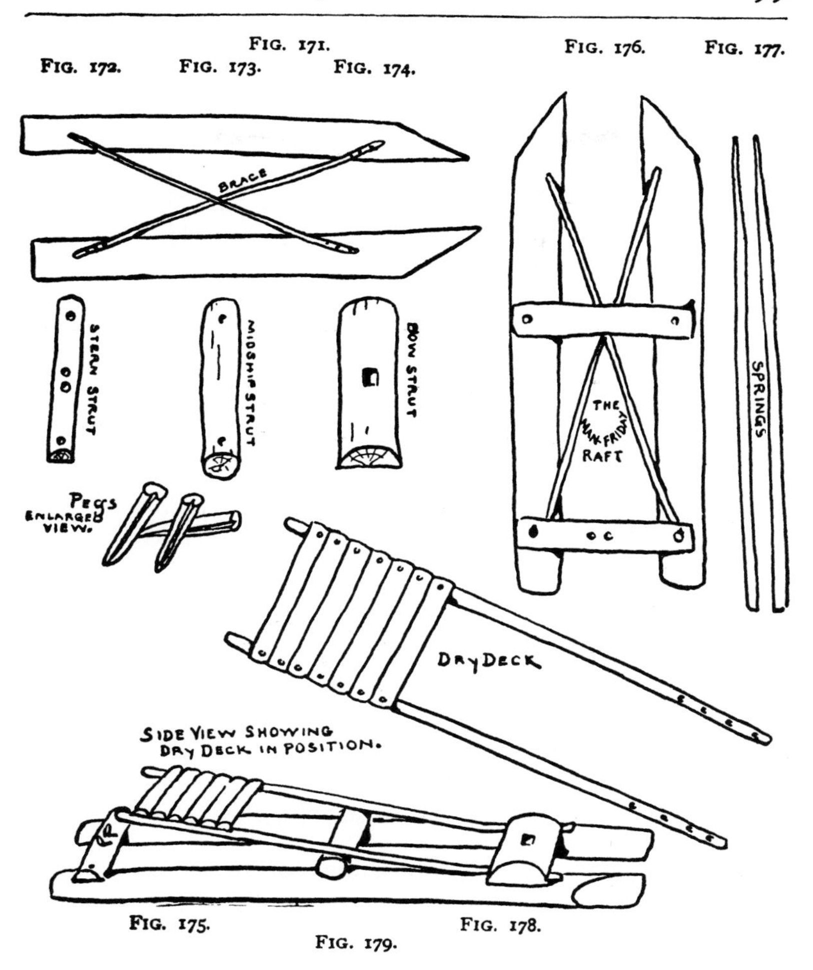

PARTS OF MAN-FRIDAY SAILING RAFT.

FIG. 171.—Logs in Place with Braces. FIGS. 172, 173, and 174.—Struts. FIG. 175.—Pegs. FIG. 176.—Raft with Middle and Stern Strut in Place. FIG. 177.—Springs for Dry Deck. FIG. 178.—Dry Deck. FIG. 179.—Dry Deck in Place.

In the centre of the bow cross-piece bore several holes close together and chip out the wood between to make a

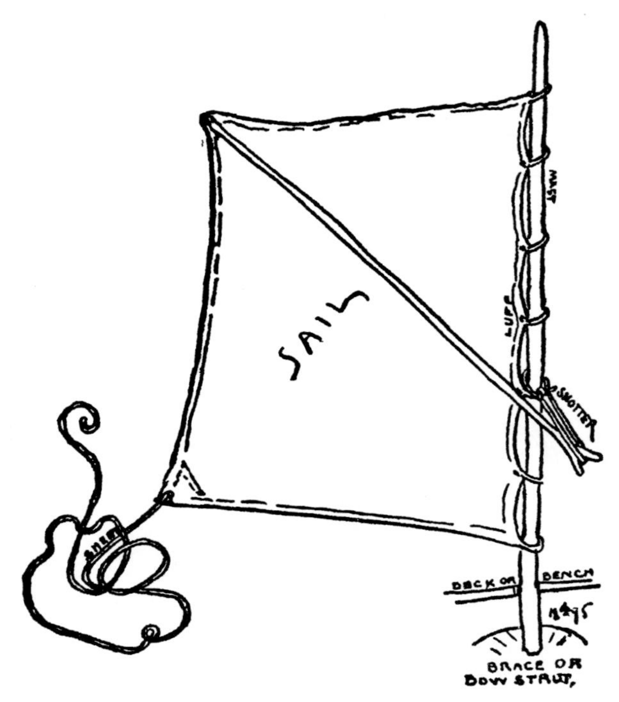

FIG. 18a.—Sail for Man-Friday.

hole, as square a one as possible, for the mast to fit or "step" in. With the wood from a packing box or a slab from a log make the bench for the mast.

Bore a hole through the bench a trifle astern of the step or hole for the mast below. It will cause the mast to "rake" a little "aft." You have done a big day's work, but a couple of days ought to be sufficient time to finish the craft.

The Sail.

Turn over the raw edges of the old sailcloth and stitch them down, as in Fig. 180—that is, if you have the needle and thread for the purpose; if not, trim the cloth to the proper form and two inches from the luff (the side next to the mast). Cut a number of holes; these should be stitched like buttonholes, if possible, but if the sailcloth is tough and we

FIG. 181.—Scudding Before the Wind.

have no needle, we shall have to let them go unstitched. A small loop of rope must be sewed or fastened in some other manner very securely to each corner of the sail.

From spruce pine or an old fishing pole make a sprit, and of a good, straight piece of pine manufacture your mast somewhat longer than the luff of the sail (Fig. 180).

Through the eyelets lace the luff of the sail to the mast, so that its lower edge will clear the dry deck by about a foot.

Through the hole made for the purpose in the bench (Fig. 181) thrust the mast into the step or socket that we have cut in the bow cross-piece. Tie to the loop at the bottom corner of the sail a strong line about twelve feet long for a sheet with which to control the sail.

Trim the upper end of the sprit to fit in the loop at the upper outer corner of the sail, and make a notch in the lower end to fit in the loop of the line called the "snotter."

Now, as you can readily see, when the sprit is pushed diagonally upward the sail is spread; to hold it in place make a loop of line for a "snotter" and attach the loop to the mast, as in Figs. 180 and 181. Fit the loop in the notch in the lower end of the sprit, and the sail is set.

The Keelig.

We need anchors, one for the bow and one for the stern. It takes little time to make them, as you only need a forked stick, a stone, and a piece of plank, or, better still, a barrel stave. Figs. 186, 187, 189, and 190 show how this is made. Down East the fishermen use the "keelig," in preference to any other anchor.

Make fast your lines to the "keelig" thus: Take the end of the rope in your right hand and the standing part (which is the part leading from the boat) in your left hand and form the loop (A, Fig. 182).

Then with the left hand curve the cable from you,

bringing the end through the loop, as in B, Fig. 183; then lead it around and down, as in C, Fig. 184.

Draw it tight, as in D, Fig. 185, and you have the good, old-fashioned knot, called by sailors the "bow-line."

To make it look neat and shipshape you may take a

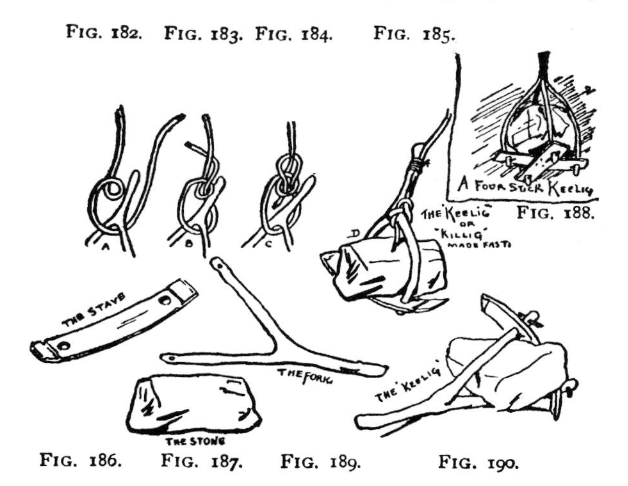

FIG. 182. FIG. 183. FIG. 184. FIG. 185. FIG. 188.

FIG. 186. FIG. 187. FIG. 189. FIG. 190.

piece of string and bind the standing part to the shaft of your anchor or keelig—keelek—killick—killeck—kelleck—kellock—killock, etc., as you may choose to spell it.

A paddle to steer with and two pegs in the stern cross-piece to rest it in complete the craft; and now the big bass had better use due caution, because our lines will reach their haunts, and we are after them!

A Home-Made Catamaran.

Possibly after you have built and sailed on the rude catamaran described above you have grown ambitious and wish to try a real catamaran. In this case it is, of course, necessary that you should be in some locality where you can have access to ordinary building materials and tools.

In place of the two unwieldy logs substitute two narrow boats. If such boats can be found already built, so much the better. Two old-fashioned dugout canoes make most excellent hulls for a catamaran, but unfortunately dugout canoes are now few and far between. In these modern days we must look for something more up-to-date, and probably the shortest way out of the difficulty is to build two long, narrow boats. This is not a difficult piece of work. Any boy who has successfully built either of the preceding craft, or is sufficiently skilful to build even a rude skiff, will be able to put together two long water-tight boxes, and it does not require much additional skill to make boxes pointed at each end.

Make each side of the boat of one straight-grained white pine board, twelve or fourteen feet long, and put the boat together after the fashion shown in Figs. 160a, 161, 162, 163, and 164 (Rough and Ready), with this difference: You must make the bow and stern just alike, and leave the four stretchers or moulds in their places, to add strength to the hulls. This, of course, divides the hulls into five compartments, each of which is liable to hold water. To prevent this saw a triangular notch in the bottom of each mould to allow the water that may leak in free passage from bow to stern; then it may be all bailed out from one trap or hatch. Particular attention must be paid to making the two side boats exact duplicates of each other. If white lead is applied to all seams and joints before they are fastened together, it will make them very nearly water-tight, but a new boat will leak until the water has caused the wood to swell.

A Trap-Door or Hatch,

large enough to admit one's hand and bailer, should occupy an accessible position near the stern of each boat. The trap should be built to fasten as tightly as possible to prevent any water that may splash over the boats from leaking in through the openings in the deck. Make each deck of a single board, trimmed to conform with the lines of the boat, and make holes in the deck for the bands to pass through. With bolts and bands, that have been made for you at the nearest blacksmith shop, you fasten the cross-piece supporting the deck to the moulds in the boat. Fig. 193, A, shows one of the bolts. It is understood that these bolts are securely fastened to the moulds before the hulls are decked. The holes are then bored in the deck, and the screw ends of the bolts come up through the deck and through the holes made for

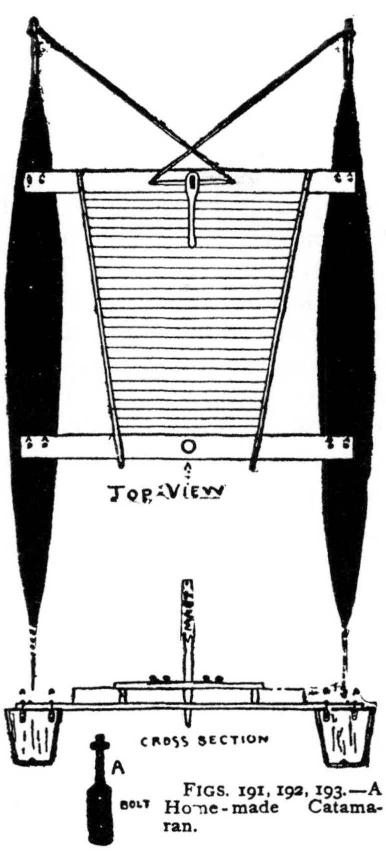

FIGS. 191, 192, 193.—A Home-made Catamaran.

that purpose in the cross-pieces supporting the deck. A piece of india-rubber from an old hose can be used for washers to fit under the bolts. The nuts are then screwed home.

The deck is now floored, as shown in Fig. 191, and

The Rudder and Mast

benches are put in place, the latter at the forward and the former at the after end of the deck. Underneath the deck a keel-piece is securely bolted on. If you wish a sloop rig, a bowsprit is fastened to the keel-piece, but in regard to sails, you may make your own choice of the many styles. A good lateen will look best and is easily made, as described in the chapter on rigs. If one sail does not work to suit you, a dandy or a jigger may be added.

This style of craft may be built as large or small as you choose to build it. In a very small catamaran that would only hold one boy he could probably steer it with a paddle or an oar, but in the larger ones a somewhat more complicated steering apparatus is necessary.

Steering Apparatus.

Evidently it would be a most difficult undertaking to steer the catamaran with independent rudders, and we must devise a method by which one tiller will control both. Fig. 201 shows how it may be done with a system of pulleys or blocks and tiller-lines, or you may make a short oaken stick of the form shown in Fig. 194, A. Bore a hole through the centre, as is shown in Fig. 195, B. Trim off the top to fit the tiller-handle (Fig. 196, C). Saw into all the four corners of the square stick to form a shoulder to rest on the bench. Fig. 197 shows the shoulder at S. Plane off the square corners of the wood below the saw cut. After this it is quite a simple matter to round it off below the shoulder (Fig. 197, E).

After slipping the rudder-post through the two holes

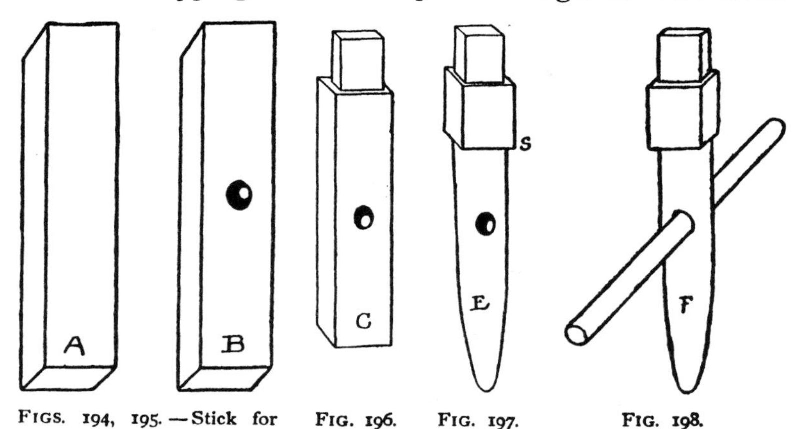

FIGS. 194, 195.—Stick for Rudder-post of Catamaran.

FIG. 196. FIG. 197. FIG. 198. Rudder-post of Catamaran.

bored for the purpose in the rudder bench, drive through the post a good, strong oaken or hickory peg (Fig. 198, F),

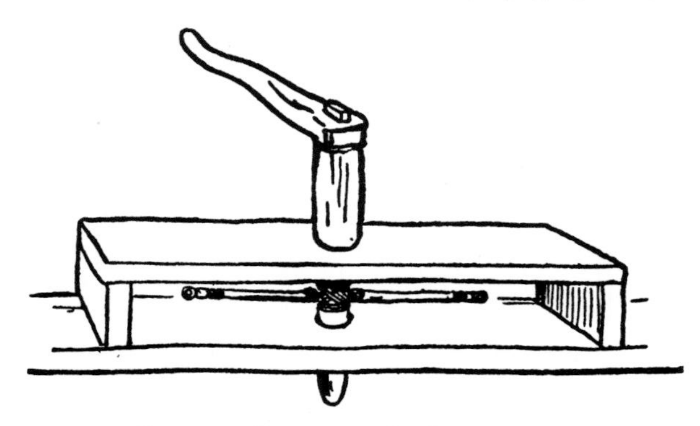

FIG. 199.—Rudder Bench of Catamaran.

and bind the cross-pieces tightly with tarred twine. The end of the cross-sticks should be firmly lashed with tarred

FIG. 200.—Half Hull of Catamaran.

or painted twine. A large screw-eye may be now put in each end of the cross-stick or near the ends, allowing the screw-ends of the eye to protrude far enough to screw on a nut.

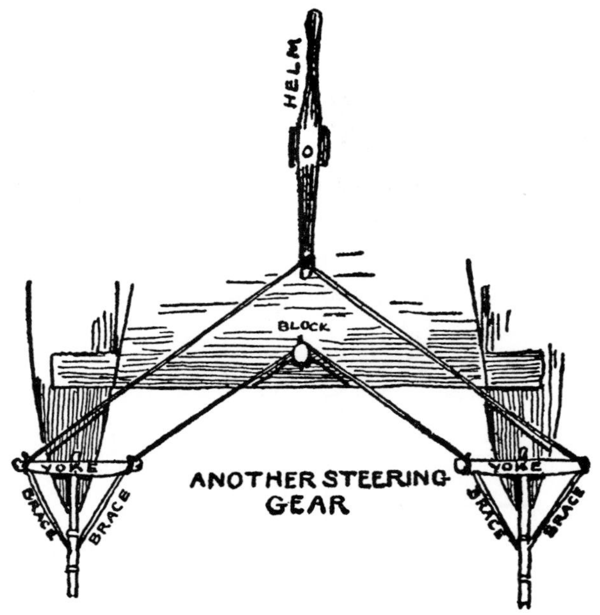

FIG. 201.—Tackle for Steering a Catamaran.

Now we must have two long, strong hoop poles to connect with the rudders by means of bolts and rings, as

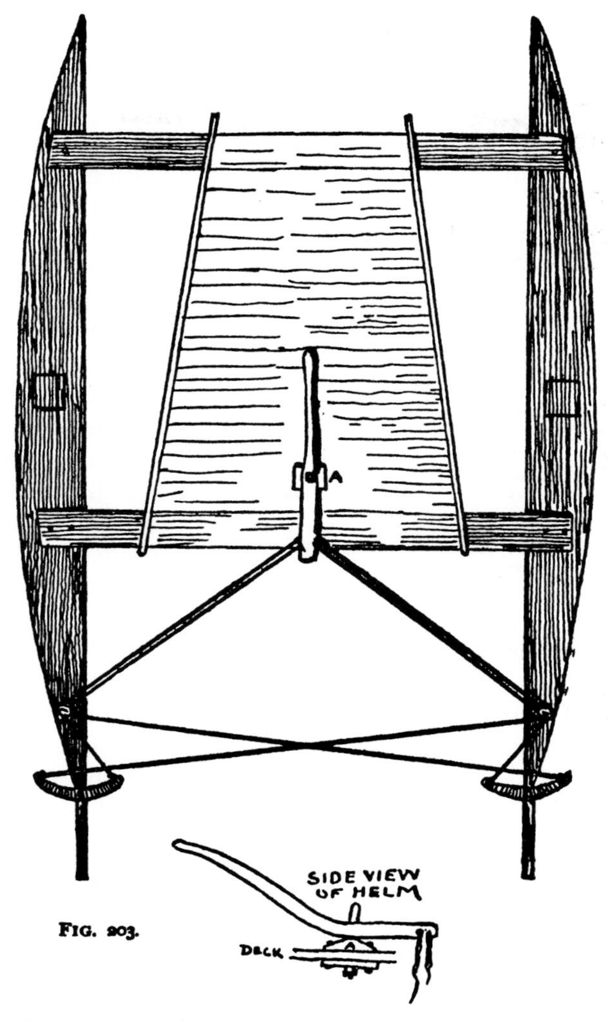

FIG. 202.—The Half Hull with Double Block Steering Gear.
FIG. 203.—The Side View of Helm.

shown in Fig. 191. All that is now necessary is to fit your tiller-handle over the top of the rudder-post, and the steering apparatus is finished. Fig. 201 shows another plan for steering with a helm like Figs. 202 and 203.

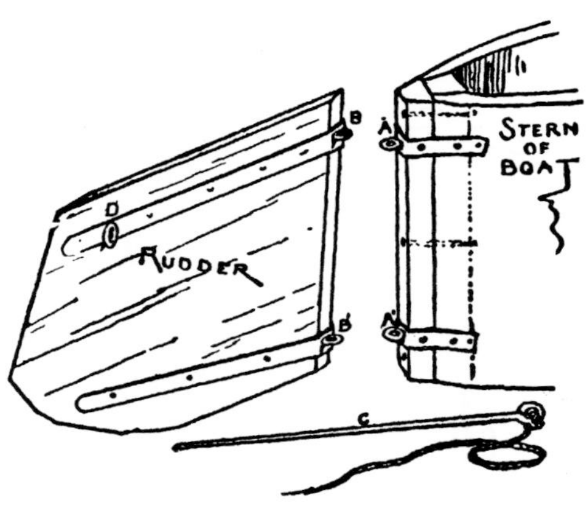

FIG. 204.—Detail of Rudder, Showing Braces and Rings, AA′ BB′, for the Rudder-pin, C, to fit in. D is the Ring for Attaching Steering Gear.

The mast is stepped in a bench at the bow similar to the rudder bench. Each consists of board benches bolted to heavy plank supports and bolted to the deck. The material used should be as light as possible, consistent with strength. The dry deck can be made of neatly planed boards, and the whole craft may be as neat and well done as the skill of the maker will admit. Hulls with a swell on each side jam the water between them and retard the boat; so if you build the catamaran with half hulls you will do away with this objection. Fig. 200 shows diagram of hull; Fig. 202, plan of craft; Fig. 203, the helm.

A Tom Thumb Catamaran

could be built just large enough to hold one boy. The dry deck may be made with bamboo poles, in the form of a seat for the sailor, and if a foot-rest is added below, he may sit perched in his dry seat like a horse-jockey in a sulky, where he can manage his little craft in weather that no other small boats could stand. Some people say that under a heavy sail and a hard blow this style of boat will rear up at the stern and go end over end. If this is true, it is because the craft is too short and dumpy, or has too large a spread of canvas. Even full-rigged ships have been known to run their bows under.

FIG. 205.—A Home-made Catamaran.

There was a good-sized catamaran wrecked in Flushing Bay the same day that the writer upset in his canoe, but from the looks of the wreck, with its sails torn to ribbons, it seemed probable that the sails had been carried away, and the craft had then drifted ashore. The wreck showed no signs of having turned somersaults.

Two old single shells would make a beautiful Tom

Thumb catamaran, and they would be far more likely to sail up in the air than to stand on end, but all these gymnastics on the part of the boat can be avoided by not venturing out during a gale or by shortening sail when the wind is strong. Never be misled into thinking it seamanlike to carry full sail when other boats are reefed. Too much sail retards the boat as much as too little. In all yacht races the skippers never hesitate to take in sail when it is necessary any more than they do to shake out a reef when more sail is thought to be beneficial.

Danger of False Pride.

Learn to manage a small sail first and then a larger one. Do not be ashamed of blunders. Why should you? Is a baby ashamed to creep before it learns to walk? On the contrary, the baby is very proud of its newly acquired powers of locomotion. Nobody is a born sailor. The best seaman was once a land-lubber.

CHAPTER XVII

SINGLE SHELLS AND UMBRELLA CANOES

How Old Shells Can Be Turned into Boys' Boats—The Cause of Upsets—Landing from and Embarking in a Shell—What an Umbrella Canoe Is and How It Is Made.

WHERE there are oarsmen and boat clubs there you will find beautiful shell boats of paper or cedar, shaped like darning needles, so slight in structure that a child can knock a hole in them, and yet very seaworthy boats for those who understand how to handle them. The expensive material and skilled labor necessary to build a racing shell puts the price of one so high that few boys can afford to buy one; but where new shells are to be found there are also old ones, and when they are too old to sell they are thrown away. Many an old shell rots on the meadows near the boat-houses or rests among the rafters forgotten and unused, which with a little work would make a boat capable of furnishing no end of fun to a boy.

Checks or Cracks

can be pasted over with common manilla wrapping paper by first covering the crack with a coat of paint, or, better still, of varnish, then fitting the paper smoothly over the spot and varnishing the paper. Give the paper several coats of varnish, allowing it to dry after each application, and the paper will become impervious to water.

The deck of a shell is made of thin muslin or paper, treated with a liberal coat of varnish, and can be patched with similar material. There are always plenty of slightly damaged oars which have been discarded by the oarsmen. The use of a saw and jack-knife in the hands of a smart boy can transform these wrecks into serviceable oars for his patched-up old shell, and if the work is neatly done, the boy will be the proud owner of a real shell boat, and the envy of his comrades.

The Cause of Upsets.

A single shell that is very cranky with a man in it is comparatively steady when a small boy occupies the seat. Put on your bathing clothes when you wish to try a shell, so that you may be ready for the inevitable upset. Every one knows, when he looks at one of these long, narrow boats, that as long as the oars are held extended *on the water* it cannot upset. But, in spite of that knowledge, every one, when he first gets into a shell, endeavors to balance himself by *lifting the oars*, and, of course, goes over in a jiffy.

The Delights of a Shell.

It is an error to suppose that the frail-looking, needle-like boat is only fit for racing purposes. For a day on the water, in calm weather, there is perhaps nothing more enjoyable than a single shell. The exertion required to send it on its way is so slight, and the speed so great, that many miles can be covered with small fatigue. Upon referring to the log-book of the Nereus Club, where the distances are all taken from the United States chart, the author finds that twenty and thirty miles are not uncommon records for single-shell rows.

During the fifteen or sixteen seasons that the author has devoted his spare time to the sport he has often planned a heavy cruising shell, but owing to the expense of having such a boat built he has used the ordinary racing boat, and found it remarkably well adapted for such purposes. Often he has been caught miles away from home in a blow, and only once does he remember of being compelled to seek assistance.

He was on a lee shore and the waves were so high that after once being swamped he was unable to launch his boat again, for it would fill before he could embark. So a heavy rowboat and a coachman were borrowed from a gentleman living on the bay, and while the author rowed, the coachman towed the little craft back to the creek where the Nereus Club-house is situated.

In the creek, however, the water was calmer, and rather than stand the jeers of his comrades, the writer embarked in his shell and rowed up to the boat-house float. He was very wet and his boat was full of water, but to the inquiry of "Rough out in the bay?" he confined himself to the simple answer—"Yes." Then dumping the water from his shell and placing it upon the rack, he put on his dry clothes and walked home, none the worse for the accident.

After ordinary skill and confidence are acquired it is really astonishing what feats can be accomplished in a frail racing boat.

It is not difficult to

Stand Upright in a Shell,

if you first take one of your long stockings and tie the handles of your oars together where they cross each other in front of you. The ends will work slightly and the blades will keep their positions on the water, acting as two long balances. Now slide your seat as far forward as it will go, slip your feet from the straps and grasp the straps with your hand, moving the feet back to a comfortable position. When all ready raise yourself by pulling on the foot-strap, and with ordinary care you can stand upright in the needle-shaped boat, an apparently impossible thing to do when you look at the narrow craft.

How to Land Where there is no Float.

When for any reason you wish to land where there is no float, row into shallow water and put one foot overboard until it touches bottom. Then follow with the other foot, rise and you are standing astride of your boat.

How to Embark Where there is no Float.

Wade out and slide the shell between your extended legs until the seat is underneath you. Sit down, and, with the feet still in the water, grasp your oars. With these in your hands it is an easy task to balance the boat until you can lift your feet into it.

Ozias Dodge's Umbrella Canoe.

Mr. Dodge is a Yale man, an artist, and an enthusiastic canoeist. The prow of his little craft has ploughed its way through the waters of many picturesque streams in this country and Europe, by the river-side, under the walls of ruined castles, where the iron-clad warriors once built their camp-fires, and near pretty villages, where people dress as if they were at a fancy-dress ball.

When a young man like Mr. Dodge says that he has built a folding canoe that is not hard to construct, is inexpensive and practical, there can be little doubt that such a boat is not only what is claimed for it by its inventor, but that it is a novelty in its line, and such is undoubtedly the case with the umbrella canoe.

How the Canoe was Built.

The artist first secured a white-ash plank (A, Fig. 206), free from knots and blemishes of all kinds. The plank was one inch thick and about twelve feet long. At the mill he had this sawed into eight strips, one inch wide, one inch thick, and twelve feet long (B and C, Figs. 207 and 208). Then he planed off the square edges of each stick until they were all octagonal in form, and looked like so many great lead-pencils (D, Fig. 209).

Mr. Dodge claims that, after you have reduced the ash poles to this octagonal form, it is an easy matter to whittle them with your pocket-knife or a draw-knife, and by taking off all the angles of the sticks make them cylindrical in form (E, Fig. 210); then smooth them off nicely with sand-paper, so that each pole has a smooth surface and is three-quarters of an inch in diameter.

After the poles were reduced to this state he whittled all the ends to the form of a truncated cone—that is, like a sharpened lead-pencil with the lead broken off (F, Fig. 211) —a blunt point. He next went to a tinsmith and had two sheet-iron cups made, large enough to cover the eight pole-ends (G and G′, Figs. 212 and 213). Each cup was six inches deep. After trying the cups or thimbles on the poles to see that they would fit, he made two moulds of oak. First he cut two pieces of oak plank two feet six inches long by one foot six inches (H, Fig. 214), which he trimmed into the form shown by J, Fig. 215, making a notch to fit each of the round ribs, and to spread them as the ribs of an umbrella are spread. He made two other similar moulds for the bow and stern, each of which, of course, is smaller than the middle one. After spreading the ribs with the moulds, and bringing the ends together in

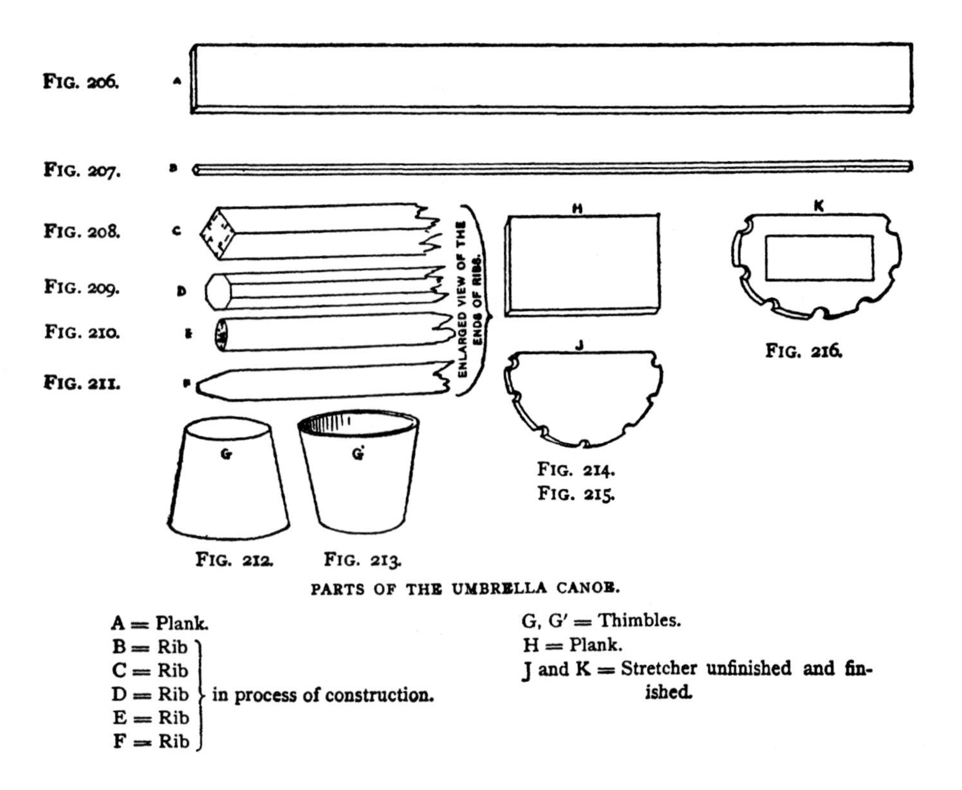

FIG. 206. FIG. 207. FIG. 208. FIG. 209. FIG. 210. FIG. 211. FIG. 212. FIG. 213. FIG. 214. FIG. 215. FIG. 216.

PARTS OF THE UMBRELLA CANOE.

A = Plank.
B = Rib, C = Rib, D = Rib, E = Rib, F = Rib } in process of construction.
G, G′ = Thimbles.
H = Plank.
J and K = Stretcher unfinished and finished.

the tin cups, he made holes in the bottom of the cups where the ends of the ribs came, and fastened the ribs to the cups with brass screws, fitted with leather washers, and run through the holes in the tin and screwed into the ends of the poles or ribs.

A square hole was then cut through each mould (K, Fig. 216), and the poles put in place, gathered together at the

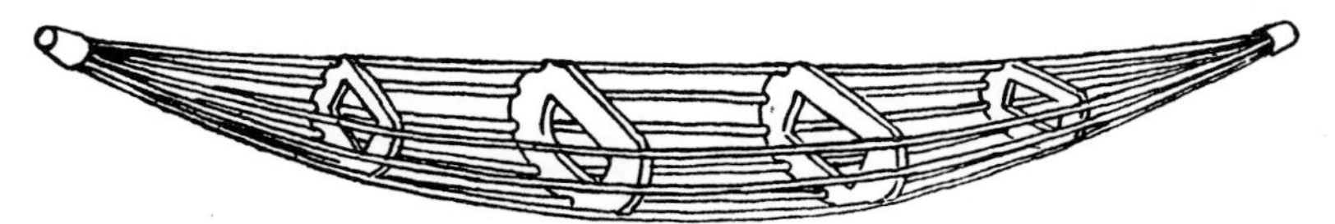

FIG. 217.—Frame of Umbrella Canoe.

ends, and held in place by the tin thimbles. The square holes in the moulds allow several small, light floor planks to form a dry floor to the canoe.

The canvas costs about forty-five cents a yard, and five yards are all you need. The deck can be made of drilling, which comes about twenty-eight inches wide, and costs about twenty cents a yard. Five yards of this will be plenty. Fit your canvas over the frame, stretch it tightly,

FIG. 218.—Umbrella Canoe.

and tack it securely to the two top ribs only. Fasten the deck on in the same manner.

When Mr. Dodge had the canoe covered and decked, with a square hole amidship to sit in, he put two good coats of paint on the canvas, allowed it to dry, and his boat was ready for use (Fig. 218). He quaintly says that "it looked like a starved dog, with all its ribs showing through the skin," just as the ribs of an umbrella show on top through the silk covering. But this does not in any way impede the progress of the boat through the water.

Where the moulds are the case is different, for the lines of the moulds cross the line of progress at right angles, and must necessarily somewhat retard the boat. But even this is not perceptible. The worst feature about the

FIG. 219.—Canoe Folded for Transportation. Canoe in Water in Distance.

moulds is that the canvas is very apt to be damaged there by contact with the shore, float, or whatever object it rubs against.

With ordinary care the umbrella canoe

Will Last for Years,

and is a good boat for paddling on inland streams and small bodies of water; and when you are through with it for the night all that is necessary is to remove the stretchers by springing the poles from the notches in the spreaders, roll up the canvas around the poles, put it on your shoulder, and carry it home or to camp, as shown in Fig. 219.

To put your canoe together again put in the moulds, fit the poles in their places, and the umbrella is raised, or, rather, the canoe is, if we can use such an expression in regard to a boat.

CHAPTER XVIII

HINTS FOR COLLECTORS

How to Capture and Preserve Moths and Butterflies—A New Cabinet.

WITH some marked exceptions, among which we are apt to place wasps, hornets, scorpions, and spiders, insects may be held of slight account as individuals. Collectively, however, they certainly at times demand serious consideration.

We can scarcely regard with contemptuous indifference tribes, for instance, like those of the dreadful African ant, before whose armies of tiny, but savage, soldiers men and beasts fly in terror, or the destructive termites, or white ants, whose countless hordes eat their way into everything made of wood, and hollow out tall telegraph poles until nothing remains but the merest shell, too weak to support their weight of wires. Sometimes, too, these wires are rendered useless by cobwebs, such as are woven by South American spiders, which form conducting lines and steal the messages.

Nothing seems to be more preposterous than the idea that any number of insects can bring an engine and a train of cars to a standstill; and yet every year the newspapers testify that it is not an uncommon occurrence. Caterpillars and, in some cases, grasshoppers appear in such quantities that the rails are rendered slippery with their crushed bodies and no progress is possible until the tracks are cleaned. In August of last year the daily journals had many graphic descriptions of "hold-ups" of locomotives by the innumerable multitudes of potato-bugs that were endeavoring to pre-empt a right of way on the various lines of the Long Island Railroad.

Practical Value of the Study of Insects.

The study of insects is really a matter of no small importance to humanity, and the boy collector who imbibes a taste for this most intensely interesting study, when he breaks out of his boyhood state, to shake out his strong mental wings as a perfect man, may become the wise naturalist who shall show us how to do away with the danger of such small fry as potato-bugs "holding up" express trains or of robbing the hard-working truck gardener of his crop of new potatoes. He should also be able to tell the farmer how to prevent the devastating effect of a horde of grasshoppers, or the vegetable gardener how to protect his cabbage from the larvæ of the white butterfly, or the shipbuilder how to secure his lumber from the ruinous effect of "borers," and in a hundred ways be of great service to his country and to the world.

All the great things that are to be done in the next fifty years will be done by men who at the present time are either unborn or are now common, every-day boys. They wear no badges to tell you they are to be great scientists, artists, authors, engineers or statesmen, but they are certain to occupy those positions. The greatest man who ever lived was a boy to begin with, and the next to fill his place may be now reading this book—may perhaps be you!

The Popular Classification.

With the exception of butterflies, the general public class the whole insect world under two heads—worms and bugs—and regard them with unqualified disgust. But this is only a sign of universal ignorance.

Some insects are veritable living jewels; many possess all the iridescence of an opal. There are few of our precious stones that cannot be matched in beauty by some despised creeping or buzzing insect.

Baby butterflies and moths are properly called caterpillars, not *worms*. The caterpillar's taste is as varied as that of any other animal. Roots, wood, buds, flowers, wool, fur, flour, wax, lard, and meat, are some of the articles selected as food by different individuals, but the majority of these creeping infants live on the leaves of trees, shrubs, and other vegetables.

If you take a sausage and tie bits of string around it at short intervals, you will have a very good model of a caterpillar. Supply a little lump at one end for a head, some warts along the back, add from ten to sixteen small legs, and your sausage will be sufficiently lifelike to alarm any timid people who see it.

The Life of Caterpillars.

Caterpillars are as varied in their mode of life as in their choice of food. Some hide in the earth and only steal forth to feed; others dwell in crowded silken tenement-houses, while their relatives of different taste lead the solitary life of hermits or make themselves small tents of silk or huts of folded leaves.

Every boy knows at which end of its body the spider's spinning apparatus is placed, but the caterpillar carries his thread at the other end, the silk issuing from a little tube in the middle of the lower lip. Inside the body there are two long bags of sticky stuff. The bags connect with the tube in the lower lip, and as the sticky fluid is forced out it is hardened into silk by the atmosphere.

When a caterpillar grows too large for his skin he crawls out, dressed in a bran new suit of clothes that fit his increased dimensions comfortably. About four suits of clothes answer for the young butterfly, and he is ready to be born again. The change is all inside, and when he is good and ready and feels all right, he bursts open the skin on his neck and wiggles out; but his own brothers would not know him.

He is shorter and thicker than ever before, has lost all of his ten or sixteen legs, and has no eyes, nose, mouth, or head. All he can do is to wriggle his funny ringed tail. This is what is called a chrysalis or pupa state.

Not Ready to Fly.

After hanging by the tip of his tail under a fence-rail, or after sleeping in his soft silken bed inside his waterproof cocoon, or covered in his bed of earth, as the case may be, for a sufficient time to regulate his internal anatomy, he again cracks open the skin on his back and crawls out a six-legged winged insect, but his wings are sadly crumpled from being folded in the narrow quarters within the chrysalis skin.

This, however, is a small matter, and still clinging with all six feet to his cast-off shell, he trembles and shakes until wrinkle after wrinkle and fold after fold is shaken out, and four beautiful wings move slowly up and down; gradually their delicate framework is dried and hardened, and then we see one of the most beautiful of sights—a perfect butterfly or moth.

The reason they are called lepidopters, or scaly wings, is because all that fine powder that rubs off so easily on one's fingers is not powder, but minute scales, which may be seen by examining what adheres to the fingers with a magnifying glass.

As a rule, butterflies fly by day and moths at evening or night. Butterflies have knobbed "smellers," "feelers," or antennæ, and moths have feathered antennæ. Most moths are much thicker and shorter in the body than butterflies, but this is not invariably the case (Figs. 220 and 221).

Important Differences.

In studying insects examine and note the form and proportion of the heads, the length and form of the feelers (antennæ), the plan of the veins in the wings, and the size and proportion of the latter, and you will soon see greater difference than there is between Irishmen, Germans, Hebrews, Englishmen, negroes, and Indians.

FIG. 220. FIG. 221.

FIG. 220.—A Moth with Feathered "Feelers."
FIG. 221. — A Butterfly with Knobbed "Feelers"

The preservation of caterpillars for cabinet use is very difficult on account of their soft, perishable bodies. Some of the more minute ones may be prepared by heating a bottle in the oven until it is a little glass oven itself, and then inserting the small larvæ in the bottle, where it will bake and dry, and may be then pinned in the cabinet or box the same as a moth, butterfly, or beetle.

FIG. 222.—A Day in the Country.

Drying Better than Alcohol.

Alcohol will preserve almost any sort of specimen. I have bottles at home filled with all manner of creatures—bats, baby bats, mice, fish, lizards, and shrimp-like animals from salt water. For ten years they have remained undisturbed and practically unchanged, but there is an unpleasant look about alcoholic specimens that is not present in cabinet collections of dried insects.

For the purpose of study, however, those specimens preserved in spirits have many advantages over the dried ones. It is claimed that larvæ (young insects, grubs, caterpillars, etc.), if immersed in boiling water for half a minute and then placed in bottles containing half water and half alcohol, will retain all their natural colors and form. Mr. Packard, in his most valuable book on this subject, advises the use of whiskey as a preservative for a few days before placing the caterpillars in their final resting-place in vials of alcohol, the latter being so strong that all soft specimens will shrivel and shrink when placed in it without preparation.

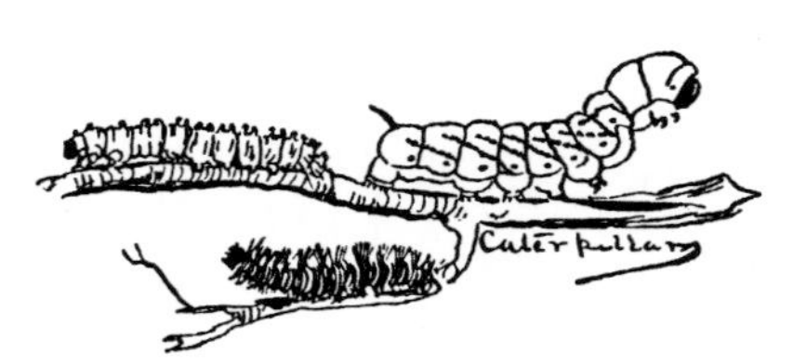

FIG. 223.—Caterpillars.

The careful and methodical German collector prepares beautiful, if frail, specimens by first squeezing the insides out of the baby butterflies, and then with a blowpipe made with the nozzle fitted over a fine straw, and worked by a bladder filled with air, he blows up the larvæ skin by squeezing the bladder under his arm or between his knees, while with his hands he holds the little skin over a small lamp, so that it dries in its distended form.

The perfect insect—that is, the full-grown winged butterfly or moth—may also be preserved in alcohol, after the manner described for the larvæ, but the most artistic and beautiful specimens are the dried ones.

Common-Sense Needed.

The best specimens are only procured by rearing the young and collecting the full-grown butterflies after they have freed themselves from their horny chrysalis. The space allowed for these hints is too short for a detailed account of the science of caterpillar farming, but this I can say: By experiment you can learn more than can be taught by * books.

If a larva is found eating willow leaves, it does not require a ponderous volume on natural history to tell a bright, intelligent boy that willow leaves are good food for that particular young insect. If the experimenter finds that sprinkling the food leaves in his farming box with water causes the caterpillars to swell up with a sort of fungus growth, killing them, he is bright enough to keep his leaves dry the next time. If his pets seem restless and pained by the sunlight, his common-sense will tell him to put them in the shade; so I must rely on his good American common-sense observation, judgment, and ingenuity to supply the information that want of space makes impracticable to insert here.

How to Make a Cabinet.

Any broad, flat box will answer, but it should be neatly joined, with a cover that fits closely. Some collectors use

---

* Chapter XXV., American Boys' Handy Book, gives many novelties which, of course, are omitted here.

flat strips of cork, glued in the bottom, to pin their specimens on; others stretch a piece of drawing-paper on a frame that fits closely in the box and leaves a half or quarter of a inch air-space underneath, for the purpose of stowing gum camphor or other drugs to keep the moths, buffalo beetles, and other small pests from destroying the dried insects. But the following plan will be found most convenient:

Make a false bottom of wood or card-board; fit it securely in the box on a frame that holds the false bottom,

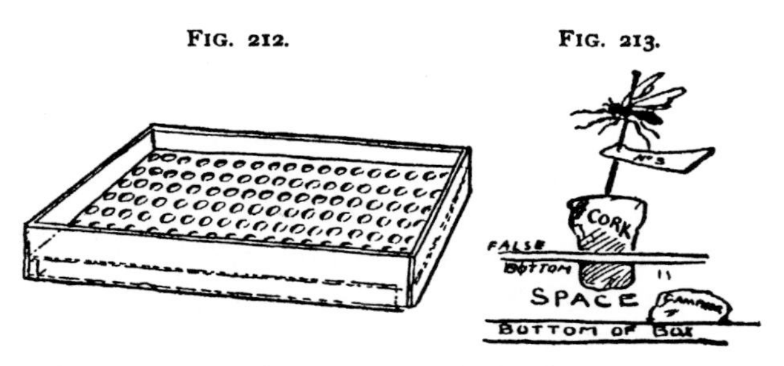

FIG. 212. FIG. 213.

FIGS. 224, 225.—The American Boy's New Box for Insects.

about half an inch from the real bottom. Through the false bottom bore a series of round holes of a size to fit a number of small corks. In the top of these corks the specimens are pinned (Figs. 224 and 225).

This cabinet has a great advantage over the others, for the collector can remove any cork, with the specimens attached, for examination or show with the least possible danger of injuring the frail object (Fig. 213). Lumps of camphor or other moth-preventive drugs can be freely inserted under the false bottom with no danger of damaging the collection by the heavy particles of the drug coming in contact and breaking the dried insects.

At any drug store, and many candy stores, you can for a trifling sum buy wide, open-mouthed bottles with a metal top that screws on, in place of the clumsy, old-fashioned cork; these make perfect collecting bottles. Take a piece of common blotting-paper, cut from it several pieces in the form of circular disks just large enough to fit tightly in the bottom of the bottle. Push one piece down until it rests snugly on the bottom of the bottle. Saturate it with chloroform, ether, benzine, or creosote; then fit a dry piece of blotting-paper over the wet one, and another dry piece in the metal stopper. Screw the top quickly on, and the fumes of the drug will fill the bottle, forming a death-deal-

FIG. 226.

FIG. 227. FIG. 228.

FIG. 226.—A Killing Bottle.
FIG. 227.—A Grub in Spirits.
FIG. 228.—A Beetle on Flat Cork.

ing atmosphere to any unfortunate insect you may capture and drop in the fatal glass chamber (Fig. 226).

Often the opportunity presents itself of capturing a small moth or butterfly without touching its delicate wings with your clumsy finger, for if the insect is carefully approached, the top removed from the bottle and the latter inverted and placed over the victim, it will cease to live without a struggle and, with its dainty wings unmarred,

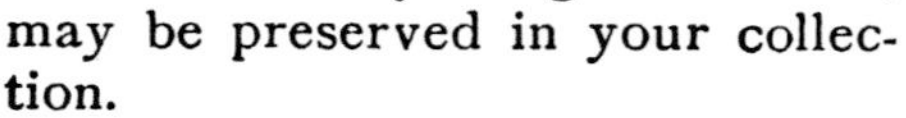

may be preserved in your collection.

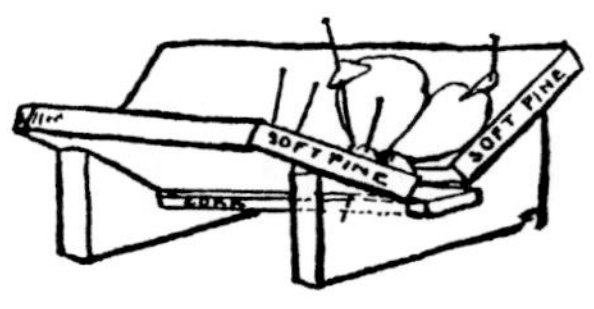

FIG. 229.—Insect on Drying Board.

Before going hunting insects, fill your pockets with all the pill boxes and glass vials that you can conveniently carry, and, armed with a net made of light gauze or mosquito-netting, sally forth. No game laws protect your game, no badly spelled and ungrammatical notices warn you not to hunt insects on the farms, because the farmers are all glad to have you make war on their little but expensive enemies.

Useful Occupation.

You will experience as much joy in securing a rare specimen as any hunter does in his successful efforts to help exterminate the beautiful, harmless, and useful birds, and you are conscious of the fact that while enjoying yourself and adding to your stock of health and useful knowledge, you are also in a small way making war on the enemies of the trees and flowers.

While it is true that many insects are of absolute benefit to mankind, it is also true that the moths and butterflies and many other insects, though they be dreams of loveliness in form and color and add beauty and interest to the flowers and fields, make us pay for their beauty by the destruction of crops which each year amounts to thousands and thousands of dollars.

CHAPTER XIX

HONEY-BEE MESSENGERS

How to Send a Cipher Message by the Bee Line—The Key—Bee Stings and How to Avoid Them.

MONSIEUR TAYNAC, the celebrated French bee expert at Versailles, has a hive of several thousand bees trained like carrier pigeons, which he offers for the French military service.

This is an idea for boys to follow—not to be used in any such old-fashioned, barbarous practice as the wholesale murder called war, but in healthy, modern, up-to-date, intelligent play. If one of my readers or one of his friends, anywhere within ten or fifteen miles of his home, owns a hive of bees, the two can use the little insect to carry messages between their respective homes.

With your butterfly net catch some honey-bees, or, better still, trap them with a box set in front of the doorway of the hive. Make a hole in the box like the hive door, and the insects will enter the box under the impression that by that means they can reach their home. The boy who lives at a distance takes

The Box of Bees

home with him, and liberates them in a closed room, where he has placed a saucer of honey or syrup. After the bees have fed on the syrup he opens the windows and they, of course, will go directly home. Bees have been known to travel fifteen or twenty miles, but these are long distances. Monsieur Taynac's bees traversed ten miles with messages on their backs; they travelled at the rate of twelve and one-half miles per hour. Boys at school used to catch blue-bottle flies, and with fine thread fastened bits of paper to their legs and let them loose in the school-room, to the delight of the other pupils, and the annoyance of the patient and long-suffering teacher; but the paper message is glued on the bee's thorax between the wings and the head.

How to Make the Message.

With a little pair of scissors cut some small slips of paper in the form of Fig. 233. Make a slit at the bottom, and

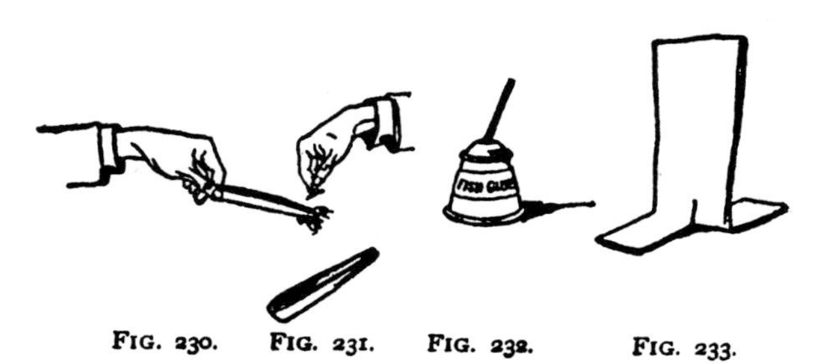

FIG. 230. FIG. 231. FIG. 232. FIG. 233.

FIG. 230.—Sticking the Messages on the Bee.
FIG. 231.—The Tweezers.
FIG. 232.—Bottle of Fish Glue.
FIG. 233.—Paper for Message.

bend the divided parts in opposite directions. Monsieur Taynac used isinglass with which to glue the paper to his bees, but there are other glues that will answer. Mucilage can be made to serve the purpose; but great care must be taken to prevent daubing the sticky stuff on the poor insect's wings or legs.

How to Handle the Bees.

The best manner of handling bees, and the safest way to prevent being stung, is to use a small pair of tweezers to pick them up with and to hold them (Figs. 230 and 231). Monsieur Taynac uses a little gauze cage to transport his bees. When a bee with a letter on his back reaches the home hive, the message standing upright on his back prevents him from entering the doorway, and the owner on watch finds the messenger bee crawling around and captures him.

FIG. 234.—Enlarged View of Honey Bee with Message. Drawn from a photograph.

How to Write the Message.

The bit of paper is so small that it would be difficult to write even a sentence on it, but any boy with a hard, sharp pencil can make a few figures on the slip, and if his friend has a key he can read the message. Each figure may stand for a sentence, and with 1, 2, 3, 4, 5, 6, 7, 8, 9, 0, you will have ten sentences. If you add the alphabet to this and allow each letter from A to Z to stand for a sentence, you will have twenty-six more, or thirty-six sentences in all; and, with thirty-six well-chosen sentences a great deal can be said. You may add thirty-six more by adding a dot over each letter and number, thus, $\dot{3}$ or $\dot{D}$; and thirty-six more by a dash over each character, thus, $\bar{3}$ or $\bar{D}$. Here we have 3 for one sentence, $\dot{3}$ for another, $\bar{3}$ for still another. With the aid of a magnifying glass and a finely pointed pencil several sentences may be put on one bit of paper.

Suppose A to stand for some such sentence as this: "If to-morrow is pleasant," and B to stand for "Meet me after school at the old chestnut-tree," and nine with a dot over it ($\dot{9}$) to mean "We will go a-fishing," A $\dot{9}$ B will be read by your friend: "If to-morrow is pleasant we will go a-fishing. Meet me after school at the old chestnut-tree."

How to Make Your Key.

Write the numbers, beginning with 1 and ending with 0, in a column, 2 below 1, 3 below 2, etc. Opposite each number write the sentence you wish it to represent, below the first column of figures place a second column, in every way similar to the first, except that each figure has a dot over it; then a third, each figure with a dash over it; then three alphabets, one plain, one with a dot, and the third with a dash above each letter. Opposite each character write the sentence you desire it to stand for in your code.

Of this key make a duplicate, which is to be given to your correspondent.

Bee Stings and How to Avoid Them.

Some cousins of mine and myself had been gathering nuts on the shores of Lake Erie and were sitting on an old log to rest and crack a few walnuts. We had not hammered long on the old log before we were aware of a peculiar buzzing noise inside, and the next thing that claimed our attention was a stream of very angry yellow-jackets pouring out of a hole in the log, all intent upon wreaking vengeance upon the disturbers of their peace. I fled in dismay, wildly swinging my hat, but my two country cousins stood stock still and were passed unnoticed by the angry insects, all of whom devoted their entire attention to me with a persistency that baffled my most energetic efforts to fight them off. They stung me in the back of the neck, in the edge of my hair, behind the ears, and even crawled down inside my collar and left their stings in my back until I howled with pain.

Experience is a Good School.

I have seldom been stung since, and the few times I have suffered have been what might be called accidents. Once I put on a hat that had a lot of bumble bees in it; once I took up a pail and a wasp at the same time, but I never since have been attacked by a swarm, although it has happened that bees, wasps, and yellow-jackets have rushed out of their homes with murder in their hearts, and finding only a perfectly motionless figure, have either passed me by or alighted on me, crawled around for awhile, and then flown away without once unsheathing their sharp little swords.

A Bee's Stinger.

Under a powerful microscope the point of a cambric needle looks like the blunt end of a crowbar, and the point of a pin is no point at all; but the sting of a bee is sharp even under the powerful magnifying glasses of the microscope, and when magnified a thousand times it still looks as a fine needle-point does to the naked eye.

I have always found almost immediate relief when the sting left by a bee or wasp has been removed. This may be done with a needle or with the pointed blade of a pocket-knife. But the best plan is to use care and then you will not be stung.

CHAPTER XX

A "ZOO"

For the Housetop or the Backyard—How to Build a Coop for Animals on the Roof or in the Yard—The Way to Provide Homes for Various Kinds of Pets.

ASCENDING any of the modern "sky-scraper" buildings and gazing around at the vast city beneath, one is interested in the acres and acres of wasted space of tin and gravel roofs. I know of no good reason why this space may not be utilized for pleasure. Roof-gardens are not difficult to construct, and can do no possible damage to the buildings if they are properly made.

Boys in the city have "no place to be," as I heard one of them express it. They are fretful and a nuisance in the house, and on the street they are a constant source of anxiety to their parents, and annoyance to the policemen. All boys with healthy minds are fond of pets, and as I look out of my studio window on the unoccupied fields of red tin and white gravel roofs I wonder that the space is not used for the neglected young people of the city, or that the young people do not pre-empt claims, as their ancestors did the sites upon which the buildings are built.

Strange Birds on the City Housetops.

Up aloft, above the crowded, noisy streets, you are more free to breathe, to see and to enjoy life. Overhead is the blue sky, as yet unmarred by "no trespass" signs, and unfrequented by policemen. Even the wild birds know this, and I have myself seen a bald-headed eagle calmly roosting on a flag-pole, gazing with dignified curiosity upon the crazy lot of human beings hurrying along crowded Broadway. Not long ago, casually looking over a roof on

Fig. 235.—A City Boy's Zoo.

Fifth Avenue, I saw a black-crested night heron patiently standing on one leg in a pool of rain-water, awaiting the appearance of some unwary fish or frog, all unconscious of the fact that such creatures do not, as a rule, frequent red tin roofs.

Once, while experimenting with a new kind of kite for the boys, and losing my patience over the network of wires that then covered the downtown roofs, I was startled to see that I was watched by a great Virginia horned owl, perched upon a neighboring smokestack.

A friend whose business is among the great warehouses along the river-front tells me that on more than one occasion he has seen yellow-legs running over the roofs and shy woodcock boring for worms in the soft black mud accumulated in the gutters on the tops of high buildings.

FIG. 236.—End View of House.

Material Easy to Get.

Now, since these wild creatures visit the tops of buildings of their own accord, why cannot the boys use the vacant housetops for private zoölogical gardens of their own, where white rats, coons, crows, herons, pigeons, and chickens could be reared and enjoyed? Coops, pens, and inclosures can, with little ingenuity, be built for the shelter and protection of the pets. Wire-netting is an ideal material for such structures. All boys, however, are not supplied with the requisite amount of money, but I never yet saw the boy who could not obtain a few old barrels, and the barrel-staves are most excellent material for pigeon- or chicken-coops and rabbit-houses. What will do for these animals will do for any creature a boy is likely to possess.

You Must Be a Carpenter.

Select two sticks for uprights, and let them be exactly the same length and long enough to enable you to stand up inside the coop when it is finished.

FIG. 237.—End Pieces Set Up.

Cut two more uprights a foot or two shorter, to give a pitch to your roof. Lay these on the floor, and nail on firmly cross-pieces, as shown in Fig. 236, the frame for the ends of your house. Place the largest upright against the fire-wall of the roof, and fasten it there; at the proper distance—say six feet, set up the other end piece (Fig. 237); connect the front and rear with cross-pieces, as in Fig. 238, and erect two more uprights for door-jambs (see A B and C D, Fig. 238); nail all firmly together, and fasten on the roof the stringer (E F, Fig. 238) and the braces G H, I J, G L, and J K; split a number of barrel-staves, and nail them on, as in Fig. 235.

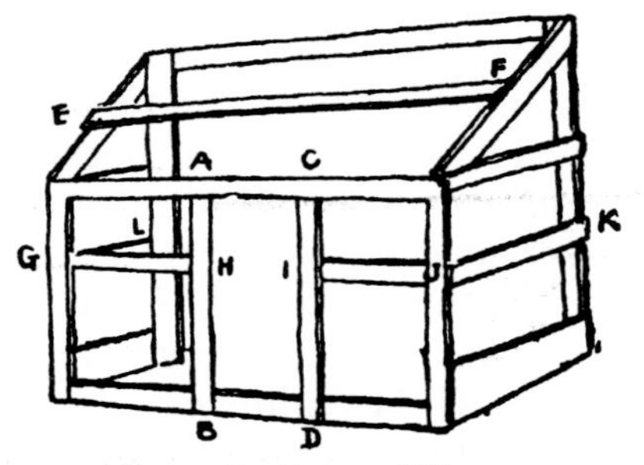

FIG. 238.—Frame of House.

For the roof of the coop use whole staves in place of shingles, and lay them tile fashion. Make one row on the lower end of the roof, all with their hollow, or concave, side up, and place them several inches apart. At the upper end place a second row in the same manner. Commence again at the bottom, and place a second row of staves, each overlapping the staves on each side, and covering the open spaces left between the first ones; these last must have their round, that is, their convex, side up. Repeat the process for the second tier, and the roof is complete and water-tight.

FIG. 239.—Finished House.

Make a door-frame of four sticks. Cross it with slats of split staves. From the soles of cast-off shoes make a pair of leather hinges, and, with the addition of a hook and eye, the thing is done.

Plank the back end up solid above the fire-walls, and you have a good, substantial chicken-coop, rabbit-house, or cage for other pets. A run-way for exercise room for your pets may be connected with the coop by a door, as in Fig. 240.

Splendid for a Yard, too.

This same house is first-class in a yard, if any of you city boys are fortunate enough to have one, and when neatly built looks well, and, if you choose, its cost will be absolutely nothing, except the exercise of your muscle and brain.

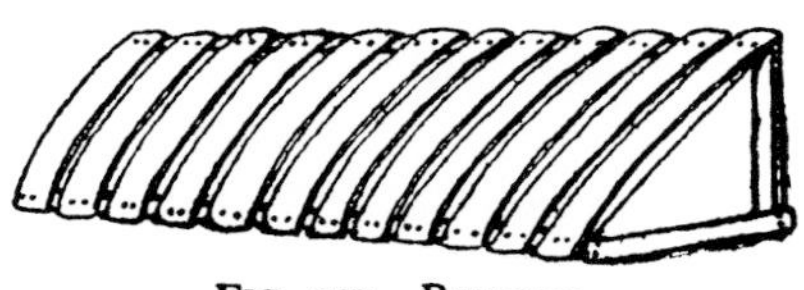

FIG. 240.—Run-way.

There are boys, and many of them to-day, who have spending-money freely given to them by their wealthy parents, and who can consequently buy whatever they wish. This is an unfortunate condition for the boys to be placed in, for, as a rule, they will never know the real pleasure of being a boy. But even these boys may have some fun if, in place of buying things outright, they spend their money for materials and then make their own playthings—rabbit-houses, kites, and sleds. The boy with money may have beautiful carpenter-tools, plenty of selected timber, and wire netting, and with these and a little skill he may build houses for his pets which will be an ornament to his father's grounds. But while his wire-netted cages will look more expensive, the barrel-stave cage will answer all purposes, and, if neatly made, will look more picturesque.

FIG. 241.

CHAPTER XXI

CHOOSING UP AND "IT"

"Which Hand is It in?"—"Pick'er Up, Wipe'er Off, and Stone-holder"—"Last One Over"—Short Straw—Handy, Dandy, Riderly Ro—"Whole Fist or Four Fingers"—"Odd or Even?"—"Wet or Dry?"

TWENTY-FIVE years ago a popular method of deciding which boy should be "It" was called "Which hand is it in?" A boy, in the party about to engage in some game, would pick up a pebble, and facing his companions he would put his hands behind him and place the stone in either hand to suit himself. Then extending his closed fists to a companion he would exclaim, "Which hand is it in?"

The companion, after due study and deliberation, would say, "Not that!" as he slapped one extended fist with his open hand. If the hand he chose was empty he would "go free;" if not, he would take the stone and go through the same performance with the next boy, and thus the process would continue. Each lad went free when he passed the stone on, and each lad who guessed the empty hand went free, until all had had a chance and one boy was left holding the stone in his hand.

The evident objection to this method is that the first boy has every chance to go free—that is, if there are six boys the first one has only one chance in six of being caught, and the next one one chance in five. But the last one has only one chance in two of going free. This does not appear to affect the popularity of this method, although the eagerness of the boys to hold the stone first, or to have first choice, plainly shows that they fully understand the importance of first choice.

Of course the last boy to hold the stone is "It."

"Pick'er up, Wipe'er off, and Stone-holder"

stands as evidence that the boys see nothing unfair in the old method of "Which hand is it in," and that they deem it right that the boy whose wits are the quickest is entitled to go free.

As soon as a game is proposed nowadays one lad shouts "Pick'er up!" as he stoops and picks up a pebble. The words are not out of his mouth before another cries "Wipe'er off!" and a third "Stone-holder."

Pick'er-up hands the stone to Wipe'er-off. Pick'er-up is then free, Wipe'er-off makes a great show of wiping the stone off on his trouser leg, and hands it to Stone-holder. Wipe'er-off is then free and Stone-holder puts his hands behind him, arranges the stone as described in the preceding method and allows the next boy to choose which hand it is in. The last lad to hold the stone is "It."

"Last One Over is 'It!'"

This is a simple but exciting mode of deciding who shall be in that terrible position described as "It."

Suppose that a group of boys are standing by a fence and one of them proposes a game of "I spy." No sooner is the proposition made than another lad shouts "Last one over the fence is 'It!'"

Immediately all is confusion and hubbub. Each boy is trying his best to scramble, leap, vault, or tumble over the fence before his companions can perform the feat. Sometimes the cry is "Last one across the street!" or "Last one to the corner and back!" etc.

Whatever it be, a trial of speed, agility, or skill, that is proposed, the last boy to accomplish the feat is "It."

Short Straw.

From a handful of straws or grass, one of the boys selects as many pieces as there are to be players in the proposed game. One of the blades of grass or pieces of straw is cut off so that it will be much shorter than the other pieces.

"Straw-holder" arranges the straws so that the top ends protrude from his closed fist, either perfectly even or irregular in their height above the hand according to his fancy. It may happen that the first boy to choose a straw will select the short one. This in a measure spoils the fun, and to guard against it the lads are often made to stand up in a line and each one in turn pulls a straw from the fist of "Straw-holder." Each one is expected and required to put it behind his back immediately and keep it there until all the boys in the line have straws behind their backs.

Then "Straw-holder," holding up the straw left in his own hand, cries, "Who is short straw?" At that each boy produces his straw and compares it with the others.

While it adds greatly to the interest to have all the straws of different lengths, it is best to make the short straw unmistakably shorter than any of its fellows. Otherwise the game may be broken up by a heated and angry dispute, a state of affairs never desirable and one which is easily avoided by the precaution suggested above.

After comparison of the relative length of all the straws, the boy found with the shortest straw in his possession is "It."

"Handy, Dandy, Riderly, Ro."

This is another form of "Which hand is it in," only in this case the fists are put one above the other. One hand contains a button, stone, piece of coal, or any other object, and the other hand is empty. The two hands are then clenched tightly and are extended out in front of the "Stone-holder," who shouts "Handy, dandy, riderly, ro! Which will you have, high or low?"

The boy appealed to makes a guess. If he guesses the empty hand he goes free. If he guesses the hand with the stone in it he takes the stone and says, "Handy, dandy," etc., to the next player, who guesses high or low as suits him. The last one to hold the stone is "It."

"Whole Fist or Four Fingers?"

shouts one of the boys, as he grasps with his right hand the middle of a base-ball bat or broom-stick. Immediately the other boys fall in line and the lad with the stick tosses it to the first boy in such a manner that the stick does not lose its upright position. The first boy must catch it with his left hand, and he is not allowed to move his hand after catching it until the test is over, or until his turn comes around again and he puts his other hand on.

Number two in the line now grasps the stick with his right hand just above and close against number one's hand. Number three does the same with his left hand and so on until the first boy's turn again comes. Then this boy puts one hand on and number one puts his right hand on the stick until at last one boy is unable to get his whole fist or four fingers on the stick. When that happens, the boy that fails is "It."

This is a poor method where there are four or more

boys in the game, but for any game where the captains choose their sides it is a very popular method of deciding between the two captains which shall have first choice. When only two are choosing, the first tosses the bat, as described, the second catches it with his left hand, then the first puts his right hand on top of the second's left, the second places his right hand on top of the first boy's right; and in this manner the hands climb to the top of the bat or stick until the time comes when one is unable to get four fingers on the bat.

When this occurs the other boy has first choice of his playmates for the game that is to follow, which is usually a game of ball. While evidently not invented for that purpose, still the author has often seen "Whole fist or four fingers" used to decide who should be "It."

"Odd or Even?"

is also generally used to decide who shall have first choice in a "choosing up" game, but like "Whole fist or four fingers" it is sometimes used for counting out. One boy takes the contents of his pocket, a handful of marbles, Jack-stones, pebbles, coin, or whatever is handy, and holding out his closed hand cries "Odd or even?" meaning, "Have I an odd or even number of objects in my hand?" The other boy makes a guess, and if it is correct he has first choice, and if not the first choice falls to the share of the one who holds the objects.

When used in counting out the boy who guesses correctly goes free, while he who does not turns to the next and cries "Odd or even?" with his extended hand filled with the contents of his own pocket. When all are free but one, that one is "It."

"Heads or Tails?"

It seems absurd that any one should deem it necessary to describe in detail this method of deciding a disputed point, but the author has written a great many things for boys, and consequently learned much by experience. He knows that he will be forgiven much more readily for describing something the reader is perfectly familiar with than he will for taking it for granted that the reader knows all about it, which, if true, would do away with the necessity of books altogether.

Throw up a cent or other coin and cry "Heads or tails?" Your playmate must make his choice and call out his guess while the coin is in the air. Then both stoop and examine the piece of money as it rests on the ground. If the side *with the date on it* is up, that is "heads"; if the other side is up, it is "tails." If your playmate's guess was correct, he has first choice for sides in the game you are about to play; otherwise you have first choice.

When this game is used for counting out, each one goes free who makes a lucky guess, and each one who fails tosses the coin for the next one to guess. If at any time the coin does not lie flat on the ground, but rests wholly or partly upon its edge, that toss does not count, and it must be tossed over again.

When all the boys but one have gone free, the boy who is left is "It."

"Wet or Dry?"

This was formerly the method of deciding who should have first choice for sides in a game of ball. Not base-ball, for it was before that now popular game had made its appearance. It was used for "town-ball," a game played with a flat bat like a cricket bat. One boy would dampen one side of the bat, and then send the bat twirling in the air, and the other boy would guess which side would come up, wet or dry. Often one side of the bat would be marked with a piece of chalk or soft brick, and that side was called wet. But the old flat bat and the old game have both been swept aside.

"Wet or dry" has not disappeared, however, with the bat that originated it. If any one will watch the boys carefully as they scream and shout at their play, he will no doubt, sooner or later, see the youngsters decide "first choice" by throwing up a chip and crying "Wet or dry?" The choice is decided exactly as it is in "Heads or tails," or "Odd or even," and when the chip is used in counting out, as in "Heads or tails," "Odd or even," or "Which hand is it in," each boy has a turn to guess. The boy who fails, tosses the chip, until another unlucky playmate fails, when he in his turn tosses the chip, crying "Wet or dry?" This goes on until all the boys are free but one, and as this one, should he choose to toss the chip, would have no one to guess but himself, he gracefully accepts the situation and becomes "It."

CHAPTER XXII

COUNTING OUT RHYMES

How the Game is Played—Various Rhymes—An American Version of an Ancient Rhyme — Causes of Variations — Rhymes of Different Nationalities.

THE full-grown man who hears the once familiar words, or rather articulate sounds, of "On-ery, ore-ry, ick-ery, Ann!" without a pleased smile o'erspreading his face, is a man devoid of sentiment, or a man with no fond memories of his own boyhood days.

For untold centuries the boys have handed the queer, whimsical rhymes down to their younger playmates with only slight variations. "On-ery, ore-ry" is sometimes "one-ry, two-ery," etc., but the author has made diligent inquiry among his young acquaintances and has been unable to find more than one or two verses that were not familiar to him in his own childhood.

After consulting the rhymes contributed by H. Carrington Bolton, of Trinity College, to the Boston *Journal of Education;* those published in the New York *Mail and Express* of May 9, 1885; a collection in the *Journal of American Folk-Lore*, and a collection by William Wells Newell, in his interesting book of "Games and Songs of American Children," the author is still unable to add many new ones to his list.

How to Count Out.

These quaint rhymes seem to be the common property of all children, especially those of the Anglo-Saxon or Anglo-Norman race. We all know how these rhymes are used. A game is about to be started and one boy chooses to count out. After a brief clamor of protests from his playmates, all of whom are anxious to do the counting themselves, the first boy is generally allowed to proceed.

Standing his playmates in a row in front of him, or in a circle around him, he places his forefinger on his own breast and impressively pronounces the word "one-ery." Placing his finger on the breast of the first playmate to the left he repeats "two-ery" or "ory" according to his version of the rhyme. With each mystic word he places his finger upon the chest of a playmate until he comes to "buck." Buck is out, or free, and the count commences over again, each buck going free until only one boy is left, and he is "It."

Sometimes it happens that there are more boys than words in the counting rhyme, or the counter foresees that he himself will be "It." In both cases he adds to the verse something like this:

One, two, three,
Out goes he!

Often he will add a whole verse and dialogue as follows:

One, two, three,
Out goes he
Into the middle
Of the deep blue sea!
Are you willing to be IT?

Here the boy indicated answers "yes" or "no" as it suits him, and the counter continuing, repeats, "N—O spells No," or "Y—E—S spells Yes, and you are out. O—U—T spells Out!"

This is spoken with long pauses between the words or letters. "Out" is free, and the counting commences again:

One-ry, or-ry, ickery, Ann!
Fillison, follison, Nicholas, John.
Queevy, quavy, English Navy,
Stinckelum, stanklum, buck!

Or, as it is sometimes repeated:

One-ery, two-ery, hickory han,
Fillison, follison, Nicholas, John.
Queevy, quavy, Virgin Mary,
Stingelum, stangelum, berry buck!

Some say "English navy," some "Virgin Mary," some "Irish Mary," etc. As a rule, "English navy" is for boys, and "Virgin" or "Irish Mary" for girls. Some end with simple "buck," some with "berry buck," some with "John buck," others with "Jericho buck," etc. According to Mr. Bolton there are at least thirty variations of this rhyme, but the lines given here will be all that are necessary for our purpose.

A Counting Verse.

It is evident that "Mother Goose" and various other nursery books have contributed some of the verses used, but none of these have the true ring in them. It is apparent that the following has been adapted by the boys for the purpose of a counting verse:

One a penny bun,
Two a penny bun,
One a penny, two a penny;
Out goes one!

And this :

One a penny bun,
Two a penny bun,
One a penny, two a penny
Hot cross buns !
If your mother don't like 'em,
Give them to her son.
One a penny, two a penny,
Out goes one !

The following rhyme is unmistakably

An American Versiern of an Ancient Verse.

Enna, mena, mina, mo,
Catch a tiger by the toe;
When he hollers, let him go,
Enna, mena, mina, mo !

It is evident that the above American verse has been built on the framework of the antique Cornwall rhyme which has the reputation of coming down from the Druid priests of ancient Britain :

Ena, mena, mona, mite,
Pasca, laura, bona, bite,
Eggs, butter, cheese, bread,
Stick, stock, stone, dead.

Another verse springing from the same root is familiar to the boys all over the land in some one of its many variations :

Ana, mana, mona, Mike,
Barcelona, bona, strike ;
Care, ware, frow, frack,
Hallico, ballico, we, wo, wack !
Huddy, guddy, boo,
Out goes you !

The last two lines are frequently added to other verses, and do not belong to any one rhyme in particular.

Another form, or variation, very commonly heard, is the same as the last with this exception, in place of "Barcelona, bona, strike," we have "Tuscalona, bona, strike."

Many differences in the sounds or words which compose these verses are due to the different pronunciations of the boys. West of the Alleghany Mountains the boys will say "Wee, wo, *whack!*" But in New York and along the Atlantic coast the boys drop the "h" in whack as they do in "white," "what," and "whip," which they pronounce "wite," "wat," and "wip." Consequently the New York boy says "Hallico, ballico, we, wo, *wack*." Here is another ending that the counter sometimes adds to his verse to lengthen it or to save himself from being "It."

Three cheers for the red, white, and blue!
All are out but you!

In this case the one named "you" is "It," and all the others go free.

Some Good Rhymes.

Among the many notes made for this chapter there are some for the explanation of which it was evidently intended that the memory should supply the data. But in the case of the following verse memory has failed to do its duty. The lines, however, make good counting out rhymes with the real swing in them.

Fip Dick, bumphrey gig,
Mother Hop-foot milled a pig;
Ithy, mithy, owery, gout,
Lytle tinkar, thou art out!

One-azall two a-zall, titter zal zan,
Bobtailed Britisher, little girl Nan;

Harum, scarum, ball of hot rorum,
Knuckle bone, crackle bone, bloody bone,
uck!

Mr. William Wells Newal gives a verse very similar to the last which he gets from Salem, Mass. It is interesting because it plainly shows that the phrase "One-azall, two a-zall" was originally "One is all, two is all," etc.

One's all, zuzall, titterall, tawn,
Bobtailed vinegar, little Paul ran,
Harum, scarum, merchant marum,
Tiger, turn-pike, toll-house out.

There are few of my readers but have either used or heard the following:

Monkey, monkey, bottle of beer,
How many monkeys are they here?
One, two, three,
Out goes he!

But I doubt if many of them are familiar with this:

Ane, a-zall tane a-zall titterzall zee,
Striddledum, straddledum, chicken knee,
Ham, slam, musty jam,
Stingum, stangum, bumble bee.

A Quaint One from Georgia

is given in "Games and Songs of American Children:"

One-amy, nery, hickory, seven,
Hallibone, crackabone, ten and eleven.
Peep,—O, it must be done,
Twiggle-twaggle, twenty-one!

A gentleman from Cambridge, Mass., gives the following one as a favorite rhyme used when he was a lad some twenty-five years ago. There is nothing ancient either in the words or in the theme, but it has the elements of popularity which cannot fail to please some of my readers:

Bee, bee, bumble bee,
Stung Jacob on the knee,
Stung Sally on the snout,
Oh! golly, you are out!

This Cambridge verse reminds me of one sometimes used in Kentucky:

Ole Dan Tucker clum a tree,
He clum so high he couldn't see.
A lizard caught him by the snout
And he hollered for a fella to pull him out!
O-U-T spells out.

Dan Tucker was also very popular as a dance, and the verse was sung by the dancers.

Another nursery jingle sometimes used for counting out is:

Hickery dickery dock
The mouse ran up the clock
The clock struck one
And down he come,
Hickery dickery dock!

But this nas the genuine swing of the counting rhyme:

Haley, Maley, Tipperley Tig,
Teeny, Tiney, Tombo Nig,
Goat throat, bank note,
Tiney, Toney, Tiz!

And this is a familiar old timer:

Five, six, seven, eight,
Mary at the cottage gate,
Eating plums off a plate,
Five, six, seven, eight,

1—2—3—4—5—6—7—8!
Susan at the garden gate
Eating grapes off a plate,
1—2—3—4—5—6—7—8!

Now she leaves the gate, changes her name, and goes to the door:

One, two, three, four.
Kitty at the cottage door,
Eating plums off a plate,
Five, six, seven, eight!

Susan and Kitty are both left out in the following and Mickey takes their place:

One, two, three,
Mickey caught a flea,
The flea died and Mickey cried,
Out goes he!

Mickey had no plate, and evidently it was neither plums nor grapes that bothered him. But a lady from "down East" gives the following in which Kitty takes Mickey's place:

One, two, three,
Kitty caught a flea,
The flea died and Kitty cried,
Out goes she.

This is evidently a version that has been adapted to fit girl players. In New Haven the boarding-school girls have still another variation. They claim that it was mother who caught the pest:

One, two, three,
Mother caught a flea
The flea died and mother cried,
One, two, three!

But no self-respecting boy will use a girl's verse to count out by. So they may use "Mickey" or "Father" in the place of "Susan," "Kitty," and "Mother," or, better still, take another rhyme, for there are plenty of them. The verse most familiar to the author, because with the boys of his acquaintance it was the most popular, is:

Intry, mintry, pepery corn,
Apple seed and apple thorn!
Wire, brier, limber lock
Three geese in a flock,
One flew east, and one flew west,
And one flew over the cuckoo's nest.

Rhymes of Different Nationalities.

Upon the wind-swept mountains of Scotland the bare-legged, kilted descendants of Rob Roy when preparing for a game in the heather count out with this verse:

Eatum, peatum, penny, pie,
Babyioni, stickum stie,
Stand you out there by!

The little Irish lads have a very original rhyme of their own which the author believes few if any Americans have ever heard:

A lirripeg, a larrapeg,
A bee, a nail, a stone, a stack,
A bonny Billie Gelpie,
A Belia-bug, a warum rock,
Crib-i-stery, Hick!

According to the New York *Sun*, Mr. Bolton says that the little Turks and Armenians used this count:

Allem, Bellem, chirozi,
Chirmirozi. fotozi.

Fotoz, gider magara,
Magarada tilki bash,
Pilki beni korkootdi,
Aallede shooullede Edirnede,
Divid bashi
Ben Olayen kehad bashi,

and we suppose that if the counter does not fall ill after the first count or lose control altogether of his tongue from the hard knots that he has tied in it, he continues his "Allem, Bellem, Chirozi" until all the "bashi" have gone free, leaving some little red-capped Mahomedan or Armenian as "It."

The Turkish jingle is all about ghosts in a cave and foxes' heads and other queer things, with about as much sense in them as the English and American boys have in their rhymes. The Bulgarians have one about a strange sort of frog that jumps screaming from fence to fence, and a little white bone. The polite little French boy, as he bows to his companions, counts out in this fashion:

Un, deux, trois,	One, two, three,
Tu ne l'est pas;	Thou art not "it";
Quatre, cinq, six,	Four, five, six,
Va-t'en d'ici!	Go away from here!

The sturdy little Dutchman, in his wooden shoes, counts out too:

Een, twee, een kopje thee;
Een, klontje er bij,
Af ben jij!

While the North German boy has evidently taken his rhyme from the same source we get ours from, for he says:

Ene, tene, mone, mei,
Paster, lone, bone strei.
Ene, fune, herke, berke,
Wer? Wie? Wo? Was?

A verse from India that Mr. Bolton gives also has a familiar sound in it:

> Ha, hoo, too,
> Pooska, bramina padala stoo!

Antiquity of the Rhymes.

Where the ancestors of our present crop of young people found these verses is a question that has troubled many a wise old head, but there seems to be little doubt that the verses which our boys use for play served a far more serious purpose for our ancestors. It is claimed that in ancient Britain, when the wild-eyed Druid priests ruled the people, and built funny sorts of play-houses with stones set up on end, the priests used to sacrifice human beings in their mummeries, and in

> Ena, mena, mina, mite,
> Pasca, laura, bona, bite,
> Eggs, butter, cheese, bread,
> Stick, stack, stone, dead!

the first two lines are the identical words the old priest sang when the victims who had been fattened on "eggs, butter, cheese, and bread," were being killed with "sticks, stacks, and stones."

Possibly some, if not all, of these jingles were originally incantations used by the old humbugs who pretended to practise magic, often fooling themselves as well as the poor, ignorant, awe-stricken, common people by their rites. "One-ry, two-ry, ickery, Ann" is thought to be a gypsy magic spell. There is small doubt that you, my readers, are all unconsciously making fun of your poor, ignorant, old forefathers every time you count out to find who is "It."

And "It"—what did that mean? Well, we will not

make too many guesses into the mysterious rites that the people once thought to be religion; but we will let "It" go, as the boys understand it to be—the most undesirable part of the game that is to be played; and, whether the reader is "It" in the boyish game of "I spy," or in the great game of life, the author feels certain that his reader will play his part with that cheerful, manly spirit that makes a good play-fellow and a desirable citizen.

George Washington was "It" for the Revolution. Abraham Lincoln and General Grant played "It" in the last war; and in both cases it was the nation that counted out to the end that all should "go free."

FIG. 242.—The American Boy's Wooden Swimming Master. Fig. 243 Shows the Bow-line-knot.

CHAPTER XXIII

IN THE WATER

How to Swim—A Wooden " Swimming Master "—Suspension Bridge, Chump's Raft, and Tub Races.

EVERY boy's book, with the exception of the " American Boy's Handy Book," has a chapter telling boys how to learn to swim. This was left out of the " Handy Book " because the author believed no boy could learn to propel himself in the water while sitting in the house reading about it. Such a chapter appeared to him very much like the old bit of advice to " hang your clothes on a hickory limb, but don't go near the water."

Still there are many practical hints that will not be

amiss to those who are already good swimmers, and who are good-natured enough to devote some of their time to their more backward or less fortunate companions. There are thousands and thousands of boys in this vast country who have never seen big rivers, like the Ohio and Mississippi, or beheld the broad ocean, with its white sandy beach and small quiet bays, or the great blue lakes, and whose only chance to swim is in the deep holes of some small stream, a mill-pond, or small lake.

Beginners are just as liable to meet with serious accidents in such places as in the large rivers or the salt sea. For it must be remembered it is not the width of the water, but its *depth*, that troubles a beginner. Fig. 242 shows a simple contrivance that will make it absolutely safe for any lad who cannot swim to go "over his head," as the boys call it when they enter deep water.

It will require work to make one of these swimming masters; but the machine, of any use, is yet to be invented that does not need work to build, and there is nothing in the construction of a "swimming master" that a crowd of boys could not accomplish in a few hours.

How to Build a Swimming Master.

Dig a hole about three feet deep on the brink of the swimming pool. Plant in this a good stout post, six or seven feet long, and see that the earth is packed solidly around the post, so that it will stand firm and immovable. This is called the "ducking post" (Fig. 244). Next select a long pole for the sweep, the length of which will depend upon the extent of the swimming hole. With an auger*

---

* In case you have no auger get a piece of iron rod of some sort, heat it red hot, and burn the holes, or use a chisel and cut square holes.

bore a hole in the top of the post and a trifle larger one through the sweep, at such a distance from the butt, or big end, of the latter, as will allow the small end to reach well out over the deep water (Fig. 245).

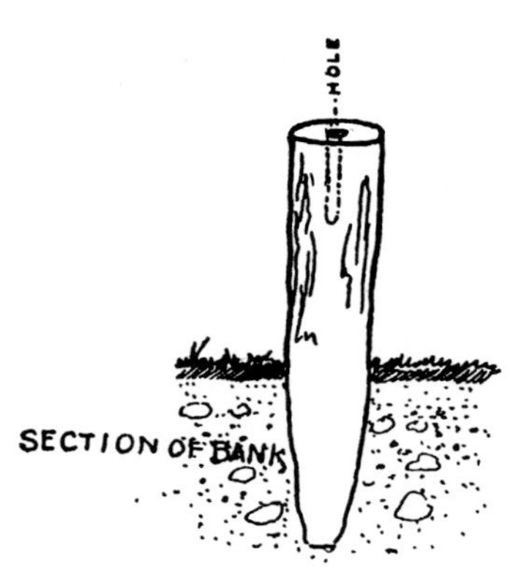

FIG. 244.—Post for the Wooden Swimming Master.

The principle of this machine is a very old one: it is the model of a well-sweep of ancient times. Even to-day a few such sweeps may be seen in old-fashioned farm-yards.

Make a good long hickory or ash peg with a groove in the end that enters the stump. The peg must be large enough to fit tightly in the post. Pour some water in the post-hole and drive the peg home. The groove will allow the water to escape and the water will make the wood swell and hold the peg tightly in place.

To the end of the sweep lash a good strong rope, starting with a clove hitch (see Index) and binding the rope around the sweep. In this case, however, you allow one end to hang down in place of cutting it off. Place the sweep on the ducking post so that the ash peg holds it in place. At the butt end of the sweep nail some boards in the form of a rude box (Fig. 242).

FIG. 245.—Sweep for Wooden Swimming Master.

At this point let

One of the Good Swimmers

strip and swim out to the hanging end of the rope, fasten it into a loop with a bowline knot which will not slip (see Fig. 230). Before drawing the knot tight he should slip the loop over his head and under his arms, making the rope of sufficient length for the weight of his body suspended in the water to lift the butt of the sweep a couple of feet clear of the ground.

While the swimmer occupies this position the other boys must load up the box at the end of the sweep with stones or any heavy material they may have, until the weight of the swimmer and the weight of stones make an even balance.

Ready for the Novice.

When this is done and all the good swimmers have tested it, the small end of the sweep may be swung around and the novice may slip the noose over his head and under his arms and bravely push out into deep water. Here he can flounder and splash after the manner of all beginners until he is tired, or until he learns the trick of propelling himself through the water and of keeping his head above it.

Should the novice be stricken with a panic and try to climb the rope, the weight of his body when lifted out of the water will bring the end of the pole down and he will still have only his head above water. But should he be one of the rattle-brained boys, a boy whose mind is like a badly trained dog that refuses to obey its master in times of emergency, he must not be allowed to work himself into a state of panic, for he can drown even while the "swimming master's" rope is around him. Such a lad needs watching, but most of all he needs just this sort of training to give him command over himself.

In Case of Fright.

When a beginner is seized with fright one of his comrades must rest his weight on the stone box and slowly swing the novice in shore and allow him to regain his composure at leisure.

Never try to frighten a timid boy; it is not only cruel, but you may spoil the "makings" of a good fellow. Some of the bravest soldiers the world ever knew were badly frightened at their first battle, and, no doubt, many an expert swimmer and noted life-saver was seized with terror when first he found himself in deep water. A boy who, because he knows how to swim himself, will try to duck or terrify a beginner has no business to associate with good fellows and should be avoided by them.

Hints for the Beginner.

It is best not to try to swim immediately on swinging out into the deep water. Allow your legs to sink if they will and your arms to hang idly down—the rope will keep your head above water. In this pose loll around awhile until you become accustomed to your surroundings and gain confidence in the sturdy wooden "swimming master" who holds you. This is of vital importance, for without confidence in your ability to keep your head above water you can *never learn to swim*. Even if you put in two or three days in floating around it will not be time lost, and when you begin to experiment with kicking and striking out with your hands and arms you will learn the more readily because you are not retarded by the fear that perhaps your head may go under water for a moment. What if it does? You will come up smiling in place of gasping or shouting for help.

The Frog

is a good swimming teacher, but he has the advantage of us in possessing a pointed head, with bulging eyes on top, so that it is not necessary for him to throw his head back to see. And, as for breathing, one breath every ten minutes answers his purpose. The frog does not use his arms in swimming, as is commonly supposed; he holds them close to his sides, and swims by kicking his long legs and disproportionately long feet.

If you watch a frog swimming you will see that he draws his knees up on each side of him, as shown in Fig. 246, and then pushes them back as if he were pushing something away from him (Fig. 247). And, indeed, that is just what he is doing, for he is pushing the water back. At the end of the stroke his legs are straight and close together,

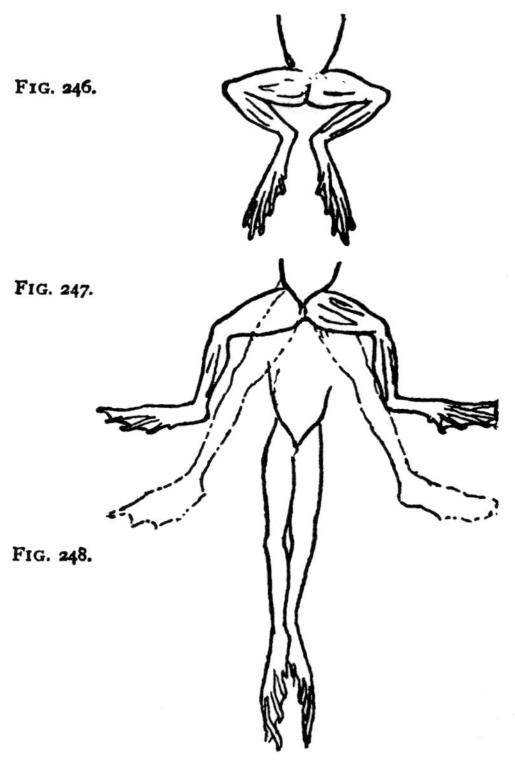

The Beginning and End of a Kick.

his toes pointed down and heels up (Fig. 248). In this position he shoots a long distance through the water before he again draws up his legs for another stroke.

Kicking.

After you have gained confidence in your support, practise the frog's kick. Never mind your arms; it is possible to swim without them, as the frog has shown us. Do not draw your knees up under you, but spread your legs apart like a dancing-jack (Fig. 249) with your knees on each side. This, as has been shown, is the bull-frog's style. He knows his business and will take no points from us, though we may with advantage take some from him. In kicking, strike the soles of your feet against the water as you would against the foot-board, were you lying face downward on your bed, and, like the frog, push the water from you. Finish the kick with the feet wide apart, then bring your legs close together, extending them in a straight line. At this point your toes must be turned down and your heels raised as far as possible, to lessen the resistance as you glide through the water. And glide you will, if the peg in the ducking-post is well greased and the kick properly made.

FIG. 249. — Dancing-jack Showing the Position of Legs for Swimming.

Do not be in a hurry to make the next kick. There is time enough to do that when the impulse forward that the first kick gave is dying out. Many old swimmers make the mistake of hurrying their kick and thus losing speed while making double the exertion necessary.

The Breast Stroke.

Gus Sundstrom, the champion long-distance swimmer and swimming master at the New York Athletic Club, in an article published ten years ago in the *Harper's Young People*, states that "this is the stroke that frogs use and always have used." Well, we will go to Gus to learn to swim, for he is a past grand master of the art. But we prefer to watch a frog ourselves, and by so doing we shall see that he does not use his little short arms, or his funny hands, with *no web* between the fingers. As already stated, he depends entirely upon his long muscular legs and big webbed feet to propel him through the water. So, in place of going to Mr. Frog for the breast stroke, we prefer to go to Gus, for he has no webbed feet and does depend upon his hands and arms to help propel himself.

He says that when you strike out you must "hold your fingers close together." Perhaps one of the principal uses of man's hands in the water is keeping his head up, so that he may breathe, and that is why he makes the stroke a little downward, for by pressing on the water he lifts his head.

How to Make the Breast Stroke.

Bring your hands together under your chin with the palms down, fingers straight, close together, and pointing in the direction you are about to move. Next shove the two hands straight out in front of you, keeping your thumbs touching. As your hands are pushed forward kick backward with your legs, as previously described. When the knees are straight the legs will be spread wide apart (see dotted lines above Fig. 248). Bring them together and, if you time this properly, your position will now be that of an arrow, the point being your extended hands.

In this pose you will shoot through the water some distance, and not until your speed begins to slacken perceptibly must you sweep your hands to the right and to the left with the palms slightly hollowed, and bearing down hard enough to force the head sufficiently above the water for you to breathe through your nose without taking in water. When your stroke is finished, bring the hands back to the same position they first occupied under the chin.

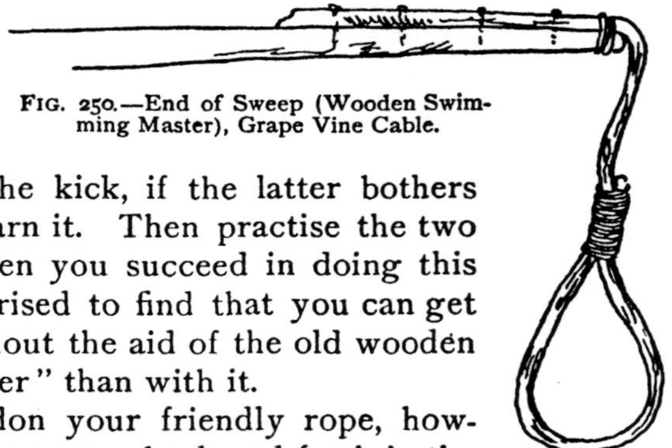

FIG. 250.—End of Sweep (Wooden Swimming Master), Grape Vine Cable.

Practise this stroke without the kick, if the latter bothers you, until you learn it. Then practise the two together, and when you succeed in doing this you will be surprised to find that you can get along better without the aid of the old wooden "swimming master" than with it.

Do not abandon your friendly rope, however, until you have gone back and forth in the semicircle it describes a sufficient number of times to assure yourself that its support is no longer needed.

The Grape-Vine Cable.

If it should so happen that the rope is the most difficult thing to procure, a wild grape-vine will answer your purpose, and it may be nailed securely to the end of the sweep as in Fig. 250, and the loop made by lashing the end to the vine, as shown in Fig. 250.

The Suspension Bridge.

Make two pairs of shears by binding two stout poles together, as shown in Fig. 251, for each pair. Set the shears on each bank, and use a good strong rope or wild grape-vine for a cable. Fasten the cables to a tree, stump, or some other unyielding object on each bank. If it is a rope, fasten with a lark's head, as shown in Fig. 252. If you use grape-vine, wrap once around the tree and nail it there. Erect the shears under it on each bank, and the suspension bridge will be found firm and strong.

Short lines, which will reach the water, must be fas-

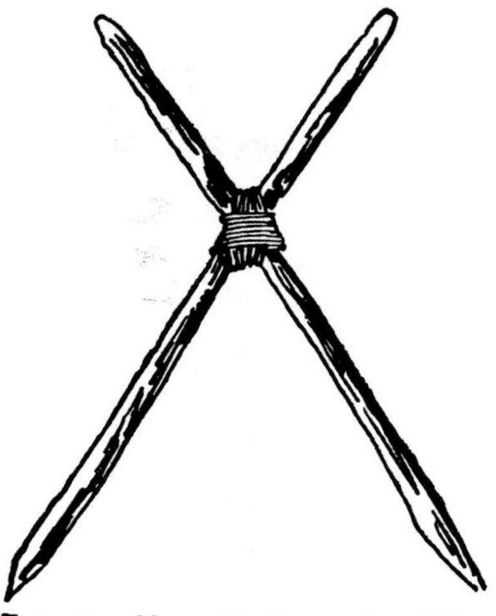

FIG. 251.—Shears for Suspension Bridge for Swimming Pool.

FIG. 252.—Diagram Showing the Suspension Bridge and Cross Section of Ground and Water.

tened at brief intervals to the cable, before it is swung across the stream; little wooden handles tied to the ends of the lines will add to the security of the bather. With this contrivance beginners may enjoy themselves even in deep water, crossing and recrossing the hole with no danger, for so long as the bather holds one of these handles he is supported by the cable above, and by kicking and paddling he can reach another life-line before he lets go the last. Another aid to the novice, and a very useful thing to the swimmers, when they are sky-larking in the water, is

The Chump's Raft.

Its construction is simple. Four boards, each about six feet long, are nailed together in the form of a square, with

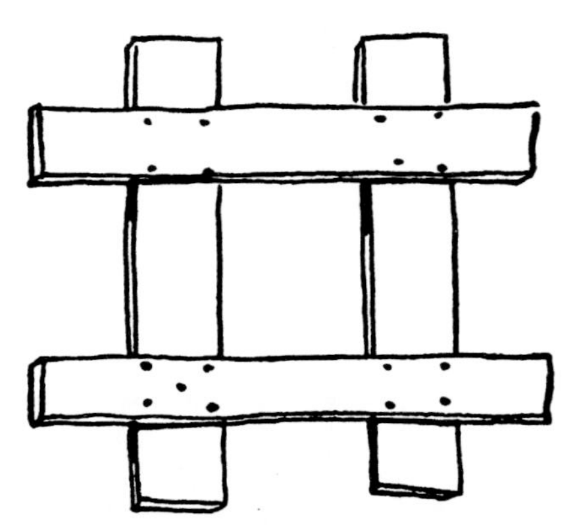

FIG. 253.—The Chump's Raft.

the ends of the boards protruding, like the figure drawn upon a school-boy's slate for the game of "Tit, tat, toe."

All nail-points must be knocked off and the heads hammered home, to prevent serious scratches and wounds on the bather's body when he clambers over the raft or slips off in an attempt to do so.

Beginners get in the middle hole, and there, with a support within reach all around them, they can venture with comparative safety in deep water.

FIG. 254.—A Beginner in a Chump's Raft.

Water Bladder.

While inflated bladders can and are often used by boys learning to swim, in the game of Water Bladder they are used for an entirely different purpose. Water Bladder is a game, and all the players must be perfectly at home in the water, because the "field" is all "overhead." In some deep pool or hole erect two goals after the manner of those used in football. But in this game have the cross rods only a foot or two above the water.

Divide the party into two sides and take your positions as in an old-fashioned game of football. At the word "Ready," the umpire, who is on the shore or at some convenient point, throws an inflated bladder between the opposing sides. The object of the players is to send the bladder over the enemy's goal, and the rules are very simple. It is foul to interfere with an opponent by putting your hands on him, it is foul to use more than one hand in handling the bladder, but you may swim in front of a man, dive under him, in fact, "interfere" in every way you can. Each goal counts one point, and five points make a game.

A similar game is played in the swimming tanks of the big athletic clubs in New York, and is called Water Polo. In place of an inflated bladder these full-grown boys use an india-rubber ball.

Tub Races.

One might suppose that this would come under the head of boating, but one would be mistaken, for it properly belongs to swimming, as any one who has witnessed or taken part in such a race will tell you.

Each contestant supplies himself with an ordinary wash-tub. At the word "Go!" he places it in the water, climbs in as best he can, and paddles with his hands for the taw line.

In most of the races the writer has taken part in the winner was the most deliberate and slowest moving fellow of the lot. He took more time to get into his tub, took more time to balance himself properly, but at last, when more than half the other tubs were upside down and their late occupants floundering in the water, this methodical, cool-headed racer, with his legs hanging in the water, the tub listed slightly forward, began with deliberation to paddle with his hands; and usually, before he reached the taw line he had the satisfaction of knowing that he was the only racer who still occupied a tub.

Sometimes another would pursue the same tactics. Then the fun was at the finish, for here both would risk sinking in their efforts to come in ahead. There is possibly no water sport more enjoyable to all concerned and provoking more laughter and excitement than a well-conducted tub race.

Springing Boards.

Upon all those rivers where the big lumber rafts come down and are moored to the banks, the boys not only have

FIG. 255.—Springing Board.

excellent floats to swim from, but the material is always at hand for a good springing board, from which they can try any circus trick that suits their fancy. For when they fail the worst that can happen is the smart slap of the water as they strike it on their backs or sides, and the hearty laugh of the lookers-on.

There are few better devices for developing and at the same time keeping supple the growing muscles of a boy than a good springing board. At the sea-shore, at boat-club houses and places of resort they are supplied by the proprietors of the clubs and hotels, and are made by carpenters. But when you are inland and in the country, that is the very time you long for one and the very time there are none on hand. All you need to make a springing board is a good elastic plank, and that is seldom a difficult thing to borrow or buy.

How to Set up a Springing Board.

Place the plank on the edge of your swimming pool, and under it a box, log, stone, or any other object strong enough for a rest. Now if two or three lads will stand on the shore end, another boy can spring from the other end into the water. This is a very rude plan, but often the time is too limited to waste in work, and all are desirous of a swim, and a rude springing board is better than none. When you have time at your disposal you may fasten the shore end securely to a board and nail the board fast to a log, beam, or other like object, or drive a number of stakes deeply into the ground with their heads flush with the earth and nail the board to the heads of the stakes. (See Fig. 255.)

Back Somersaults.

In attempting a back somersault from a springing board there is always danger of coming down in the exact spot you spring from, and striking the board, with more or less serious results. To avoid this push yourself away with your feet as you leave the board and there will be no danger.

Never enter the water when you feel exhausted or shortly after eating a meal. You will derive no pleasure from it and it is injurious.

CHAPTER XXIV

GAMES OF TAG

Origin of this Sport—King's X—Last Tag—Iron Tag—Cross Tag—Old Bloody Tom—Bad Man—Prisoner's Base and Other Variations.

WHEN you observe one kitten hiding behind a tree or other object, and another creeping cautiously around in search of its playmate, you see the original and primitive game of "I Spy" as it was played long before there were any boys to enjoy the game. Some ancestors of our kittens invented "I Spy," some ancestors of our puppies invented "Tag," and some common ancestors of four-legged animals invented "Racing." All that the boys have done is to take these games as played by young quadrupeds and make fixed rules to govern them; and from these three simple sports almost all of the out-door games that boys play have been evolved.

Home.

There must be a place of refuge for every one. The wild beasts have their dens in the heart of the jungle, where they can retire in safety; wild men have their secret hiding-places in the mountains or forests; the old pirates had their islands, surrounded by shoals and rocks that would pierce the hull of any vessel attempting to land without a pilot; and civilized man has his home, which is sacred from the invasion of friend or foe, a place to which he need admit no man.

In all games there must be some such spot where the players are safe for the time, where neither the Wolf with

FIG. 256.—A Typical Plan of Various Games of Tag.

a Brown Ear, the Woolly Wolly Wolf, The Black Man, Old Bloody Tom, or "It" can catch him. This place is called goal, taw, den, base, or home.

King's X.

Away back in those times that are so dry to study about in our school histories and so intensely interesting to read of in "Ivanhoe," "The Hunchback of Notre Dame," and "The Black Arrow," King's X had its origin.

FIG. 257.—King's X.

Everything was queer in those days. Men like Robin Hood really lived outside of the pages of a story-book. Foot-ball, golf, and other popular games were forbidden because they might take time that otherwise would be devoted to archery, and the law in England compelled small boys to practise a certain number of hours each year with the long bow.

Men on the streets dressed like the clowns in Barnum's circus, and blacksmiths did a tailoring business; for gentlemen wore iron clothes and heavy iron pots for hats, even under a broiling hot summer's sun, because it was the style. The horses these iron-clothed men rode were resplendent in gorgeous crazy-quilt coverings which reached to their heels.

It is strange how dull a historian can make these interesting old times, when farmers who worked in the fields wore only a shirt to cover their nakedness, and barefooted priests with shaved heads trod the highways; when there were no railroads, no steam-engines, and no telegraphs, kerosene lamps, gas, or electric lights.

It was then that everybody, from the beggar to the king, ate with his fingers; but nobody smoked, because they had no tobacco. Without tobacco they got along very well, but how did they manage to make a meal without sugar, tea, coffee, potatoes, corn, or turkeys? The streets were never cleaned, watered, or lighted, and every house of any pretensions was a fort and the people all knew how to fight. There was among them a dim idea of fair play, and conscious of the fact that the courts were seldom just, they provided sanctuaries or places of refuge where the poor persecuted people might fly and be safe from the law and their neighbors. These sanctuaries were sometimes in the monasteries or churches, and sometimes in the King's house.

All that remains of this quaint old custom of our funny old ancestors is preserved by the boys in their games, and they call it "King's Cross," "King's X," or "King's Excuse," and cross their first and second fingers to proclaim a truce. Here we have a combination of the king and the church that insures the safety of the player.

Notwithstanding the fact that out-door games are largely provided with retreats in the form of goals, homes, taws, or dens, it is often convenient to have some other safeguard to protect the player from "It;" this is supplied by the crossed fingers and the cry of "King's Ex!" As long as the boy giving this cry keeps his fingers crossed he is safe, for to "It," the sign of the cross is sacred.

King's X is used only in times of accident or emergency, for instance when a player's shoelace becomes untied, or when he is disputing some point in the game. Then he cries "King's Ex until I fasten my shoestring!" or

"King's Ex until we settle this," and the truce lasts until the shoestring is tied or the disputed point decided. Often boys of weak character will give the cry and cross their fingers to save themselves from being caught. This is called "the baby act," to show the contempt with which all real manly boys hold a comrade who will seek safety under the cross because his legs are lazy.

Last Tag.

As a crowd of boys are coming out of school one of their number slaps a friend on the back and cries "Last tag!" No boy with any spirit will allow this to pass unnoticed, for that would be against the ethics of a schoolboy. Immediately upon hearing the words "Last tag" the boy struck darts for his nearest playmate and slaps or touches him, crying "Last tag!" and so the game goes on until the boys are tired.

The only rules of the game are these: A touch is a tag and the boy touched last is "It" until he tags some one else; and he cannot tag the boy who has just tagged him.

Iron Tag, Wood Tag, Stone Tag, and Cross Tag.

All of these games are alike in their simple rules and unlike only in their goals or homes. In Iron Tag no player can be caught so long as he has a hand or foot touching iron; in Wood and Stone Tag it is the touching of wood or stone with hand or foot that brings safety from "It." In other respects the games are like the first described games of tag.

Cross Tag.

This game is usually played on the ice by skaters, but it is also played during the summer on the streets or in the fields. "It" selects a victim and starts after him, but whenever another player crosses between "It" and the boy he is after, "It" chases the boy *who crosses his path* and no other unless another boy crosses out the second.

FIG. 258.—Cross Tag. Dotted lines show where a boy has crossed out the lad "It" is after.

Then "It" again changes his pursuit. In this manner the boys continue to cross each other out until "It" succeeds in tagging one before a playmate can cross between him and his prey.

Korungattam or Monkey Tag.

"It" is a hunter who, we may suppose, wishes to supply some hand-organ men with monkeys. At any rate he is a monkey hunter, and all the other players are monkeys. There must be as many trees, stones, or bases of some kind as there are monkeys, and the boys to act their part must keep in constant motion, running from base to base as in the game of Pussy Wants a Corner, while the hunter uses his best endeavors to catch them between their bases.

The bases are supposed to represent the branches of trees and are called branches. No two monkeys can occupy the same branch, and if any monkey stands still for an instant and the hunter catches him while he is not moving, that monkey is "It." The monkeys endeavor by their constant chatter to disconcert the hunter and tantalize him with the oft-repeated rhyme of:

> "Monkey, monkey, bottle of beer,
> You can't catch a monkey here!"

Korungattam is said to be the East Indian name for this game, which is played by the boys in India in the wide-spreading branches of some forest tree, each little Indian occupying a branch of the tree. Like the little animals they are supposed to represent, they jump from branch to branch while "It," the hunter, tries to catch them. A circle is drawn around the trunk of the tree and all the monkeys try to drop to the ground inside that circle. Any one putting a foot outside the ring is "dead," any one ceasing to move is dead, any one touched by the hunter while in the act of climbing or jumping from limb to limb is dead, and the game ceases when all are dead. The first monkey killed is "It," or the hunter for the next game.

Old Bloody Tom, Black Tom, or "Pull Away!"

What the original meaning of this last cry was, is lost in the mist that veils so many of the expressions of boys. Old Bloody Tom and Black Tom are probably names for an ogre, while "It," no doubt, also represents one of these monsters. The game, under any of its names, is a simple one. "It" stands in the middle of the street while the other players are gathered on one of the sidewalks which form the two homes. "It" cries: "Pull away once! Pull away twice! Pull away three times!"

At the conclusion of the last cry the other players make a rush for the opposite sidewalk, while "It" tries to tag them. Each boy tagged joins "It" and helps him tag the others until all are caught. The first player caught is "It" for the next game. No boy can be tagged after he has crossed the home curbstone or while he touches it with hand or foot, unless all the players are on the same side of the street. In this case "It" may tag them while on home-grounds. (See Fig. 256.)

In some places "It" cries:

"One for the money,
Two for the show,
Three to make ready,
And four for to go!"

in place of "Pull away," but the game is the same, and is in no respect different from the following game of "Bad Man," except in the words used to set the boys running.

"What Are You Doing in My Vineyard?" or Bad Man.

"What are you doing in my vineyard?"
"Stealing grapes!"
"What will you do when the bad man comes?"
"Rush right through like we always do!"

This is the whole of the game of the Bad Man. Yet I have had as much fun playing this simple game as any sport of my boyhood that I can recall. We always played it at dusk, and Bad Man on one side of the street calls out the first question. The boys upon the opposite side give the answer as above; then the Bad Man threateningly asks what the boys will do when he comes, and the boys bravely respond with the boast that they will "rush right through like they always do," which, strictly speaking, is not the truth, because it often happens that one of the vineyard robbers is caught half way by the Bad Man, and is then compelled to give up his pilfering and become a Bad Man himself and help guard the vineyard. (See Fig. 256.)

So the game goes on until all are Bad Men. Then the boy first caught is "It" for the next game. The rules of the game are simple. The two curbs form the home lines and the sidewalk is home, or two lines are drawn for home lines. If a boy is on this goal, that is, if his feet are on the home side of the curb or line, the Bad Man cannot touch him, but between the goals if the Bad Man catches him, the boy caught joins this vineyard guardian in chasing his late comrades. (See Fig. 256.)

The simplicity of this last game you will find upon trial in no way detracts from its enjoyment, but on the contrary adds zest to the sport, as the mind being unencumbered with tiresome rules is free to devote its whole attention to the swiftness of the heels.

Prisoner's Base.

War is the probable origin of this sport, and originally the two sides faced each other, but it was found that while in real war the armies oppose each other in two lines of battle, this is not necessary for the game, it being much easier to have only one line occupied by both sides.

Usually in town the curbstone forms the boundary and the sidewalk is home. The boys choose up for side and then select two trees diagonally opposite home for the prison-pens, called the bases, one for each army.

The game begins as the battles did of old by the leader of one army stepping out in the field and daring the other captain to meet him. Any player of one army can tag any one of his opponents who has left home before he did, and all players tagged must go to the prison-pen of their captors and remain there until they are released or until the game is finished.

A prisoner can only be released by one of his own side evading the other soldiers, reaching the base and touching the prisoner before a foe tags the lad attempting the rescue of the prisoner. This done neither can be molested on their way back home, or until they again leave the curb line.

The game ends when all of one side have been made prisoners.

The Den of Wild Beasts—A Jungle Game.

There is no " It " in this game or it might be said that all are " It."

Each player represents some wild and ferocious animal, and each one chooses a convenient tree, post, or stone for his particular den. All then make a terrible noise, the lion roars, the panther screams, and the wolf howls as a signal for the game to commence.

The most venturesome and alert lad leaves his den. Keeping a close watch upon his neighbors he dances around to entice them from their dens and soon succeeds in drawing a crowd to the centre of the field.

The fun then begins. No animal can be captured while at its own den, and no animal can be captured while bringing home a captive. Any animal which leaves its den last may capture any one of those already in the field. If the lion is away from his den and the tiger is not, the tiger may leave his den and give chase to the lion, and if the wolf from his den sees them, he may give chase to one or both. But if the lion in the meantime touches his own den he may start out in pursuit of both tiger and wolf.

It often happens that all the animals are in the field at the same time. Captures are made by tags or touches with the hand. The animal tagged deserts his former den and joins with his captor in pursuit of the others. Often one den will contain a lot of animals, and a few moments later it will be cleaned out by the skill and dexterity of some wolf, panther, or lynx. The game ends only when all the animals are collected in one den and there are none left to capture.

Dixie's Land, or Yank and Johnny Reb.

This is a relic of the last war, and evidently the grandson of the old game of Tom Tiddler's Land, which, during the four years of bloodshed that visited this country, was modified by the boys to fit the occasion. Of course it was a simple matter to change Mr. Thomas Tiddler's Land into Dixie's Land. That change once made, the popular Southern song supplied the rest of the verse.

But as the game represents both the Federal and Confederate sides, there must be taunts for each, more or less appropriate to the occasion. The South supplied one verse, the North supplied another, both taken from old war-time songs, which are now forgotten by most of those who sang them, and, with perhaps the exception of the few lines that are used in the boy's game, are unknown to the younger generation.

As in Tom Tiddler's Land a section of the playground is marked off to represent the land, and after counting out to see who shall be "It" or Johnny Reb, Johnny takes his place on his land, and shouts:

"On Dixie's Land I'll take my stand,
I'll live and die on Dixie's Land!"

This is a signal for hostilities, and all the little "Feds" commence to invade the South. Of course they use what taunts they can to excite Johnny Reb, as

"Eighteen hundred and sixty-one,
That's the time the war begun.
Eighteen hundred and sixty-three,
Georgey Meade beat Robert Lee!
Oh, Johnny Reb, you can't catch me."

Now if Johnny Reb can catch and hold any "Fed" while on Dixie's Land long enough to repeat

"Any, taney, tother, ted,
Now I've caught you little Fed!"

that "Fed" must change his blue coat for a gray one, that is, join Johnny Reb in his efforts to capture more Union soldiers. And so the game goes on until all are caught, with mutual bantering and jingles, historical and nonsensical. The following comes under the latter heading:

"Skeedaddle, vamose,
Counterband goose,
Mason and Dixon's line,
I'll catch you this time!"

To which they reply:

"Jeff wore hoops! Jeff wore a dress!
Jeff has no army now,
Y—E—S!"

And,

"I'm on Dixie's Land,
Dixie's not home.
Dixie's got a sore foot,
And he cannot roam!"

Johnny, nothing daunted at the personal nature of the rhymes, sings out:

> "Mud sills, Mud sills, dirty dealers;
> Blue back, Blue back,
> Barnican Peelers!"

or,

> "If you want to see Yankees just tremble with fear,
> Tell them Johnny Reb has got in their rear.
> Hooray! Hooray! for the people they dread!
> Hooray for Jeff Davis and the Red, white, and red!"

After the Johnnies capture all the players a new game begins, and the first one caught in the last game is "It" for the next.

I felt some hesitancy about incorporating this game among the boys' sports. For, at first thought, it appeared likely to keep the old sectional feeling alive. But, on second thoughts, I believe it has quite the contrary effect, for whoever plays must sooner or later take both sides, and I also notice that the boys find no deeper significance in the game than in any other hereditary sport, and that to most of them there is no more meaning in the verses than in the old familiar button-count:

> "A rich man,
> A poor man,
> A beggar man,
> A thief.
> A doctor,
> A lawyer,
> A merchant,
> A chief!"

So let them play their game of Johnny Rebs and Little Feds, and jumble it up with their queer folk-lore for future wise men to try and decipher and guess its source.

Tommy Tiddler's Land.

Tommy Tiddler represents a miserly old dwarf, the owner of some mineral property. The dwarf attacks all trespassers on his domain. Tommy's land must have been very rich in mineral deposits, for the boys cry:

> "I'm on Tom Tiddler's ground
> Picking up gold and silver."

Sometimes Tommy is the King. Then the boys say:

> "I'm on the King's land
> Stealing his gold and silver."

But whether it is Tommy Tiddler's, the King's, Van Dieman's, or the Ogre's land, there seems always to be plenty of gold and silver. On Dixie's Land, however, if it is anything that they are stealing, it is colored people.

Cow-boys, or Cattle Rustling.

This game descends to us through our Highlander and Lowlander ancestry, and originally represented the struggle between these ancient people over the possession of cattle which had been stolen and restolen so many times that no court could have decided who had a just right to them. Indeed, no court was necessary, for the old-fashioned, bare-legged cattle thieves decided the question in a manner that was always perfectly satisfactory to themselves when they *won*, and more cannot be said of a modern court decision.

It is a slander on the American cow-boy to call this game after him, for the cow-boy is not a cattle thief, though he may sometimes work for one. On the whole, cattle rustling is a perfectly proper name, and the one that should be adopted hereafter in place of cow-boy.

Choose up for sides in the usual manner, and after the sides are made up let each player provide himself with a cow; not a real live cow, but some object to represent one, such as a stick or a stone.

If the game is played in the street, as it usually is, the sidewalks will represent the ranches of the opposing factions, the street will be the battle-ground, and the curb-stones the boundaries. Each side must place its cattle in a line in its own ranch.

The object of each player is to guard the cattle on his side from the rustlers across the street, and to watch his opportunity to "rustle," or capture, a cow from the boys on the other side. Any boy found in your ranch or on the street may be made prisoner by slapping him on the back three times or holding him long enough to repeat "one, two, three." Every prisoner captured takes sides with his captors, and tries to rob his late friends across the street of the very cows he was so carefully guarding before he was captured. The game lasts until all the cows, or all the cow-boys, or both of one side, are captured by the other.

As a rule, this game is played in the twilight, and there are great opportunities for slyly creeping into the enemy's ranch, when they are all busy defending a united attack from your side, or when they are all busy in a raid on your cattle and leave their own unguarded. Your ranch is home for your own side, and no one can capture a rustler on his own ranch, or on his own side of a line drawn in the middle of the street.

There is plenty of racing, dodging, shouting, and laughing; and, in spite of the low state of morals it depicts in our ancestors, as a game Cattle Rustling is a thoroughly moral and enjoyable sport.

"Lil! Lil! Over the Hill!"

This is a Yankee form of Tag or Black Man, and is played with two homes, or goals, with Lil or "It" in the middle. The players line up, half at each goal, with Lil in the middle, on the battle-ground.

At the cry of "Lil! Lil! over the hill!" the players make a wild rush, the boys on each side doing their best to reach the opposite side without being caught, while "It" uses his best endeavors to capture one or more of the players before they can gain their goal. To make a capture, he must slap his captive three times on the back. All captives help Lil to catch their free comrades until all are caught. The first one caught is "It" for the next game.

Wolf and Sheep.

"It" is the wolf, and the boy who is to play this part is selected by one of the numerous methods of counting out. The sheep select one of their number for a shepherd-boy. When this is arranged, the wolf departs to some place of concealment, a short distance from the spot selected for home, or the fold.

When the wolf has concealed himself he sets up a most dismal howling, and the shepherd-boy, followed by his sheep, seeks to discover the wolf, and all the sheep cry "Bah! bah!" As soon as the shepherd-boy discovers the wolf he announces the fact with these words, "I spy a wolf!" Immediately he and all his sheep take to their heels, closely pursued by the wolf. If the wolf catches or tags a sheep or the shepherd before he reaches the fold, the one caught is wolf for the next game.

In Brooklyn the shepherd or any one of the sheep who

spies the wolf, cries "Stand!" At the cry of "stand" all, wolf, sheep, and shepherd, remain stationary until the shepherd counts ten. As the word "ten" is pronounced the spell is broken, and there is a wild race for the fold.

"What Time do You Dine?" or, The Brown-eared Wolf.

Take a piece of old newspaper, wrapping-paper, or any other similar material, and tear it into as many bits as there are players. Mark each piece of paper with a number representing some hour of the day, until there is only one piece left. Mark this piece with the same number as any one of those already numbered.

This will make two of a kind; that is, the papers will read one, two, two, three, etc., or one, one, two, three, four, etc. There can only be twelve numbers, as there are only twelve hours on the clock; but, if more boys are playing, you can make some of the numbers half hours until the required number of papers are marked.

Under one of the twin numbers mark a cross, thus $\overset{4}{\times}$. No one but the lad chosen as marker must see the numbers until they are drawn, and then each player must keep his number a secret.

To draw the numbers the marker places them all in a hat, and each boy in turn reaches in the hat without looking and selects a bit of paper; the piece of paper left in the hat belongs to the marker. The boy who finds that he has drawn the paper with a figure and a cross is "It."

A simpler form of the game is played by omitting the duplicate number and counting out to see who shall be "It." "It" then retires a short distance while the sheep decide among themselves what o'clock they shall each represent.

"It" announces himself in this way:

> "I eat no meat but woolly sheep,
> My stomach is very good;
> It's their blood, I think, that I will drink,
> If caught inside my wood!"

With a cry of alarm all the sheep hasten to form themselves in a ring around the wolf, for, if the ring is not complete before he finishes his verse, he is allowed, by the rules of the game, to catch any boy who is not grasping the hands of two other boys, one on each side. Consequently the end boys of the line hasten to join hands and form the circle.

Now this funny old wolf is hemmed in by his prey, and, in spite of his blood-thirsty nature, he is either not allowed or is afraid to catch anyone until a proper signal is given. The signal is given in this manner: All the sheep dance around the wolf, shouting together this verse:

> "Wolf! Wolf! Wolf with a brown ear,
> Tell us what time you will dine
> On one of the sheep gathered here!"

Then the wolf shouts out "Two o'clock," "three o'clock," or whatever he chooses, and the sheep holding the ticket answering to the time given darts out of the ring with the wolf after him. The wolf cannot call the same number twice. If the sheep can run around the ring three times without the wolf catching him, and regain his place, he is safe, and the wolf sings out again:

> "I eat no meat but woolly sheep,
> My stomach is very good;
> It's their blood, I think, that I will drink,
> If caught inside my wood!"

And the sheep reply, repeating the verse first given. The wolf then guesses another hour, and so the game goes on until a sheep is caught, when the sheep becomes a wolf and the wolf a sheep, and all the boys trade numbers, being careful not to allow the brown-eared wolf to hear them.

In case the wolf guesses the twin number of his own, it is unnecessary for him to catch that sheep, for the sheep becomes a wolf as soon as his number is mentioned, and there are two wolves inside the circle. Happy then is the sheep that escapes them when his time is called.

The Red Ogre.

The ogre appears in various forms in a majority of the children's games, more frequently, perhaps, in the girls' and small children's play than in that of the boys; but even in the boys' sport he is to be found.

It may be that he likes girls and little children best because they are more tender, and avoids boys because they are tough. Probably it was this same ogre, "Old Rawbones," who invented these lines:

> "What are little girls made of?
> Sugar and spice and everything nice.
> That's what little girls are made of!
> What are little boys made of?
> Snaps and snails and puppy dogs' tails.
> That's what little boys are made of!"

If he did I trust he is happy, because these silly lines have made more small boys indignant than any others that I can recall. But, on the whole, one is led to believe that Old Rawbones's ugly face is only a mask that hides a laughing countenance, and that his bloody talk is only a make-believe to disguise his jovial disposition. Other wise, why should he take part in so many games, and always be found on the playground and in the best storybooks?

When the boys have decided who is to be Ogre, the latter hides around the corner, and in his deepest voice growls out these gory lines:

> "I'm the great Ogre Red!
> I will eat you when you're dead!
> I must be fed!
> Your bones are my bread.
> Come, come, and be bled!"

The other players, to show how little they fear the Red Ogre, rush by the corner shouting challenges to the

Fig. 259.—Red Ogre.

monster, who darts out and usually manages to catch one or more of the players. These captives then help him catch their playmates in the following manner:

The players who escaped the Ogre's first rush, retreat to their starting-point. The captives then clasp hands and shout together:

> "We are the great Ogres Red!
> We'll eat you when you're dead!

We must be fed!
Your bones are our bread.
Come, come, and be bled!"

Again the players rush by the corner, while the Red Ogres try to intercept them, as they string across the street with joined hands, and thus the game goes on until all are caught.

In Brooklyn the boys call this game Red Robin, but the rules are the same, and the same game possibly has twenty names in various parts of the United States.

The American Game of Three. Fox and Geese Modernized.

An even number of boys are necessary to play this game. They decide who shall be "It" and who shall be "Three."

The remaining boys form themselves in a double circle or in concentric circles; that is, one ring of boys is inside the other ring of boys, and so arranged that they stand in couples. (Fig. 260.) "It" takes his position opposite the outer circle, and "Three" takes his position opposite to him, also outside the outer ring.

When ready, all the couples join hands, "Three" taking the hand of the boy next to him, and all facing the same way. The boys now shout in unison a jingle making fun of "Three:"

"Three, Three!
Ric, stick, stee!
High ball, low ball,
Long-legged *Three!*"

This is supposed to anger "Three," and he retaliates with a verse of his own. While the boys recite their verse

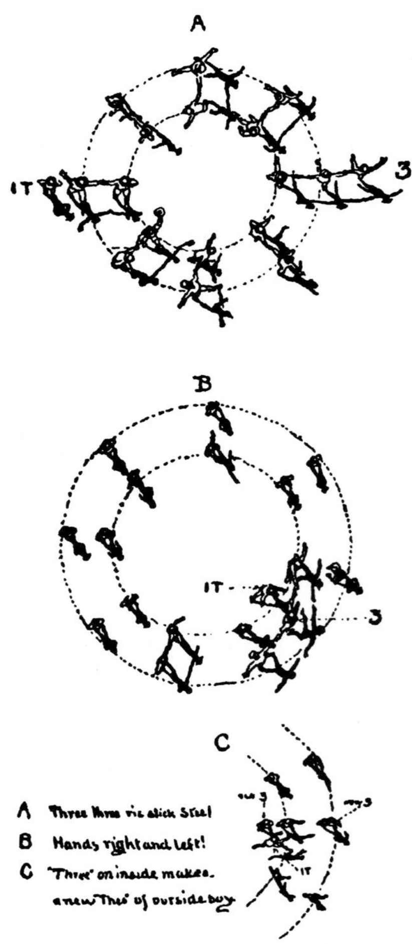

FIG. 260.—American Game of Three.

they march around in a circle, and "It" stands still. When "Three" passes "It" he shouts:

> "There stands he,
> High ball, low ball,
> Red-headed he,
> Will never catch me!"

The word "me" is the signal for the circle to come to a stand-still and for "It" to dash after "Three," who must run around, outside the ring, at least once, after which, if hard pressed, he may shout: "Hands right and left!" Then he grasps the right hand of the boy nearest to him with his right hand, and the left hand of the next in order with his left hand, one hand and then the other, right and left, as in a square dance. (B, Fig. 260.)

"It" follows close at his heels, going any way he can and watching for "Three" to make a mistake. If "Three" gives his right hand when he should have given his left, or his left when he should have given his right, and "It" touches him before the mistake is rectified, then "Three" is "It," and the game begins again. But if "Three" gets out of breath he may suddenly stop on the inside of the circle next to one of the ring boys. This move puts the outside boy of the couple next to which "Three" stands outside the circle. (C, Fig. 260.) The outsider then becomes "Three" and "It" must try to catch him.

In case "Three" is caught while running, the outside boy that he stood next to when the game commenced is "Three," and "It" takes his place, while the late "Three" becomes "It."

It is a noisy game, furnishing plenty of exercise of muscle and ingenuity, and the jingle, as it is changed to suit the different players, creates any amount of laughter. Sometimes it is "Little dude three," "Freckled-face three," "Long-nosed three," "Short-legged three," "Curly-headed three," "Pretty boy three;" and "Three," when he sings his verse, retaliates upon poor "It" with some apt or comic allusion to this particular boy's peculiarities. "It" always stands stock-still until he hears the word "me."

Bull in the Ring.

"It" in this game is the most sought-for position, for "It" is the bull. After it has been decided who shall be the bull, the other boys all join hands in a circle around him. The bull then examines the different hands where they are clasped together, asking: "What is this lock made of?"

"Brass!" answer the boys.

"Well, brass is strong. What is this lock made of?" he again asks of the owners of two other clasped hands.

"Iron!" they answer.

"And this?"

"Steel!"

"I think I can break steel;" and making believe to try, the bull suddenly turns and breaks his way through the circle where it is unguarded and runs with all speed up the street with all the players running pell-mell at his heels. The boy who catches the bull is bull for next game.

FIG. 261.—Bull in the Ring.

It must not be supposed that the bull always succeeds in breaking through the ring the first time. Sometimes the locks of brass, iron, gold, or even lead are too strong for him, and he makes believe examine some other locks, while the circle of boys jeer him, and tell him that he cannot escape. But sooner or later he breaks through some weak point in the ring and scampers away. If the bull is a fast runner he often leads the boys a long chase, over the fences and through back-lots of the city; or, if the ring is in the country, through pasture-lots, where real bulls gaze in wide-eyed wonder at the scampering boys, through the woods, with the rabbits and gray squirrels flying ahead, and over the brooks, where the speckled trout hide under the banks. Over fences and ditches, with never a stop, the bull rushes on until he is at last headed off and caught.

Then all go back to the playground, and a new ring is formed with the victor for a new bull, and new locks of brass and iron are forged to keep him in the ring.

CHAPTER XXV

I SPY

With Instructions also How to Play Hunkety and Kick the Wicket.

WHEN the world was young the little folks played I Spy, and the game is still popular, and will be, I venture to say, as long as there are young people to play it, even though the world becomes old and gray in the meantime.

And, if there are no children left, the young beasts of the forest will play it as they do now. A pair of young foxes once owned by the writer never seemed to tire of playing I Spy. First one would hide and then the other, and great would be the race when the hider was discovered. The race generally ended in a rough-and-tumble fight and then the game was started afresh. They had no rules determining which should be "It" that I could discover, nor did "It" count a hundred with his eyes shut to give the other a chance to hide as a boy does. Nor was the young fox intelligent enough to use the unfair methods of counting sometimes employed by boys. For instance, when "It" agrees to count one hundred, and the other boys are seeking a hiding-place, they are sometimes caught unaware when "It" shouts "Ten, ten, double ten, forty-five, and fifteen!" opens his eyes and goes in search of his half-hidden playmates. Any hider gaining home before "It" can do so is in free, and generally announces the fact by shouting as he runs. "In free! in free!" But if "It" spies a boy, calls his name, and reaches home first, the boy is caught. The game goes on until all are in free or caught. If "It" fails to catch one, then "It" must be "It" for the next game, but if he catches one or more boys, the first one caught is "It" for the next game.

As Played in the Evening.

As this game is played in the evening, or after dark, it is frequently difficult for "It" to distinguish one boy from another. This difficulty is often increased by those hiding turning their caps and coats inside out or exchanging caps and hats, and purposely allowing the disguised heads to appear from behind a tree or the front steps of a house. When the boy who is "It" sees the head and recognizes the covering, in nine times out of ten he will be deceived, and cry out, "I spy Tom Jones!" when it is really Billy Smith with Tom Jones's hat or cap on. In this case both Jones and Smith are free. Usually, while this affair is going on, several others slip in crying, "In free!" and "It" learns by experience to be more cautious the next time. The exchanging of hats and coats or the turning of them inside out adds greatly to the difficulty of detection and to the interest of the game.

Freeings.

If the last hider to come in succeeds in reaching home without being caught and cries "Freeings!" then all go out and hide again, and "It" is "It" for another game.

Hunkety: A Long Island I Spy, with a Wicket.

After "It" has been chosen by one of the usual methods he selects a tree, fence, lamp-post, or the corner of a house for his den, home, or goal. First leaning a stick against home, "It" turns his face to his den, and, covering his eyes with his hands, counts five hundred by fives as rapidly as possible, while the other boys run and hide.

At the end of the count he shouts "Five hundred, com-

FIG. 262.—Long Island Hunkety.

ing, ready or not!" As in ordinary I Spy, or Hi Spy as the boys term it, "It" searches for the other boys, and when he discovers a playmate he rushes home to his den, and, placing his hands upon the goal, shouts "One, two, three!" and calls the boy's name that he has spied. If the hider discovered by "It" does not reach home or kick the stick over before "It" finishes his sentence the hider is caught, and "It" goes out to seek the others, and the game goes on.

"It's" power to move is governed by the stick, for, while that is down, he is not allowed to spy any one. Consequently he guards the stick with great care for fear some hider-out may rush in and kick it over. When a hider-out succeeds in kicking the stick over without being caught, then those who have previously been caught are free, and all that are in go out and hide again while "It" is fixing the overthrown stick.

Often one of the players will hide within ten paces of the den, and as soon as "It" leaves his goal the boy inside the ten-pace limit rushes in, kicks over the wicket, and is free. To guard against this last move "It" sometimes shouts "Anybody hiding around my den is 'It.'" The boy, if there is one, who is hiding within the limit of ten paces is now "It," and the former "It" goes out and hides. Frequently it happens that the last boy out succeeds in knocking over the stick before "It" can prevent him. This, of course, frees all that have been previously caught, and all rush out and hide again.

When at last all the boys are caught or in free a new game is started with the first one caught in the last game for "It."

Kick the Wicket.

This is a game of Flushing, Long Island. The boy who is to be "It" is decided upon after the manner in vogue with the boys, and the rest take their numbers according to the order in which they call them. "I choose number one!" shouts one boy. "Two for me!" cries another, and so it goes until all are numbered.

Then "It" places the wicket, which is simply a stick, against a tree. Three other trees are selected for bases. Number One gives the wicket a kick and sends it as far as possible and runs for the first base, while "It" hurriedly chases the wicket and replaces it with all possible speed. As soon as the wicket is in place the runner is supposed to be suddenly stricken with paralysis, or is enchanted, so that he can move neither hand nor foot. If perchance the runner is detected by "It" in lifting a toe, he must take "It's" place.

The enchantment can only be broken by Number Two kicking the wicket. When Number Two has sent the wicket flying he runs for the first base and Number One for the second, provided he has reached the first base before he became enchanted, and both continue to run the bases until the spell is thrown over them by the magic wicket being again replaced against the home-tree by "It."

The object of the players is to run all three bases and home again, and the object of "It" is to prevent them from moving at all. Often it happens that all the boys are bewitched at one time between the first and home base. In this case they must endeavor to steal along until one reaches home without being detected by "It," in which case he kicks the magic wicket, and sets all his comrades in motion again. But this is a very difficult feat to perform, because "It" is lynx-eyed and he will if possible keep close watch and as soon as he sees a boy move cry,

"I saw you stir,
Yes, sir!
Don't say nit,
You're 'It.'"

Nevertheless it sometimes happens when the boys are well scattered that little by little they will steal ahead until one can reach the wicket and give it a kick, which he is entitled to do if he touches home base before being detected by "It."

In Brooklyn, when all the players are enchanted between bases, "It" is compelled to kick the wicket himself. This he does reluctantly, making many false passes first in order to deceive the players and cause them to move.

This interesting and queer game is new to the writer, though without doubt it is as old as all the others, and only chance has prevented him from becoming acquainted with it until he took up his residence in the old Quaker village of Flushing. The game savors distinctly of the old times, when people believed in fairies, gnomes, witches, and magic spells.

CHAPTER XXVI

LEAP-FROG.

Teaching the Game to the Esquimaux — Foot-an'-Half—With First Back and a Leader — A Game Requiring Skill — Spanish Fly —The Danger of Quarrelling—Dick's Hat-band.

When Mr. Landon Gibson was with Lieutenant Peary on his polar expedition he often had very jolly times with the hardy, good-natured, ice-dwelling folk of those cold climes. Among other things the explorers taught the natives the game of leap-frog, and used to have great fun allowing the little fur-clad, laughing Esquimaux to go straddling over their bent backs. It is possible that all of those in the polar region now know how to play the game, for the sport pleased them beyond measure, and no doubt they took advantage of the first opportunity to teach it to all their neighbors.

How to Play Leap-frog.

However, the Esquimaux will not read this book, and there may be some poor little chap so unfortunate as to be born and bred in one of our big cities, whose careful parents have had tutors for him in place of sending him to school, and whose life has been narrowed in various ways by his surroundings, so that he has never taken part in a game of leap-frog, or seen it played. For this unfortunate, possible boy it is well to explain that this simple game is performed in the following manner: One boy, with his back to the player, stoops down and rests his hands on his knees. This is called

"Giving a Back."

The other boy places his hands on the first boy's back and leaps over him by straddling his legs wide apart on each side like a frog. The second boy then assumes the stooping posture and the third boy leaps over the first and second, and the fourth over all three, one at a time, of course.

This goes on until there is no boy left who is not stooping. Then the first boy's back straightens up and he goes leaping over his fellows and again gives a back, while the second one follows, and so on until they are all tired and the game ceases.

FIG. 263.—Leap-frog.

Foot-an'-Half, or Foot and One-Half.

The foot mentioned in this title is not the foot marked on a United States standard rule, but a boyish foot enclosed in a rusty shoe and owned by the leader in the game. The boy who is

"It" in this game is called First Back. He stands at a taw line and gives a back. The leader is supposed to be the best jumper in the game, and is selected by the First Back for this reason. He tells First Back the height to hold his back and places his hands on First Back's shoulders, gives a leap, spreading his legs, and over he goes. Where the leader's heels strike he makes a mark, and First Back takes his position at this line, astride the line and with his side toward the taw and the other players. All the other boys stand at the taw line and one after another jump over First Back.

FIG. 264.—Foot-an'-Half.

When the leader's turn comes around again he makes another jump, not from the taw line but from a point a foot and a half in advance of the first starting point, measured with his own feet. Again he marks where his heels strike, and First Back takes his position at this mark.

This goes on until one of the players fails to clear First Back, usually tumbling him over and rolling both together on the ground. The player who fails is "It," or First Back, for the next game. Any player may direct First Back to give him a high, low, or medium back before he jumps. Usually each boy calls for as high a back as the leaper thinks he can possibly jump, each player taking pride in making good jumps and being loath to call for a low back unless the distance is great.

Any jumper is allowed to place the middle of his foot on

the line, but more than that in advance of taw is called "toeing over the line." If a boy alights with one heel on the taw side of the line which First Back is straddling, it is called "heeling behind the line." Any one of these errors, or jumping out of turn, may "bring a player down." Generally some one shouts "Something up," and if he first names the error the boy who is caught becomes First Back. If the right error is unnamed the game proceeds.

Foot-an'-Half, with a Leader and a Foot-an'-Half.

Count out to find who shall be "It," or First Back. The First Back then selects the *poorest* jumper for leader and a good player for Foot-an'-Half, or "header" and "footer." The object of this arrangement is evident when the game proceeds, for it soon becomes plain to the dullest observer that Foot-an'-Half is First Back's friend and is doing his best to set tasks that it will be beyond the powers of the leader to perform.

First Back stands with one foot on each side of the taw line, with his side toward the players, and "gives a back." The leader, followed by all the other players in turn, jumps over First Back. Foot-an'-Half, coming last, jumps as far as he can and marks the spot where his heels strike by a line drawn parallel to the taw line. First Back moves to the line drawn by Foot-an'-Half, and, placing a foot on each side of the line, again gives a back.

The leader may now take a foot and a half measured by his own feet from taw, or take a step beyond the taw line, if he deems the distance too great for a single jump. But should any one of the players following the leader be able to make the jump from taw, the leader becomes First Back and the game commences over.

With good players and a good Foot-an'-Half the distance of First Back from the original taw line sometimes becomes so great that a successful jump is only accomplished by taking a hop, skip, and a jump from the starting point, marking the spot where the heels strike, or three jumps and a hop and making the final jump over First Back from this mark. First Back stands high or low as he may be directed by each player in turn.

Par

is a game of Foot-an'-Half in which the leader marks his jump, which each boy following must equal or exceed. After all have marked their jumps, First Back measures a foot and a half from taw line and takes his position at this point; the leader now jumps from taw over Foot-an'-Half and he must surpass all previous jumps. Failures bring the culprits "down."

Spanish Fly.

After settling who is to be leader the boys start the game as in the preceding by the leader placing his hands on the shoulders of First Back and leaping over. As the boys go over in turn some good player, desiring to win glory for himself and to increase the fun, shouts "Spanish fly!" before he touches.

Up to the moment that the player makes this announcement it is supposed to be an ordinary game of Leap-frog or Foot-an'-Half. But now all realize that excitement and difficult feats are ahead of them. The next time the self-appointed leader goes over First Back he cries

"Torchlight!"

and jumps with only one hand on First Back's shoulders, while with the other he waves his cap for a torch. All the otner players follow suit, and encouraged by their applause the leader selects more difficult feats to perform.

"Hats on Deck!"

he now shouts, and placing his hat or cap on First Back's shoulders he leaps over without disturbing his head-gear. The next player places his cap on top of the leader's and leaps over it. The last boy in "Hats on deck!" or "Hats in a pile," as some call it, has the most difficult part to perform, often having five or six hats to jump over. Now the last boy makes another jump and takes his hat off the back without disturbing the others, and all the other players follow suit.

If none fail the leader next cries

"Hats Full of Water!"

and picking his hat up he balances it upside down on his head and makes the jump without jostling it off his head. This act being performed by all the players, the leader next cries

"Hats in the Water!"

and jumping over First Back he deftly shakes off his hat on the other side. Each player following must do likewise, without touching another hat with his feet or with his own hat.

When the hats are all in the water the leader must jump over First Back and alight on one foot without touching any of the hats scattered around; and still without coming in contact with hat or cap, or touching his uplifted foot to the ground, he must manage to hop to his own hat, kneel down and pick it up with his teeth, and hop back to First Back, turn his back to taw and First Back, and with a toss of his head send his cap backward over his own head and clear of First Back, toward taw. The touching of another hat or of the uplifted foot to the ground before the last feat is performed, will bring the leader down, or if he touches his own cap with his hands, or if his cap strikes First Back in going over, the leader " comes down, that is, takes First Back's place."

Each of the players must perform the same feat in turn. A failure to perform the part in accordance with the prescribed rules brings the player down and the game begins over. Generally some one fails before the hats reach the water. If not the leader taxes his memory and invention to its utmost for difficult acts to perform, until some one fails, and the game starts afresh.

Spanish Fly is a jolly game, full of fun and noise, two elements that seem inseparably connected; but sometimes the rougher boys introduce rowdyism into the game that eventually results in doubled fists, blows, or bad names. This is the invariable result of such deportment whereever it may be found, and all such acts as "spurings," "knucks," and "ramming the cannon" are to be tolerated only by toughs.

Effect of Bad Names.

Speaking of bad names, which with boys as well as with men are the invariable prelude to a fight, I once saw a little fellow in Kentucky close up the mouth of a low, vulgar bully in a truly boyish, but to me, a most novel and effective manner. Many of the horrid names that a retentive memory had stored in fifteen years of life among the "river rats" were hurled by the bully at the little Kentuckian. The latter turned pale, hesitated a moment, while a crowd of boys looked curiously on to see the result. It was evident to all that the little fellow would stand but a poor chance for victory in a scuffle with the bandy-legged, broad-shouldered young tough from the levee on the river front. Yet, at first, it appeared as if the smaller boy meant to fight, for his little fists were clenched as if he intended to resent the insult with a blow; but it was only a natural impulse of a brave boy, and was but momentary.

Soon his little fingers unclasped and his hands were thrust carelessly into his trousers' pockets, the color came back to his cheeks, and with a bright smile on his lips, he gently said, "Fen for me, all on you, twice as many as you call me."

This reply was greeted with a roar of applause and checkmated the levee bully, who, low as he was, did not care to call himself all the vulgar names he had applied to the little Kentuckian, and according to boys' etiquette it was evident that the only way he could prevent the names reverting to himself with doubled intensity was by keeping his bull-dog jaws closed.

Dick's Hat-band.

One of the players consents to act the part of Dick; the others are his band, and since all their hats are used in the game the other boys are called his hat-band. Dick's own hat is placed in front of a row of those of his band, which are ranged in a line parallel to a board-fence or dead wall, at a distance of about a foot from it and a couple of inches or thereabouts from each other.

The game is begun by Dick, who, placing the heel of one foot against the toe of the other, and then the heel of the latter against the toe of the other, alternately, measures off from twelve to fifteen of his foot-lengths directly away from the line of hats. At this distance he marks his taw line. He then measures off five more of his foot-lengths and marks the distance line.

Standing upon the taw line Dick tries to toss a ball into his own hat. If he succeeds in doing this he cries "Even score," which is twenty points, the game being one hundred; if he fails, the other players shout "Odd," and each gains a point, while Dick gets a "scratch," which is one against him. Whether he wins or loses, however, he puts his hat on his head and throws the ball a second time, trying to make it drop into the last hat in the row on the right. If he fails, the boy to whom the hat belongs, together with all the players but Dick, again shout "odd," and gain a point, Dick losing one, and the said owner of the hat becomes "Dick," while he who was Dick places his hat to the left of the others. If, however, Dick succeeds in making the ball fall into the hat, he puts it on his head on top of his own, while the owner of the former hat gives a back, as in Leap-frog, at the distance line, and Dick, standing at the base line, tries to leap over him without jolting off either one or both the hats from his head. Should he do this he shouts "Even score" and gets twenty more points; should he fail, the band shout "Odd," and get a point apiece, while Dick has a scratch and loses one, and becomes one of the band, the owner of the extra hat becoming Dick. If, however, Dick gets his "even score," he tries to make the ball rebound into the next hat on the right from the one in which the ball was last, and, succeeding, puts this hat on his head in addition to the two already there, and again attempts the same feat with the owner of the third hat he has successfully performed with that of the second.

And thus the game goes on. As Dick's hats increase in number the other boys try to disconcert him by shouting

"Wig, wag! wig, wag! Dick with a hat-band!" Dick cannot very well carry more than half a dozen hats on his head, and consequently the game is generally limited to that number of players, the odd number, five, being the band, and the extra one Dick.

Much sport may be had at this game. It is simple and yet requires considerable skill and activity to play it well. An ordinary tennis ball, or, better still, a child's rubber ball, is the best one to use. The score may be kept by marking it down on the wall or fence with a bit of chalk, or each player may have a shallow hole in the ground in which a bit of stick is put for a point and a stone for a scratch.

CHAPTER XXVII

VARIOUS SPORTS FOR HOT DAYS

Jack's Alive!"—Spirit Tortoise and Dead Turtles—Jack and the Candles—Bowlder On, or Duck on a Rock—Nine and Ten Pins—Skittles, Ancient and Modern.

HAVING built a small bonfire in some vacant lot, all the boys squat around it like so many Indians about their campfire. A cork on the end of a stick is thrust into the blaze and allowed to remain there until it becomes well lighted. Then by using the stick for a handle one of the boys withdraws the cork and, blowing out the flame but leaving the red glowing end of the cork, exclaims

"Jack's Alive!"

and passes it to the next boy to the right. This boy blows the cork to see that the end still glows and repeats the words, "Jack's alive!" as he hands it to his companion at his right.

FIG. 265.—Been Playing Jack's Alive.

As the hot end becomes duller the boys pass it with greater haste, each repeating, "Jack's alive," until the time arrives when no amount of blowing will bring to life the dead embers on the cork. Then "Jack is dead," and the boy holding the dead Jack must submit to having the score marked on his face. One black mark only can be made for one dead Jack. The first mark may be on one side of the player's upper lip representing one-half of a mustache.

The cork is then again placed in the fire while the boys sit around and wait for Jack to come to life again. Then the cork is again passed around with the same remarks, until Jack again expires and another lad is decorated with the half of a mustache or a big black eyebrow or a round black dot on his cheek.

When Jack shows a ruddy red light he is passed along carelessly, but as his light pales it is laughable to see with what haste the boys shout "Jack's alive!" and pass the dying ember on to the next player.

Spirit Tortoise and Dead Turtles.

There is no necessity of counting out in this game, for all are "It." The game commences by each lad choosing what sort of turtle he intends to represent. "I'm a soft back!" "I'm a snapper!" "I'm a mud turtle!" "I'm a diamond back!" "I'm a red belly!" and "I'm a land tortoise!" they shout. Then they all squat down in a row, resting their chins on their knees and crossing their hands, each holding his right foot with his left hand and his left foot with his right hand.

A short distance from the line of boys is some object, a fence or wall, which they have decided upon as their taw line or goal. It is the object of all the turtles to waddle along without removing their hands from their feet until they have touched goal and returned to the starting point. When all are ready they shout out a comical verse, which is probably intended to represent the awkward motions of the turtles by words—

"Kumbo, kuzetoo, rungetoo, zee!
When we start, fun you'll see!
Wiliy, wally, wully, wake!
See this turtle take the cake!"

At the word "cake" all start in their queer race amid general laughter, boasting, and banter. Sooner or later some one of the boys is certain to loose his grip on either one or the other of his feet. Then the others shout "Dead turtle!" and the player whose hand slipped must lie motionless where he is until the return of his more skilful companions.

The first racer who reaches his goal and returns successfully is the victor, and is supposed to be endowed with supernatural powers. After reaching the starting point he goes back to the dead turtles, and of each he makes the same inquiry, "Dead turtle, what are you doing there?"

Now, while all who fail are considered dead, yet they are not supposed to be deprived of the power of speech, and so no one is surprised when the dead turtle answers in these words: "I am waiting for the spirit tortoise to blow life into me." The victor, or spirit tortoise, still retaining fast hold of his feet with his hands, manages to waddle around the dead turtle, repeating these mystic lines:

"Hunyab, Punjab, chiz row zie,
I bring life to all near me!
I touch a turtle on the snout,
Life blows in and death blows out!"

Loosening his grasp on one foot for an instant, the spirit tortoise touches the nose of the dead turtle with his finger, and instantly the dead turtle returns to life, grasps his right foot with his left hand and his left foot with his right hand and wiggles back to the starting point.

After the victor has restored all the dead to life he manages to regain his position at the starting point and the game is finished.

It is no easy matter to win in this game, and the victor

must have the pluck and force of character to hold hard with both hands, no matter how great the temptation to let go and be a dead turtle.

This game is said to be of Indian origin. In the Indian game neither the turtles nor the tortoises repeat verses, but in other respects it is practically the same as the Indian tortoise race.

Jack and the Candles.

"School is out and it will be hours before it is dark. What shall I do to fill in the time?" says the healthy boy.

FIG. 266.—Jack and the Candles.

Well-meaning parents sometimes answer: "Come home, be washed and dressed, and go out with nurse for a walk."

Old Mother Nature says: "Shout, run, jump, and have a rollicking good time. After a good romp you will need no walk and no nurse. You can wash yourself as clean as soap and water will make you, put on your good clothes, and eat as hearty a meal as your parents can provide; study as hard before bedtime as your young mind is able, sleep as soundly as good health will admit, and wake up as bright as a dollar next morning."

It is hard in cities to find games that can be played in the awful presence of cable and trolley cars and big brass-buttoned policemen, none of whom have much sympathy with boys or their sports, but there are few places, even in crowded New York, that have not a comparatively quiet side-street near by where such a game as Jack and the Candles can be played with little danger of the direful interference of the street cars or policemen.

Choosing the Master.

There ought to be at least half a dozen boys in the game. One boy is chosen for master by drawing straws previously described; the boy holding the longest straw is "master," and the lad with the shortest straw is poor "Jack." The game begins by the master sending Jack after some candles.

"Jack!" calls the master in a domineering manner. "Yes, sir," answers Jack, meekly. "You lazy rascal, come here!" "Yes, sir," replies Jack, edging cautiously up. "We expect company to-night, and need more light; go and fetch me some candles." Jack, apparently glad to escape from the presence of his master, hastens away. While Jack is out of hearing, the other boys range themselves in a row on any convenient seat, and each selects a name for himself, as "Baked Beans," "Tripe," "Onions," "Mutton Chops," "Mush," "Sauerkraut," "Plum Pudding," or any other set of names they may choose.

After all have chosen names and told them to the master, the latter, in a loud tone, summons Jack, who, of course, comes back empty-handed. This apparently enrages the master, and he threatens Jack with a pocket-handkerchief that has a knot in one end. Jack begins to make excuses, saying that he went to the hardware shop and the clerk told him he had nothing in light ware except tin lanterns; at the bakery they told him that the only light they had for sale was light bread, and the blacksmith told him to light out, and some one else said that if he did not snuff himself out mighty quick he would let daylight through him, and the butcher that he would sell him liver and lights, etc. In fact, Jack tries in his excuses to be silly or witty enough to make the other boys laugh. The master then tells Jack that he is light-headed enough to answer the purpose, and since he has brought no candles they must eat in the dark. Then he commands him to bring on the "sauerkraut," or any other name chosen by the boys.

It is

Now Jack's Duty

to select the one of his playmates whom he thinks may have chosen sauerkraut for his name. If the servant fails, as he is most likely to do, Jack is told to get up on the back of the boy he has selected, and that boy passes sentence on the unlucky servant in this manner: "Master, let him have three hard eggs and three soft eggs," or "four soft eggs and two peppers," always limiting the amount of the dish to six. For soft eggs the master gently flaps Jack on the back with the loose or soft end of the handkerchief; for hard eggs he applies the knotted end; for pepper he snaps the handkerchief at that part of Jack's clothes which is drawn the tightest, after which he is told to try again and to bring on some other dish named.

But if Jack selects the boy whose name has been called,

then that boy must mount on Jack's back and Jack passes the sentence and the master administers the punishment accordingly, giving him pepper, soft or hard eggs, as the case may be, after which Jack becomes master. The master takes his place in the line, and the boy whose name was guessed becomes Jack and is sent for candles, while the

FIG. 267.—Hard-boiled Eggs.

others choose new names, and so the game goes on. Each boy in the line is careful, as a rule, not to make Jack's punishment too severe, for fear Jack may guess his adopted name and pay him back in his own coin.

In many cities in the United States there are hundreds of Jacks hunting for candles every summer evening, and some that I have heard of have become so proficient in their part and create so much fun by their witty excuses that the merry shouts of boyish laughter that greet their remarks may be heard for a block away. And some boys make excellent masters, imitating with rare ability the harsh, unreasonable language of a churl in authority, while Sauerkraut, Baked Beans, Pickles, and Mush sit in a line on curbstone or fence and applaud their young dramatic stars.

Bowlder On; or, Duck on a Rock.

It was hot. The boards of the lumber-piles visibly shrank and lost color under the direct rays of the sun. The yellow-clay banks of the river dried and cracked until what was lately mud now appeared to be a mosaic work of irregular flat stones. Between the bricks of the uneven sidewalks the ants were busy piling up little cones of dry pellets of yellow earth. The angle-worms had retreated so far below that a spade would scarcely reach them, and on the gate-post the song sparrow perched himself, that being the most exposed and unprotected spot available, and there he gleefully sang his little tune. In the vacant lots the bumble-bees buzzed and feasted on the red clover that grew among the weeds.

Where were the boys on this hot day? All were in swimming, except those who had already soaked themselves in the water until the ends of their fingers shrivelled up like a washer-woman's. And these lads were gathered under the wide-spreading branches of a giant oak playing "Bowlder On," the local name for "Duck on a Rock," and the author of this book was with them gaining his first knowledge of the charms of this simple but popular game.

How the Game is Played.

It is not customary to count out for the one who is to be "It" in this game. As soon as the game is proposed each boy searches for a cobble-stone, and when he finds one announces the fact by shouting "My duck!" The last boy to shout is "It," and he cries "My drake!" and places his cobble-stone or small bowlder on the larger one selected for the purpose and stands guard over his drake.

The other players stand at a taw or scratch line and throw their ducks at the drake with the purpose of knocking it from its perch. Each player who has thrown and missed must recover his duck and run the risk of being caught by the lad guarding the drake. The guardian stands by the rock, but cannot tag a playfellow until the latter has touched his duck. Often all the boys make a rush for their ducks at the same time, each one trusting to luck that he will have the good fortune to escape over the taw-line free, and sometimes they all escape. More frequently, however, some one of the crowd receives a tag from the guardian of the drake, and he must then drop his duck and assume the guardian's place, while the latter picks up the duck and joins the rest of the crowd of duck-throwers at taw-line.

If at any time one of the players succeeds in knocking the drake off of his perch then all the boys scramble for their ducks that are scattered around, and the guardian, or "It," as quickly as possible replaces his drake, for he may not tag any one until his drake is in place.

There is always an appearance of danger in this game on account of the flying bowlders, but the danger is only apparent and is nothing like as real as it is in base-ball or foot-ball. "Bowlder On," however, is quite exciting.

Nine- and Ten-Pins.

Because some people used nine-pins as a gambling game, the authorities thought to stamp out the evil by making the game unlawful. But after the law against nine-pins was passed the proprietors of the bowling alleys hung out signs "*Ten*-pins played here," and as the law said nothing about ten-pins the authorities were unable to interfere. Ten-pins thus became the American game. At first all games with balls and pins as bowls and skittles were out-door games and played on smooth, level grass-plots similar to the old Bowling Green in New York City.

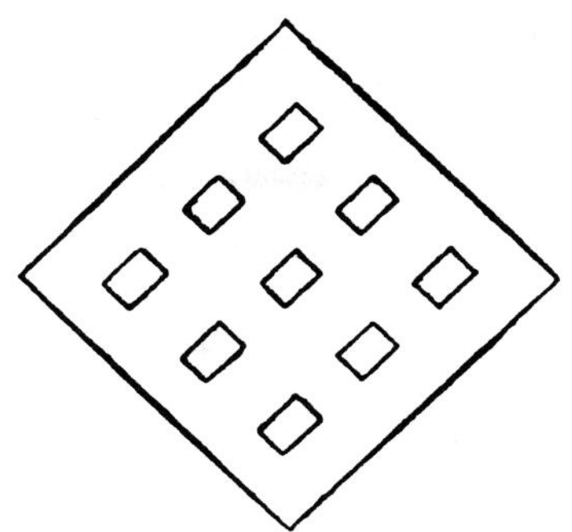

FIG. 268.—Brick Skittles.

Skittles

is an old English name for wooden pins and the game in which they were used. The game of

Bowls

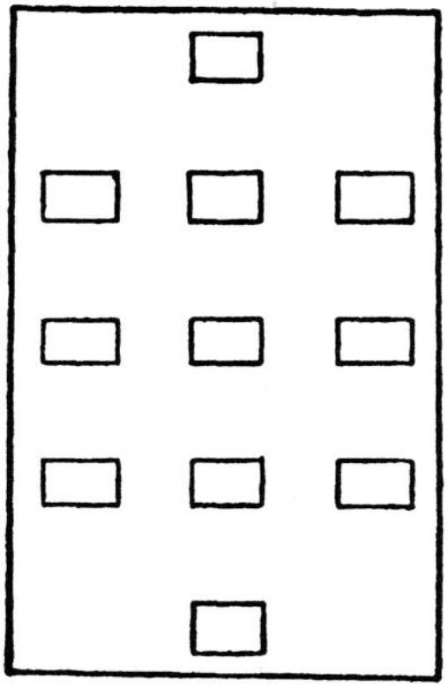

was like a game of marbles, with this difference, that in place of shooting a small marble from the fingers a large wooden ball was rolled at a number of other wooden balls placed some distance away on the green.

FIG. 269.—American Bowls.

British Skittles.

British skittles is a game allied in character to bowls. In the last century skittles was a fashionable game. An old print of 1786 represents a skittle-alley of that period. The alley is fringed with poplars, and has at one end a summer-house. Here three gentlemen in cocked hats read the news and partake of refreshments. More refreshments are carried by a waiter. Old-fashioned "dudes" in cocked hats look on, while a friend rolls a ball at the pins. The moral is:

> "In Reason's Eye the world's a Skittle Ground
> In which mankind will tott'ring pins be found."

Skittles in China and Persia.

The book which is adorned with these reflections is a complete guide to "Old and New Methods of Forming General Goes and Tips," and includes a discourse on the Chinese and Persian modes of playing skittles. From this it appears that skittles in olden times was considered a most scientific affair. The frame (the name of the arrangement of pins) and other features of the game were all calculated on mathematical principles, with arcs and curves and plenty of goodly learning.

The Chinese use twenty-five pins, and the game counts 457 points. The different pins are called Tong-hw, Tsi-shu, Nang-Mw, etc., and refer to the resemblance between the standing pins and a wood or forest. The Persians set up the pins in concentric circles—that is, one circle inside another circle—and use seventeen pins. The ball was like that used in English bowls.

Such are the rude outlines of British and foreign skittles; but mastery of the details of the game can be acquired only by special aptitude and serious application, and is hardly to be attained by an American boy, who has so many equally good games at hand. According to an old English book of games, skittles proper is what we call nine-pins.

Brick Skittles.

Ordinary bricks, or, as the Ohio boys call them, "brick bats," make good skittles, and cobble-stones will make very fair bowls for a game. On a vacant lot or open space draw a diamond-shaped figure and set up three rows of bricks at equal distances from each other. At a distance agreed upon from this "frame" draw the scratch or taw-line, and with your cobble-stones or small bowlders bowl the bricks down as you would the pins in a bowling-alley. Count a point for every brick fairly upset. Make the game as many points as you wish, and take turns in bowling.

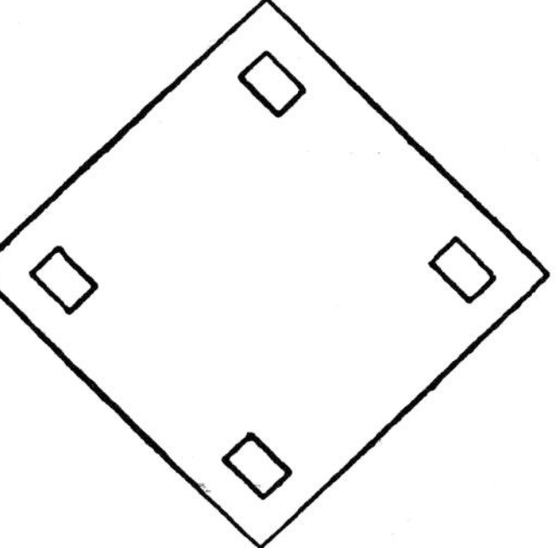

FIG. 270.—Frame of Four Bricks.

Fours

is played in the same way as nine-pins or skittles, with the exception that bricks are used for nine-pins, and that only four bricks are set up in the frame, one at each of the four corners of the diamond.

Dutch Pins.

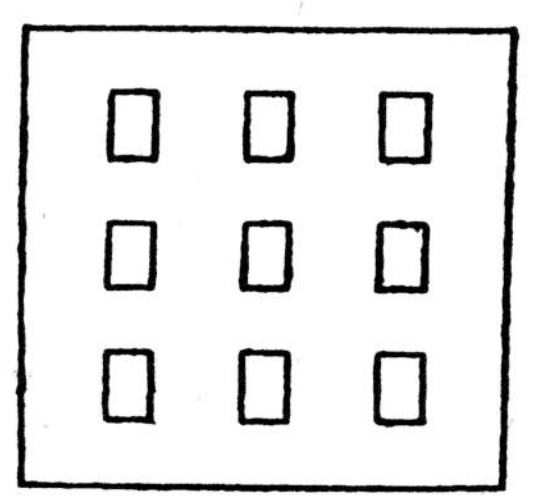

FIG. 271.—Dutch Pins.

In the real game of Dutch pins the skittles are larger and taller than in the other games here described, but as bricks are made of one size you will use the same bricks for Dutch pins that you do for nine-pins, but a square is used in place of a diamond for the frame, and nine bricks are set up in three lines.

CHAPTER XXVIII

TIP-CAT

How the Cat is Made — English-Cat — Country-Cat — American-Cat — A Game Requiring Skill and Quickness.

THERE are many quaint laws in this and other countries that are never enforced, and there are many games in boys' books that are never played. Once on a time the old laws were active and were obeyed; and once on a time some boys somewhere played the old games, but to-day they are dead.

Trap-ball is one of these dead games, but Tip-Cat is a revival of the old game and is anything but dead. Not only does it show signs of renewed popularity, but it is spreading rapidly all over the world where there are boys to play. It is popular all along the Atlantic Coast, in Germany, Italy, and even in Hindostan. Fifty years ago Tip-Cat was practically confined to the rustics in England, and fifteen years ago was uncommon in the United States and unknown in many sections.

The Cat

is a piece of wood about half a foot long and two inches in diameter at the middle, from which it narrows down to a point at each end, forming two elongated cones joined at their bases (Fig. 272). When the cat is placed upon the ground and struck upon either end with a stick it will fly up in the air.

English Cat.

In this game there are from four to eight bases, according to the number of players. Usually the bases are simply holes in the ground, like "rolly poly" or "nigger baby" holes. These bases are arranged on the circumference of a circle at equal distances apart. The Outs take the field, and the Ins, each with a stick for a bat, station themselves at the bases or holes. One of the fielders tosses the cat to the nearest batsman. The latter endeavors to strike it, and if he hits the cat then all the boys on the bases must change places. If the cat has been knocked a long distance they continue to run from one base to another as long as they feel safe in doing so. Each base gained scores a point, but if one of the Outs catches the cat the striker who struck it is out, and if one of the Outs stops the cat and throws it in front of a player after he has quitted one base and before he reaches the other, that player is crossed out.

Fig. 274.
Figs. 272-274.—Cat, Bat, and Player.

When all are out the other side take the bases and have an inning, while those lately at the bat take to the field and toss the cat as before described. When a striker misses the cat he tosses it back to the fielder, and the latter tries another toss.

Country Cat.

Make a ring on the ground as large as a big circus ring, and stand the striker in the centre. The fielder or fielders, as the case may be, stand inside the ring in front of the striker, and toss him the cat. If the boy at the bat misses, it counts nothing; if he hits and fails to knock the cat outside the circle, he is out. If a fielder catches the cat when struck by the stick of the batter, the batter is out.

When the striker succeeds in sending the cat outside of the ring, he carefully measures the distance with his eye, and calls out "Twenty," "Thirty," or "Seventy," as the case may be, and if his call is not disputed, his score is credited with that number. But if the fielders challenge the score, the stick used by the striker for a bat is used as a measuring rod, and the distance is measured from the point where the striker stands to the spot where the cat has fallen.

If it is found that the striker has claimed too much he scores nothing, and resigns his stick to the fielder whose turn comes next. But if it is discovered that there are twenty-one stick-lengths where the striker has only claimed twenty, or seventy-two where he has only claimed sixty-eight, that is, if it is found by measurement that he has not claimed too much, he is credited with the number called and the game goes on.

Where there are more than one fielder they decide among themselves the numbers they take. Number One has the first inning, and Number Two's inning begins when Number One is out, etc.

American Cat.

The American cat is smaller than the Country or English cat, the double cone not being over four or five inches long. If the game is played on the sidewalk, as the boys play it in New York City, a small circle is drawn on the paving stones, where the striker stands; but if the game is played on the bare earth, a hole is made, where the striker stands. It is the duty of the batsman to defend the hole or ring with the stick he uses for a bat, and it is the object of the giver or pitcher to toss the cat in the circle or hole.

If he is successful, the striker is out. If, on the other hand, it falls outside the circle, the striker places the cat inside the ring, strikes it on one end, which causes the little piece of wood to fly up in the air, and before it reaches the ground the striker endeavors to hit it again and send the cat as far as possible.

If he Misses

he throws the cat back to the fielder, who again attempts to toss it into the circle, but if he succeeds in sending it a good distance he does not call his score, as described in Country Cat, but the pitcher offers him five points or ten, as the case may be. The striker, however, is not compelled to accept the offer, and may keep the pitcher bidding for some time, and if his last bid is refused the pitcher proceeds to measure the distance from the circle to the cat in jumps. If he can make the distance in fewer jumps than he has bid, the striker, or the striker's side, loses the number of points named in the last bid of the pitcher, and the striker is out.

Sometimes the score is measured by feet, that is, the length of the pitcher's foot is the unit of measure, or one point in the score. If a fielder or the pitcher catches the cat when struck by the batter, the batter is out.

CHAPTER XXIX

GAMES OF BALL

How Town-Ball is Played—One or Two Old-Cat—House-Ball—Hand Up—Ballie Callie—Crackabout—Over the Barn—Stool-Ball—Corner-Ball—Black Ball—Hat-Ball.

It is almost a waste of space to describe in detail any of the National popular games, such as base-ball, as the rules which govern them for one year will not answer for the next. And, furthermore, there is possibly not a reader of this book that does not keep himself thoroughly posted upon such games. But there is the "father" of base-ball, which is a first-rate game, and not played enough to be constantly changing its form and rules. In England, this game, or its immediate ancestor, is called Rounders, and possibly it may go by this name in some parts of the United States, but in the West it was formerly called

Town-Ball.

The ball and bat used in Town-Ball are both different from those used in base-ball. In place of bases there are corners, in place of a pitcher there is a giver, and the fielders are of any number, with no distinctive names.

The Ball

is sometimes a small rubber ball, such as can be found at most toy-stores—not those of solid rubber, which are generally black in color and too heavy, but the hollow ones of a whitish color. The real town-ball, however, is a home-made affair, consisting of a small ball of tightly wound yarn, usually unravelled by the boys from old yarn socks, and wound up into a spherical form. This is covered with leather that is cut in the form of a three-leaved clover, or may be you will understand better if it is likened to an

FIG. 275, 276.—Town-ball; showing How it is Made. FIG. 277.—Delilling. FIG. 278.

orange-peel when you make three cuts in the orange-skin and then take the rind off without breaking it (Fig. 275). This leather covering is sewed on the ball with shoemaker's thread by means of an awl and a waxed-end, and should fit tightly and evenly without wrinkles. A well-made ball is a work of art that boys are proud of exhibiting and talking about.

The Bat

is either very short, resembling a dwarf base-ball bat (Fig. 277), and is called a "delill," or it is broad and flat after the fashion of a cricket-bat (Fig. 278).

The Corners

are usually three in number, with a home-base, making four, but this varies according to the whim of the players or the locality where the game is played. Ordinarily with three corners the distances are about the same as between the bases in base-ball. In place of home-base there is a rectangle marked on the ground where the striker and catcher stand.

The Giver

stands in the same position that the pitcher occupies in a game of base-ball; but in place of pitching or making the underhand throw, he throws overhand and "gives" the ball to the catcher over the right shoulder of the batter.

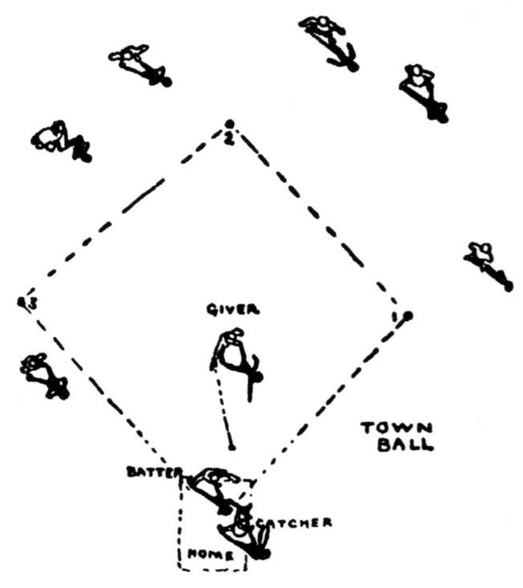

FIG. 279.—Game of Town-ball.

The Batter

stands at the front line of the home-base and holds his bat above his shoulder and strikes from that position, with both hands grasping the handle of the bat, if he is using a flat bat. But if he is using a "delill" he holds it with one hand and allows the swiftly thrown ball to strike his club and glance off at an angle to a part of the grounds where no fielders are on the outlook for it. Every time the ball touches the bat it is considered a fair hit, and the batter must run for his first corner and reach it, if possible, before some fielder, the catcher, or giver secures the ball and "burns" or "stings" him, as they call it when they hit a player with the ball. No one stands on guard at the bases to catch the batter out, and the ball, in place of being thrown to the base, is thrown *at the man running the corners.* When one batter makes a hit or is put out the next batter takes his place, as in base-ball.

The Catcher

stands behind the bat and without gloves, and with no protection for his face or body he catches the "hot" balls the giver sends to him. The balls are not heavy enough to be dangerous.

The Fielders

scatter themselves over the field, according to the directions of the captain, and try to catch or stop all balls from the bat, or those that are thrown at and miss the runners between corners.

When Out.

When a man is out he is out until the next inning, and the game proceeds without him. If a striker sends a ball in the air and it is caught before it touches the ground by the giver, the catcher, or any one of the fielders, the batter is out. If the ball touches his bat it is counted a hit, and if it is caught by any one of the opposite side he is out.

If any one of the fielders, the catcher, or giver make a successful throw at a man running the corners and strikes him with the ball when he is not touching his corner, he is out.

If the batter misses a ball that he strikes at, and the catcher catches the ball before it strikes the ground, the batter is out.

When a man is put out, he is out for that inning, and cannot strike again until the next inning for his side. When all are out but one, that one has a very difficult task to make a score, unless he can make a home-run strike. There are no other batters to help him by sending a "sky-scraper" over the fielders' heads; but he must run his corners while the giver and catcher, standing in their regular position, pass the ball between them. This always produces a great deal of excitement and sport, as all the batter's side coach him, and if he succeeds in stealing a corner or successfully dodges the ball thrown at him, he is greeted by wild cheers from his own side.

Should he at last succeed in reaching home-base untouched, he has the privilege of "putting in" the best batter on his side, and there are then two men in and a better chance to score.

Any number of boys may play in one game, and since all the really necessary properties consist of a ball and a bat, both home made, it makes a game much better suited to boys than base-ball, with all its array of expensive balls, bats, bases, home plates, armor, wire masks, sliding gauntlets, and gloves. As far as skill is concerned, no good town-ball player need hang his head in the presence of the best of base-ball players.

Fig. 279 shows the proper method of laying out the field. In this case, wands, with colored flags on them, are stuck into the ground for corners. These are strong enough, for the runner only touches them with his hand and does not fall all over them, or slide to them, as in base-ball. The distances between bases are regulated according to circumstances and the dimensions of the play-ground.

One or Two Old Cat, Striking Out, or Feeder.

This is town-ball modified to suit the occasion when only three or four boys play the game. Of course a giver, a catcher, and a batter are necessary, but there is usually only one corner for the batter to run. Generally the run is from home to the pitcher's stand and back again. If the game is played with a small ball the runner must be "stung" with the ball; if played with a base-ball, he must be touched with the ball while in the hand of the pitcher or catcher. In other particulars the rules of the previous game govern this. When the striker is on his corner the catcher and giver, or pitcher, pass the ball back and forward, between them, while he tries to run home.

When there is only one striker, the game is One Old Cat; when there are two strikers, it is called Two Old Cat, the game being named according to the number of strikers.

House-ball.

In this game the house takes the place of the pitcher or giver. Two boys, a batter and a catcher, stand facing a blank wall, usually the side of a brick house. The catcher throws the ball against the side of the house and as it rebounds the striker, or batter, endeavors to hit it, and then runs to the house and back home before the catcher can touch him with the ball. If the batter misses the ball and the latter is caught by the catcher, the batter is out, and must take the catcher's place. If the striker reaches the house, but is unable to return before the catcher secures the ball, the catcher throws the ball against the house and catches it on the rebound, and the runner is expected to run in home, or attempts to do so before four balls are passed. Otherwise the striker is out, and must give up his bat to the catcher and take his place behind the bat.

Hand Up.

The blank side-wall of a brick house and a bit of hard, flat ground form an ideal field for Hand Up. With a sharp stick trace three sides of a square on the hard ground in front of the wall, and let the wall form the fourth side and complete the square. These are the boundary lines. Make

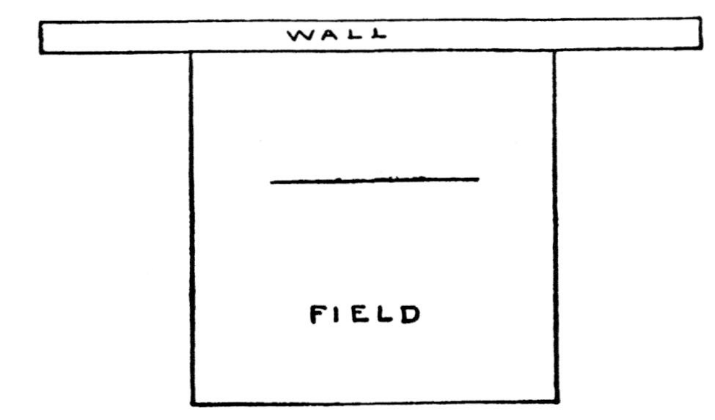

FIG. 280.—Hands Up.

another line on the wall, three feet from the ground, and a taw line, nine feet from the wall, on the ground, and you are ready to choose up for sides or toss for "first hand up." You may have one on a side, or as many as you choose; there is no limit.

First Hand Up takes a small rubber town-ball or a base-ball and drops it in the square at the taw line, so that it will bound, or bounce, as the boys would say. As the ball rises from the earth the player strikes it with the flat of his hand, sending the ball against the wall, above the three-foot line. with sufficient force to cause it to rebound and fall outside the taw line. The next player uses his hand as a bat, and sends the ball back against the house in the same manner. He must hit the ball on the first bound or before it has touched the earth. The next player is ready to take his turn and strikes the ball on the rebound, and so the game proceeds, until someone misses, or sends the ball below the three-foot mark or outside the boundaries.

If it is the first striker who misses or sends the ball out of the boundaries on the ground or side of the house, then he loses his inning, and the boy on the other side drops the ball and strikes it as already described.

If it is a player on "outs" that makes a miss, then the "inners" count one for each miss or foul. A foul is when the ball goes below the three-foot line on the house or rebounds outside the boundaries.

The Outs cannot count when the Ins miss, but they take the place of the Ins and the Ins are out. After the first hand up or play it is unnecessary that the ball should rebound beyond the taw line. Fifteen points make a game. In England the boys have the same game under the name of Fives.

Ballie Callie.

As in the preceding game the ball is thrown against the house while all the players group themselves around the giver. As soon as the latter sends his ball against the house he shouts the name of one of his playmates who must catch the ball on the rebound. If he misses or drops the ball the other boys scatter in every direction, but come to a halt when he picks up the ball and cries, "Stand!" He then selects a victim and throws the ball at him. If he hits the boy aimed at, the latter throws the ball against the house, and the game goes on, but if he misses he must stand against the wall with head down and allow each of the other players to have one throw at him with the ball from a distance of ten paces.

Crackabout

is played with a town-ball or a soft rubber ball. For noise and activity Crackabout excels all other games. The boy owning the ball cries "Crackabout!" and throws the missile at his nearest comrade. All the others make a mad rush to gain possession of the ball, and as soon as one of their number has secured it, the others make an equally mad rush to escape; and alternately rushing together to secure the ball and scattering far apart to escape being hit by it, shouting and laughing, the boys are soon tired out and are ready to rest or play some quieter game. Twenty years ago Crackabout was the favorite recess game in Southern Ohio and Northern Kentucky, and when the boys came in at the call of the bell they were all mopping their heads with their handkerchiefs, and brighter eyes and rosier cheeks never faced a tired and patient school-teacher than those which came fresh from a rollicking game of Crackabout.

Over the Barn, House Over or Haley Over.

Choose up for sides. When all are ready, form two separate groups, one on each side of a house or barn. The boy with the ball cries, "House over!" and throws the ball over the house where the others are watching for its appearance in the hopes of catching it before it touches the ground. If they are successful in this, the boy who makes the catch rushes around the house and throws the ball at some one on the other side.

Since there is no way for the side who threw the ball to

know whether or not it was caught until the lad from the other side appears with it in his hand, it is no wonder that there should be wild cries and a scurrying of feet upon the sudden appearance of the boy with the ball.

If the latter hits one of the other side, the boy hit must follow his captor, who returns to his own side of the house with his prisoner, shouts, "Over the house!" and throws the ball. Each miss counts nothing. Each catch brings with it the right to invade the enemies' camp, and to select a victim and even run after him, so as to shorten the distance and increase the chance of hitting him with the ball. Each boy hit joins the side of the boy who threw the ball, and the game ends only when all the players are gathered upon one side of the house. This game will do for the suburbs of cities and villages, where detached houses of moderate height are to be found.

In olden times

Stool-ball

appears to have been quite a popular game, but it never took root in American soil.

The second Christmas after the founding of the colony of Massachusetts, Governor Bradford took the balls and stools away from the players; and he it must be who is responsible for the killing of the ancient game in America, for apparently it never revived.

Corner-ball.

The number of corners depends upon the number of players. If you have six boys, then there are three corners, making the boundaries of a triangular form. If you have eight boys, then there are four corners, and the boundaries form a square. There should be more than four players, because with this number you would have only two bases and the boundaries would be a straight line.

The Ins take the bases and the Outs group themselves inside the triangle, square, or whatever the figure may be formed by the corners. The Ins pass the ball around the corners, throwing and catching until they see a good chance to hit one of the Outs grouped inside the boundaries. The ball is then thrown at the Outs, and if it hits one he is out of the game; and if it misses, the thrower is out of the game. But, if one of those in the centre catch the ball, there is a laugh and the ball is thrown back to a corner man with no score either way.

When all of one side are put out of the game the opposite side has won, and all are entitled to a throw with the ball at the boy on the losing side who was first put out. The victim stands with head down and back arched facing a wall, while the victors line themselves at thirty feet distant and take turns "burning" the captive—that is, hitting him with the ball—if they can. It must be remembered that the dangerous base-ball is never used in these games, and the other ball does no injury to the lad struck.

Black Ball.

A much noisier and more active game is that of Black Ball. It is a game of ball and can only be played in such parts of the city as still possess bare earth, level and soft enough for the series of shallow holes necessary for the game.

There must be a hole for each player, and a common, hollow India-rubber ball or a soft yarn ball covered with leather. On no account use a hard ball, as the game is too rough for the use of a missile that can do injury when thrown with force.

First, with your heel make a number of holes about three feet apart and all in a line, one hole for each boy in the game. When there is a shallow hole for each boy let every boy stand by and guard his particular hollow, while the boy at one end attempts to roll the ball slowly over the line of the holes, so that it will rest in the hole at the extreme end in front of the lad at the opposite end. In case the ball passes safely over, the player at the other end rolls it back again in the same manner.

FIG. 281.—Game of Black Ball.

This cannot go on long before the ball stops in one of the holes. As soon as this happens all the players except the one at the hole where the ball stops scamper away for dear life, shouting, "Black ball! Black ball!" while the remaining lad seizes the ball as quickly as possible and throws it (a New York boy would say "fires it") with might and main at his nearest playmate. If he fails to hit the fleeing mark all return to their places, and a little piece of coal, a "black ball," is put in the hole lately occupied by the ball; but if he strikes the mark, the boy hit must quickly pick up the ball and throw it at his nearest playmate, and a game of "crackabout" ensues until someone makes a miss. As soon as this occurs all return to their places, and the failure is marked by a "black ball" placed in the hole belonging to the lad who failed, and the game of rolling the ball is continued by the boys at the end holes. As soon as a boy receives two "black balls" he is called "black ball half whitewashed."

The game goes on until some one player receives three "black balls." As soon as this occurs the culprit takes the ball, retires to a wall, fence, or tree, and with his left hand and right foot resting against the tree, wall, or fence, which he must face, he throws the ball over his shoulder as far as he can. The spot where it strikes the ground is marked by the other boys with a taw line, and from this line each player in turn has the privilege of throwing the ball at the unfortunate owner of three "black balls," who stands with his back bent and his head resting against the wall.

This may appear hard on the unlucky "black balls" boy, but—and here is the chance for which he is watching —every miss entitles the "black balls" to a throw at the bad marksman. After each thrower has had three shots at the culprit then the misses are called, and each in turn takes his place at the stake and receives his punishment until all debts are paid.

One game will give to a crowd of boys sufficient exercise and harmless fun to occupy the time between the close of school and tea-time. Then home you go, glowing with health and good nature, to wash and dress for the evening meal.

Rolly Poly

is only another name for Black Ball is played in the same manner.

Hat Ball

is a variation of the same game, the difference being that in place of holes in the ground each player places his hat on the sidewalk or play-ground in the same order in which the holes in the other game are arranged. Of course it is evident that the ball cannot be rolled into the hats, and the boy who has the ball tosses it in one of the hats. All the boys scatter except the one whose hat contains the ball. Five "babies" put a boy out and condemn him to the penalty prescribed in Black Ball.

CHAPTER XXX

MUMBLY PEG, HOP-SCOTCH, AND JACK STONES

The Motions of Stick-knife—Universality of the Game of Hop-Scotch —As Played in Different Countries—Different Games with Jack Stones.

A SUMMER'S day, a shady nook, a close-cropped green sod, two or three boys, and a jack-knife are the things necessary for a quiet game of Mumbly Peg.

The first player takes the knife and goes through as much of the game as he can without a blunder. The second follows in turn, doing the same. The last one to perform all of the difficult feats is beaten, and must pull a peg, two inches long, from the ground with his teeth. The winner drives the peg with the knife-handle for a hammer, being allowed, by the rules of the game, three blows with his eyes open, and three with his eyes closed.

This usually drives the peg out of sight in the sod, and in that case the boys cry:

"Root! Root!"

as the defeated player, unaided by aught but his teeth, literally roots, until, with a dirty face and a broad grin, he lifts his head, showing the peg between his teeth. From the penalty that the loser pays comes the name of Mumbly or Mumbelty-Peg.

The Feats

are these:

First.—Hold the right fist with back to the ground and with the jack-knife, with blade pointing to the right, resting on top of the closed fingers (Fig. 282). The hand is swung to the right, up and over, describing a semicircle, so that the knife falls point downward and sticks, or should stick, upright in the ground (Fig. 283). If there is room to slip two fingers, one above the other, beneath the handle of the

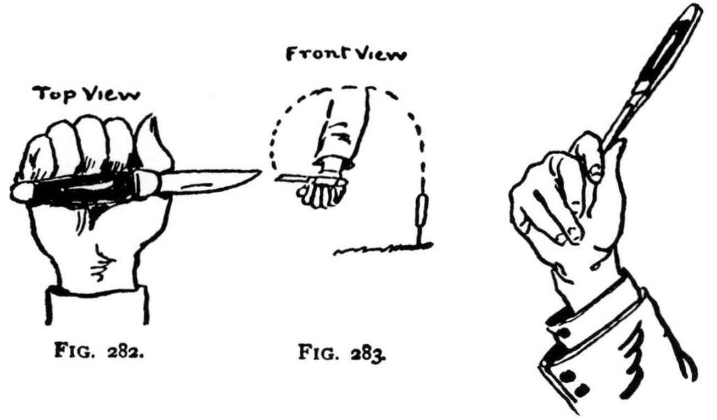

FIGS. 282, 283.—First Feat.

FIG. 284.—Third Feat.

knife and if the point of the knife is hidden in the ground, it counts as a fair stick or throw.

Second.—The next motion is the same as the one just described, but is performed with the left hand.

Third.—Take the point of the blade between the first and second fingers of the right hand, and fillip it with a jerk so that the knife turns once around in the air and strikes the point into the ground (Fig. 284).

Fourth.—Do the same with the left hand.

Fifth.—Hold the knife as in the third and fourth positions, and bring the arm across the chest so that the knife-handle touches the left ear. Take hold of the right ear with the left hand and fillip the knife so that it turns once or twice in the air and strikes on its point in the earth (Fig. 285).

Sixth.—Do the same with the left hand.

Seventh.—Still holding the knife in the same manner,

FIG. 285.—Fifth Feat. FIG. 286.—Seventh Feat.

bring the handle up to the nose and fillip it over through the air, so that it will stick in the ground (Fig. 286).

Eighth.—Do the same with the handle at the right eye.

Ninth.—Repeat, with the handle at the left eye.

Tenth.—Place the point of the blade on top of the head. Hold it in place with the forefinger, and with downward push send it whirling down to the earth, where it must stick with the point of blade in the earth (Fig. 287).

Eleventh to Fifteenth.—Hold the left hand with the fingers pointing up, and, beginning with the thumb, place the point of the knife on each finger as described above, and

FIG. 287.—Tenth Feat.

the forefinger of the right hand on the end of the knife-handle. By a downward motion, throw the knife revolving through the air, so that it will alight with the point of the blade in the sod (Fig. 288).

FIG. 288. — Eleventh Feat.

Sixteenth to Twentieth.—Repeat, with the right hand up and the forefinger of the left hand on the knife-handle.

Twenty-first, Twenty-second.—Do the same from each knee.

Twenty-third.—Hold the point of the blade between the first and second fingers and, placing the hand on the forehead, fillip the knife back over the head, so that it will stick in the ground behind the player ready for the next motion (Fig. 289; dotted lines show flight of knife).

FIG. 289.—Twenty-third Feat.

Twenty-fourth.—After twenty-three the knife is left in the ground. Then with the palm of the hand strike the knife-handle a smart blow that will send it revolving over the ground for a yard, more or less, and cause it to stick in the ground where it stops. This is called "ploughing the field" (Fig. 290; dotted lines show flight of knife).

FIG. 290.—Ploughing the Field.

When a miss is made the next player takes his turn, and when the first player's turn comes again he must try the feat over that he failed to perform last. A good player will sometimes go through almost all the twenty-four motions without failing to make a "two-finger"—that is, a fair stick, each time; but it is very unusual for anyone to run the game out in one inning. This is the game in twenty-four motions; many boys play it with double that number.

Hop-Scotch.

One would suppose that where thousands of children are every year killed by wild beasts and poisonous snakes, and where boys and girls are compelled to marry like grown-up people, the boys would be so busy fighting tigers, killing snakes, and attending weddings that they would find no time in which to play. But in India, where all these things take place, such is not the case. The games the young East Indians play are perhaps as numerous as those in vogue in America, and many of them are the same. Often the little natives may be seen hopping around on one brown, bare foot regardless of snakes—intent upon the game of hop-scotch.

From far Hindoostan, all the way across the map of Europe and Great Britain, in every town, chalked on the sidewalk or scratched on the ground, may be found the boys' hop-scotch courts. Not content with crossing the English Channel, this popular game has traversed the wide Atlantic and spread all over the United States, and it is only a matter of time when, by the way of California and the Pacific Islands, it will reach Japan and China. The whole world will then be encircled with a chain of hop-scotch courts, and who will dare to say that it is not a popular game?

The Hop-Scotch Court

is drawn with chalk or a soft brick on the stone flags of a sidewalk, or is scratched with a stick on a piece of hard, level ground. It is about twenty feet long and five or six feet wide. Figs. 291, 292, and 293 show some English courts, and Fig. 294 shows an American court. Fig. 295 is a modification of the American court made so that the flags of the pavement make the courts and only require a few cross lines and numbering.

A taw line is drawn a short distance from the court. In England the last division or sub-court at the top of the main court is called "cat's cradle" or "plum pudding;" in Italy, the "bell;" in New York, the "pot," and in Austria, the "temple."

The little Italian boys give a religious significance to the game by calling the last three divisions Infernal Regions, Purgatory, and Paradise; and it must be very encouraging to them, because if they play long enough they are sure to reach Paradise.

The Potsherd.

Originally a broken piece of crockery, a shell, or a small flat stone was used for the potsherd to play with, but now a bit of old tin folded and refolded, and hammered flat with a hammer, brick, or any other heavy object, is the favorite potsherd, though a piece of brick or a stone is often used.

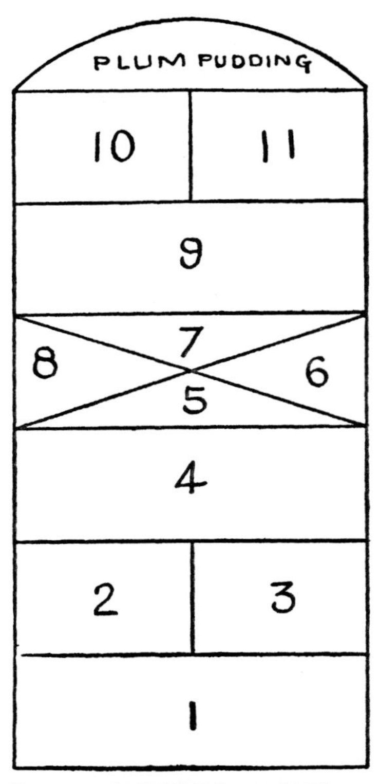

FIG. 291.—An English Court with Eleven Subdivisions and a Plum Pudding.

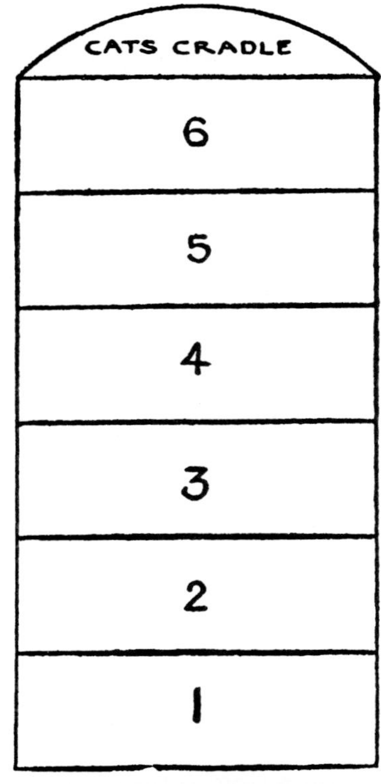

FIG. 292.—The Six Divisioned English Court with Cradle.

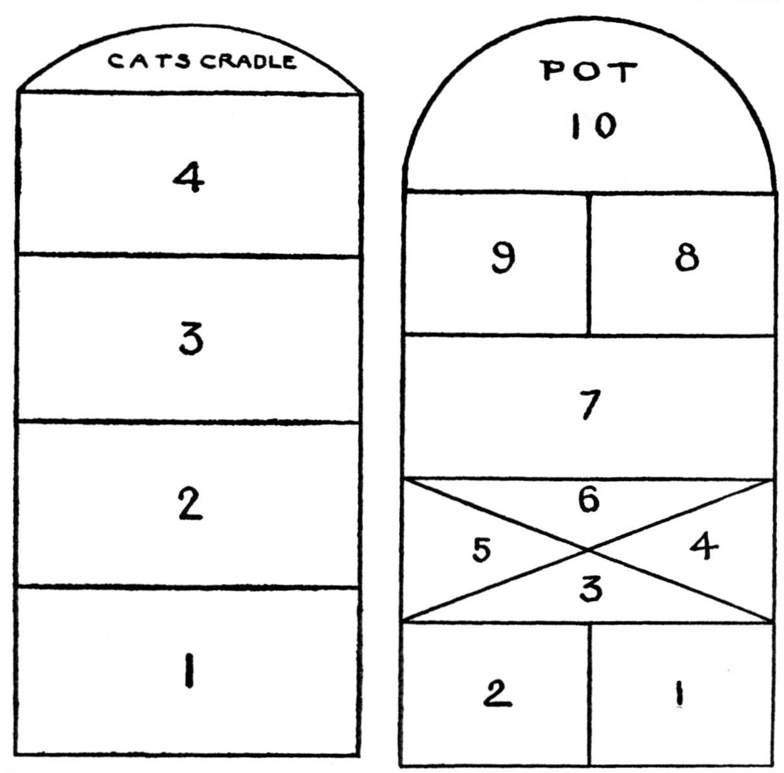

FIG. 293.—The Simplest English Court with Cat's Cradle.

FIG. 294.—A Typical American Court with Ten Subdivisions.

The Game.

After deciding who shall be first, second, etc., the player stands at taw and tosses the potsherd into division number one (Fig. 294). Hopping on one foot over the line into number one and still keeping one foot raised, he makes a hop-kick with the other and sends the potsherd out of the court. Whenever he fails to do so the next player takes a turn.

After kicking out of number one the player returns to taw and tosses the tin into number two. Then he "jumps a straddle," that is, he jumps so as to straddle the division line between number one and number two, with one foot in each of these divisions of the court, and without lifting up either foot he makes a sliding kick, sending the tin into number one. Then hopping into that division he makes another hop-kick, sending the potsherd out.

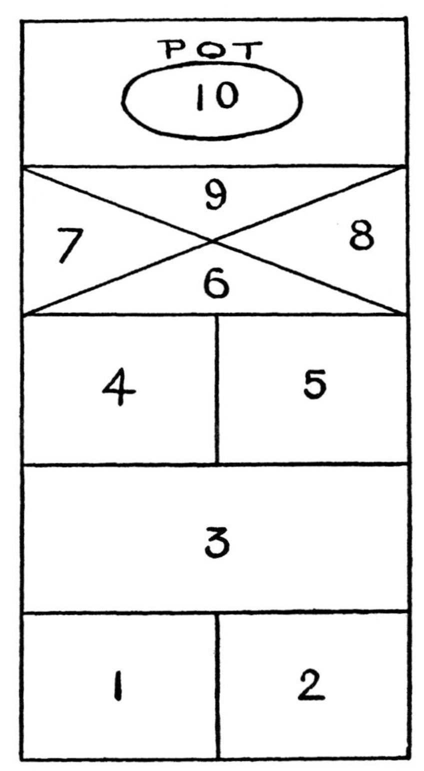

FIG. 295.—An American Court Adapted to Stones of Sidewalk.

In this manner all the divisions are played, with a straddle jump over the dividing lines at four and five and eight and nine, the player always going through the lower divisions as he came, with a hop or a straddle. At ten, after hopping three times around in the "pot," he strikes the potsherd with his toe and sends it through all the divisions toward the taw line, clear of the court, returning with hops and straddles the way he came.

Sometimes at seven and ten he is required, while still standing on one foot, to pick up the potsherd, place it on the top of his ground foot, and then with a hop-kick throw it toward taw, clear of the court. Or with an upward jerk he may send the potsherd up in the air, catch it with his hands, replace it in the court, and kick it out without touching his foot to the ground. After doing the "pot," "plum pudding," "cat's cradle," or paradise, he goes backward through all the divisions to number one, and the game is finished.

In Fig. 293, with four divisions and a cradle, there are no straddles. In Fig. 292, with six divisions and a cradle, there are no straddles, but in Fig. 291, with eleven divisions and a plum pudding, there is a straddle at two and three, eight and six, ten and eleven, and a "pick up and kick," as described above, at four and nine and the plum pudding. In the American game (Fig. 295) there is a straddle at one and two, a single at three, a straddle at four and five, a single at six, a straddle at seven and eight, and a single at nine. When the potsherd is pitched into ten, the player hops into one, straddles into one and two, hops into three, hops into four, straddles into four and five, hops into six, straddles into seven and eight, hops into nine, hops into the space surrounding the small pot ten, and then, without putting his foot to the ground, hops three times around the centre pot and into it.

If he is successful so far, he kicks the potsherd toward taw out of the court, and returns the way he came.

If there is any one who looks with contempt upon this game, thinking it a simple baby play, let him attempt this last feat and ever afterward he will consider Hop-scotch a sport in which it requires no small amount of skill to succeed.

Grounds Out.

When the player touches his foot or hand to the ground it is called "grounds," and he is out.

When a player pitches the potsherd in the wrong division or on a line, he is out.

When he kicks it into the wrong division or on a line, he is out; and in each case the next in turn plays from taw, and the other players, when their turns come around again, begin at the division they failed in.

Hop-Scotch on Stilts.

If any one of my readers wishes to try a game that will test his athletic skill, let him try hop-scotch on the simplest English court (Fig. 293) with a pair of "gadabouts," such as are described in Chapter VIII., strapped to his legs, and he will find it no simple game.

Jack Stones.

This is another game that was old when Greek civilization was young. "Chuckie stanes," "chuck stones," "five stones," and "knuckle-bones," are some of the names by which the game has been known. Knuckle-bones were in favor for use in this game two thousand years ago and are still used. White, water-washed pebbles; crockery stilts, which are little three-legged bits of earthenware upon which china and earthenware are placed when firing; iron stilts, made in imitation of the crockery ones; "lucky stones," which are bones from the inside of the head of the fresh-water fish called sheepsheads; and marbles, are all used in this country for jacks. But perhaps the best are the earthenware stilts with an agate (marble) for the jack.

Jack is the name given to the stone which is thrown up while the different feats are performed.

First Jack.

The game opens with one player taking the five stones in his hand. Holding the hand, palm up (Fig. 296), he tosses them into the air (Fig. 297). Before the stones have time to descend the player turns his hand over and catches as many as he can on the back of the hand (Fig. 298). These, he again tosses up (Fig. 299), and before they descend he picks up those jacks that he failed to catch on the back of his hand (Fig. 300). Quickly turning the hand he catches the descending jacks, and now holds all five in his fist (Fig. 301).

Whenever a player fails the next in turn takes the jacks. After successfully catching the jacks on the back of the hand, or picking up all that fell off, the player does the second feat, called

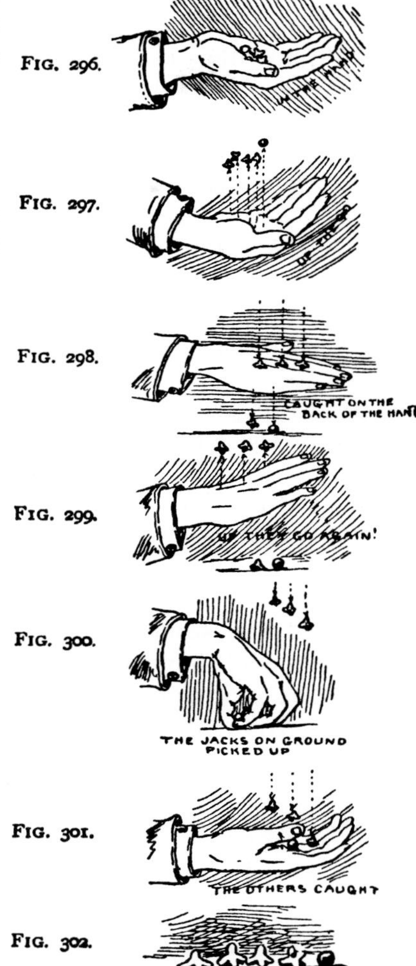

FIG. 296. FIG. 297. FIG. 298. FIG. 299. FIG. 300. FIG. 301. FIG. 302.

Ones.

First rolling the stones from his hand on to the ground, he throws his Jack up, and before it falls, picks up a stone. Again tossing up Jack he picks up another, continuing until all are successfully picked up from the ground. The next play is called

Twos.

Again rolling the stones on the earth and tossing Jack aloft, the player picks up two stones at a time, and, sending Jack up again he picks up the remaining two. This same process is repeated in

Threes ;

but in this play one is picked up first and three at the next toss, or three first and one afterward.

Fours.

All four stones must be picked up while Jack is in the air.

Drive the Horses in their Stalls.

Roll the stones from the hand on to the ground, and place the left hand with fingers spread apart on the ground near the jack stones. Toss Jack aloft, and before he comes down, drive one of the stones between the outspread first and second fingers. This is called putting the horse in the stable or stall. Do the same with all the other stones. Then in succession

Drive the Horses Out of their Stalls.

Toss Jack up, and while he is in the air fillip one horse out. Repeat the action with all the others, then bunch them together and pick up all four, and catch Jack as he descends.

Jumping the Hurdles.

Place the four horses (jack stones) in a line. Then toss Jack up, and before he comes down, pick up the first and third stones together and catch Jack as he comes down. The second and fourth are next caught up together and Jack is caught as he falls.

Base-ball.

Four of the Jacks are placed to represent the four bases on the base-ball field. Jack is sent aloft and the jack stone at home base is picked up and deposited at first base and Jack is caught as he falls. Jack is again tossed up, and the second base is run in the same manner, and then the third, and then the home base.

Now the first-base man is picked up and set down at the second, then the first and second are picked up together and set down at third, then the first, second, and third are all taken up at one time and set down at home base. Then as Jack is again tossed up all four are taken up at the same time and Jack is caught before he reaches the ground.

Cats in the Well.

The Jacks are rolled from the hand on to the ground; these are the cats. Then the left hand of the player is placed near them with the fist lightly closed, the thumb and first finger forming the opening to the well. Jack is now thrown up, and while he is in the air, one of the four cats on the ground is picked up and put in the well. The same operation is repeated with the second, third, and fourth cat, until all have been drowned in the well. The left hand is now taken away and the dead cats are left in a bunch. Jack is tossed up and all four of the cats are picked up before Jack comes down.

Sending the People to Church.

Again the stones are spilled upon the ground. This time they have changed from dead cats to well-dressed people, but people who need urging before they will go to church. The left hand is placed with fingers crooked and spread apart. The ends of the fingers resting on the ground form the bases to the arched doorways of the church, while the hollowed palm forms the ceiling and the back of the hand the roof.

Jack is now sent up and one of the Sunday idlers is driven through one of the five doorways into the church. One at a time, all four are sent to church. Then all four are gathered up while Jack is above, and Jack joins them when he is caught as he returns to earth.

When girls play Jack-stones they use a pretty marble for Jack, select a stone step to play upon, and allow Jack to strike the step and catch him on the rebound. They also have a number of feats generally ignored by the boys. This being a boys' book, these feats, such as "peas in a pod," "setting the table," "doves in a cot," "spinning the plate," "knock at the door," "pick up a pin," "light a match," "washing the clothes," will be left for books written for girls.

CHAPTER XXXI

PRACTICAL HINTS FOR BICYCLISTS

Regarding Baggage and how to Carry it—A Photographer's Outfit on a Wheel—A Collector's Box—How to Deal with Punctures—An Extemporized Handle Bar—A Rope Tire—A Cleaning Rack, and a Bicycle Stand.

THERE is only one way to learn to ride a bicycle, and that is, to straddle a wheel and try; but there are thousands of practical and useful things to learn after you are able to ride. Every boy knows how to strap his coat on the handle bars, and most of them can carry various parcels, but there are some articles of

Baggage

that need special care. It is customary in ordinary wheeling to strip a machine of every ounce of weight not absolutely necessary. Many riders travel without even a tool-bag, pump, or wrench. This is absurd, for the additional weight of a few tools cannot possibly be sufficient to make any appreciable difference to an ordinary road-rider.

Of course, if you are a "scorcher," and are out to pass everything you meet on the road, the less weight you carry the better time you can make. But the wheel is used by most boys for other purposes. In Flushing, Long Island, it is no uncommon thing to see one of the local colony of artists wheeling merrily along with sketching easel and umbrella strapped to his handle-bars, and paint-box and canvas swung in the frame beneath him. Nor is it an uncommon sight, in the spring, to see the trout fishermen, men and boys, passing by on their bicycles with their jointed fishing-rods strapped to their handle bars and their creels on their backs.

This suggests a variety of uses that boys may make of their wheels.

How to Carry Photographic Outfit on a Wheel.

The top diagram shows the arrangement of straps on Mr. Hemment's camera, Fig. 303. This gentleman is the official

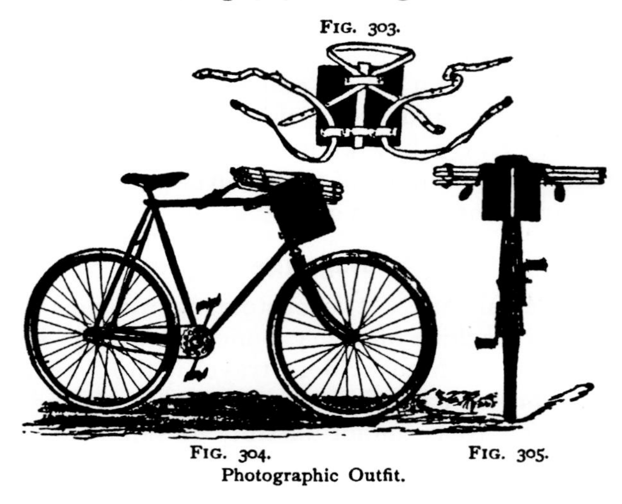

Fig. 303.

Fig. 304. Fig. 305.

Photographic Outfit.

photographer for *Leslie's Weekly*, and carries his eight-by-ten camera and five-feet tripod on his wheel. The tripod is strapped to the handle-bars and the camera is strapped on in front, as shown in Fig. 304, side view, and Fig. 305, front view of the same. The straps allow a certain amount of movement, which is necessary for safety. If the camera is fastened too tightly to the machine the constant jarring of the bicycle will be more than likely to result in injury to the plates or other apparatus.

But all boys are not photographers. Some are fishermen and need only to strap their rods to their handle-

FIG. 306.—Bicycle Stand and Naturalist Outfit.

bars. Most of them are great collectors of something, and many are interested in making cabinets of beetles, butterflies, and moths; or in collecting various small creatures, such as toads, frogs, snails, and even snakes. These boys will be glad to know

How to Rig the American Boy Naturalist's Wheel.

The drawing, Fig. 306, it will be seen, shows a wheel loaded with bags for tools, bottles, boxes, lunch, and various knick-knacks essential to the outfit of a naturalist collector. Cut paper patterns for the different boxes, so that they will fit the particular machine for which they are designed. Make the boxes of stiff pasteboard. Divide the largest box or bag into as many subdivisions as will best meet your requirements. Make the compartments of pasteboard, and keep them in place by pasting cloth along the edges on both sides.

After all the divisions are made, line the whole inside of the box with cloth and sew it in neatly, turning in all the rough edges. Next make a cover of pasteboard and cut a door for each compartment. Cover the inside with cloth, sewed on neatly. Sew the cover itself to the box. Make the doors or lids for the compartments, and make each considerably larger than the opening it is to cover. Line the inside of each lid with cloth, leaving a flap for a hinge, and cover the outside with enamelled cloth. Sew the linings to box so that the lids will cover the proper openings, and cover the whole outside of the box with enamelled cloth. Use an awl or big darning-needle with which to punch holes, when you are sewing the pasteboard. Do not sew the enamel cloth to the box. Cut holes to correspond to the various doors, leaving flaps to turn in, and sew the flaps to the lining on the inside.

There is no mystery about the art of sewing a thing of this kind. It is not a girl's work, and few of them could do it; but any boy who will take pains can, and a boy who will not take pains will never make a collector.

All that remains to be done now is to

Add the Straps and Buttons.

Sew short straps or pieces of tape to the box to fasten it by buckling or by tying it to the frame, and small straps on the lids with slits in the ends for button-holes. Put some round buttons on the box to which you can button the straps, thus fastening the lids. The small boxes under the seats can be made in the same manner; but, being without divisions, they are so simple that they need no further explanation.

As to Punctures.

The dreaded carpet-tack, the lurking horseshoe, with rusty nails sticking up like the fangs of a serpent, the treacherous broken bottles, and the innocent-looking clam-shells, are all mortal enemies of the inflated rubber tires and lose no opportunity to stab or cut the rubber and spoil the cycler's ride. It is supposed that every rider goes prepared for such emergencies, but observation teaches that many do not, and all should know

How to Stop a Puncture with Chewing-Gum,

or any other sticky substance that can be procured. A nail or tack hole can be temporarily mended with chewing-gum in the following manner: Let all the air out of the tire, make a small wooden paddle, and with this implement poke the gum through the hole from the outside of the tire, flatten what is left over the outside and bind on a piece of rag or a part of your pocket-handkerchief. Do this neatly. Then pump up the tire, and the compressed air on the inside will flatten the wax over the inside of the hole and prevent the escape of air, so that you may reach home without another application of the pump.

Not long ago the New York *Journal* told of a cyclist who broke his handle-bar and patched it up so that he was able to ride his machine a long distance, reaching home in safety. His method is a common-sense one, and all boys should know

How to Rig a Jury Handle-Bar.

Take two elastic saplings and bind them securely to the front fork, as shown in the front view (Fig. 307). Lash a stout stick to the handle-bar, holding the broken part in place. Bind the ends of the fork-sticks securely to this and you have a jury bar that, though it may work a little stiffly, will enable you to ride home, which, even in a short distance, is a much pleasanter ending to a ride than walking and leading a crippled wheel.

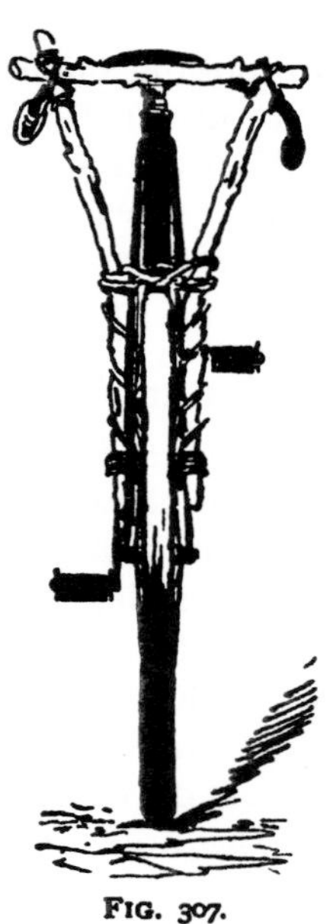

FIG. 307.

It sometimes happens that from contact with the knife-like edge of a piece of tin or glass, a slit is cut in the tire, so large that it is impracticable to attempt to mend it on the road. In such a case

A Rope Tire

will often enable the rider to reach home without humiliating himself by walking and leading his wheel. A few yards of clothes-line borrowed, begged, or bought from some wayside house, will enable you to make an old-fashioned solid tire. Remove the rubber tire, tie it to your handle-bar, and take the rope and bend one end diagonally across the hollow in the rim of the wheel. Then wind the rope carefully around, over the bent end of the rope, around again alongside of the first length until the rim is covered. Keep the line tight and wind it until it fills up the hollow and is considerably higher in the middle than at the sides. The neater this work is done the more comfortable will be your ride home. When the rope tire is complete pry up the side lap and force the free end of the rope diagonally under until it comes out on the other side. Draw it taut and cut off the end flush with the outer wrapping. Now pour water all over the rope until it is thoroughly wet, this will cause it to shrink and become firm and hard. All that remains to be done is for you to jump on your wheel and start for your destination.

When you reach home after a ride you should always clean your wheel. To do this it is best to turn the wheel upside down. The work of cleaning is made more pleasant if you have a repairing stool.

How to Make a Cleaning and Repairing Rack.

It is a simple but most convenient affair, and varies in dimensions with the wheel that it is intended to support.

FIG. 308. FIG. 309.

The first drawing, Fig. 308, shows a side view with the wheel upside down, ready to be cleaned; the second, Fig. 309, shows the construction of the bench. The front slots for the handle bars must be covered with cloth, stuffed with cotton; and the bench in the rear must have a cushion made by tacking on a piece of cloth and filling the upper part loosely with hair, moss, cotton, or excelsior.

The only safe way to stable your machine is to have a stand of some kind for it, and the most simple stand is the best.

How to Make a Bicycle Stand.

Select a good straight-grained piece of plank, of any kind of wood, an inch and one-half or two inches thick, and twelve or fourteen inches wide. Saw off a piece eighteen inches long for the base of your stand. Saw out a slit in the middle of the stand nine inches long and a trifle wider than the tire of your wheel. With your pocket-

FIG. 310. FIG. 311.

knife, or chisel, round off the sharp edges of the slit, and cut a slot from the bottom of the plank, at the end of the slit, to the top. Round this out so that it will fit loosely to a wheel pushed in the slit. At the end of this hollow bore two holes, about a quarter of an inch in diameter, to hold a stiff wire which is bent over in a loop to receive the tire of the wheel (Fig. 306). This wire can be taken out and the board set up against the wall when it is not in use, or both may be hung up in the hall closet, out of the way. When you wish to stable your wheel take down the base, set it on the floor, put the wire in place, and back your wheel in the slot until the rear tire is held by the wire loop. This will keep the wheel upright, with no danger of its being knocked over.

The last two diagrams, Figs. 310 and 311, show how to decorate a wheel for

A Night Parade.

The illustrations are made from the two wheels which took the first and second prize in a parade. The first, Fig. 310, was simply a very large Japanese umbrella, with Japanese lanterns suspended from the ribs. The lanterns illuminated the whole umbrella, which, when seen at a distance, had the appearance of a large colored balloon. The second, Fig. 311, was rather sparsely decorated with lanterns, but plentifully supplied with streamers of all colors, which the light from the lanterns brought out in brilliant effect. In appearance the rider was sailing in a boat.

Autumn

CHAPTER XXXII

POINTS ON CAMPING OUT

How to Make a Fire in the Woods on a Rainy Day—To get a Light Without Matches—The Diamond Hitch, and a Home-made Cinch.

"LAFE, I can't make a fire; we have no paper and the wood's all wet."

Lafe is a Pike County backwoodsman. He only smiled; then shouldering his axe he walked over to a moss-covered log that lay on the ground as soggy and wet as a sponge in the water. With a few blows from the butt end of his axe he knocked out of the rotten wood the remnants of what were once the noble limbs of a giant pine-tree. These remnants were now nothing more than spike-shaped clubs, the largest not over two feet long.

FIG. 312.—The Fire Won't Burn.

"Here's what we use in the woods for paper," said Lafe.

Upon examination, we discovered that the spike-shaped clubs were almost as heavy as lead, but it was not water that gave them weight; it was the sap of the tree, the pitch, that colored them a rich red and made them hard and impervious to rain. Lafe pulled out his one-bladed jack-knife and began to whittle the pine stick, but he allowed no shavings to become detached (Fig. 313). When he had three cut in the manner shown in the accompanying drawing (Fig. 314), he set them up on the ground, with the small ends down and the big ends resting against each other, placed as the sticks are that form the frame of an Indian wigwam. He touched a lighted match to the shavings, and immeidately a flame burst forth with a black smoke. Selecting some sticks he had previously split in halves, he piled them around the blazing pine-knots in a conical wigwam fashion, and soon we had a fire that was hot enough to ignite the wet, unsplit wood we gathered.

Fig. 313. — A "Fat" Pine Knot.

Fig. 314.— Starting the Fire.

Building a Fire Without Matches.

After the coffee was boiled and the fish fried and the boys' clothes partially dried, they made haste to ply Lafe with questions.

"How would you build a fire, if your matches were wet, or if you had none?" asked Tom.

"I generally calculate to keep my matches dry and always keep some about me," answered the woodsman; "but in case, as you say, I had none, I'd put a light charge of powder in my gun and a loose wad of cotton rag and shoot in the air, and then double the red-hot ashes of the rag up and blow on it until it flamed up.

"Or, if I find that I am running out of matches, I take a piece of cotton cloth and dry it at the fire, heating it until it is almost charred; then I dampen the rag and rub gunpowder into its fibres as hard as I can until I can rub no more powder in. After that I dry the rag thoroughly again and put it in a bottle, tin box, or horn, cork it up tight and keep it until I need it. With the back of my knife-blade for a steel and a piece of flint, I strike a spark that sets the rag a-burning and fold the glowing rag up, cover it with shavings, twisted straw or punk, and blow it into a flame."

Things Worth Remembering.

" Tamarack is a very good wood,
If you can get it dry,
But to make a fire of green tamarack,
I'll be a fool to try."

An Indian builds a small campfire and hugs it, a white man makes a roaring big fire and stands away from it.

In selecting a camping-place never forget that the presence of good firewood in abundance is a matter of grave importance. A standing dead cedar will furnish the best of kindling wood. Green, soft woods, spruce, and white birch, burn badly and are difficult to ignite.

To build a fire that will burn all night, select a couple of good heavy sticks for andirons, and a

FIG. 315.—A Camper.

quantity of green hardwood, maple, yellow birch, or beech, for fuel. Across the andirons lay all the fuel sticks in the same direction parallel with each other; in this position they will burn slowly and smoulder for a long time. A large tree, or, better still, a large rock at the back of your fire will retain and reflect the heat.

FIG. 316.—The Author's Camp at Big Tink, Pike County, Penn.

Always select a well-drained spot, or a slight elevation for a place to pitch your tent or build your shack; this will prevent an exceedingly disagreeable experience of awakening during a rain-storm to find your tent, floor, and blankets soaked with water. The presence of a neighboring spring, or other water-supply for drinking and cooking, of course, must not be overlooked.

Never pitch your tent in a hollow or depression, or you may find yourself in the middle of a pond. Soldiers always dig a ditch around their tents. The floor, which is often your bed, can be covered with straw, if straw is obtainable; if not, fir-boughs; these lie flatter than spruce. It is best to lay the foundation of good-sized branches, cover them with smaller ones, and over all place a deep layer of fir-twigs broken off the length of your hand, and laid shingle-fashion, commencing at the foot of your bed, or the door-way of your shack or tent, each succeeding row of boughs covering the thick ends of the previous row. A properly made bough-bed is as comfortable as a mattress, but one in which the ends of the sticks prod your ribs all night is not a couch that tends to make a comfortable night's rest.

Candles, lamps, and lanterns add to the luggage of a camper, and may be dispensed with, yet it often happens that you will need a light at night. If you do, remember that almost any sort of fat or grease will burn. I have made a passable lamp of an old clam-shell filled with melted rancid butter and a twisted rag for a wick resting in the butter, and I have seen most dainty little candles moulded in willow bark of tallow from the deer, with a wick of the inside bark of a cedar-tree. But such things are only made by guides for ladies, or as souvenirs to take home. A torch will answer all needs of camp life.

A Birch-bark Torch.

Peel off several strips of birch bark, four or five inches wide; double and fold them two or three times if the pieces are long.

Split one end of a stick for a torch-handle and slip one or more of the doubled strips into the end of the stick. The Northern Indian always keeps a lot of neatly folded bunches of birch bark, tied with cedar-bark rope, on hand for use as torches in spearing fish at night.

Remove the outside bark of a cedar-tree, and then from the bottom up strip off the fine inner bark, and from these fibres twist what ropes or strings you need around camp.

FIG. 317.—Supper at Camp.

Keep your feet dry; that is, keep them dry while in camp. To do this take an abundant supply of old socks with you and two pairs of shoes—one pair for dry shoes and an old pair for wet ones. With an old pair of trousers and some leaky shoes you may wade a trout stream and stand in the water for hours without suffering any ill effects if you are prompt in removing the wet clothes and replacing them with dry shoes, socks, and trousers as soon as you leave the water. Experience has taught many sportsmen that this method is far more comfortable and healthful than wearing expensive hot and clumsy rubber boots.

I was never lost in the woods, but once. I remember that I had read in books that the moss grew thickest on the north side of the trees. Upon careful examination I could distinguish no difference between the moss on one side of the trees and that on the other side; the moss grew all around! The thick interlacing branches overhead concealed the sun. After wandering around in a circle for hours I at last heard the rushing of water, and, following the sound, soon discovered the brook I had been fishing, down which I waded until I struck camp at 4 P.M., having left there at 4 A.M. I was wet, cold, and hungry, but otherwise all right.

An Indian in starting out always carefully notes the direction of the wind. Where the sky is not obscured the sun and stars serve as guides, but the safest way is to blaze trees as you go (mark them with your hatchet), or every now and then break a twig or branch, bending the broken end in the direction you are pursuing, thus making a trail that is easily retraced. Streams always flow toward greater bodies of water, and somewhere along these water roads, farms or settlements are located; so if you are really lost, follow the first stream until it leads you, as it invariably will, to some road, settlement, or camp.

While the trapper, scout, and guide, can sleep peacefully wrapped in a blanket with his feet to the fire, it takes a green city boy some time to accustom himself to the katydids, "pinching bugs," and various other harmless but more or less annoying small creatures of the wood. If the "tender foot" will get his mother to make him

A Sleeping Bag

of an old blanket, he can creep into it at night and cover his head with a bit of mosquito-netting and sleep as soundly as his guide, with no fear of insects or other small creatures interrupting his slumber.

If you have a pony, horse, or mule for a pack animal, it greatly facilitates the transportation of camping material, and furnishes you with many more conveniences, such as additional cooking utensils and extra clothes. All campers travelling with pack animals owe a debt of gratitude to an old Spanish muleteer who many, many years ago invented

The Famous Diamond Hitch.

As the boys' counting-out rhymes are told by one boy to another, so one muleteer told his fellows until it reached Mexico, was learned by the hardy prospectors and trappers, and from some one of them, Captain A. E. Wood, of the Fourth United States Cavalry, discovered the trick in 1879 and taught it to his men; and my cousin, a civil engineer, who has spent much of his time in the Wild West, learned the Diamond Hitch and taught it to me.

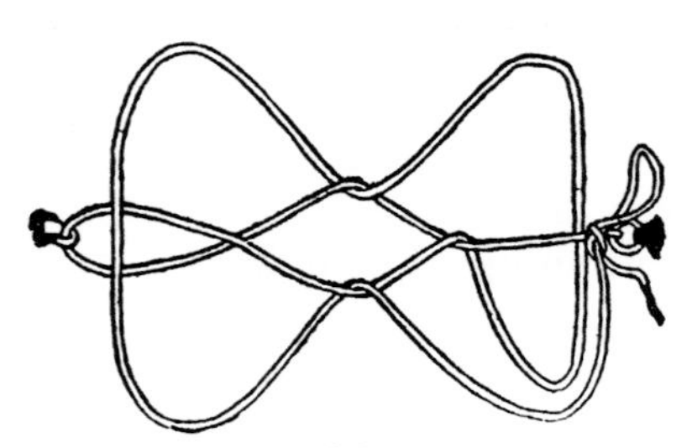

FIG. 318.—Plan of the Diamond Hitch.

The Aparejo.

The pack-saddle of the Mexicans is called an aparejo,* and is used in preference to the old saw-buck saddle. It is

* As pronounced it would be spelled Ah-pahr-ai-ho in English.

made of a leather bag attached to a very broad leather breeching. Inside is a slight springy framework of willow, and the space between is filled with straw.

Of course such a saddle is not to be found east of the Mississippi River; but one can easily be made of canvas, which in many respects is better than leather and is not so easily damaged by water. This saddle must be stiff at the bottom edges and corners, where considerable strain comes when the pack-rope is bound on. Before placing the saddle on your pack-horse, fold a blanket neatly on the animal's back and secure it with a wide girth. This will prevent the pack-horse's back from being rubbed and becoming sore.

For two whole days I worked with a rope to try and learn the diamond hitch, and though I had a printed and illustrated account which claimed to disclose the secret of this far-famed hitch, I might still be working at the problem had not my cousin, Wolcott LeCléar Beard, chanced to come in. He showed me that on account of the lack of familiarity with the terms used, the writer and proof-reader had so mixed up things that no one could follow the description and throw the hitch. Taking a rope in his hand Mr. Beard then showed

How the Trick is Done.

First, you need one short quarter-inch rope for a "sling rope" to hold the baggage in place while throwing the diamond hitch.

There must be two boys to do the packing. The boy on the near, nigh, or left-hand side of the pony or donkey, takes in his left hand the two ends of the sling-rope, and with his right hand throws the loop or "bight" of the rope across the pony's back and leaves it hanging there. The boys now lift two bags or parcels and place them lengthwise, one on each side of the animal's back-bone.

The loop is now passed up and over the pack on the far, "off," or right-hand side. The loose end of the sling-rope nearest the animal's head, on the near side, is now passed up and over the near pack through the loop, brought down and tied in a square knot to the other end of the sling rope. The two packs are thus *temporarily* fastened to the animal's back and we are ready

To Throw the Diamond Hitch.

The cinch is the band that goes under the horse's belly. In the West it is made of a number of parallel strings of horse-hair rope. A first-rate substitute can be made from the grass rope of a hammock; but a broad canvas or webbing band will answer our purposes.

The cinch must have an iron ring on one end and an iron hook on the other (Figs. 318 and 326). Pass the cinch under the horse's belly, bringing the ring to which the pack rope is attached on the near side. The packer on the near side must throw the line to his companion on the far side, who passes it through the hook and throws it back so that it lies forward of the portion previously passed over.

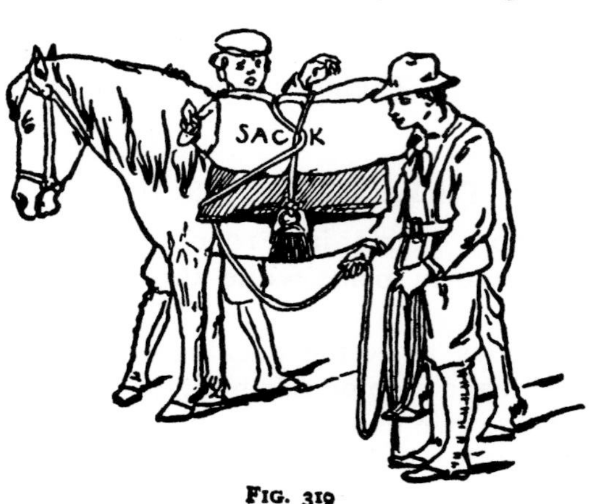

Fig. 319

The near pack

er passes the free end of the rope down and under the standing part (which is the part fastened to the cinch) where it binds on the near pack, which of course brings the free end to the rear of the standing part.

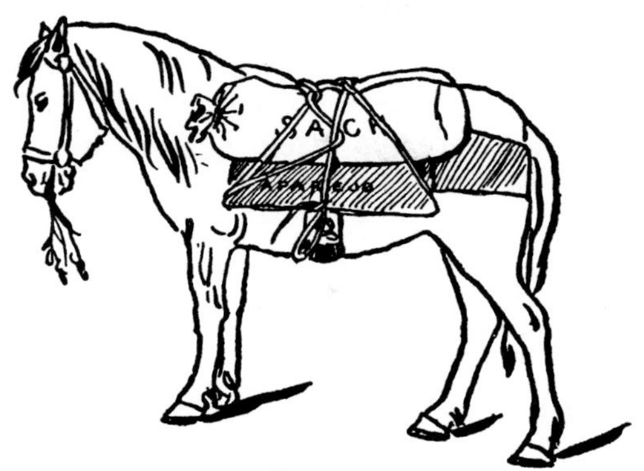

Fig. 320.

Bring the free end forward and diagonally down to the front of the saddle and under the front end of the aparejo or pack saddle (Figs. 318 and 319). Bring it back under the standing part and under the rear corner of the aparejo. The free end is now thrown over the animal to the packer on the far side. The near packer guides the line diagonally forward over the packs, and the off packer pulls everything tight. In order to hold it the near boy grabs the rear corner of the aparejo and the rope under it with one hand and "pinches" it over the corner to prevent it from slacking, while the far packer passes the free end over and under the standing part at the middle of the horse's back between the two packs (Figs. 318 and 320). The far packer then passes the free end under the rear corner of his side of the aparejo and passes it forward under everything to the forward corner of the aparejo. He passes the line up over the forward corner of the aparejo and throws the free end over and back to the near boy. The near boy hauls everything tight while the far packer guides the pack rope diagonally back over the packs.

The far man now "pinches" the line at the forward corner of the aparejo, while the near packer passes the line over and under that part of the pack rope which passes over the horse's back nearest his head (Fig. 318). He brings the free end diagonally forward and down under the forward corner of the aparejo (Figs. 318 and 321).

FIG. 321.

Everything is tightened for the last time, and the free end is brought back and fastened with a single bow-knot to the standing part at the ring (Fig. 321). The axe, the frying-pan, and all such articles are thrust under the ropes (Fig. 321), and, if the directions have been properly followed, the luggage will stick in its place even if the animal rolls over a cliff. There was once a mule that tried this, and although he fell thirty feet and did considerable damage to his luggage, he failed to dislodge it, and his pack broke his fall and saved his life.

How to Make Your Own Cinch.

Procure some thick wire, and if you have no conveniences for iron work, go to the blacksmith shop and show the smith how to bend the wire, so as to make the ring (Fig. 326 D and Fig. 324). The base should not be less than eight or nine inches. Let him make another ring, elongate it and give it a twist, as in Fig. 322. Bend it over in a hook, as in Fig. 323; but, if you have a hammer, a hot fire, and an old paving stone for an anvil, you can make your own hook and ring.

Now take some hammock string and fasten it with a lark's head to the ring (A, Fig. 326). Bring the two ends over to the base of the hook, around and up again, as shown by B in the same diagram, and tie in a square knot (Figs. 122 and 123, page 173). Repeat this, with a lark's head first at A, and a knot at B, and then with a lark's head at C, and a knot at D, until the parallel strings fill up the space on the bases of the hook and ring. The length of the cinch depends upon the size of the animal that is to wear it. The ring and hook should come just under the edge of the pack saddle. Two inches on each side of the centre of the cinch weave a small piece of twine, and tie the ends (Fig. 325). Weave two more strings four inches apart near the ring, and two more four inches apart near the hook. These are for spreaders. All that remains to be done is to fasten two broad sole-leather pads to your cinch, one under the hook and one under the ring. Punch holes with an awl

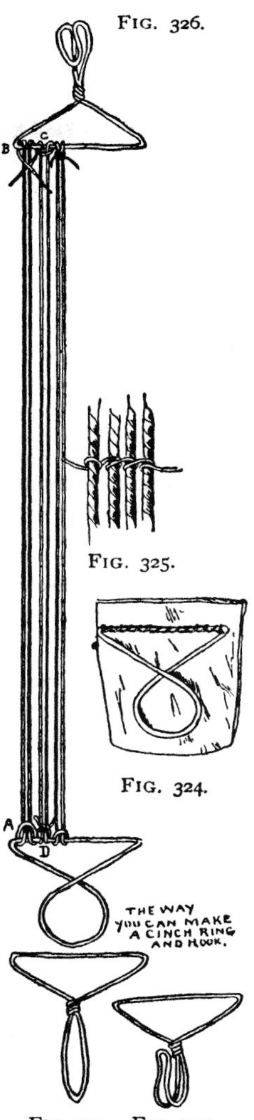

FIG. 326.

FIG. 325.

FIG. 324.

FIG. 322. FIG. 323.
Home Made Cinch.

or a nail in the leather, and bind it with twine on to the base of the hook and the ring (Fig. 324).

The advantage of a horse-hair cinch is that it will not slip, and the grass-twine of a hammock makes a first-class substitute. My cousin, who, as I have already said, has spent much of his time in the land of cow-boys and diamond hitches, assures me that the grass-twine cinch possesses all the qualities claimed for it.

Cooking Utensils for Camp.

The following articles are almost indispensable: A long-handled frying-pan, a bunch of half a dozen pieces of telegraph wire, each two feet long, with which to make a spider or broiler; by simply laying them across the fire or over the hot coals, you have a gridiron; you may bundle it up when its work is done; three or four assorted tin buckets for cooking purposes and for water; a tin coffee-pot; a long iron fork; a long iron spoon; some cheap tin cups, plates, and spoons, and some forks and knives.

Food.

If you do not want to go hungry, do not depend upon the fish and game you intend to capture for food supply, but take along some boneless bacon and fat pork. With the latter, you can cook your fish, and the former is good for a relish with whatever fresh meat you may secure. Then you should have some good ground coffee in a tightly closed tin box. Some tea in a screw-top glass preserve-jar, sugar, salt, prepared flour, corn meal, rice, beans, oat-meal, condensed milk, evaporated cream, crackers, and as much canned or dried fruits as you can transport without overloading—these are not necessaries, but all of them will come handy in camp, and will help out a meal when the fish do not bite and the game fails to come and be shot.

CHAPTER XXXIII

THE BOYS' BABY BALLISTA

How to Build this Warlike Engine, and the Fun That Can be Had With It—Blow-guns and Their Use—Blow-gun Parachutes—The Lariat, How to Make and Throw it.

In the autumn much fun may be had with a Baby Ballista, which is constructed in this way:

From a two-inch plank make a base plank of any size that may suit your fancy, say four feet long. Near the front end of the baseboard (C, Fig. 327) and at equal distances from the edge, saw and chisel out two notches, four by two inches each. These mortises are for the uprights A and B (Fig. 327) to fit in, where they must be secured by screws or nails. Make A and B of two by four inch plank. Next select a board that is broad enough to form the spreader D (Fig. 328). D is simply a board a trifle longer than C is broad and a little wider than A or B. In each end a mortise is cut so that the distance between the edges

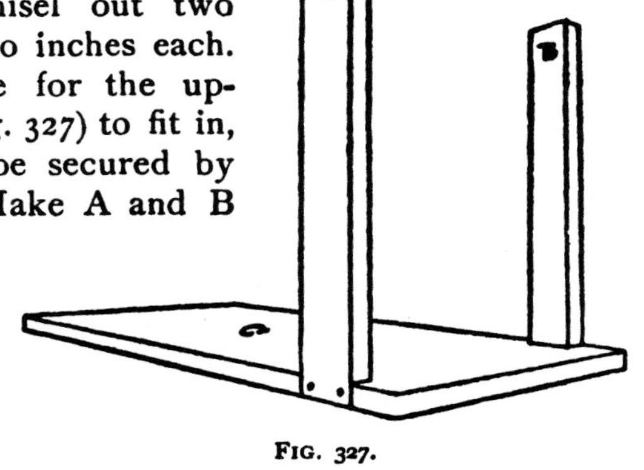

Fig. 327.

of the rectangular notches or mortises is exactly the distance between the uprights A and B where they join the

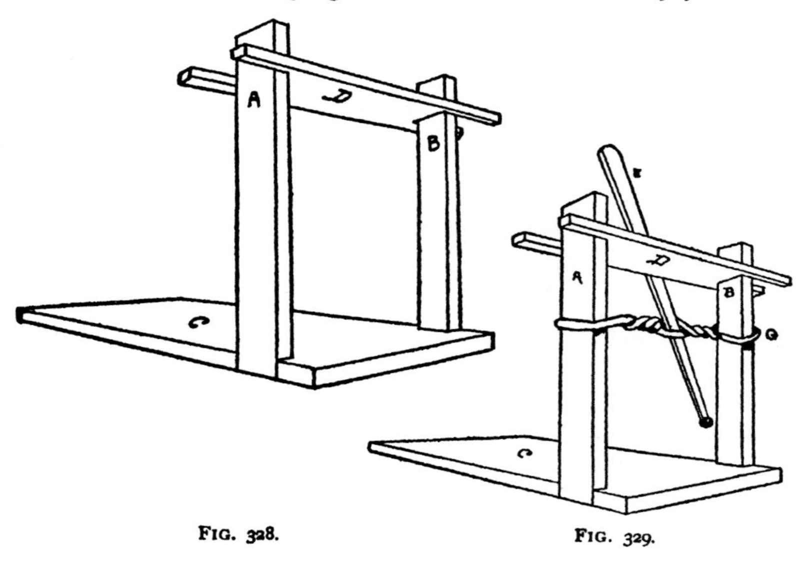

FIG. 328.

FIG. 329.

base, plank C. Fasten D in place near the tops of A and B by driving nails above and below.

Take a piece of good, strong clothes-line and bring the ends around the uprights A and B, and tie them securely together so that the rope forms a loop which is tight enough to support itself. Now from a long, flat piece of strong wood make the bat E (Fig. 329), make it a little longer than the base-board C. Take a short stick, somewhat thicker through than the bat-stick E, and with it thrust between the sides of the loops of rope, wind the stick over and over, twisting the rope G until it is very tight. Now carefully slip the end of the bat-stick E into the space occupied by the thicker stick you have used as a winder, and remove the short stick, leaving E in place. The spring of the rope will force the bat-stick into the position shown in Fig. 329, and if the upper end of the bat is pulled down and suddenly let go it will strike the stretcher D with a resounding whack.

From an old tomato-can, or any other convenient source, secure a piece of tin, which may be flattened out and cut into a square. With a nail, make four holes near the centre. Next cut four slits in the tin, from the corners of the square to four points near the centre of the tin. At the long end of the bat-stick (E, Figs. 330 and 331) place the piece of tin, near enough to the end of the stick to allow free play for a trigger that is fastened on the end of the base-

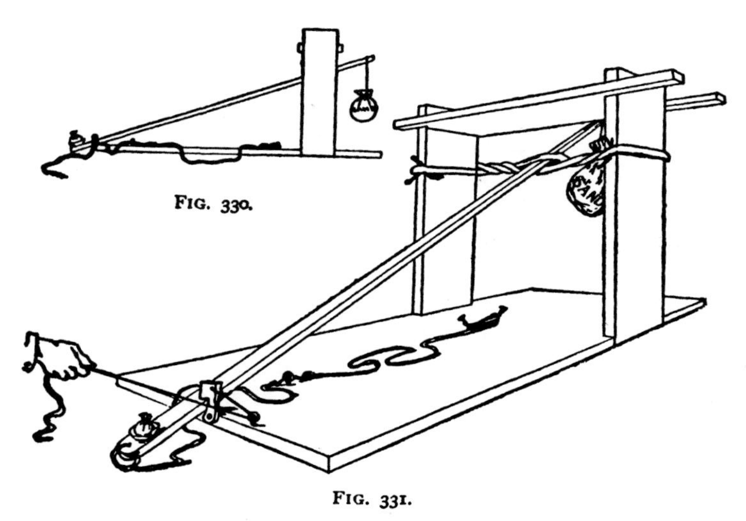

FIG. 330.

FIG. 331.

board (see Fig. 331). After you have adjusted the tin in its proper place, with a pencil thrust through the nail-holes in the tin, mark the spots on the back-stick underneath, and with a gimlet or a hot iron bore four holes at the points marked. Then fasten the tin to the bat-stick with a piece of wire. Next bend up the edges of the tin, allowing them to overlap each other until they form a cup or basin-shaped chamber for holding the shells (Figs. 330 and 331).

The base-board should be fastened to the ground to prevent the recoil from displacing the ballista at every shot. Two screw-eyes are screwed in the base-board.

The trigger is fastened to the end of the base-plank C. To the end of the bat-stick fasten a check-string; allow the other end of the string to pass through a screw-eye a short distance back of the trigger, thence to a rude cleat made by driving two nails slanting into the base-plank (as may be seen in Fig. 331), where the end of the string is to be made fast to the cleat.

To the short end of the bat-stick fasten a weight—a sand-bag, a flat-iron, a dumb-bell, or anything heavy, and now your ballista is ready for war. But you have no ammunition! Stones and rocks are out of the question, as the serious consequences that almost certainly would follow the use of such missiles would deter any self-respecting, law-abiding boy from using them, and if the boy is malicious and fond of cruel tricks the certainty of detection in this case will prevent such a use of the baby ballista, which was invented solely for fun-loving boys. The baby ballista throws shells that burst with a cloud of smoke, and it would do no injury to a boy if a bomb burst on his head.

The Shells.

These are made of tissue, or thin, light paper, flour, and dough. Place some flour in the paper, then a piece of dough to give it weight, then some more flour; gather the corners of the paper and twist them together like a big paper torpedo; reinforce the twist with a piece of thread or string, and the shell is complete. Elevate the front of the ballista by placing some object under it—boards or stones—fasten the other end securely, with the check-string draw back the bat and fasten it back with the trigger. Place a shell in the chamber, pull the trip-string, and—bang! your flour bomb is hurled through the air at great speed, and when it strikes a hard object the paper bursts, and a cloud of flour flies out just as smoke does from a gunpowder shell.

By a few experiments the range can be very accurately measured, so that it is possible to strike repeatedly the same spot, or very near it. This is done by shortening the check-string and marking the length with a knot at the screw-eye. Now load and fire, and mark the spot where the bomb bursts, let out some more check-line, make another trial and mark the length with a knot, thus a knotted check-string will mark just where the shells will reach, and you can always reach the point you wish by letting out or winding up the check-line to the proper knot.

The foregoing description is intended for an engine to work in the city. In the country it is often possible to find two young trees of green growing wood that will answer for the uprights A and B. Out in the woods or fields you may shoot with almost any object without endangering life or limb.

Blow-guns.

The fierce cannibals of Borneo, the quaint and artistic little Javanese, and the wild tribes of South America all use blow-guns in hunting, and even to fight with. When people depend for their dinner or personal safety upon a "putty-shooter" you may be sure that they learn to shoot with great accuracy. Some of these natives use poisoned arrows, but we must admit that even a poisoned arrow can do but little execution unless it hits the mark.

The naked youngsters of Borneo and South America acquire great skill with a blow-gun, and there is no reason why the bright, intelligent boys of this country should not be able to become just as good marksmen. I have seen

FIG. 332. FIG. 333.

some wonderful shooting with a putty-blower in New York City, and I recall one very amusing incident.

I was returning from luncheon and had reached Broadway when my attention was attracted by a crowd. I found a fakir in the middle of the crowd. He opened his big mouth to shout his wares, then suddenly began to splutter, and finally spat a clay pellet out of his mouth. After the pellet came emphatic words and phrases that amused the crowd, but did not tend to elevate their morals. It was odd, and I laughed heartily, which so angered the fellow that he accused me of filling his mouth with mud.

No one in the crowd knew what on earth was the matter with the man, or where the clay came from; many evidently thought it was part of the programme. At that moment I caught sight of the laughing countenance of a well-known artist * in a window on the opposite side of the street. Knowing the artist very well, it was not difficult for me to imagine where the clay came from. As if for the purpose of dispelling all doubts in my mind, the mischievous fellow put a long glass tube to his mouth. and the next instant a piece of blue clay flattened itself on the fakir's hand. The street pedler was now in a towering rage, and I saw that he was looking over the crowd for me. Being peaceably inclined, I quietly left.

Great Skill with a Blow-gun.

This particular artist, by the way, was exceedingly skilful with a blow-gun. Twice I have seen him, using a common glass blow-gun, on the top of a five-story building, put a pellet into the mouth of a fakir on the sidewalk opposite. His good marksmanship, you may be sure, kept the corners around that building clear of street fakirs.

Years ago the Indians inhabiting the banks of the Mississippi River manufactured beautiful blow-guns from the stalks of cane that grows in the cane-brake along the shore. These toys were taken to New Orleans and other cities by the aborigines and sold to the boys. Unless the art of

* Before this book went to press my genial and fun-loving friend ceased his merry pranks. The brush and pen by which he gained honor and fame are laid aside forever. You will miss him, for you all know him.

making them has been preserved by the negroes of that section there are probably none to be had now, but the long glass tubes, such as are used by the artist, and the common tin putty-shooter can be bought in all parts of the country.

From the World's Fair I secured two beautiful blow-guns made in Java, and a few split bamboo arrows. Each of these arrows had a lump of loose raw cotton on the rear end, big enough to fill the blow-gun so that it might be expelled by a smart puff of air from the marksman's lungs. Anxious to see how they worked, I set up an old high hat and the first arrow pierced it to the cotton butt. If you use arrows in the place of clay or putty, you can derive plenty of amusement and sport, and develop remarkable skill by shooting at a target.

To Make the Target.

Hunt up an old wooden hoop; one from a barrel will do (Fig. 334). Take a piece of a sheet, or some similar cloth, dampen it thoroughly and lay the hoop over it (Fig. 335), and with a pair of shears trim the cloth in the form of a circle around the hoop to fold over. From your mother's work-basket borrow a large darning-needle; thread it with cotton string, and sew the cloth to the hoop by a stitch running over and over the hoop (Fig. 336).

A good piece of strong paper is the next thing required. Place the cloth-covered hoop over the paper, and with the shears trim off the paper, as is shown in Fig. 337. Cover the paper with flour paste, and paste the paper on the damp cloth, turning the edges of paper over the hoop as in Fig. 338. Allow it to dry. When it is perfectly dry it will be as tight as a drumhead.

Fig. 339 shows the front of the target as it should now

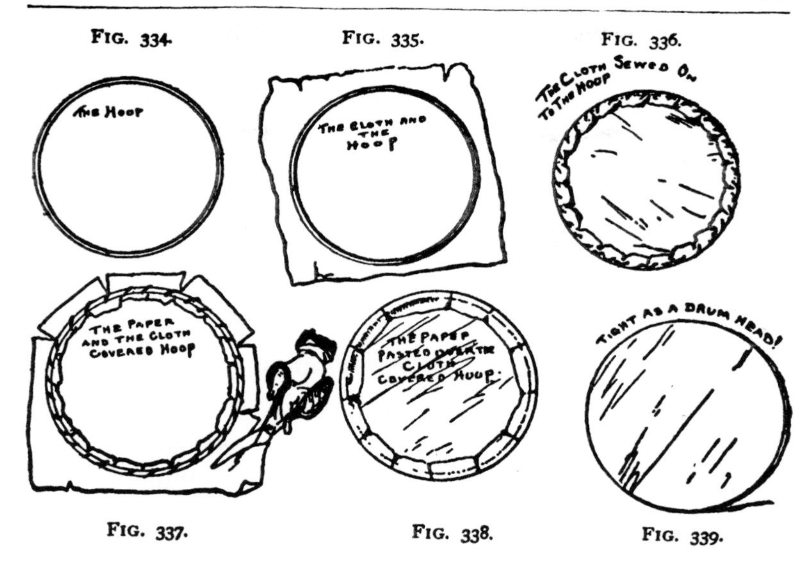

FIG. 334. FIG. 335. FIG. 336.

FIG. 337. FIG. 338. FIG. 339.

appear. Fig. 340 shows how to fasten the legs on. Fig. 341 shows the hind leg, which must be fastened only at the top by a piece of flexible leather for a hinge. In Fig. 342 can be seen all three legs attached.

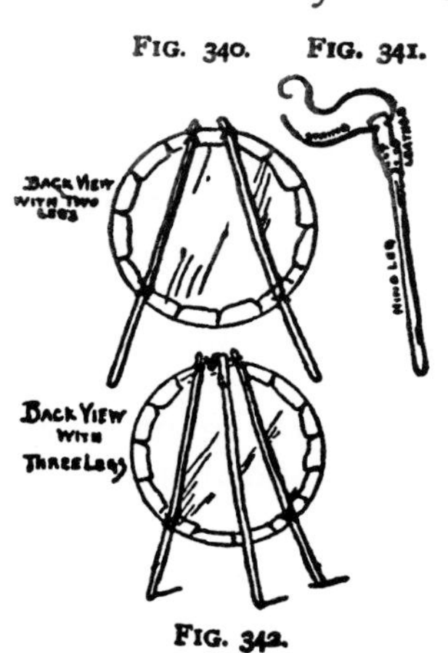

FIG. 340. FIG. 341.

FIG. 342.

With a pot of marking paint, or with common ink, paint a centre bull's-eye and a couple of circles on the paper covering the target and you have the finished butt. Split pieces of bamboo, or an old fishing-pole, into small pieces of about the thickness of a match and twice as long, sharpen one end of each piece and roll a bit of cotton very loosely around the blunt end of the arrow. Fasten the cotton at the point nearest the point of the arrow with a bit of thread or chewing-gum. Do not put too much cotton on the blunt ends of your arrows, only sufficient to make the bamboo fit loosely in your blow-gun.

With a long cane or bamboo blow-pipe from Java I sent such an arrow through a heavy curtain in my studio. Arrows that can be sent with such force are dangerous and should only be used in target practice.

Blow-gun Parachutes.

If you cut out a small, circular piece of very fine cloth or silk, and with a tack made of a pin that has been filed off, tack the centre of the cloth to the end of a bamboo arrow, using a bit of writing paper as a washer to prevent the pinhead from pulling through the cloth, you may make a dainty little parachute. Fasten a number of pieces of thread neatly to the edges of the cloth, and make them long enough, that when the cloth is folded the strings will just reach the cotton end of the arrow. The threads must all be exactly the same length and neatly tied to the stick about a quarter of its length from the butt end.

Shoot this arrow up in the air, and if you have made it properly when it descends the heavy end will fall first and will spread your little parachute like a tiny silk umbrella, and it will float airily down.

After you have made a few experiments you will discover how much weight you need at the blunt end of the arrow, and this may be adjusted by bits of chewing-gum or putty.

When you once succeed you will feel rewarded for your labor by the sight of the beautiful little air-ships sailing so lightly through the air, and no one not in the secret can tell how it is possible to shoot such things from a blow-gun.*

If the reader looks upon blow-guns as playthings for small boys, let him try

La Riata—The Lariat.

Properly speaking, there is no such thing as a "lasso." You may lasso things with *la riata*, but you cannot carry a "lasso," because lasso is a verb, and no cow-boy carries a verb coiled at his saddle-bow though he may have strings of forcible adjectives under his tongue.

The American cowboy learned the use of *la riata* from the Mexican, and he shortened the name and called it lariat, which has become the accepted name among Americans; but even this to the cow-boy's ears sounds far too alien and awkward, so he now calls it lass-rope or simply rope, and when he lassos a steer he briefly says he "roped it."

Boys' books are full of accounts and rules for archery and cricket, both of which are essentially English sports and have never become thoroughly naturalized in this country, but the graceful and useful art of throwing the lariat has never received the attention it deserves or been seriously adopted as a sport by our boys. Many of them, however, after visiting the Wild West show have played cow-boy, and with a bit of old clothes-line have made awkward efforts to lasso their comrades, who, it is presumed, represented the buffalo of the Wild West.

The very best lariats are made of raw hides. On Rosebud River there lives, or formerly lived, an old man who

* This toy is not altogether original with the author. He saw something of the kind described in a paper, but regrets that he is unable to remember what paper it was, and is thus unable to quote or give credit for the suggestion. Its application to the blow-gun is believed to be original.

was so skilful a workman that he could with propriety be called a lariat artist. One of the raw-hide ropes that he made I have in my studio, and it is admired by every cattle-man who chances to see it.

Fig. 343.

How the Raw-hide Lariat is Made.

The raw hide is first cut into strips as long as the hide will allow. The hide is half-tanned without removing the hair. The strips are next soaked in water and stretched over a block, after which they are neatly braided into a rope. During the latter process they are carefully pulled as tight as possible.

When this is done the rope is buried in the ground and allowed to remain in the earth two weeks to soften, after which it is dug up and again stretched over a block by means of heavy weights. After the hair has been sand-papered off, the rope thoroughly oiled or greased with mutton tallow and properly noosed, it is ready for use.

The lariats are made either forty or fifty feet long, according to the preference of the maker. Mr. Charles Lummis says the standard lariat is forty feet in length, but from other sources I learn that there are two standards, one of fifty and one of forty feet. The lariats vary also in thickness from three-eighths of an inch to half an inch. It takes a hardy, tough man to wield one of such dimensions. A rope twenty or thirty feet long is long enough for any boy to handle.

How to Make a Boy's Lariat.

A small iron ring, or eyelet, such as is used on sails and awnings, may be obtained at the hardware shop for a few cents. One end of the small rope, selected for the lariat, must now be unravelled, and the loose ends brought carefully around the ring from opposite directions, meeting again at the unwound part of the rope. Here they must lie neatly upon each side of the rope, bound tightly in place with a strong piece of twine as described in Chapter XXXIV., Figs. 355–364. The other end of the rope should be wound in the same manner to prevent it from unravelling. This will make as good a lariat as that used by many an expert cow-boy.

FIG. 344.

In certain parts of the country this form of "lass rope" is used exclusively. Of course when a boy becomes an expert he will be ambitious to have a raw-hide rope, and by writing to a Chicago firm, or some Western saddlery shop, he may procure one at market rates, which vary from eight to twenty dollars. There is also a braided linen line that is very good. But the home-made rope will answer all boyish purposes and afford him more pleasure than the heavy raw-hide "wolly" Western one can.

How to Throw the Rope.

Mr. Lummis recommends a loop of seven feet diameter to begin with, while the expert, Mr. Louis Ohnimus, starts with a noose only a foot or a foot and one-half in diameter, allowing the rope to slip and the noose to grow larger as he swings it; but most of my rope-throwing friends advise the large loop.

Take your position in front of a target, a post for instance. Run the end of the rope through the ring or "honda," as it is called. Coil the rope in your left hand, carefully leaving about six feet of loose rope between the coil and the noose, and see that there are no kinks in the line and that the coils will slip easily off when the noose is thrown (Fig. 343). Take hold of the noose with your right hand about a foot from the ring, and with the same hand grasp the rope the same distance below the ring or honda (pronounced onda) (Fig. 343). Do not hold your wrist stiffly, but allow it to move easily as you swing the noose over your head from right to left (Fig. 344). Let your wrist act as an axle, and swing the rope as if it were a wheel revolving horizontally around your wrist and over your head. Let it move with sufficient force to lengthen the noose, if you use the small noose, and swift enough to enable you to guide it if you have started with a large noose. When you feel that the proper time has arrived for making the cast, choose the moment as your swinging hand comes

FIG. 345.

around from back to front, give a quick step forward, bring your hand, with palm down, forward and down to the level of your shoulder, let it stretch to a full arm's-length without interrupting the swinging motion of the noose, and let it go at the post (Fig. 345).

In throwing the rope the right side of the loop should be lower than the other; then this side will strike first and throw the other side over the object.

If you have followed these rules without a slip it will not be a bad throw even though it is your first, and if you failed to circle the post you at least saw the noose sail straight at it without losing its circular form, and this will encourage you to try again and again until the poor post will become red in the face from the chokings it receives.

First strive to send the noose sailing on a level course. When this is achieved more than half the battle is won, and you can begin to teach your playmates this sport. Besides being typically American and great as an educator of the eye and developer of the muscles, it may be an exceedingly useful acquisition to a boy's list of accomplishments. Many a life of skater and swimmer has been lost that would have been saved had any of the panic-stricken spectators been able to cast a rope with even a small degree of accuracy.

The Lariat on Horseback.

Here you do not coil the rope, for it is ready coiled at your saddle-bow. The loop, however, when the rope is coiled at your saddle-bow is only the size of the fakes, or coil-loops; so the noose must be lengthened. You simply lift the rope from the saddle, and throw as described. The lariat is not made fast to the horn of the saddle, because that is exceedingly dangerous. A big bull, steer, horse, or even some of the smaller animals, when improperly roped, can throw horse and man. When the strain comes the rider makes a hitch over the saddle-horn that will hold if necessary, or that he can cast loose if the occasion demands. A cow-puncher who ties the riata to the saddle-horn is looked upon with scorn by his more proficient neighbors. The end of the rope should be held loosely in the left hand until the animal is caught, and then a couple of quick turns are taken with it around the saddle-horn.

Said a Western friend to me, "In roping from your horse the horse is trained to brace back as the rope tightens. In roping a cow or a steer the forefoot is always the target, never the head. All you have to do," he continued, "is to throw the rope in front of the beast so that the side of the noose nearest the cow is on the ground and the *other side in the air*. Then the animal will step right into it. See?"

I saw and tried it many times. It can be done after practice, no doubt, for cow-boys do it, but it is not so easy as it sounds.

CHAPTER XXXIV

"TALLY-HO" AND OTHER CRIES

The Origin of "Hello" and "Tally-ho"—Indian War-whoops and College Yells—Boys' Cries.

WOLVES were formerly very numerous in England. It was some time after the introduction of firearms that the last one was killed. A legend similar to that told of General Putnam credits a man and his son by the name of Polson with killing the last English wolf. The celebrated Sir Ewen Cameron of Lochiel killed the last wolf in Scotland in 1697. In the bog of Kilcrea, in Ireland, wolves remained until the beginning of the last century.

Wolf-hunting in England

was formerly not only an exciting sport but a duty which the government enforced upon its subjects. King Edgar remitted the punishment for certain crimes if the criminal could produce a given number of wolves' tongues. There was formerly a law which forced all the barons "to hunt and chase the wolfe and wolfe whalp (whelps) four times a year and as often as they see them. The Scherrif and Baille to hunt them thrice a year, with power to raise the country to their assistance."

When we remember how the wolves ran in large packs in the great forests we may imagine what a time they must have had in those wolf-hunts. How the burly old English hunters must have shouted! And what did they shout?

The French language was the language of the court, and they used the French wolf-hunter's cry of "Hab le loup! à lou loup!" or "au loup!" Gradually the French words were modified to "a-loo!" The wolves became extinct and the English added their favorite H and shouted "Ha-loo!" In this country the ancient wolf-hunter's cry is principally used to call up "Central" on the telephone, and we call it "Hello."

It will be noticed that all cries have a marked similarity. This is not because they all come from the same source, but because only such calls as possess great carrying qualities are retained in use. Two hundred years ago, according to a magazine of that date, the English fox-hunter's cry was

"Tallio, Hoix, Hark, Forward,"

which is a corruption of the French hunter's call. Four hundred years ago the gay French hunter encouraged his dogs with the musical cry of "*Thia-hilaud a qui forheur!*" * sometimes printed "*Tya-hillaut a qui forheur.*" From this the English manufactured "Tallio, hoix, hark, forward." Later it has been abbreviated to simply

"Tally-ho."

In very ancient times each soldier wore for a uniform whatever clothes he could procure, and no two were dressed alike. They had no banners or flags, but fought after the manner of our own American Indians, and like them they had their war-whoops. Every boy in America has felt the

* These huntsmen's shouts are given in a quaint and rare old French book illustrated with the queer pictures of the day and entitled "La Venerie de Jacques du Fouilloux, à Paris 1573."

cold chills run down his back as he has read of the silence of the frontier settlement being suddenly broke by the "blood-curdling yells of the Indians." A neighbor of mine who formerly employed an expatriate Indian tells me that on rare occasions his employee allowed the children to persuade him to give a war-whoop, "which he did with such energy that every living thing within hearing would stand spell-bound with astonishment or terror, until the echoes had died away."

I never heard this Indian, but have heard what purported to be the

War-cry of the Wild Tribes,

and I think it no worse than, nor indeed half as bad as, some of the yells given by the college or foot-ball teams. If you can imagine that one of these foot-ball teams was intent upon scalping you and burning your house, and if the stillness of the night should be suddenly broken by their "Rah! rah! rah! siss-boom-ah!" it would, without doubt, make your hair stand on end.

The Greeks had their "Eleleu!" the Scripture Alleluia, the Welsh their "Ubub," the Irish, "Ullulu," the Scots their various slogans.

"The Rebel Yell."

The old backwoodsmen that formed the rear-guard in our Revolution swept down on the redcoats with a yell that made British hearts stop beating, and in the Civil War of 1861–65 the descendants of these old backwoodsmen in the Confederate Army gave the same cry, and it was then known, and is still spoken of, as the rebel yell. It was borrowed from the Indians by the first settlers.

In olden times the Frenchman when he charged the

enemy cried "Monte Joye, St. Dennis," which was changed to "*Tue, tue!*" and the ancient Irishman shouted "Farrah! farrah!" The Scotch kings yelled "St. Andrew!" but every clan in Scotland had its own particular slogan. The Johnstones cried "Light thieves all!" the MacGregors, "Ard choille!" while the MacFarlane's watchwords were "Loch Sloidh!"

At first war-cries were only used by chiefs, princes, or commanders, and at tournaments the heralds thus proclaimed them. Now the degenerate descendants of these burly old fighting men use the self-same watchwords or war-cries as mottoes. In place, however, of being shouted from the hairy throats of men-at-arms to arouse warriors, they are embroidered on handkerchiefs, painted on private coaches, and used for book-plates!

"Coo-ee!"

is the call for help and the signal for recognition throughout Australasia. The yell is borrowed from the natives, and has remarkable carrying powers. It has been heard over the plains at wonderfully long distances. This cry is given in a head-tone something like the New York City milkman's early morning whoop. In the Australian bush anyone hearing the "Coo-ee!" is bound by the laws of the bush to reply, as it invariably means that some one has lost his way, or has met with some accident and needs assistance.

In the great Southwest of our own country, on the plains and in the mountains, the woodsmen and travellers use the Indian yell of

"Yaqui!"

from which the tribe of Indians takes its name. This cry is only used as a "hello." The first syllable is given in chest-, the second in head-tones, and the latter is generally prolonged. It is claimed that this call will carry farther than "Coo-ee."

Small Boys' Call.

All small boys in America have a peculiar method by which they signal or call to each other. This they do by a yell in which they suddenly change from a head-voice to a chest-voice, and produce a sort of warbling shriek that it is impossible for me to indicate with letters, but can easily be understood by any one who has ever heard the cry of the Loon or Great Northern Diver. After the boys grow older and their voices change it is impossible for them to give the call of their childhood.

"Whoo-ah!"

In parts of the South the boys use a cry which is probably an importation from Africa, brought over by the slave children. As near as I can spell it it is "Whoo-ah!" or "Hough-ah!" to which is generally added the name of the playmate who is thus greeted or called, as "Hough-ah, Ralph!" The cry is uttered in a loud but peculiarly soft tone, with a rising inflection on the hough. The rather long-drawn "ah!" is given in a lower tone.

"Mee-ma Red Eye!"

Another odd cry, the meaning of which I never learned, is from Kentucky. It is "Mee-ma! mee-ma!" Often the words "Red eye" are added to the cry, making it Mee-ma, red eye! mee-ma!" Generally this cry is used in derision. If one boy excels another in jumping he cries "Mee-ma!" or the victorious ball-nine will "Mee-ma" the vanquished nine.

"Oh!"

In the East one boy calls to another by simply shouting his name, as "Johnny!" or, "Say, Johnny!" but in the Southwest the boys cry "Oh, Johnny!" with a long-drawn "Oh."

For some reason little attention has been paid to these peculiar cries by students of folk-lore and their origin is doubtful.

"Lil!" "Track!" "Way!"

are the shouts of warning sounded by boys when coasting. In Cincinnati, O., and Covington, Ky., they cry "Track! Clear the track!" as they come tearing down the hill on their long sleds with solid runners bound with half-round iron. In the vicinity of New York the bob-sleigh's pilot shouts "Way!" an abbreviation of "Clear the way;" but in certain parts of Yankeedom the bob-sleigh lads cry "Lil! lil! lil!" the origin of which is lost in the forgotten and unrecorded lore of boyhood.

The Nereus Boat Club boys of Flushing, L. I., have a very effective yell which can easily be heard and distinguished for long distances over the water. It begins with a head-note and ends with three chest-notes:

"K-e-e Yoy! Hoo! Hoo!"

The first syllable is long drawn out, the second is a little shorter, and the last two are short and quick.

Most of the college yells consist of a repetition of an abbreviation of "Hoorah," repeated over and over again with the name of the college thrown in the middle or at the end of the cry. This is sometimes varied by the addition of an imitation of the ascent of a sky-rocket and of the exclamation of the spectators when they behold the bursting rocket shed its shower of golden fire. This is rendered "Siss!" the rocket ascending; "boom!" the rocket exploding; "ah!" the people's expression of admiration and pleasure.

The notes of frogs, dogs, and crowing cocks are often introduced. One Brooklyn military company has a "tiger" composed of a provincial expression borrowed from the farmers. When drawled out by a hundred throats the phrase, "I-wanter-know!" always produces a laugh.

Princeton.

All who have visited the foot-ball fields where the desperate contest for the championship between the colleges takes place are familiar with the wild yell of the Princeton tigers which is delivered in thirty seconds' time at each good play or bad play of the striped-legged gladiators, "Hurrah! Hurrah! Hurrah! Tiger-siss-boom-ah! PRINCETON!" And the sturdy sons of

Yale

reply vehemently and vociferously three times three, "Rah! rah! rah! Rah! rah! rah! Rah! rah! rah! YALE!" quickly and sharply enunciated. The crimson

Harvard.

Harvard boys cry, with long-drawn deep notes, "Rah, rah! rah! Rah! rah! rah! Rah! rah! rah! HARVARD!"

Cornell.

Better than any one of the foregoing, in my opinion, is the "Cornell I yell! yell! yell! CORNELL!" This yell will make more noise for a few men than any other except, possibly, the *old* (not the present) Lehigh yell. Then there is the odd, "chewy" cheer of the

Williams College

boys, with its emphatic start and finish, "Rah, rah, rah! Yums! yams! yums! WILLYUMS!"

Trinity College

boys hurrah with a "Rah! rah! rah! Trinity! Boom-rah! Boom-rah! TRIN-EYE-TEEE!"

Wesleyan College

lads are rivals of the Trinities and send back an answering yell of "Rah! rah! rah! rah! Wesleyana! Rah! rah! rah! rah!" which is answered by the

Brown

fellows with a hearty "Rah, rah, rah, rah! BROWN!"

After all the monotonous "Rah! rah! rahs!" it is quite refreshing to hear the original wild and woolly cry of the

Colorado

boys, as with Western enthusiasm they swing their hats and shout "Rah! rah! rah! Pike's Peak or bust! Colorado College! Yell we MUST!"

The Leland Stanford, Jr.,

boys borrowed their yell from the red-men, "Wah hoo! Ya hoo! L. S. J. U! STANFORD!"

In the

Dartmouth

cheer the soft notes suggest Indian origin, but they are very musical compared with the rasping yell of some of the others: "Hi! hi! hi! Rah! rah! rah! D-d-d-d-Dartmouth, wah, who, wah!" or, "Wah, who, wah! Wah, who, wah! Da, di, di Dartmouth! Wah, who, wah!"

The old Knickerbockers have left an heir-loom in their rally which has been incorporated in the

Union College

cheer of "Rah, rah, rah! U-N-I-O-N. Hikah! hikah! hikah!"

Possibly the honor of having a yell that consumes the most time in voicing belongs to the

University of Illinois,

but time is no object to these boys so long as they continue to make a noise, and, if possible, drown the cries of their rivals with "Rah, hoo, rah! Zipp, boom, ah! Hip-zoo! Rah-zoo. Jimmy blow your bazoo! Ip-sidi-iki U. of I. campaign!" The length of the above is in strong contrast with the brevity of the yell of

Hanover.

The Hanover boys think they can make just as much noise with their short cry of "Han! Han! HANOVER!" and doubtless do when their lungs are in good condition. Like the Knickerbocker Dutchmen, the early French settlers of Missouri have left a bit of their mother tongue in the watchwords of

Westminster.

Of course the inevitable "'rah" is the opening note of their slogan. "Rah, rah, rah! Oh, yes, sir! Vive-la, Vive-la! WESTMINSTER!"

Cornell, of Iowa,

does not want to be confounded with the other Cornell, and though they have had numerous war-cries, I believe they have now settled down to a sort of sky-rocket noise, represented by "Zip-siss-boom! Cor-cor-nell! C-C. tiger-la! Zip-siss-hurrah!"

Amherst

has a cheer of the conventional type: "Rah! rah! rah!" etc., and terminating with the name of their institution. Boston people are modest folk until they mention their beautiful city of crooked streets. Then they swell with pride, and the pupils of

The Boston University

modestly give their cry under their breath until they come to the final Boston, which word is given with the full force of their lungs, thus: "Boston, B-B-BOSTON! Varsity! Varsity! Varsity! Rah! rah! rah!"

It is told of the

Cumberland University

that they once gave an out-door banquet on the mountains, and in the discussion that arose as to what their war-cry should be, some one suggested that they leave it to the echo to decide. Now there was more than one echo hiding in the mountains, and when the college shouted out the inquiry, "Where are you?" all the echoes made haste to repeat the sentence, and jumbled the words so that it sounded like "Roo raw roo?" Thereupon the boys decided that their cheer should be: "Roo. rah! Roo. rah!

Roo, rah! Rau! Roo, rah! Roo, rah! CUMBER-LAND!"

They once had a mascot in the form of a dog at

Rutgers,

and the boys now yell "Rah, rah, rah! Bow-wow-wow! RUTGERS!"

The Rochester University

cry is "Waxico, waxico, waxico, wax! Waxico, waxico, waxico, wax! Brek-k-ks—Brek-k-ks, ah-h-ah! ROCHES-TER!"

University of Washington

has this cry: "U. of W.! Hiah! Hiah! U. of W.! U. of W.! Siah! Siah! Shooken! Shookem! WASHINGTON."

Hobart's Cry

is: "Hip-ho-bart! Hip-ho-bart! Hip-ho, hip-ho, HIP-HO-BART!"

Syracuse University

cry is: "Srah—Srah—Srah—Sy-ra-cuse!"

The University of Pennsylvania

has a cheer of old Dutch origin. Besides these university slogans each class has its own call, which varies every year, but they are all of the same general style. One that I remember is: "Johnny, get your gun! Johnny, get your gun! We're the class of 'Ninety-one!" The Class of Ninety-one of the Quaker boys of Swarthmore had a unique cry of M.D.!—C.C.C.!—X.C.I.!—S.C!"

The number of club, class, school, and university yells is unlimited; but if any one of the readers of this book wants to invent a cheer, remember to choose first such sounds as will make the most noise; second, to end up with the name of his club or organization, the idea being first to attract attention, and second, to advertise your society, school, or university, by impressing its name on the willing or unwilling ears of your hearers. In the same way the old Scots would yell the name of their leader, prince, or clan, so that their foe might know who were the valiant men they were fighting, and might always afterward remember their name or the name of their leader.

CHAPTER XXXV

INDIAN GAMES ADAPTED FOR BOYS

Squaw, Saddle-bags, or Sky Shinny—The Way the Game is Played—An Exhilarating Sport—Mandan Ring—A Fine Game for Autumn or Winter.

In place of a bung or a golf-ball a pair of bags are used for the game of Squaw, Saddle-bags, or Sky Shinny, as it is variously called. These are made of soft leather or buckskin, and are connected by a strap twenty-four inches long, securely sewed to the bags at each end. The bags are seven by four inches, and usually contain corn, beans, or some similar material. The bags should not be heavy enough to make dangerous missiles, but should be of sufficient weight to render it possible to throw them a considerable distance (Fig. 347).

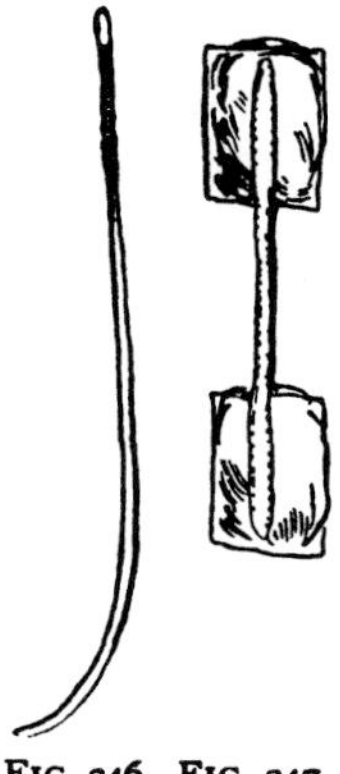

No one is allowed to touch the bags with his hands or feet. Each player is supplied with a light, strong ash or hickory stick curved at one end like a shinny or golf-stick. (Fig. 346). It is with these sticks that the bags are picked up from the ground, skilfully caught on the fly, and carried, while the player makes a rush for goal; or the sticks may be used like slings or throwing-sticks, with which to send the twin bags sailing over the heads of the tribe.

Fig. 346. Fig. 347. Saddle-bags and Squaw Stick.

The Rules

governing this game are similar in many respects to those governing the old game of foot-ball as played at Rugby. But in this game there is no kicking another fellow's shins or legs below the knee, as the Rugby boys do. No player is allowed to kick either below or above the knee, or to trip another player with foot or stick.

The ground on which Saddle-bags is played is called the "prairie," and is the same size as the foot-ball field, with the same boundaries. There are two goals, one at each end of the field, consisting of two uprights with cross poles about ten feet from the ground.

There may be any number of

Players,

divided as in foot-ball, but with different names.

The rushers are called the *tribes*, the half-backs *braves*, the full-backs *bucks*, and the captains *chiefs*.

The game begins by the two chiefs tossing up for choice of goals or first cast. If the winner chooses first cast, the loser has choice of goals; if the winner takes choice of goals the loser has first cast.

After these preliminaries are settled the two chiefs place their men, sending the bucks back to guard the goals, and the braves to a position between the bucks and the tribe. The duties of the braves are liable to begin immediately upon the opening of

The Game,

particularly if the opposing side makes a good cast, and the saddle-bag comes whirling over the tribe to where the braves are placed. The braves must be ready and are expected to catch the bags, and whoever does so must run for dear life, with the bags swinging from the end of his stick. When he sees that he can carry them no farther he must cast them with might and main for the goal, or, if necessary, pass them from his stick to that of one of his tribe, who receives them and does his "level best" to carry or cast them to the goal, or pass them to still another of his own tribe.

It is the duty of the opposing braves to do their utmost to intercept or tackle the foe, who carries the bags on his stick, or to lift the bags from the enemy, and having obtained them to run as fast as possible in the opposite direction, and go through all the tactics already described.

The bags are free to all when in play, but you are not allowed to capture them by forcibly striking the enemy's stick or person with your stick, though it is considered perfectly fair to lift them by thrusting, poking, slipping, or inserting the end of your stick under the bags and lifting them from their perch on the enemy's rod.

It is the duty of the tribe to gain possession of the saddle-bags when a brave is stopped, and to fling them with all possible force toward the goal. The duty of the bucks is similar to that of the braves, whenever the bags pass over the heads of the latter.

The Score.

No advantage that counts in the score is gained by either side until the bags are cast over the goal or carried beyond the enemy's goal-line. A run over the goal-line counts one scalp; a cast under the goal-stick and over the goal-line counts three scalps; a goal, that is, a cast over the goal-stick, counts ten scalps. If by accident the saddle-bags catch and hang on the goal-stick, it is called a straddle and counts eight scalps. When the bags fall outside the boundaries they are placed on the "prairie" by the umpire at the point, as near as he can judge, where they crossed the line for a scrimmage as in foot-ball, only in this case the bags must be sent overhead.

The Umpire.

It is the duty of the umpire to watch that no player kicks, strikes, or butts another, and warn him for the first offence and rule him off the field for the second. All doubtful points are decided by the umpire by the rules of football. The side that first scores forty-five points is the victor.

Considerable skill is required to play a good game of Saddle-bags, and besides this there is any amount of excitement and exercise with a minimum amount of danger. Once a crowd of boys learn the game well enough to make an occasional goal with a long cast across field they will become fascinated with the good American game of Saddlebags, which is adapted, with few changes of any importance, from an old game of our red-skinned brothers.

Mandan Ring

is a beautiful game and originated in America. It has no ancestor on the other side of the ocean, but was introduced among the American Indians by the Mandans, who now muster scarcely enough warriors to make a good game.

The ring used by the Indian sportsmen is laboriously carved from stone, but a good iron or metal ring, four inches in diameter, can be obtained at most hardware shops or made to order by a blacksmith, or bought from a junkman. The "tchungkees," or spears, you must manufacture yourselves.

How to Make the Tchungkee.

Hunt up a piece of ash or hickory about the size of a hoop-pole. Cut off the extra wood so that the stick will measure six feet in length. With a good jack-knife you can whittle the stick down to something of the proportions of a billiard-cue, except that the butt end should be considerably smaller, not larger, than a medium-sized walking-stick. Taper the spear to a blunted point at the top and see that it is well balanced. With a piece of broken glass scrape it smooth and be careful to make it straight. When, in your judgment, your tchungkee is finished, mark off four divisions, each a foot apart, and the first a foot from the top or point of the spear (Fig. 353).

Leather Barbs.

Next you must procure enough good thick leather to cut into ten pieces, each three inches long by one and one-half inch wide. With a sharp knife make a slit at one end of the leather, dividing it equally for one and one-half inch (Fig. 348). With the same sharp knife taper off the other end of the leather as shown by Fig. 349. Make twelve of these leather barbs, and then with an awl or some similar instrument bore holes as shown in Fig. 349.

These barbs are to fit on the foot-marks on the lance, and must be fastened on in the following manner: Bend the legs of the barb in opposite directions (Fig. 350); with a small brass or copper brad tack one barb at each mark on the spear; divide each foot marked on the rod into three divisions of four inches each, and one-third the distance around the spear, that is, one-third of the circumference measured from the leather barbs already nailed on; fasten another row of barbs, one at each four-inch mark (Figs. 352 and 354).

Two-thirds of the distance around the tchungkee fasten on the remaining leather barbs at the eight-inch marks. To give a good finish the legs of each barb should be tightly and evenly wound with shoemaker's waxed thread (Fig. 352). Start off with a clove hitch. Bend your line in a loop as in Fig. 355. Make another loop as shown in

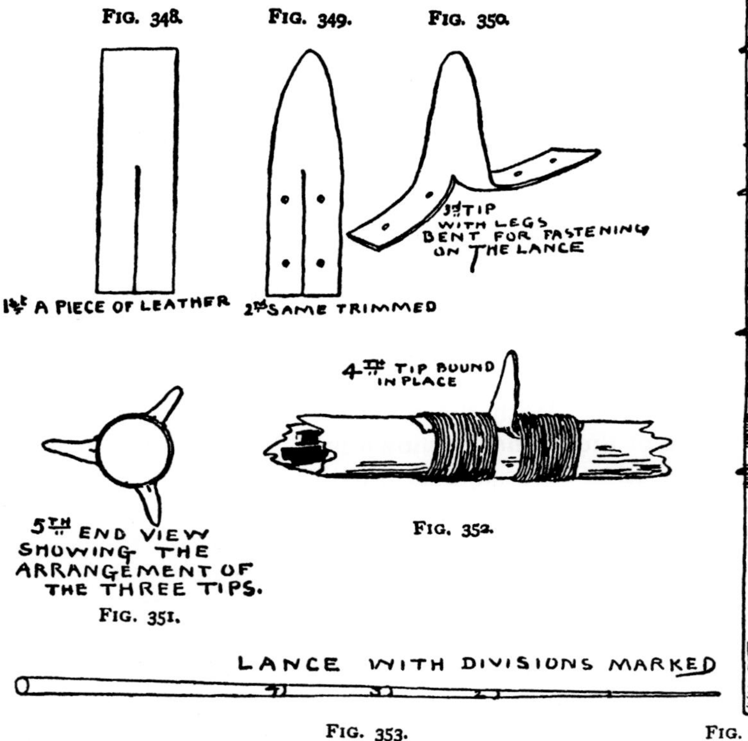

FIG. 353. FIG. 354

Construction of the Tchungkee.

the next diagram. Fig. 356 shows the double loop. Place the first loop over the second as shown in Fig. 357. Thrust the rod through the double loop (Fig. 358). Draw the lines tight as in Fig. 359. Bring the end A to one side and lay the end B along the rod (Fig. 360). Take the end A and wrap the line neatly around the stick and over the line B for the required distance, leaving a small margin for a few additional wraps (Fig. 361). Now take B and make a long loop, bringing the end B up as shown in Fig. 362. Make a few additional wraps and thrust A through the protruding loop as in Fig. 363. Pull B tight so that A is brought up under the binding. Then cut both ends off close to the stick (Fig. 364). You will find that this will not unwind or leave any exposed ends. Finally give a coat of varnish or paint.

If you have followed the directions carefully your tchungkee when placed upon the ground will always pre-

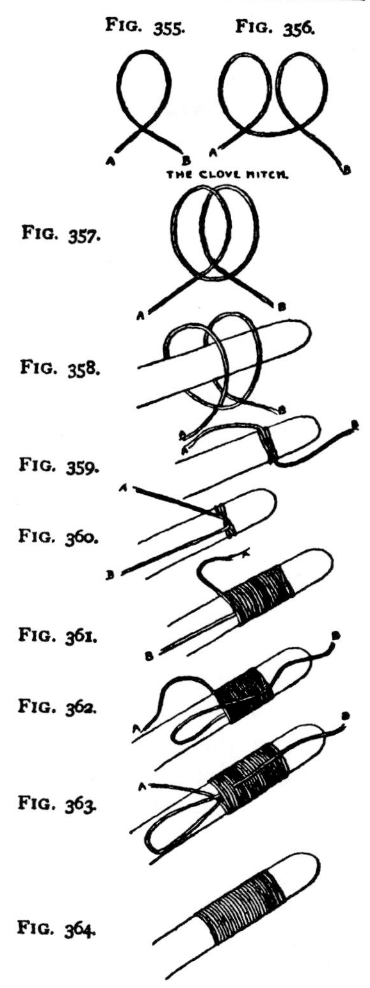

How to Bind the Lance, a Fish-rod, a Bow, or for Mending any sort of Rod or Stick.

sent a row of upright leather barbs, while it rests on two other rows. Fig. 351, an end view, explains this.

How to Play Mandan Ring.

If there are more than two boys, choose up for sides, and toss up for first inning. This decided, the chief of the Ins takes the ring and his tchungkee, and the chief of the Outs follows him with his tchungkee, ready for use. Shoulder to shoulder they start on a run, and when under good headway the Ins' chief throws the ring so that it will roll like a hoop. Both chiefs follow and throw their lances before them as they run, in such a manner that the tchungkees slide along the ground or pavement one on each side of the ring. This they do—picking up their lances and throwing them again as long as the ring keeps rolling.

How the Score is Made.

No count can be made in the game if your lance is on the other boy's side. The object of the player is to have his lance alongside the ring when it stops, and if the ring falls over one of the leather barbs, that counts a number of points in the game, regulated by the location of the barb. The first leather counts one, the second two, etc. The loser of the first run is out, and the winner rolls the iron ring with the next boy from the opposite side. This continues until the game is won by one side or the other. The game may be any number of points you may agree upon.

This should become a popular American boys' game, as it possesses all the qualities necessary to make a popular sport, and can be played upon any hard, smooth surface.

The composition street-paving that is now becoming common in the cities makes the best of play-grounds for Mandan Ring. Where the ground will admit the players may wear roller-skates, and in winter it makes a fine game on the ice, in which case all the players of course wear skates.

CHAPTER XXXVI

ON THE FOOT-BALL FIELD

The Antiquity of the Game—The General Principles of the Game as It Is Played by the College Teams at Present.

POSSIBLY the foot-ball players are unaware of the important fact that they have a patron saint. At Lincoln, in England, in 1520, a boy named Hugh was a champion foot-ball player, and he met his death from kicking the ball through the open window of a Jew's house. The old verse says that

"Four and twenty bonny boys
Were playing at the ba',
And by it came him sweet Sir Hugh
And he played o'er them a'.

"He kicked the ba' with his right foot
And catched it wi' his knee;
And throck-and-thro' the Jew's window
He gar'd the bonny ba' flee."

It seems that the Jew did not take the same interest in the game that we now do, and so he or his daughter enticed "sweet Sir Hugh" into the house and cut him up with a big knife after the fashion of the day. After the crime was discovered sweet Sir Hugh had a great funeral, and he was made a saint. According to the legend, "miracles were performed at his tomb."

But foot-ball was

An Old Game

before Sir Hugh was born. As far back as 1349 we find a public edict prohibiting the game. It is not to be supposed that the ancient game bore any striking resemblance to the modern American foot-ball, and there is little doubt that another ancient game of ball called "hurling," in which two towns battled for a ball of wood or precious metal, has been mixed with plain foot-ball; and from the mixture of kicking the ball and rushing with it in the arms was evolved the Rugby and then the American game of foot-ball.

FIGS. 365 and 366. —A Place Kick at Princeton.

FIG. 367.—A Snap Back.

FIG. 368.—A Pass.

FIGS. 369, 370, and 371. — A Place Kick at Yale.

FIGS. 372, 373, and 374. — Some Good Tackles at Yale.

SKETCHED ON THE FIELD.

The Only Way

in which to learn the modern American game is by careful study, not of books alone, but of the players in match and practice games. A paper-covered copy of Spalding's official foot-ball guide, containing the latest revised rules, can be obtained at an expenditure of about ten cents, and with this in your pocket to refer to, you will soon learn to see science where the untrained eye sees only an apparently heedless rough-and-tumble scrimmage.

When you yourself play, keep the rules handy for reference, and when in doubt as to the real meaning of a rule, never hesitate to address a note to some famous player asking an explanation. You may almost invariably count upon his interest in the game being great enough to insure you a speedy and satisfactory reply.

The Game.

By looking at the plan of the field you will see that it resembles a gridiron. In reality the foot-ball field is a sort of giant chess or checker board with long strips in place of squares and with but one chessman or checker, and that is the oval, leather-covered ball. The moves are made by main force and strategy and consist of a number of "downs," runs, or kicks as the judgment of the player may dictate.

The Points in the Game

are counted as follows:

Goal by touch-down ...... * * * * * *	2
Touch-down without goal. * * * * * *	4
Goal from field kick ...... * * * * * *	5
Safety by opponents...... * * * * * *	2

The Ball

is egg-shaped and called the "intercollegiate match ball." Many boys in the rural districts have the leather cover for their ball made at the shoemaker's or harness shop. Inside the leather cover they put a bladder which is inflated by the use of a quill and a healthy pair of lungs. The nozzle is then tied fast with a bit of string and pushed out of sight and harm's way and the leather cover is laced up.

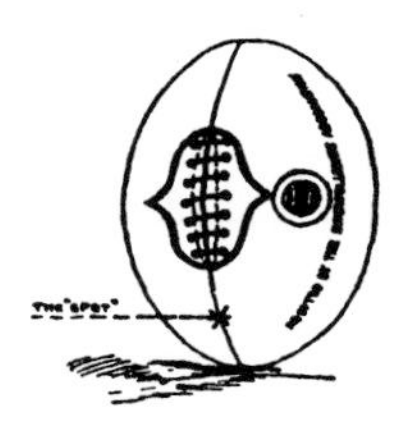

FIG. 375.—The Ball and the Invisible Spot.

Most of my readers will find it cheaper to purchase the regulation ball, which is similar to the rustic one. It is egg-shaped, of course, but in place of a bladder it has an India-rubber oval inside, which may be inflated by a little pump similar to those used for inflating bicycle tires.

The Field.

Upon a level stretch of ground mark out a rectangular figure one hundred and sixty feet wide by three hundred and thirty feet long, and, for convenience in determining how far the ball is advanced at each down, divide the field up with cross lines every fifteen feet or five yards. You can make the lines and boundaries with ordinary whitewash and brush.

Measure eighty feet from one corner along the end line of the field and mark the point. Do the same on the opposite end, and as the end lines are each one hundred and sixty feet long the two points will mark the centres of the lines. Measure nine feet three inches to the right and to the left of the centre points on the end lines and plant your four goal-posts, two at each end of the field. This will leave

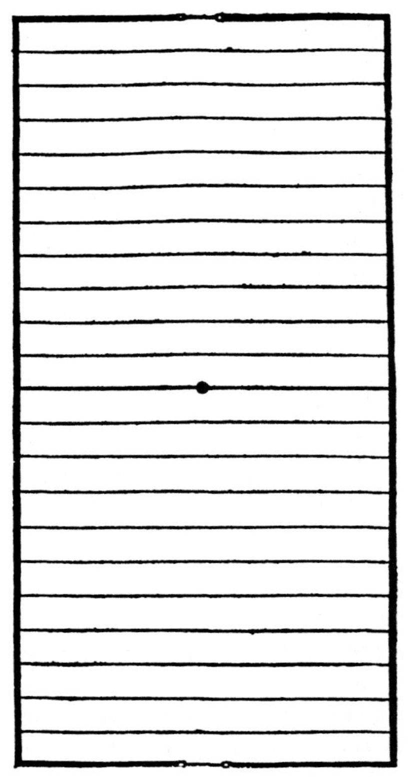

FIG. 376.—The Field.

the regulation space of eighteen feet six inches between the posts. The cross bar should now be placed on these poles ten feet from the ground. The uprights should extend over ten feet above the cross bar.

The Teams

in regulation games consist of eleven men each, but for practice or impromptu games among boys, as few as four on a side will make a game full of fun and exercise.

The eleven men in the regulation game are divided into rushers and backs. A quarter-back, two half-backs, and a full-back. The first seven or line men who are known as centre, right-guard, right-tackle, right-end, left-guard, left-tackle, and left-end. The captains of the respective teams number the plays and keep the numbers secret. But they ofttimes first call false numbers to confuse their opponents and not "give away" the proposed play.

The Kicks

all have special names, such as a

Drop-kick, when the ball is dropped from the hand and kicked the instant it touches the ground ; the

Place-kick, made by kicking the ball after it has been placed on the ground ; the

Punt, made by kicking the ball as it falls from the hands and before it reaches the ground ; the

Kick-off, is a place-kick made from the centre of the field. The kick-off cannot score a goal. The

Kick-out, when one of the players on the side which has touched the ball down in its own goal makes a punt, drop-kick, or place-kick. A

Free-kick, any kick where the rules forbid the opponents from advancing beyond a certain point.

In-Touch.

In-touch is out of bounds.

A Touch-down is when the ball is kicked or carried across the goal line and held there.

A Touch-back is when the player touches the ball to the ground behind his own goal, the ball having been propelled over the line by an opponent.

A Safety Touch-down, is when either by a kick, pass, or a snap-back, the player guarding his goal receives the ball from one of his own side and touches it down behind his goal line, or when he carries the ball across his own goal line and touches it down, or when he puts the ball in his own touch-in-goal, or if the ball, being kicked by one of his own side, bounds back from an enemy across the goal line and the player guarding the goal then touches it down.

A Fair Catch.

When a player kicks a ball and it is caught on the fly by an opponent, the catcher of the ball may plant his heel in the ground, marking the spot where the catch was made. If none of the catcher's side touched the ball it is called a fair catch. It is customary for the man making the catch to announce the fact by shouting "Fair Catch!" or by holding up one hand or by both.

The Heel-mark

is the limit beyond which the opponents of the player making a fair catch cannot advance until the ball is again put in play. The catch entitles the player to the privilege of retiring as far back of the heel-mark toward his own goal as he may see fit, and of taking there a place-kick, punt, or drop-kick, or he may give the ball to some one on his own team for a scrimmage, which is governed by the rules of a scrimmage. In case he takes a free kick he must send the ball at least ten yards, unless some opponent stops the ball.

Off Side.

A player is off side when he is between the ball and his opponent's goal. If, however, the ball first touches an opponent, an off-side player is thus put on side.

A player is

On Side

when he is not between the ball and his opponent's goal, except, as noted above, in case the ball touches an opponent.

When a ball goes

Out of Bounds

by crossing the boundary line of the gridiron, it is said to go "into touch," and one of the players must immediately bring it back to the point where it crossed the line. It is then put in play by a member of the side which carried it out of bounds, or which was first to capture the ball after it crossed the touch line. He may touch-in in bounds at right angles to the side line and then kick it, or run with it, or he will probably call out the number of paces he intends to walk in, so as to give his opponents a fair show, and then he must take the agreed number of steps; but the distance cannot be less than five yards or more than fifteen yards.

If the player carries the ball across one of the end lines, he obtains a touch-down at the spot where the ball after being carried over is held. Any player on his team may now bring the ball out, making a mark by a twist of his heel on the line as he walks. When a point is reached which he considers best suited to his purpose, he places the ball for one of his own team to kick while the opponents retire behind their goal line.

When the progress of the game has advanced the ball to a point within kicking distance of the goal, it is an open question whether it is best to take a drop-kick at goal or make an effort to carry the ball across goal. If the latter play is successful it is a touch-down and entitles you to a try-at-goal; but when no score is made by a drop-kick on a first down inside the twenty-five-yard line the ball can be brought out for only a ten-yard kick-out, which means that your side can line up at ten yards.

This compels the players guarding the goal to kick-out

practically within their own goal line. From this it may be seen that the running attempts or drop-kick must be wisely chosen at this point of the game in accordance with the relative risk and gain, but all these problems should be studied on the field.

At any time a player may kick, pass, or carry the ball across his own goal line and touch it down there for safety. This scores two points for the other team, but his side may take the ball out to the twenty-five-yard line and there have a kick-out. He may punt the ball or take a drop-kick or a place-kick.

Much has been said and written on the different plays in the modern game of foot-ball, and pages have been devoted to the proper manner of making one move in the game. When I lately visited Princeton and Yale to study the game I found the men devoting their odd moments to experiments and practice on

FIG. 377.—A Place-kick. View looking down on players' head.

Place-kicking.

We have already seen that a place-kick is made after the ball is placed on the ground. In the accompanying sketches Figs. 365, 366, 367, and 377, it will be noticed that the player on the kicker's side is holding the ball with the lower end just off the ground (Figs. 365 and 377). As long as it continues in this position it is not "in play." The moment the ball touches the ground it *is* "in play," and the enemy lined up on their goal line will charge and block the kick, if possible.

The Formation

is to a great extent governed by the plays to be made, but as a general rule the seven rushers stand in line of battle facing their opponents. Just behind the rushers stands the quarter-back, and a few yards in the rear of him the two half-backs are placed; while a dozen yards farther back, alone in his glory, the full-back guards his precious goal.*

The Toss-up.

If a strong wind is blowing the winner of the toss-up takes the side favored by the wind, and the other team have the kick-off. If there is no wind to speak of, and no great advantage in either goal, the winner of the toss-up chooses the kick-off, and the other side have the choice of goals.

Lining Up.

The two teams now line up in their respective positions, and the ball is placed upon the exact centre of the field by the side having the kick-off.

As a rule the full-back is a good kicker and is selected to open the game.

To the right of the ball on the line stands right-guard, alongside of him is right-tackle, next to him is right-end, then comes right half-back and quarter-back, while stretched out on the line to the left of the ball are the centre, left-guard, left-tackle, left-end and left half-back. All these sturdy men are ready to rush upon their opponents the moment full-back's toe touches the ball.

As the rules require the opposite side to stand at least

---

*Lately there is a tendency to make full-back do more work, and he is often seen playing in much closer proximity to the others.

ten yards back of the middle line, they form themselves in a sort of rough triangle so as to be able to guard the whole

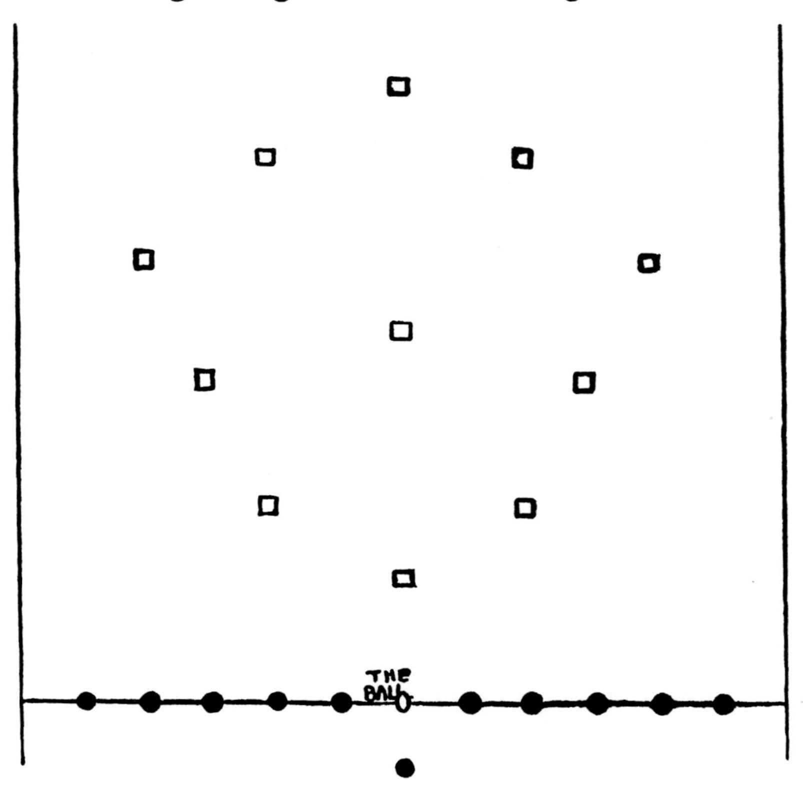

FIG. 378.—The Rounds are about to open the game by a kick-off. The Squares are ready to receive the ball and the rushers.

field and stop the ball with the least possible waste of time. At the required ten yards back of the centre line, centre of the opposing side is posted, back of centre stand the two guards, back of them the two tackles with the quarter-back between them, behind them the two half-backs are stationed with full-back "plugging the centre" in front of his goal. There are no rules for placing the men on the field, and the formation here given may be, and is, altered to suit the ideas of the different captains of the various teams.

The player selected to kick the ball must send it at least ten yards into the opponent's camp, and it is usually sent as much farther as the judgment of the kicker directs. It is not expected that half-grown boys will play the game as scientifically as the college experts. When a boy makes a kick-off his judgment usually tells him to kick the ball as far as possible. When the ball comes sailing over into their ranks the enemy catch it and either return it by a kick or one of them runs with the ball.

The Scrimmage.

Now when the player made the kick-off he calculated that the rushers on his side could reach the ball in time to prevent the enemy making much headway with it, and the enemy calculated to interfere in all lawful ways with the kick-off's rushers. If the enemy who holds the ball starts for a run, the men on the other side tackle him and down he comes. Just as soon as the player and ball are brought to a standstill the runner cries "down." Then someone on the runner's side, usually the fellow called snap-back or centre-rush, places the ball on the ground at the spot where it came to a standstill, and the ball is put in play by the snap-back kicking it or snapping it back, generally with his hand but sometimes with his foot, to the quarter-back of his own side, who has taken a position just behind snap-back. Up to this moment the men of each team have kept their positions upon their own side of the ball, but as soon as the ball is put in motion both sides may press forward and the scrimmage commences. Quarter-back, when he receives the ball quickly passes it back to half-back or full-back who runs with or kicks it.

When

A Snap-back

is to be made the boys arrange themselves in the following manner. Centre has the ball (squares in Fig. 379), back of him stands quarter-back ready to receive it, and still farther in the rear is full-back with left half-back and right half-back little in advance, and flanking them on either side a short distance farther in advance are the two ends. Each one of the five is ready to receive the ball from quarter-back according to the signal. Centre is flanked upon each side by the two guards and two tackles, and the five face their opponents, who are lined up with their centre in the middle, and the two guards, two tackles, two ends, and two half-backs standing on their relative sides of centre forming the line, while a short distance behind centre stands quarter-back, and still farther in the rear full-back. (Black dots in Fig. 379.)

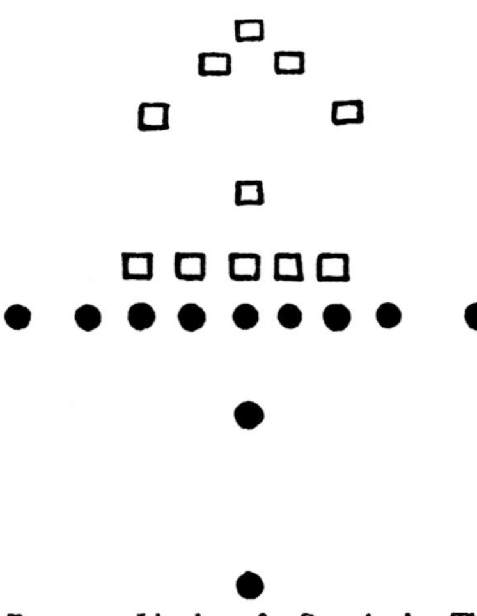

FIG. 379.—Lined up for Snap-back. The Squares have the ball.

After looking over Fig. 379 a college friend recommends the following changes in the formation: Bring the five squares up much closer to the front line and place them farther apart. Place the quarter-back of the black dots close behind the centre of his own side. Move the full-back of the black dots to a position just behind the quarter-back, and place the two half-backs of the same side just behind the ends. All this is a matter of choice to be governed by experience, and each side is formed according to its captain's ideas on the subject.

As soon as the ball is put in play there is a general rush; those on the side of the ball surround the runner and try to force their way through the ranks of their opponents. When snap-back has sent the ball behind him, he has placed the men in his own line between the ball and the enemy's goal off-side. The men on-side have the best claim to right of way, and the rules of the game only allow the off-siders in this case to use their bodies to obstruct their opponents, while the on-siders may use their hands and arms to open a passage for themselves, but they are not allowed to catch hold of their opponents.

It can readily be seen that one side might keep the ball for a long time with no material benefit to themselves, but the possibility of this "dog-in-the-manger" act is prevented by a rule which says that a side not making five yards toward the opponent's goal or retreating twenty yards toward their own goal, in three downs or efforts to advance the ball must give the ball to the other side.

Such a surrender seldom occurs, because if after two attempts to advance the ball there appears to be no chance of making his distance the player may kick the ball in so savage a manner that it will go sailing away down field.

CHAPTER XXXVII

GOLF, HOCKEY, AND SHINNY

How to Lay Out Golf Links and Play the Game—Explanation of the Terms Used in the Game—How Hockey and Shinny Are Played.

THE King and Parliament decided in 1457 that the Scotchmen and boys were neglecting archery to play golf, and so decrees were issued against the game, and that settled the matter. But not in the way the wise rulers intended, for the Highland game of cluich-dhesog increased in popularity until it became the national game of Scotland. In the reign of Edward III. they called it "cambuæ;" but we know it as plain golf, the most fashionable game in the United States, as it was on the other side of the Atlantic at the beginning of the seventeenth century, when Prince Henry, James I.'s son, played golf. Golf is a game that any boy can learn to play, and one in which he can soon excel his father, big brothers, or uncles, for the reason that however skilled the older people may be they have all taken the game up since it became popular and had no kindergarten training. A boy's limbs are supple, and, best of all, he has no fear of being awkward or undignified; consequently he goes at

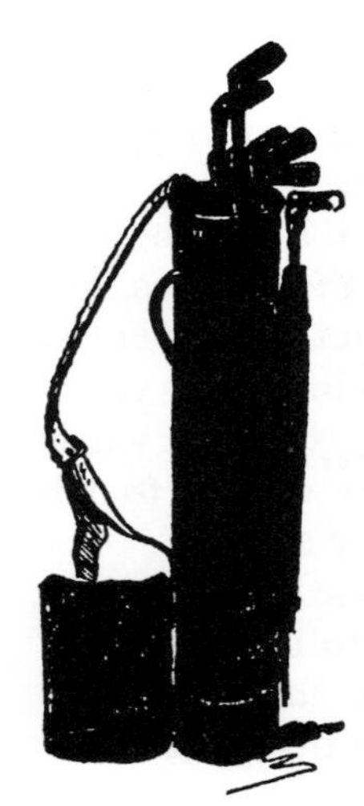

FIG. 380.—Case for Golf Clubs.

FIGS. 381, 382, 383, 384, 385, 386 and 387.—A B and E, are different points of views of a man in full swing; C is a front view after the stroke is made. From instantaneous photographs.

such a thing as golf heart and soul, and soon swings his stick with a grace and accuracy that make him the envy of the older players. Golf is

A Simple Game.

Starting from the tee the object of the player is to land a small ball in a hole a hundred or more yards distant, and to do it with as few strokes of the golf clubs as possible. The player who reaches the hole with the fewest number of strokes is said to win that hole, and the player who wins the most holes wins the game. Nothing could be more easily understood.

The Links.

Many of the best links in Scotland are laid out where the soil is sandy and the grass sparse and stiff. Such links, as the course is called, dry quickly after a rain, and the ball is easily played and seen in the scanty tufts of wiry grass. The course in this country for the regulation game is rarely over three miles long, and shorter courses can be laid out for informal work and practice. The reader must not understand that the links are to extend in a straight line. On the contrary, it is much better to have them wind about and end somewhere near the start. By carefully planning the curves a golf course may be made to occupy comparatively limited grounds.

Somehow in the evolution of the game it has become a rule to make eighteen holes constitute a full course. In America, however, comparatively few courses possess over nine holes, and good practice and entertainment can be had upon a course with even a fewer number.

The starting-point is called

The Teeing-ground,

and is marked by two whitewash lines at right angles to the course, forming a parallelogram with the side lines of the course five or six yards in length by two or three in breadth. Within the parallelogram the player places his ball upon a

Tee

or small hill of sand or earth from a half to three-quarters of an inch high.

The Holes

are about four inches in diameter (Figs. 388 and 389), and are lined with iron, and the ground for seven or eight feet on all sides is more level than the rest of the course and is known as the "putting green." A tomato-can, sunk in the earth, of course, so that the top is even with the turf, makes a good hole for boys' links. They are placed at distances varying from three hundred to twelve hundred feet apart, and are marked by little red flags which are removed when the player approaches.

FIGS. 388 and 389.—Cans for Golf Holes.

Now since a match game, as a rule, consists of thirty-six holes, eighteen holes gone twice over give the required number; so will nine holes gone over four times, or six holes six times, or four holes nine times, or three holes twelve times. So you see that if your ground is limited you need have but three, four, six, or nine holes, and the fewer the holes the fairer becomes the game for strangers, because in going over them so often they learn the ground and that puts them on an even footing with the home players.

The Golf Clubs

are something like our old-fashioned shinny sticks in shape but modified and better made, as the ball must be driven more accurately and much farther, and often from difficult "lies" or positions. They are known as wooden and iron clubs according to whether the heads are made of wood or iron. There are a great variety of them, but the beginner does not need more than four or five. The *driver*, a large club with a long shaft and wooden head, is used when the ball is on the tee, and the boy will find that with a little practice he can with this club send the ball a hundred yards, while an experienced player will cover nearly twice this distance. The *brassie* resembles the driver, but, as its

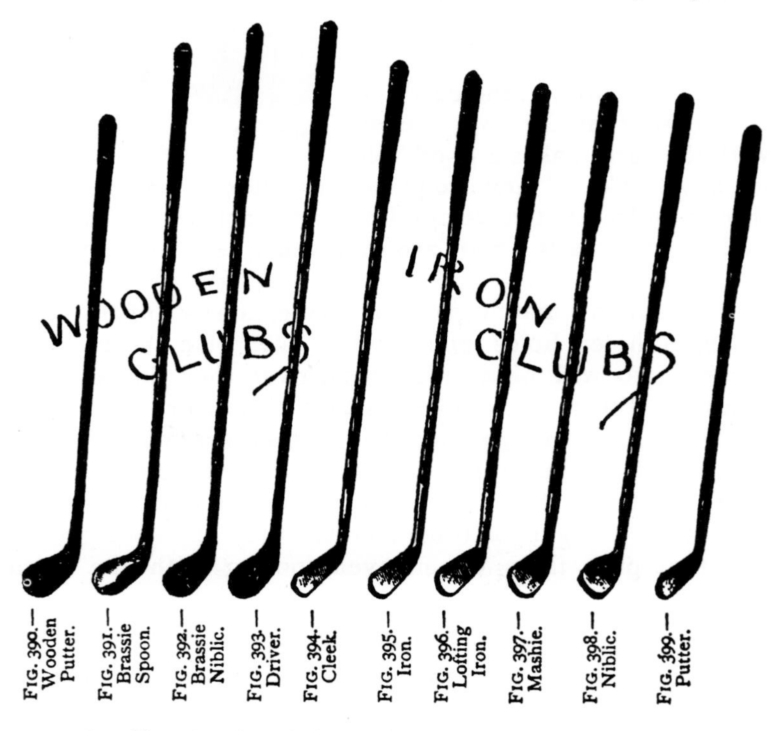

Fig. 390.—Wooden Putter. Fig. 391.—Brassie Spoon. Fig. 392.—Brassie Niblic. Fig. 393.—Driver. Fig. 394.—Cleek. Fig. 395.—Iron. Fig. 396.—Lofting Iron. Fig. 397.—Mashie. Fig. 398.—Niblic. Fig. 399.—Putter.

name implies, its head is protected with a brass plate, and it can be used when the ball lies favorably on sod or in the open ground. The *cleek* and *lofter* both have iron heads, the former being best suited to drive the ball low and far, and the latter to "loft" or lift the ball over obstructions.

In addition to these the clubs most often seen are the ***putter***, for "putting" the ball into the hole, though many experienced players prefer the ***cleek***, ***mashies*** of various sorts resembling the ***lofter***, but with a shorter iron, the ***niblic***, etc.

The Ball

used in regulation games is made of gutta-percha and is about one and three-quarter inches in diameter. Any hard

FIG. 400.—Golf Ball (natural size).

ball will answer for a boy, and with a course of three or four holes he can play with his driver until his skill entitles him to a more complicated kit.

Hazards

are all objects which interfere with the play of the ball.

A Bunker

is a hazard in the form of a sand-pit, a stone wall, or ridge. The course between the holes should be free of long grass, sticks, and stones, with only the roads, walls, and ditches as hazards. But the more hazards there are alongside of the course the more fun there is, for every bad play is punished by placing the ball in a position that will test the players' patience and skill to extricate it.

FIG. 402.—Feet Too Wide Apart in Top View.

FIG. 401.—Feet Correct in Side View.

A game of *singles* is when two persons, each with a ball of his own, play against each other. One of *foursomes* is when two partners play against two other partners, each side having a ball and the partners playing alternately.

Expert Players

often play against two, three, or more players, and this is called *three-*, *four-*, or *five-ball matches*.

When a number of players play in pairs and score for each other it is called a *score play*.

Shinny.

In this game the only preparation necessary is to procure a shinny stick. One of hickory or ash, with a curve at one end like the hook of an old man's walking-stick, is the best; but any sapling of tough wood with part of the root left on for a hook makes a good shinny stick. If the game is on the ice and you search the border of the pond for a club, be careful that you keep your hands off the white poison sumach that grows in such localities. Otherwise you will rue the day as with swollen face and closed eyes you learn the effects of vegetable poison on the skin.

The wooden bung from some barrel takes the place of the elaborate golf ball. On the ice, however, a rubber ball is better and much less dangerous. In place of plaid suits and Scotch wool stockings, rolled down from the top to show the gaudy yarn border, the ordinary every-day dress is worn.

The Game Itself.

Two goal lines are settled upon, and two captains are selected, who choose sides in the ordinary way. The bung is placed midway between the goals, and the players are stationed to suit the captain or themselves. At the call of time both captains struggle with the crooks of their shinny sticks to obtain control of the bung so as to be able to knock it goalward. After the bung is in play anyone may strike it who can, but woe be unto the lad who, in his anxiety to hit the bung, gets on the wrong side of it. "Shinny on your own side!" is the warning cry, and unless the warning is obeyed a pair of black and blue shins will record the time he got on the wrong side of the bung to strike a left-handed blow. Each goal is a game, and as many games are played as suits the players. The side A strive to knock the bung over the goal behind the side B; the Bs do their best to prevent this, and to knock the bung over the goal guarded by the As. On the ice it is not only exciting, but beautiful to see the long racing stroke of the skater, the short quick turn, and the backward glide to avoid a collision; but it is unfair to start a game on a crowded pond, as it practically drives the other pleasure-seekers ashore, and compels them to give up their sport.

Hockey

is practically the same as shinny, differing in immaterial points. In this game the bung is called the "hockey," the shinny sticks, hockey sticks; and the captains, in place of scuffling over the ball at the call of time, toss up for choice of first chance at the hockey. The winner at the call of "play" strikes the hockey with his club, and it is the business of his antagonist to strike it back again as soon as it reaches the ground, and the game consists of this alternate striking the hockey backward and forward. The side that succeeds in forcing the hockey over the goal line guarded by their opponents wins the game.

FIG. 403.—Hockey.

The great similarity of the games of "hockey" and shinny * offers no excuse for adopting the latter as an American game, for shinny was played by our fathers and grandfathers in America, and we claim it as our own, allowing those across the water the privilege of calling their game hockey.

* Shinny originally was a Highland sport and went by the name of clulch-bhal, or camanachd, and was played to the music of bagpipes.

Winter

CHAPTER XXXVIII

TURTLE HUNTING

Methods of Capturing "Snappers" and Terrapin Described—The Implements Necessary and Where to Search.

WINTER is here, but genuine winter weather with snow and ice has not yet arrived. Knee-deep in the woods the brown leaves rustle, and with every wind whirl around in russet eddies, filling up the yawning crevices between the gray rocks. The gray squirrels and the chipmunks are busy digging among the leaves for acorns and nuts for their winter store.

In the water the bass will no longer be tempted from their hiding-places by fly or bait, but the voracious pickerel, though he may ignore the spinning spoon, will bite greedily at live bait. Overhead the whistling wings of the wild duck send a thrill down the sportsman's back. The jutting logs where the turtles were wont to sun themselves during the hot summer days stand out now bare and unoccupied.

Where are the turtles? Have they emigrated with the summer birds or have they buried themselves in the mud peacefully to sleep away the cold winter, as our forefathers believed that the swallows were wont to do?

This is a practical age. If any one tells us that turtles bury themselves in the mud we will investigate and see if it be true. If our forefathers had done the same they never would have believed that the swallows were guilty of passing the winter in such a stupid manner, or that geese were hatched from barnacles, or any other of the fairy stories that made up the natural histories of their day.

FIG. 404.—Turtle Hunter and Turtle Stick.

As a boy I have dug frogs from the bottom of streams in mid winter, and was not inclined to doubt that turtles might pass the cold weather in the same manner. Still, before adopting that belief I made up my mind to investigate the subject. One raw, bleak day I sallied forth with a pole one end of which was armed with an iron hook (Fig. 403) and the other with an iron spike. A gentleman well known among naturalists accompanied me, and led me to the haunts of the "snappers." Flowing through a wide pasture was a small creek with rather high banks. Along the edge we walked until we came upon the stump of an old tree.

Hooking Turtles.

Here my guide paused and asked me to see if there was not a turtle there. Following his directions I prodded the earth beneath the roots of the old stump, and a foot or two below the surface struck something hard. I could tell by the "feel" that it was neither stone nor wood. Hastily reversing my pole I thrust the iron hook into the yielding soil, and, working it under the hard object, found little difficulty in unearthing a very large and exceedingly angry old "snapper." I think that with little labor we could have filled a wagon with turtles of all sizes from under the shores of that little Ohio creek, and among them were some veritable monsters. But our mission was not one of extermination, and after securing four for our host we returned in triumph and placed the great gasping monsters on the lawn to be admired by our friends.

I left that evening, but learned that the four turtles made a splendid soup and supplied a never-failing topic of conversation, as it was again and again related how the man and boy took two broomsticks into the pasture, were gone but a short time, and returned with more turtles than the farmers thereabouts would see in a summer.

Terrapin Hunting.

Everyone on the Atlantic coast has either read of or seen the "diamond backs" that are prized so highly by people who are fond of rich and expensive dishes. It was a sorry day for this race of turtles when they became a fashionable article of food, for they have been hunted ever since. On Long Island they are found and captured in the manner described for "snappers," but the pole is armed with a trowel or paddle-shaped blade in place of the spike, and the other end has a stiff wire loop bent out at right angles from the rod in place of the iron hook. A damaged terrapin will not bring as much money as a perfect one, and the wire loop is less liable to hurt the terrapin's feet and legs. It is claimed that wounds cause ugly warts to grow upon the injured parts, which make them less desirable in the market.

Like their fresh-water relatives, terrapins upon the approach of winter leave the broader water, and, following the small inlets and ditches at the head of the creeks, bury themselves in the black salt-meadow mud. To hunt them you should have long rubber boots, a rod as described, and an old sack for a game-bag (Fig. 405). Thus arrayed sally forth and look for signs. Experience will soon teach you to recognize the terrapin's tracks and to follow them up to the spot where he has taken a "header" into the mud. There you prod for him until the shovel end of your pole strikes his hard shell. Then you use the pole to shovel away the mud and the loop with which to fish him out.

FIG. 405.—Terrapin Hunter and Terrapin Stick.

Terrapin over half a foot in length are called by the trade "counts;" those less than a half foot and more than five inches "short counts;" females under five inches are heifers; large females are "cows," and males "bulls."

There are only a few men who are aware of the existence

of "diamond backs" as far north as New York, and fewer still who know where and how to hunt them, and these few try to keep their occupation a secret. There is no reason why boys should be debarred from this sport, and a good catch will supply cash enough to buy fishing-tackle galore for next Summer's campaign.

CHAPTER XXXIX

ON THE ICE

Plain and Fancy Skating—Begin to Learn Young—Cutting a Circle—The Spread Eagle—The Bull Frog—The Grapevine Garland—The Danger of "Follow the Leader."

SMALL feet have tested the strength of the ice morning after morning, until at last the boys hail each other with the joyous cry of "The ice will bear!"

Old skates come rattling down from their perch on the top shelves of the closets, the dust is wiped off, and the sharpness of their runners tested by boyish fingers.

What a thrill used to run through the scholars in the little frame "Academy" at my "old Kentucky home," when some boy announced, "Licking will bear!" Which, being translated, meant that the muddy stream called the Licking River had frozen over and that the ice was thick enough to bear the weight of a boy.

When at last the Saturday holiday arrived, with what feverish haste we ate our breakfast, even begrudging the time taken to consume our food. Ah, those were glorious days! In imagination now I can hear the musical notes made by the vibrating ice under the weight of a crowd of merry boys as with glad shouts we glided over the glassy surface of the river.

Sometimes even the conservative and busy Ohio River would suspend all business and close its doors of ice. At such times the flat boats, barges, and steamboats would lie helpless and idle along the shores, their only use being that of a resting-place and shelter for skating parties. I then thought that when a person reached an age when he no longer cared to skate, it was time for him to die. This opinion, like many others of my boyhood, is being gradually modified.

Little Danger.

While we older fellows look on the reader may stand on one foot and flinging out his other spin like a top.

And if he falls little harm is done; his bones are not brittle and his body is light.

Keep Your Hands Out of Your Pockets.

The only dangerous falls come from skating over sticks, leaves, chips, bits of paper or similar objects which suddenly stop the swiftly gliding feet, bringing the upper part of the body down with a bang upon the ice. Even under these conditions serious results seldom follow a fall unless the skater has his hands in his pockets. The writer still bears scars that testify to the truth of this statement.

Fig. 406.—Danger Ahead.

When to Begin.

The boy should begin skating as soon as he can procure skates small enough to fit his little feet. In Friesland, Holland, the babies learn to skate as soon as they are able to toddle, and they are expert skaters by the time they are six or seven years old. Indeed, in America, small boys generally do begin when they can get a skate of any size. One skate satisfies them at first, and if they are lucky enough to have access to two the other one is usually loaned to a comrade.

The Old Wooden Skate.

Thirty years ago the old skates that fell into the possession of the small boy were unique in pattern. Fastened to a bright red wooden foot-piece was a long, straight runner which ended in a spiral of steel that curved gracefully up over the toe and terminated in a beautiful brass acorn. The skates were fastened to the feet by heel- and toe-straps. The toe-straps crossed, sandal fashion, over the toe, ran across the instep through two iron rings in the heel-strap and back again to the buckle. A sharp spike held the shoe-heel in place. With one of these acorn skates bound on one foot, the straps tightened by sundry chips and sticks thrust between them and the shoe, the small boy was happy as he glided down the frozen gutter on one foot.

Fig. 407. — The Old Brass Acorn Skate.

Christmas came and in the bulging stocking there was more than likely to be a pair of small skates with screw heels and broad toe- and heel-straps. These were usually about an inch or one-half of an inch longer than the foot, to allow for the boy's growth. On the screw-heels the boy learned plain forward skating sufficiently well to be able to play tag and shinny on the canal, river, or pond.

The third stage in his career was when his older brother, father, or uncle presented him with a beautiful pair of club skates, with no straps of any kind.

When the glittering club skates were locked on his feet

his ambition began to grow and he was soon to be seen experimenting on the more difficult feats in skating. His efforts were now directed to

Cutting a Circle.

This is one of the first figures learned by beginners, and although it requires a small amount of outer-edge skating, it is learned before any serious attempts are made at mastering the latter art. To begin you strike out on the left foot with the body leaning toward the left, the centre of the proposed circle. When the weight of the body is on the outside edge the line described by the skate runner will be a curve directed outward (Fig. 408). As soon as you find that you can continue on that stroke no longer bring the right foot quickly forward and down. This last must be a short stroke of only sufficient duration to give you time for another outer-edge stroke with your left foot. At first you will make a very large circle, but gradually as you "catch the knack of the thing" you will be able to contract the ring to smaller dimensions. When you have mastered the left-foot circle, try it on the right foot and practise it until you are able to go either way with equal speed and grace. It is great fun to have a crowd of seven or eight boys on one circle, each trying to go faster than his fellows.

FIG. 408.—Cutting a Circle.

The Backward Circle.

This, when learned, is easier than the forward ring, for the push stroke is made with the toe. When going backward great force can be given to the toe-push stroke by slightly lifting the heel.

To cut the circle backward you must simply reverse your forward movement.

No boy can learn to skate by reading these suggestions; he can only obtain hints that will help him when he attempts the different figures described. The only way to do anything is to DO IT.

Put on your skates and try, and while trying sooner or later the feat will be performed. The best assistance is obtained in watching fellow-skaters further advanced than yourself in the art.

After you have perfected yourself in cutting the circle forward and backward, to the left and to the right, the other more difficult motions will suddenly lose their awe-inspiring qualities, because in acquiring the simpler figures you have unconsciously gained control of your muscles. The muscles were all there before, but as they had never been called upon to perform the work they were designed for, when you gave your first command they rebelled. Your foot would not go as you directed it and you thought yourself awkward. Awkward you were, but an awkward boy is a boy who has not trained his muscles, and a graceful lad is one whose muscles have been disciplined to act as he directs.

Now stand up on your skates and assert your authority over your rebellious muscles, tell them that you intend to be a skater, and to begin with you expect them to help you.

To Skate Backwards.

Work or skull yourself along any way, until you are able to detect the proper moment and proper manner of giving the strokes. This accomplished, you may call yourself a good plain skater.

The Spread Eagle

is one of the first steps in the advance from plain to fancy skating. Even when well done it lacks the elements of grace, but it is most excellent practice to render the limbs supple and make other more graceful tricks possible; and it is a favorite performance of boy skaters.

How to Perform the Feat.

You must skate straight away until you have gained sufficient headway, then at the end of the last stroke turn the toes out so that the runners of your skates make a straight line heel to heel, one skate following the other. In this position you will glide over the ice until the momentum first gained is exhausted. At first the beginner will be only partially successful, but gradually he will be able to describe a wide circle forward, and in a little while gain sufficient control of his feet to slide across the skating pond in a straight line (Fig. 409).

FIG. 409.—The Straddle-bug.

The Spread Eagle Backwards

will be found more difficult, for it necessitates turning the toes out until they point backward. In performing this last feat it is no easy matter to keep your balance, but perfection comes with practice, and soon the boy who devotes time to practice will excite the admiration of his comrades by the ease with which he turns either forward or backward. During his practice the beginner will undoubtedly bend his knees, as shown in (Fig. 409), but after he has reached that point of excellence where his whole mind need not be centred on his feet, he may learn gradually to straighten his legs until at last he can do the spread eagle forward and backward without looking like a straddle bug (Fig. 410).

Fig. 410.—Spread Eagle in Proper Form.

The Bull Frog.

This consists of a circle cut by skating spread-eagle forward and by making a succession of leaps. When the writer was still a boy of fourteen or fifteen years, it was considered the best of fun for five or six boys to group themselves in the centre of the skating pond or river and do the "bull frog." The sight is comical and certain to win applause and laughter, but no novice need attempt it. Like the clown's "drop act," described in the chapter on "Stilts," the "bull frog" requires practice to learn.

How the Bull Frogs Jump.

Spread your toes out spread-eagle fashion. Then leap into the air by raising yourself first on your toes and then springing from them. This is done all in one movement. The slightest possible inclination to the right will cause you to move in that direction; and the direction your toes point, will cause you, in a succession of leaps, to describe a circle, the novelty of which appeals to all boys. A more graceful and equally novel ring can be made without lifting your skates from the ice. This is called

A Spread-Eagle Circle,

and it is cut by spreading the feet as in the "bull-frog." But in place of leaping the skater must learn to keep his feet moving, first the right foot forward and the left foot back, then the left foot forward and right foot back, always with toes turned out spread-eagle fashion. When properly done this motion will cause the skater to glide around in a circle, his feet moving in a most bewildering manner while they weave a pretty grape-vine pattern on the ice called (Fig. 411)

The Grapevine Garland.

The momentum needed in order to cut this figure is acquired by a slight push with the toe at each movement of either foot, and as the feet are never lifted from the ice, the push is imperceptible to the observer, and the motion unaccountable to many old skaters, few of whom seem to know the garland figure or spread-eagle circle.

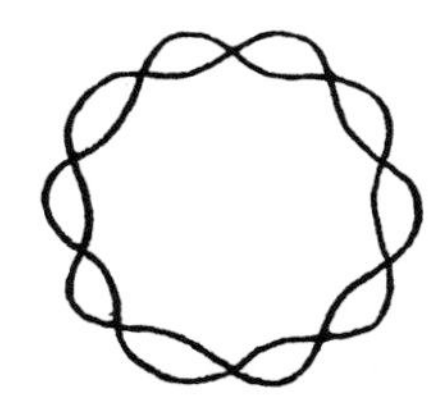

FIG. 411.—The Grapevine Garland.

When you are able to cut all the figures and skate as described in this chapter, it is safe to leave you alone. Soon the "double roll," the "single and double grapevine," the "outside and inside edge" will be familiar and easy feats for you to perform. As for the

Outside Edge,

in cutting the circle you have learned the secret of maintaining your balance while leaning outward on either foot, and it is only necessary to make this stroke first with the left and then with the right foot and you will find yourself sailing along in the most approved outer-edge style. You have learned to trust to your ankle and the sharp edge of your skate for support, and the real battle is over.

FIG. 412.—Outside Edge.
FIG. 413.—Spread Eagle Backward.
FIG. 414.—Spread Eagle Forward.

Beware of

Air-Holes.

In every group of boys there are a few hare-brained, foolish fellows who are continually getting themselves and their playfellows into trouble, often of a most serious nature. A favorite method pursued by these would-be heroes is to start a game of

"Follow the Leader," or "I Conquer,"

on the ice. Of course the would-be brave boy elects himself leader and the others must follow. The only difference between Follow the Leader and I Conquer is that when an act is performed by the leader in the first case he calls out, in a bantering tone, "Follow the leader!" In the second he tosses his head with an impudent air and exclaims, "I conquer!" This is meant as a challenge to the others, but the others must remember that the danger is apt to increase in proportion to the number of boys in turn. The leader skates along and jumps an air-hole, shouting, "I conquer!" The ice is weakened by his jump and it is more and more dangerous for each succeeding boy who jumps.

The Tickly-Bender, or Running Tommie.

The leader finds a weak place in the ice which is called a "Tickly-bender," and skating over it cries, "I conquer!" If the other boys are green they follow him. With each succeeding boy the ice bends more and more until at last one boy breaks through, often with fatal results. For the late leader, when confronted by real danger, cannot be depended upon to risk much in order to rescue his unfortunate follower. Skating over a "tickly-bender" in Yankeedom is called "Running Tommie." If any of my readers like the excitement of "Running Tommie," let them choose ice where there is not more than one or two feet of water underneath, and even then the danger of wet feet, frozen clothes, a bad cold, and a well-deserved lecture at home ought to furnish excitement enough to satisfy them.

FIG. 414 a.—Shinny.

The really brave lad does not advertise that quality by engaging his companions in a sport that brings all the danger to his followers, but he is first to act when a companion needs assistance; and it is to such a boy's cool head and "nerve" that many a rattle-brained lad owes his life.

CHAPTER XL

STUNNING MUSK-RATS AND FISH

Sport for Boys on Skates when the Ice is Thin and Clear—How Catfish and "Suckers" are Stunned and Captured.

AFTER the first freeze, and while the ice is still transparent but thick enough to support your weight, if you visit the mill-pond where you know that musk-rats abound you are pretty sure to be able to frighten them from their holes in the bank to the water. The poor rodents seem to forget that ice has formed over their pond, and they can be plainly seen and followed by the skaters who, armed with axes, strike the ice above the fleeing rat.

A Hard Blow

on the surface of the ice stuns the creature underneath, and a few quick blows with the edge of the axe open a hole from which the half-stunned animal may be fished, and thrust into a bag brought for the purpose. A frightened musk-rat can make a severe wound with his long, chisel-like teeth, so care must be taken to grasp the captive around the throat and hold him in that position until he is safe in the bag. A tame musk-rat has no more desire to bite than a tame dog.

Some boys kill the rats as they are taken from the water and preserve their skins, which have a market value; but most of the lads enter into the sport for the fun and excitement of the chase, and either free the animals after they are captured or turn them over to some companion, who may in time sell enough of their skins to secure the price of a good pair of the latest model of skates.

FIG. 415.—Stunning Musk-Rats.

Stunning Cat-fish.

We used to go "stunning cats" on the same ponds in which we hunted the musk-rats, but the sport was not nearly as exciting, for the cat-fish were numb with cold and made but feeble efforts to escape. Still a good string of these black-mustached fish brought with it a certain feeling of satisfaction that all sportsmen can understand.

We never bothered to carry an axe for "cats," but skated around with big stones in our hands, which we let drop on the ice just over the spot where the fish rested. The concussion caused the fish to turn belly up. Then the ice was broken with the same stone and the fish taken out.

This was in the Ohio valley, but there are both cat-fish and musk-rats in ponds scattered over a wide area of our country, and the sport will have the same attractions in the mountain ponds of Pennsylvania as in the muddy ponds on the bottom lands of the Ohio River valley.

I never heard of skaters in New England hunting musk-rats or cat-fish; but there are many New England boys who keenly enjoy the chase and capture of that comical, big-headed fish, whose pouting lips have given it the name of "sucker."

Stunning "Suckers."

These sturdy little New England lads, with their skates dangling over their backs, and armed with sucker-clubs, as they call the short bludgeon they carry, and an axe or hatchet, may often be seen sallying forth after the first freeze. The time they select is when the sucker stream has a new coating of fresh, transparent ice. If you should ask them where they were going, the cheery reply would come back, with Yankee accent, "Going a-stunning suckers."

The hunting "ground" that is selected is usually a shallow stretch of water not more than from six to twelve inches deep. Here the boys scatter themselves over the thin ice, which bends under their skates in an alarming manner and protests against the excursion with the peculiar musical, half-smothered, booming noise familiar to all skaters on new ice. It seems as if they were gliding stealthily over the unfrozen surface of the water. So clear is the ice that each leaf and stick that is dislodged from its resting-place by the current is as distinctly seen as it floats beneath them as if no ice intervened.

Hist! A boy in mid-stream spies his prey lying diagonally across the current, with just sufficient movement of tail and fin to keep his position. Watch the sucker-club now as it rises over the lad's head and comes down on the ice with

A Resounding Blow

that sends the cracks radiating out like a sunburst from the small hole where the water from below oozes, like life-blood, through the ice. The tail and fins of the fish have ceased to move, and his white vest may be seen, as with his dark back to the bottom and white belly upturned, he slowly floats down stream.

The shout of triumph which accompanied the blow of the sucker-club was not necessary to attract the attention of the boy with the hatchet. A few quick strokes of his skates bring him to the spot, and the keen, cold blade of his weapon soon makes a hole in the path, but below the stunned sucker. The fish is not dead and frequently escapes if the axe boy lacks judgment. When the hole in the ice is not cut in the proper place, or too much time is allowed to elapse, the fish recovers from the shock of the blow, and, although at first he may swim slowly, he usually manages to escape. Few, however, evade the trained hunter when once he has struck the fatal blow.

This sort of fishing possesses one great advantage over the ordinary pastime. When you are out stunning suckers you select only such fish as you want, passing the little ones by. When you see a New England sucker hunter raise his club you may know that an old "buster" is in sight; otherwise the fish would be passed without notice.

Caution to Beginners.

Don't become excited and strike too hard. If you do, you may smash the thin ice and do no damage to the fish, but splash the cold water in your own face and be laughed at by your playmates.

A "Buster"

weighs from a pound to a pound and one-half in most places, but in such rivers as the Housatonic and Naugatuck real "busters" weigh from five to six pounds. In poorer streams from fifteen to fifty pounds of fish are not an uncommon catch.

CHAPTER XLI

SNOW-BALL BATTLE AND SNOW TAG

The Rules of Snow-ball Battle—How Rome and Carthage is Played in Cuba—The Ingenious Game of Snow Tag.

THE two selected captains toss up in the usual manner for first choice of men. Then alternately, as in a spelling bee, each chooses a soldier until all are taken. Two taw lines are then drawn about thirty feet apart, and two flag-staffs with colored handkerchiefs for flags are erected in each camp. To bear the enemy's flag to your own camp, that is, over the taw line, wins the victory for your side. Tackling is allowed, as in foot-ball, and is limited by the same rules. No boy bearing the mark of a snow-ball on chest or back is allowed to take further part in the game, as he is considered to be a dead soldier, but the dead soldiers may coach their comrades as often as they please. No tripping, no striking, no ice balls, and no "soakers" (wet snow-balls) are allowed, as the object of this battle is to win, not to hurt or injure, a playmate who in the next game may be fighting at your side.

Rome and Carthage.

In Cuba the little insurgents play this game, using India-rubber balls in place of snow-balls, and having only one flag. This is in a fort which the attacking party try to capture. Each boy hit with a ball is considered dead, but if he catches the ball he can hurl it back and continue the fight. This Cuban ball-game closely resembles the snow-fort game described in "The American Boy's Handy Book;" but the barrel-top shields that are used by the besieging party of the snow fort are unknown in the Cuban game. They call the game Rome and Carthage.

Snow Tag.

Often in travelling through the Northern States when the deep snow covered the ground I have noticed strange circular, or rather wheel-shaped, patterns made of paths in the snow. It was never my fortune to see anyone walking in these paths, and as the form of the pattern made it impossible for the paths to lead anywhere, their use was a problem that I could not solve. Use they evidently had, for some were many feet in diameter and must have required work and hard work to make, as anyone who has attempted to shovel the snow off his own front walk must know. Inquiry at last revealed the fact that these strange circular figures were made by the boys for Snow Tag.

How to Play the Game.

Count out for "It" as in I Spy or ordinary tag. While "It" takes his place at the hub of the wheel the other players scatter around the circumference or rim, and the word "ready" is given. "It" then darts out one of the "spoke" paths and endeavors to tag some one of the other boys, and the fun begins. Two cannot pass each other on the narrow paths, and the fleeing boys often step on each others' heels, trip and tumble head first into the deep snow, forming an easy prey for "It;" but again the lads will dance around in a most provoking manner, and as "It" darts up one spoke toward the rim, the players dart down the other toward the hub and show great skill in eluding "It."

The game can be played in perfection only in very deep snow, where the rule against going out of the bounds is enforced by the impossibility of running, or even walking with any speed through the snow heaped up on all sides. When "It" tags a playmate by holding him long enough to repeat

"Snow Wag,
Snow Rag,
Snow Tag!"

the boy thus tagged is "It," and takes his place at the "hub," and the game is started again when the boys announce themselves as ready at the rim.

CHAPTER XLII

THE "GET-THERE" AND DOUBLE-RUNNERS

Instructions as to How to Build these Famous Sleds—A Safety Double-Runner.

THIS is the way in which to build the "Get-There:" For the runners take a plank one foot wide and a little over twice as long as the length of one of the proposed runners (Fig. 416, A, B, C, D). From the point B measure upon the edge of the board twelve inches, and mark the point E (Fig. 417). From E measure three feet six inches, and mark the point G. From G measure three feet six inches, and mark the point I. From A measure three feet six inches, and mark the point F. From F measure three feet six inches, and mark the point H. With a straight piece of board for a ruler, and a soft lead-pencil, rule a line from A to E, another line from F to G, another line from H to I. On the line A E measure nine and one-half inches, and mark the point K. From E measure three and one-half inches, and mark the point J. Take a saw and saw from E to A along the line E A. Saw again through the line F G, and again through the line H I. You will now have two runners of the form shown by Figs. 417 and 418.

Again take the saw, and, beginning at J, saw off the piece K E J. Then with your jack-knife round off the top as shown by Fig. 419 at L, and the bottom as shown at M. The dotted lines show the part whittled off.

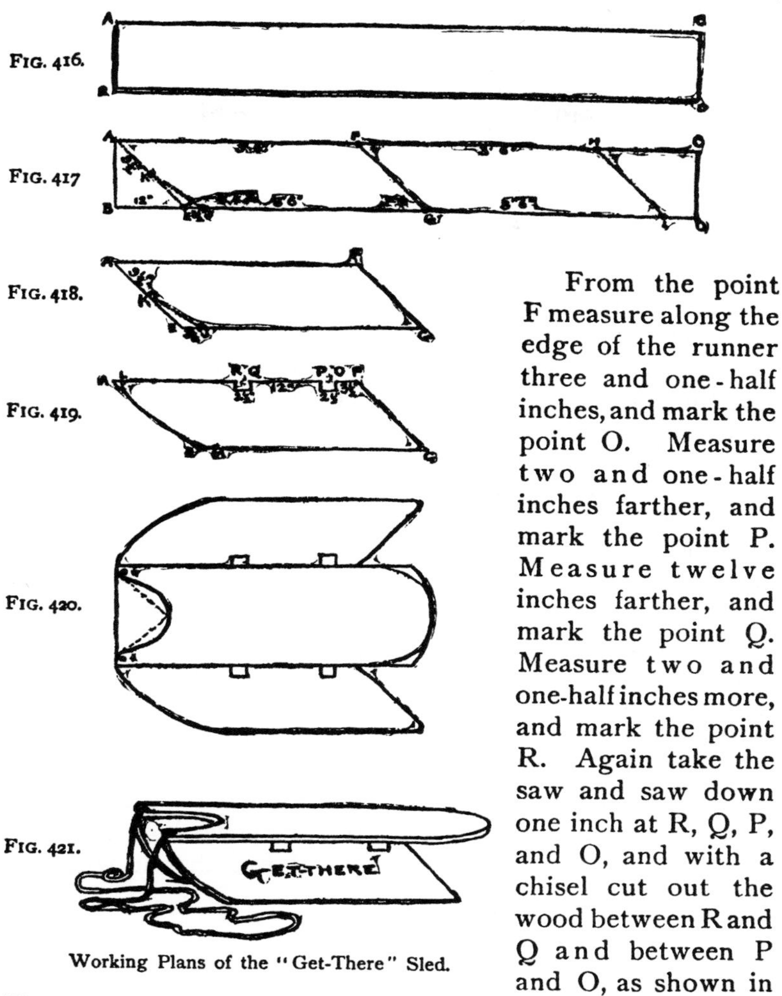

Working Plans of the "Get-There" Sled.

From the point F measure along the edge of the runner three and one-half inches, and mark the point O. Measure two and one-half inches farther, and mark the point P. Measure twelve inches farther, and mark the point Q. Measure two and one-half inches more, and mark the point R. Again take the saw and saw down one inch at R, Q, P, and O, and with a chisel cut out the wood between R and Q and between P and O, as shown in Fig. 419. With your jack-knife cut off the corner at G. Go through the same process with the second runner, and see that one is an exact duplicate of the other. Next make two braces, each one and one-half foot long, one inch thick, and two and one-half inches wide. Fit the braces in the notches R Q and P O, and fasten them in place with good screws or wire nails.

Take a piece of plank one foot six inches wide and one inch thick, and saw off a piece four feet six inches long for a top-board. Saw out a triangle in the front end as shown by the dotted lines in Fig. 420. With your knife round the sides of the triangle, as shown by the solid lines in Fig. 420. Trim off the rear end first, as shown by the solid line, and then gradually whittle it to the form shown by the dotted lines in Fig. 420, which represents the top with the runners on each side of it.

The Runners,

of course, are not spread out as shown by Fig. 420, because you have already nailed on the stretchers so that they must rest upon their edges, but the diagram is drawn with them flat upon each side so as better to show the proportions of each.

Fit the top-piece over the runners and nail it in place, and you have a good serviceable sled that only needs a visit to the blacksmith's shop to make it a better one than you usually find for sale at the toy stores.

At the blacksmith shop have your sled shod with what is called half-round irons, and after a little work on the snow has put a polish on the iron you will find that it will earn the name of "Get-There" (Fig. 421).

The Double-Runner, or Bob Sled,

as it is frequently called, possesses many advantages over the long sleds formerly used west of the Alleghany Mountains. The old-fashioned sleds were steered by the boy in front kicking with his heels on the frozen snow, or the boy at the stern by dragging one foot behind as a rudder. This answers very well for a sled of the dimensions of the "Get-There," but when the sled is seven, eight, or ten feet long, and loaded underneath with pig iron to give it weight, the boy in front who steers has a difficult and exceedingly dangerous task, especially if the hill is steep and icy; and it is next to impossible to steer such a craft from the stern by dragging one foot behind.

The double-runner is much lighter and very much easier to steer on account of the front sled being arranged so that it can be moved independently of the rear sled, for a turn to the right or the left causes the "bob" to take the direction indicated by the front runners; but double-runners steered with a wheel, lever, or yoke in front are very dangerous, as the steersman, in case of an accident, is thrown against the steering apparatus, usually with serious results.

The safety double-runner does away with this danger by having a bridle with which it is steered. It also does away with the danger of collision by having an automatic brake that will stop it, in times of danger, within the distance of its own length. These are qualities which will be appreciated by all who "slide down hill," as we called it when I was a lad, or who are fond of coasting, as our school-readers called it then, and as everyone calls it now.

How to Build a Safety Double-Runner.

Make four good runners after the manner described for the "Get-There," but make these runners not over six inches high, thirty inches on the top edge, and with more rake to the bow and stern (Fig. 422). Next make eight braces, each fourteen inches long, one inch thick, and two and one half inches broad, and mortise the ends as shown by the dotted lines in Fig. 423. At a point three inches from the rear top end of the runner, measure off on the top edge three inches, then two and one half inches, and mark the points. Eight inches in front of the last point make another mark and measure two and one half inches again, and mark it. Now set the runner upon its bottom edge and fit your braces on the two-and-one-half-inches marks, and with a pencil trace upon the top edge of the runner the outlines of the mortise.

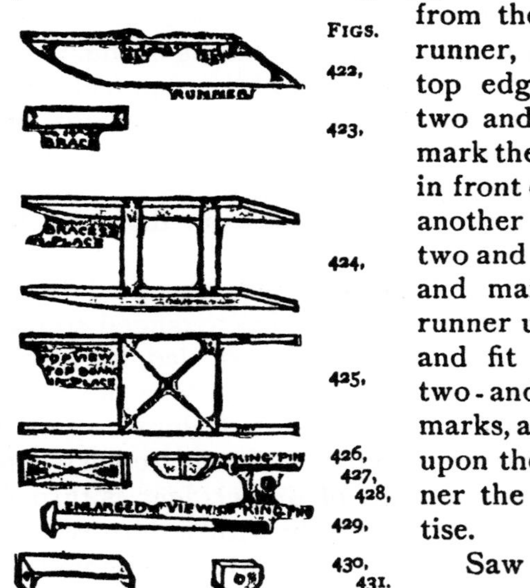

Figs. 422, 423, 424, 425, 426, 427, 428, 429, 430, 431.

Saw out the lines so that

Fig. 432.

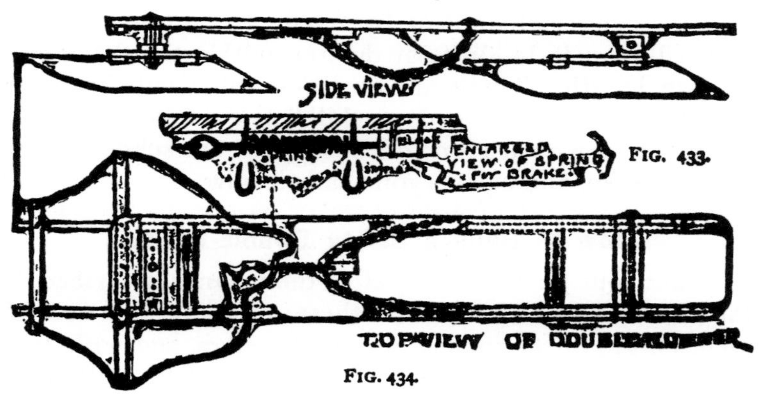

Fig. 433.

Fig. 434.

Working Plans for the Construction of Safety Double-Runner.

the braces will fit neatly in the notches, as shown in Fig. 424. The braces should be of good ash wood, free from knots, and must be fastened to the runners with good long screws, the holes for the latter being carefully bored with a gimlet.

For a top-board cut out a piece of board one inch thick, fourteen inches wide, and thirteen inches from front to rear. Fasten the top-board securely to the runners over the braces with screws (Fig. 425).

Find the centre of the top-board by ruling a line from each corner, as shown by the dotted line in the top view, Fig. 425. The centre of the top-board and the spot in which to bore a hole for the

King-pin

is placed where the diagonal lines cross each other. The king-pin is of iron, with a rounded head and with threads on the other end to hold a nut in place. Fig. 428 shows the pin and the nut proportional to the size of the sled, the diagram, Fig. 429, shows an enlarged view of the king-pin.

The Reach-Board

is the long board that forms the top for the double-runner. Each sled has a top-board of its own, but the board that joins the two sleds and upon which the passengers sit we will call a reach-board. This should be free from knots, of strong elastic wood, sixteen inches wide, an inch thick, and as long as you may desire the "bob" to be. In the one we are describing it is eight feet long.

It is evident that if we fasten the reach-board to the top of the two sleds with nails it will be as difficult to steer as the big sleds we spoke of at the beginning of this description; and if we fasten it directly to the top of the first sled by the king-pin the friction in turning will be too great To obviate this, make, of oak, a bench-block, fourteen inches long by four inches wide by one inch thick, and, finding the centre by the intersection of the two diagonal lines, as you did with the top-board, make a hole for the king-pin (Fig. 426). Place the bench on top of the sled exactly in the centre of the top-board and see that the two king-pin holes fit exactly one above the other, and that the ends of the bench are even and flush with the sides of the sled. Then securely fasten it in place with good long screws or bolts. Make a second block, now, of good oak, about nine inches long by three inches broad by two and one-half inches thick, bore a hole for the king-pin through the centre of it and trim it down to the form shown by Fig. 427. This is the reach-board block, and must be securely fastened to the reach-board by bolts. Fig. 432 shows the elevation, that is, side view of king-pin, bench, and block all in place. Fig. 434 shows a top view. Of course the reach-board, from this point of view, will hide all underneath it, but in this case we must pretend that the X rays have been turned on and the dotted lines show the skeleton underneath.

Now for

The Back Sled,

which, of course, it is supposed, was put together at the same time as the front one, and is an exact duplicate of it.

We need for the back sled a bench-block fourteen inches long, four inches wide, and three inches thick. Lengthwise through the centre, from end to end, bore a hole for the stern-pin (Fig. 430). After this is done make two side-blocks, one inch thick and a little broader than the bench-block (Fig. 431). Bolt the bench-block to the rear of the back sled and fit the reach-board on for trial. Mark the spot where the side-blocks are to go and bolt them securely in place. On the rear sled, in the side view, the bench- and side-blocks are shown in place. The dotted lines show the bench-block behind the side-blocks. The stern-pin is similar to the king-pin but runs crosswise in place of perpendicularly. It is also fastened with a nut and washer at one end, while the rounded head holds it at the other end.

If the rear sled is allowed to have too much freedom it will wrench itself loose at the first obstacle it strikes. To prevent this attach a small chain or strong cord to each runner and to the bottom side of the reach-board, as may be seen by a glance at the elevation and plan of back sled (Fig. 432). The cord is shown by dotted lines on the plan or top view (Fig. 434).

The Automatic Brake.

From a hasty glance at the plan and elevation this may appear to be rather intricate and difficult to understand; but with the exercise of a little patience you will see that it is very simple. There is a block against which a pin is kept by a spiral spring. A peg through the pin near the after end keeps the spring in place, and a staple, screw eye, or ring, behind the peg protects it and supports the brake-pin. A similar ring supports the forward end of the pin and keeps the spring confined between the two. There is a small indentation in the block to receive the end of the pin (Fig. 433). Any boy can see that a chain looped over the end of the pin, after the manner of the one shown in the two views (Figs. 432 and 434), will drop to the ground when the pin is pulled forward, and when it falls to the ground it will be directly in front of the rear runners. The latter cannot go far with a bunch of chain under each runner, and the whole thing will stop even when the headway is something extraordinary. To loosen the brake the boy in front simply puts his foot against the end of an iron rod that has one end bent over to receive the foot. A push on this pulls the picture wire-cord that runs from it to the end of the brake-pin. To bring the brake within reach of the steersman's foot two of those brass bell-cranks that all bell-hangers use when they have to turn a corner with their bell-wire, are necessary. These cranks are fastened at their middle to the bottom of the reach-board, while the wire picture-cord connects them with the brake-pin and the bolt at the side of the reach-board. The bolt is made exactly on the principles of a bolt for a door, but one end of this bolt has a hole through it to hold the wire, and the other end is bent into a crook as a rest for the foot.

Safety Reins.

A foot-rest for the bow man is made of ash, and extends at least ten inches upon each side of the reach-board, to the bottom of which it is securely fastened. In each end of this foot-rest there is a pulley-wheel, as shown by the dotted lines. Across the top of the front runners a brace is securely fastened to which the bridle is attached. The bridle runs through the blocks or pulleys at the end of the foot-rest.

With the bridle in his hands and the automatic brake ready for instant operation, the steersman may coast down what are considered dangerous hills, and feel that there is no great peril. Should an obstacle, such as a wagon, a horse-car, trolley, or steam-car, suddenly appear, one push of his foot drops a loop of chain in front of the rear runners and his safety double-runner will stop almost within its own length. If too sudden a stop unseats the steersman, he simply slides off, for there is no dangerous wheel, yoke, or helm in front for him to be thrown against.

It is not to be supposed that the reader is to make all the iron-work for the safety double-runner. This the blacksmith can do, and if the expense is greater than one boy feels disposed to stand, remember that this sled is built to accommodate a number of boys, and a club can be formed which will make the expense very light. Your brake-chain should have large links, but not necessarily very heavy ones. It must be fastened with a ring-bolt at each end to the bottom of the reach-board. The runners of the sleds should be shod with half-round irons, and everything made with the idea of strength in view. Use bolts in place of screws wherever it is practicable. The sled will not be found expensive, and if well built, it will last long enough to be used by two or three generations of boys.

Load your double-runner with a crowd of jolly fellows and start down the hill. May you enjoy the ride with that keen pleasure which only youth and health can feel. The longest hill has its foot, and the faster you coast the sooner it will be reached.

We have gone through four seasons of fun together, and although we have not seen each other, we have worked together over kites, boats, and sleds, and now, as we coast on our new bob-sled, it is with feelings of regret that I find we have at length reached the bottom of the hill and

THE END OF THE BOOK.

INDEX

A

B

C

D

E

F

G

H

I

J

K

L

M

N

O

P

R

S

T

W

Z